AESTHETICS
Approaches, Concepts and Problems

BY THE SAME AUTHOR

Studies in the Metaphysics of Bradley
George Allen & Unwin, London
and Humanities Press, New York, 1967
(Muirhead Library)

The Winged Form: Aesthetical Essays on Hindustani Rhythm
Sangeet Natak Akademi, New Delhi, 1979

Aesthetical Essays
Chanakya Publications, Delhi, 1981

Ever Unto God: Essays on Gandhi and Religion
Indian Council of Philosophical Research, New Delhi, 1988

Swinging Syllables: Aesthetics of Kathak Dance
Sangeet Natak Akademi, New Delhi, 1991

Art and Philosophy: Seven Aestheticians
Indian Council of Philosophical Research, New Delhi, 1994

Hindustani Sangeet and a Philosopher of Art:
Music, Rhythm, and Kathak Dance
vis-à-vis Aesthetics of Susanne K. Langer
D.K. Printworld (P) Ltd., New Delhi, 2001

Hindustani Music and Aesthetics Today: A Selective Study
Sangeet Natak Akademi, New Delhi,
and Hope India Publications, Gurgaon, 2009

Avenues to Beauty: Eight Essays in Aesthetics
Sangeet Natak Akademi
and D.K. Printworld (P) Ltd., New Delhi, 2009

Hindustani Sangeet: Some Perspectives, Some Performers
Sangeet Natak Akademi
and D.K. Printworld (P) Ltd., New Delhi, 2010

AESTHETICS
Approaches, Concepts and Problems

S.K. Saxena
Formerly Professor of Philosophy
University of Delhi

Sangeet Natak Akademi
New Delhi

D.K. Printworld (P) Ltd.
New Delhi

Cataloguing in Publication Data — DK
[Courtsey: D.K. Agencies (P) Ltd. <docinfo@dkagencies.com>]

Saxena, Sushil Kumar, 1921-
Aesthetics : approaches, concepts and problems / S.K. Saxena.
p. cm.
Includes bibliographical references (p.) and index.
ISBN 13: 9788124605554
ISBN 10: 8124605556
1. Hindustani music — Philosophy and aesthetics. 2. Aesthetics, Indic. I. Title.
DDC 780.954 22

ISBN 13: 978-81-246-0555-4 **ISBN 10:** 81-246-0555-6
First published in India in 2010

Published by
Sangeet Natak Akademi
National Academy of Music, Dance and Drama, India
Rabindra Bhavan, Feroze Shah Road
New Delhi - 110 001
Phones : (011) 2338 7246; 2338 7248; *Fax* : (011) 2338 2659
email : sangeetnatakak@bol.net.in

and

D.K. Printworld (P) Ltd.
Regd. office : *'Srikunj,'* F-52, Bali Nagar
New Delhi - 110 015
Phones : (011) 2545 3975; 2546 6019; *Fax* : (011) 2546 5926
email : indology@dkprintworld.com
Web : www.dkprintworld.com

Printed by: D.K. Printworld (P) Ltd., New Delhi.

To

Indian Council for Philosophical Research
New Delhi

Sangeet Natak Akademi
New Delhi

and

Mr Susheel K. Mittal

Preface

With the assistance of a Senior Fellowship from the Indian Council of Philosophical Research, New Delhi, the manuscript of this book was completed in 2005. When, on completion, it was submitted to the Council for publication, its academic director politely regretted the Council's inability to accede to my request, though in the same letter the work's quality was openly acknowledged. The decision surprised me. Anyway, now that the work has appeared in its present form, following a quick positive decision by Sangeet Natak Akademi, New Delhi, I am naturally happy and relieved.

The publication has been done in collaboration with D.K. Printworld (P) Ltd., where Mr Susheel K. Mittal spared no pains in expediting the production of the book. What is more, he kindly allowed me to check the proofs of the printed text as many times as I wanted to. So I have reason to be grateful to him.

As for the assistance received from the Akademi, and particularly from its publication expert, Mr A. Chatterjee and his colleague, Mr S.P. Saxena, I can only say that it has been so unremitting that no occasional acknowledgment can be adequate to it. This is quite as true of what I owe to ICPR. This national institute of philosophical research has been very liberal in awarding Senior Fellowships to me. It is in fact the very last one of these which has enabled me – I repeat – to undertake and finalize the writing of this book.

In the end, as I now look at its size and appearance, how can I fail to acknowledge the help given by Mr A.N. Sharma who has done all the typing, and Mr Vinay Jain who has designed the jacket in such a way that it seems to chime visibly with the general character of what the book contains, that is, philosophic reflection on matters relating to art and beauty.

I close this preface with the hope that the book will be of some definite help to our senior students of aesthetics. May this turn out to be true!

March 1, 2010

S.K. Saxena

Contents

1
Aesthetics Today

In our country it is common to think of *aesthetics* as Saundarya Śāstra, that is, as the systematic study of beauty. This view may perhaps be said to be closer to how aesthetics began than to what it is today. It was Baumgarten who first visualized aesthetics as an independent philosophical discipline. But the book in which he did so (*Philosophical Meditations on Some Requirements of the Poem*, 1735) was "very literally a defence of the relevance of sensuous perception."[1]

It tried to maintain that the senses, specially the eye and the ear, produce a certain type of knowledge. The noteworthy point here is that philosophical aesthetics, which is today brimming with intellectual ferment, originated as a plea for the value of sensibility, not as a theory of art.[2] Today, on the other hand, the focus of this subject is on art; and, what is more, beauty (or *saundarya*) is no longer regarded as a *necessary* feature of art; *meaning* alone is given that distinction, though not in the sense of verbal meaning alone. This is so because, unlike meaning or significance, *beauty* cannot be said to cover all good art. Even such a mild predicate of appeal as "pleasant" cannot be applied to Goya's *Disasters of War* or to Picasso's *Guernica*.[3] Neither work tickles the eye, and so they cannot be

---

1. Kai Hammermeister, *The German Aesthetic Tradition*, Cambridge University Press, 2002, p. 4.
2. Ibid.
3. Harold Osborne, *The Art of Appreciation*, London: OUP, 1970, p. 41.

said to be *beautiful* in the ordinary sense of the word. Yet both are universally regarded as great works of art. *Guernica* is acclaimed primarily because it is meaningful in the sense of being expressive of the artist's own indignation and revulsion at the "cruelty and injustice" involved in the destruction of Guernica (a town in North Spain) by German bombers during the Spanish Civil War. This expressiveness, however, is very far removed from the way a frown may express anger or irritation, automatically, that is, *without any effort* on the part of the person who looks angry. It is a quality of the work's structural details — of some shapes that are unusually angular. In Picasso's hands this very angularity has become a symbol or indirect index of ferocity,[4] and it is obviously *the result of his creative effort.*

Be that as it may, aesthetics is no longer regarded as the *śāstra* of *saundarya.* Even a casual look at its contemporary literature bears out the point. One of the better known books on the subject, *Aesthetics — A Critical Anthology,* for instance, opens its General Introduction as follows:

> Aesthetics is a term commonly used to refer to such diverse matters as theories of beauty and the elegance of a logician's axiomatic system. Philosophically, the term has a far more precise designation. Today, those philosophers called aestheticians are concerned with two general enterprises — the theory of art and the theory of the aesthetic that emerged in the eighteenth and nineteenth centuries from the theory of beauty.[5]

The Cambridge Dictionary of Philosophy is a little more enlightening:

> Aesthetics . . . [is that] branch of philosophy . . . [which] examines the nature of art and the character of our experience of art and of the natural environment. . . . Questions specific

---

4. Harold Osborne, op. cit., p. 263.
5. George Dickie, Richard Scalfani, and Ronald Rabbin (eds.): *Aesthetics — A Critical Anthology,* Boston and New York: Bedford/ St. Martin's, 2nd edn., 1989.

> to the field of aesthetics are: Is there a special attitude, the aesthetic attitude, which we should take toward works of art and the natural environment, and what is it like? Is there a distinct . . . [kind of] aesthetic experience, and what is it? Is there a special kind of value that we can call aesthetic value, comparable with moral, epistemic, and religious values? . . . Aesthetics also encompasses the philosophy of art . . . [Here,] the most central issue . . . has been how to define "art". . . .[6]

However, insofar as good anthologies, original works and dictionaries appear only now and then, it is mainly the regular, leading journals of aesthetics that may be allowed to determine our understanding of what aesthetics *today* is; for they alone can keep all along abreast of the latest directions and concerns of aesthetical thinking. Luckily, the two leading journals — *The British Journal of Aesthetics* (*BJA*) and the (American) *Journal of Aesthetics and Art Criticism* (*JAAC*) — both here speak almost identically, and so their conception of what aesthetics is may well be put collectively as follows:

> The term "aesthetics" is to be taken to include all studies of *the arts* and related types of experience from a philosophical, scientific or other theoretical standpoints including those of psychology, sociology, anthropology, cultural history, art criticism and education. The term "the arts" shall include all branches of art, both of fine art and of practical arts.[7]

It is here noteworthy that both journals give pre-eminence to aesthetics regarded as a *philosophical* study of the arts. Today, in fact, such a way of looking at the arts is commonly regarded as a signal intellectual achievement of the twentieth century, quite as notable as philosophies of science, logic, and mind.[8] So our emphasis too in this chapter will be on *philosophical*

6. Edited by Robert Audi, Cambridge University Press, 2nd edn., 1999, pp. 11-12.
7. The reference here is mainly to the front inside cover of the *Journal of Aesthetics and Art Criticism*, U.S.A., hereafter referred to as *JAAC*.
8. S.K. Langer, *Problems of Art*, London: Routledge and Kegan Paul, 1957, pp. 2-3.

aesthetics, as against the other ways of looking at the arts, though a brief reference to those ways will have to be made, if only with a view to highlighting the uniqueness of the philosophical approach. The word *philosophical,* specially where it occurs with *art,* may appear rather daunting to readers in general and to lovers of art in particular. But, we may note, there is nothing esoteric about philosophy today. Reflection on supersensuous realities like God and the *ātman* are no longer its primary concern. In the words of William James, philosophy today is simply "a peculiarly stubborn attempt to think clearly";[9] and, we may add, so is philosophical aesthetics in its concern with art.

It would however be wrong to confine our study of aesthetics to Western art and the contemporary modes of aesthetic thinking in the West. We must also pay due attention to some of the more important aspects of *our own traditional thinking in this context;* for, though it never assumed the form of aesthetics regarded as a unified theory of all the arts, it has given us quite a few rich insights in respect of some individual arts such as drama, dance and poetry. In this connection it is interesting to note that the value of some age-old Indian concepts and theories of art, art activity and art contemplation has been recognized by quite a few leading aestheticians of today. Thus, see the following from Susanne K. Langer's *Feeling and Form:*

> Some of the Hindu critics . . . understand much better than their Western colleagues the various aspects of emotion in the theatre, which our writers so freely . . . confuse: the feelings experienced by the actor, those experienced by the spectators, those presented as undergone by the characters in the play, and finally, the feeling that shines through the play itself — the vital feeling of the piece. This last they call *rasa;* it is a state of emotional knowledge which comes only to those who have long studied and contemplated poetry. It is . . . not like

9. Cited by Brand Blanshard in his book, *On Philosophical Style,* New York: Greenwood Press, 1969, rpt., p. 13.

mundane feeling and emotion, but is detached, more of the spirit than of the viscera, pure and uplifting.[10]

Harold Osborne too speaks of the Indian doctrine of *rasa* as "the most complex and the most subtle of emotional theories of appreciation."[11] Further, he believes that even apart from "the metaphysical and religious framework which is common to very much of Indian thought" the doctine in question "is capable of supplementing the rather meagre insights of Western thought."[12] What is more, in conformity with the contemporary demand for internationalism in aesthetics, he rightly invites our attention to *the distinctive features* of traditional Indian thinking on art and art experience. Some of these may be quickly outlined here, just for the sake of providing a more balanced overall view of aesthetics:

a. As compared to their Western counterparts, the aestheticians of ancient India have put deeper emphasis on the subjective aspects of our experience of art. It would, of course, be wrong to suppose that these aspects have been totally ignored by aestheticians in the West. Some of them have, in fact, taken care to emphasize that contemplation of great works of art is "life-enhancing" in the sense that when we are able to concentrate on a work of art which makes very heavy demands on our percipience in revealing its total form, "we are keyed up to more than ordinary vitality and alertness,"[13] and that the occasion which art contemplation provides for the successful exercise of trained and discriminating perception gives us *a kind of delight* which distinguishes aesthetic pleasure.[14] But all this is neither so deep nor so exalted as the Indian view that "both the creative function of the artist and the practice of appreciation are . . .

---

10. S.K. Langer: *Feeling and Form*, Routledge and Kegan Paul, 4th Impression, 1967, p. 323.

11. Harold Osborne, *The Art of Appreciation*, p. 116.

12. Ibid., p. 204.

13. Ibid., pp. 208-09.

14. Ibid.

modes of personal devotion demanding systematic mental discipline akin to the various forms of psychic self-control taught by *yoga* in quest of spiritual enlightenment. [Here] the pleasures of art are . . . believed to culminate in transcendental bliss akin to the spiritual rapture of mystical or metaphysical union with the Absolute."[15]

The very climate of India was such that everything was perforce to be invested with the holy spirit of religion. . . . Even the most mundane activity [could here be] viewed as religious. . . . In the widest sense [that is, as somehow reinforcing one's commitment to the divine] dance and drama, music and painting, are [to the traditional Indian] so many ways of divine worship. It does not mean, as is generally supposed, that art was a handmaid to religion, that the aesthetic approach was subordinated to dogmas of religion . . . (but only that) artists in India were religious in their personal lives and took their vocation so very seriously that they deemed their work to be on a par with the hardest disciplines like *yoga.*[16]

b. Further, in spite of its insistence on the closeness of art to religion, traditional Indian thought looks on entertainment as a quite legitimate function of art. This may seem to be no more than ordinary good sense;[17] but it is important, for (as Osborne points out) it may well serve "as a corrective to a too rigorous austerity, a too rarefied exclusiveness, which at any rate have lent a certain one-sidedness to most European aesthetic expositions."[18]

c. Finally, Indian thought has seldom lost sight of the fact

---

15. Harold Osborne, op. cit., p. 204. It may here be noted, following Osborne, that writing which likens aesthetic experience to religious mysticism is "not entirely unknown to the West." John Dewey, for instance, speaks of "the mystic aspect of acute aesthetic surrender, that renders it so akin as an experience to what religionists term ecstatic communion." John Dewey, *Art as Experience*, New York: Capricorn Books, 1958, 7th Impression, p. 28.

16. Osborne, *The Art of Appreciation*, p. 288.

17. Ibid., p. 205.

18. Ibid., p. 204.

> that the artistic impulse in man is closely allied to the sheer delight in all created things. "The *Nāṭyaśāstra* of Bharata . . . the most important source-book of Indian aesthetic thought, begins with the story that the gods approached the Creator with the request for a diversion which should delight their eyes and ears alike."[19]

At this point, however, a word of caution is necessary for understanding what aesthetics really is as an intellectual discipline. Quite a few of us feel tempted by the idea that insofar as it deals with art and beauty, aesthetics must be a very pleasing subject. Now, the focus of aesthetics today is admittedly on art. It is also true that a substantial amount of art is beautiful, and that aestheticians today are perhaps *not as generally* sceptical about the relation of art to beauty as they were till recently.[20] Yet the study of aesthetics is certainly not as directly pleasing as the sight of a rainbow or of the "cup of wonder" that we occasionally see in a little child's eye. Nor is a work of art bound to be beautiful. Many works of modern art do not tickle the common man's eye. Awareness of this fact may disappoint those who are about to begin their study of aesthetics. But it would steady them a little were their attention also invited to the fact that literary works like *Rāmāyaṇa* or *Kāmāyanī* (by Jai Shankar Prasad) cannot be credited with the *immediately seizable* beauty of an architectural marvel like Taj Mahal, though their own status as great works of poetical art is quite beyond question. Very often we admire a work of art because of what it says or signifies, as against how it looks. Today, indeed, theoretically the most stimulating kind of aesthetics is its philosophical genre; the *meaning,* and not the merely sensuous charm of art is here the main concern; and if a study of this subject yet gives us some intellectual delight, as it surely does, it is mainly because it makes us see (or check) a little better either (a) the meaning (or range) of a concept or of a theory

---

19. Harold Osborne, *The Art of Appreciation,* op. cit., p. 205.
20. That is, till before the appearance of Mary Mothersill's book: *Beauty Restored,* Oxford: Clarendon Press, 1984.

relating to art, or (b) the intricate character of art experience itself.

Illustration is here easy. Take, to begin with, the *theory* that art is essentially a kind of expression, a theory which has certainly dominated the history of aesthetics.[21] Perhaps most Indian classical singers would not only agree to, but also insist on, the view that music is nothing if not an outpouring of the singer's own heart (or feelings). The *rasika* too is here very likely to agree. The music *critic* may even be able to make us see that the expressiveness of a particular recital is due to its regulation of vocal volume, so that a semblance of the rise and fall of feeling is effectively evoked.[22] But the *aesthetician's* help yet remains necessary. As a philosopher, his concern with music (as with art taken generally) is much fuller than that of the layman, the *rasika* and the critic. It is he who is expected to make us realize that music is not mere singing, but also the music of instruments which is generally admired for qualities other than expressiveness; that even within the region of classical vocal music, the overriding criteria of excellence are sweetness to the (trained) ear, fidelity to the *rāga* and *tāla* chosen, structural beauty of *sthāyī-antarā* and *taans*, and effective execution; and that therefore expression (of feeling) cannot be regarded as the very *essence* of music. Expressiveness in our music is in fact rarely admired unless it appears as an occasional and quite unforced enlivenment of music that is already possessed of the other qualities listed.

---

21. See, here, the following: "The expression theory of art, in one form or another, has dominated the aesthetic scene for the past centuries as much, perhaps, as the imitation theory had done previously." John Hospers in his essay, "The Concept of Artistic Expression", in: *Introductary Readings in Aesthetics* (ed. by Hospers himself). The Free Press, Collier MacMillan Publishers, 1969, p. 142.

22. I have here in mind some of the greatest vocalists of modern India, specially the late Ustad Abdul Karim Khan and Pandit Omkarnath Thakur.

Consider, now, an aesthetic *concept*, say, the concept of *form*. It is of course the task of a critic to make us see how exactly the details of (say) a poem's content are organized in relation to one another. But the meaning of artistic *form*, taken generally, is not his (the critic's) *direct* concern. It is the aesthetician who argues how, in the region of art, *form* means neither what it does in the context of things — say, their outlines or abstractable shapes — nor even the identifiable sub-type of an individual art — such as *ghazal* and *mercia*[23] in the region of Urdu poetry — but the intense inner unity of a work of art's content.

Here, if in passing, a hint may be given as to how some new awareness of artistic details and aesthetic possibilities can be had if we did aesthetics in relation to *Indian* art. The integration of different human figures in a single representational painting — say, by regulating the line of their *looks* — is widely known. But when we turn to classical Indian sculpture (or dance) we are often struck by the way *the whole bodily* posture is made to lend point *to a dainty (yet meaningful) little gesture or mudrā.* Again, as we follow the changing ways in Western painting, we may come to think of impressionist art as *merely opposed to* that which is expressionistic. But the first few minutes of *ālāpa* on the (*vichittra*) *vīṇā* are a clear *blend of both.* Here, the generally fluid form not only provides aesthetic experience by projecting undivided *impressions* of the *rāga*'s distinctive character, but is variously *expressive*, say, of a yearning tenderness or deep-seated tranquillity, though because of music's inherent demands — say, of identifiable form and tonal sweetness — the artistic devices of exaggeration and distortion are just not possible here. Finally, whereas our *ālāpa*

23. *Mercia* may be likened to elegy in English poetry. It is a song of mourning. *Ghazal* holds the pride of place in Urdu poetry today. But, originally, it is a Persian and Arabic verse-form, of not more than 18 couplets, the first two lines and the even-numbered lines rhyming together; and it is mainly amatory and bacchanalian in character.

of the *dhruvapad* manner is a surpassing example (in singing) of what Walter Pater meant by "pure music," our rhythm is a whole world of purely formal charm, of sounds that have a minimum of (graded) tonal variety, but which can yet be the subject of a quite new aesthetics, *the aesthetics of mnemonic syllables,* which has happily begun to engage the attention of scholars in India.

But, to turn again to the present, what exactly is philosophical aesthetics? An obvious, though not very enlightening answer is: it is "simply the philosophical study of art."[24] Now, it would make us see the nature of such aesthetics a little better if we began by marking it off, quite briefly, from some other kinds of aesthetics. Consider, to begin with, what is known as *psychological* aesthetics. Some of the questions it addresses may be listed as follows:

Is a man's excellence as an artist related to his Intelligence Quotient? How is creativity a "magic synthesis" of the primitive, irrational forces of the unconscious with the logical, cognitive processes of the conscious mind? Can creativity be cultivated? If yes, what are the controllable factors on which it depends? Does the intake of mind-altering drugs like mescaline and L.S.D. somehow add to the artist's creative power? Again, if he is about to set out on a big creative venture, would it help if he prefaced it with a day or two of quiet relaxation? Silvano Arieti points out that a measure of "aloneness" may here be necessary. But he hastens to add that it need not be accompanied by any painful feeling of loneliness, and that it is quite different from that persistent shyness which is generally brought about by one's own psychological problems.

The psychological, however, is not the only non-philosophical way of looking at the arts. Sensible questions can also be put from the viewpoint of socio-cultural conditions. Some of these questions, which are generally left out by a

---

24. Antony Flew, *A Dictionary of Philosophy*, Pan Books Ltd., 1984 edn., p. 6.

present-day *philosopher* of art, may be put thus:

How can we explain the sudden resurgence of both *ghazal/bhajan*-singing in our country today? Is it because attendance at such concerts is a good way to at once appear socially important and to have some quick and easy entertainment; or is it traceable to the fact that neither lovers of Hindi nor of Urdu want to lag behind in their open admiration of music and poetry? Why is it that most of the better *ghazal* singers still hail from Pakistan? Does the socio-cultural setting in which an artist is born and brought up determine not only his choice of a specific musical genre but his performing ability too? And, to turn to our dances, why does the Lucknow Gharānā[25] of Kathak dance pay greater attention to softness and delicacy of expression than, say, the representatives of the Jaipur school? Is it because of the patronage which the Lucknow school received from Nawābs who were generally fond of a peaceable life of love and luxury?

Nor is *metaphysical* aesthetics, which chooses to relate art and beauty to ultimate Reality, unfamiliar to us in India. In fact, a good deal of our traditional theory of art has been frankly metaphysical. The variform *mithuna*[26] figures that fill the walls of our older temples in such abundance are said to symbolize the union of soul with God; and music has for long been regarded in India as a disciplined worship of *Nāda-Brahma* or the Absolute as *Nāda* or primal Sound. In our own day, Vinoba Bhave has spoken of beauty as the grace of the Lord granted to prayerful and ceaseless endeavour.

Now, we may not at once say that such thinking is quite without value. But the trouble is that there is no way to see what this value really is; for we are at a loss to see what

25. A *gharānā* is a traditional school of music or dance, generally having a particular family as its focus.

26. *Mithuna* signifies loving *couples*, as distinguished from erotic *groups*. *Mithuna* had been part of Indian artistic repertoire since the first century CE.

precisely such writing means. Philosophical aesthetics is different. In philosophy, today, we hesitate to speak too freely of an ultimate, supersensible Reality; and our emphasis, in principle, is on clarity of meaning. In this basic sense indeed — that is, as an attempt to clarify our ideas — philosophy is perhaps of special relevance to the arts, for our talk about them is quite often glib. Very freely, for instance, we declare that Indian music is *spiritual*, without taking care to clarify what exactly this word can be taken to mean in the context of music,[27] a great deal of which does not use any elevating or even thoughtful language. Therefore, as serious and detailed thinking about matters relating to art, philosophical aesthetics is indeed a demand of the day.

Yet a suspicion is likely to linger. One could protest that though it may be right to philosophize about matters which call for understanding, art is essentially an object of relish; and that therefore it seems improper to do *philosophy* in relation to art. Why indeed should we labour to link two quite disparate things? The doubt is however easy to dispel. Art is not merely, or even essentially, an object of mere enjoyment. It is, in this context, important to see that the "tasting" (or आस्वादन) of which our *rasa* theorists speak is no mere indulgence of the tongue, ear or the eye, but the relish of a connoisseur and a mental activity (*manasāsvādana*). The metaphor of tasting is only meant to emphasize the utter immediacy and personal character of aesthetic experience. Nor is this tasting an expert act quite in the same way in which a professional tea-taster tastes and checks a particular blend of tea. The *rasika* — or one who can experience *rasa* — is believed to be a person who is equipped with a fair *knowledge* or *understanding of the technique* of an art, along with a well trained ability to register the specific finenesses of — and artistic devices employed in — a work, such as the artist's unremitting adherence to *svara* and *tāla* in the case of music, or

27. See, here, my essay: "The Spiritual and Hindustānī Music" in *Sangeet Natak*, the official journal of Sangeet Natak Akademi (New Delhi), Nos. 131-132, 1999, pp. 3-14.

the accord of verbal meanings with the very sound or even disposition of words in the case of poetry. How indeed can any work of art be fully enjoyed unless it is contemplated discriminatingly? However, such an effort may not be easy for the average listener or reader. The *nigāh* (or discriminating perception) which a knowledgeable lover of the arts is expected to have and to exercise is indeed no isolated act of immediate attention, but an ability — acquired through long and loving communion with art, and even with artistes — to follow and admire the projection or embodiment (in actual works) of some principles which are freely talked about and discussed by the makers and "consumers" of art. It is a known fact that our poets, musicians, and dancers feel greatly encouraged by applause *at the right turn* of phrase, rhythm or melody; and that this perception of rightness is possible only for the knowledgeable.

Such a seizure of artistic significance is indeed not just a sensuous activity. Nor is *a work of art* ever meant for uncultivated perception. It calls for understanding and so is not intelligible to one and all. This is why questions such as the following, "what does it say" or "what is it about," are often freely put by us, especially with regard to a work of modern art. How then can we object to philosophy of art (or philosophical aesthetics) which discusses such questions with the throughness they demand? Nor is there any warrant for supposing that the moment we set out to *understand* what a work of art is or means, our *relish* of it is necessarily impoverished. As we have already said, the artists themselves expect their works to be praised discriminatingly; and it is quite common experience that the more conversant we become with the technique of an art, the deeper does our appreciation of creations in its region become. The alternative is to be content with just being baffled or vaguely excited by the mere surface appearance of a work of art.

Such facts are enough to justify philosophical aesthetics. A look at the problems it addresses highlights its value further.

These are essentially the same as those of general philosophy: that is, problems relating to meaning, reality, truth, value and knowledge. Of all these theoretic concerns, the question of meaning is today of pre-eminent value, for we now see it clearly that whatever be the question that faces us, we cannot even try to answer it properly unless we first take care to understand what it means. In contemporary aesthetics this question is specially important also because, as we have already pointed out, meaning or significance is today regarded as a more essential feature of art than beauty. A work can very well be good as art without being beautiful or good to look at, but it cannot claim any artistic excellence if it does not "say" something, or is otherwise significant, say, by way of lifting us above our everyday concerns for a while; by giving us some insight, maybe, into the life of feeling; or by simply teasing or refining our perception. So an important question of philosophical aesthetics is that of artistic meaning.

This question is indeed quite basic; for the meaning of *art* itself calls for some reflection. The point is easy to explain. The meaning of the words which are being used right now can also be conveyed by means of their Hindi equivalents, which means that their (English words') meaning cannot be said to be inseparable from their present (English) character. But, on the other hand, how can the meaning (or the net impact or significance) of a particular poem, painting or music composition be shifted, whole and entire, to a different set of words, colours, notes and rhythm? To take a simple example, the dictionary meanings of *glistening* and *glimmering*, are almost identical; but in a poetic line which speaks of the sea, a beach and the waves one cannot possibly replace *glimmering* with *glistening*, for only the former's phonetic quality has a slightly undulating feel which goes well with the image of waves.[28]

---

28. The reference, here, is to the following lines of Matthew Arnold's poem. *Dover Beach:*

    The sea is calm to-night,

    . . . , the moon lies fair

And, to turn to our classical music, is it not an admitted fact that a properly structured *bandish* (composition) blooms (or खिलती है, as we say in popular parlance) at — and so is aesthetically inseparable from — *its* own specific *laya* or aesthetic pace?

But of course this is not the only way to see the value of the question of meaning in respect of philosophical aesthetics. A whole list of terms that we freely use in our talk about art requires deeper analysis, for their various meanings are not always clearly distinguished. Here are some such words: art, expression, feeling, form, creation, *rasa*, and aesthetic experience; and problems here easily arise when we try to determine the meaning of these concepts philosophically, that is, in a clear and self-consistent way. For the sake of brevity, however, only one of them may here be picked for attention: the concept of *art*.

What does "art" *mean?* The question is by no means unnecessary, for we in fact use the word in different senses, and these may suggest quite different lines of enquiry. One common meaning of the word is a distinct kind of object, *an object* of art. This is the intended meaning when, say, a critic points to an abstract painting — which may look quite odd and unmeaning to a layman — and insists: "*this is art.*" Another familiar use of the word is art in the sense of an activity, or art as the making of art. This is the obvious meaning when, for instance, we talk of promoting the practice of art along with the study of science and computers in our schools and colleges. Finally, "art" may be taken to signify works of art *taken generally*, as when we speak of an institution as The National Museum of Art. All these meanings are of value to us, for they all excite

---

. . . , on the French coast, the light
Gleams . . . , the cliffs of England stand
Glimmering and vast . . .
Listen, you hear the grating roar
Of pebbles which the waves draw back and fling . . .

aesthetic thinking, if differently. Thus, to begin with the first meaning, if "art" signifies a *distinct* kind of "thing," the meaning clearly is that it is not an everyday object. But the moment we say so, at least two questions arise. If "art" *is* something and yet not in the way of things of daily use, how is it *real* at all, and how are we to *know* that it is art, and not a thing of daily life? These are both questions of *philosophical* aesthetics, for they relate to reality and knowledge. Further, should any one venture to suggest that a work of art is a distinctive something because, quite unlike our everyday objects, it is an "expressive form" or a source of disinterested *delight,* another philosophical question may be put at once. How can we be sure as to the *truth* of such general characterizations of art? Our rhythm is an independent art too.[29] A good solo *tablā* recital can be an important item in a whole session of classical music. But nobody will be found admiring it as follows: "How *expressive* the playing was!" On the other hand, if Picasso's *Guernica* is regarded as a superlative painting, it is surely not because it gives some immediate delight to the eye but because one comes to see, by exercising discriminating attention, that the artist has here used to perfection such subtle devices as making the very "unusual angularity" of shapes as "the equivalent of ferocity."[30]

The truth indeed is that, in one respect or another, the various attempts to seize the *essence* of art alike seem questionable. But what they all necessarily assume — that is, the work of art's *reality* in some sense of the word — cannot be denied. The assumption, however, is not only necessary, but invites enquiry. Is a work of art real in the manner of an everyday object? A thing is extended, and so has its "place" in

29. In support of this particular view quite a few arguments have been given in my essay on Hindustānī Rhythm which appeared in the summer 1976 issue, vol. 16. no. 3 of *The British Journal of Aesthetics*. (hereafter referred to as *BJA*) and is also reproduced in my book, *Avenues to Beauty* (Sangeet Natak Akademi and D.K. Printworld, 2009), chapter 4, pp. 113-28.

30. Harold Osborne, *The Art of Appreciation,* p. 263.

actual space. It is also generally useful or is at least usable. Now, we *can* speak of art too in these everyday ways. Thus, when we say: "Put this painting in that corner" we obviously think of it as a thing that can be handled, carried and placed. We can also so put it that it may cover an ugly patch in the wall, in which case it would become *useful* too in the everyday sense of the word. But it is clear that in all such talk about — or dealing with — the work, no attention is paid to its quality *as art*. Artistic perception would here begin only when, say, the lines, figures and masses in the work are carefully noticed, and when an effort is made to see how they all make for some unified impact or significance. Here, how the work can help us in practice is not the question at all. If a man so decides, he *can* surely use a small piece of sculpture as a paperweight, but in so doing he would in no way be concerned with its value *as art*.

But though it is surely not a mere thing, a work of art cannot be said to be wholly unreal, or a mere abstraction like number. A measure of remoteness from sheer fact may well be necessary for a good deal of art. But even where it is totally non-representational — or a very negation of surface appearances, as in the hands of the Russian expressionist painter, Wassily Kandinsky[31] — art produces specific aesthetic sensations in the spectator, or a kind of shock effect on him, maybe because of its bright colour and emphatic brushwork. On the other hand, a number as such is never seen to have the same effect on us. Further, quite unlike a number, art often amazes and delights us by virtue of its beautiful form and its magical or "virtual" elements. The literally moveless and often quite limited canvas of the painter may well be able to project a semblance of *movement* and *infinite recession* or *distance*. The former, for instance, is "seen" in El Greco's *Resurrection*[32] where

---

31. 1866-1944. Kandinsky is regarded as the first painter to develop an entirely abstract style.

32. This painting may be seen in: *El Greco* (by Lionello Puppi), A Dolphin Art Book, London: Thames and Hudson, 1967, Plate 49.

Christ seems to be *rising* back to life; and the latter, in *The Boat Padma* by Gaganendra Nath Tagore.

It would here be relevant to see, in brief, how the question of art's reality has been discussed by some important theorists of art. Of course, a mere look at works of art and literature is enough to make us see that a work of art cannot be said to be real like a material object. As a rule, things serve some practical purpose. Works of art, on the other hand, are only meant to be contemplated. But Susanne K. Langer explains the difference in a way which is not at all so obvious, but is yet not quite without sense. According to her, a work of art is a symbolic expression of how life feels. Being alone is one thing; feeling lonely or deserted is quite another; and Langer insists that art is uniquely important because it captures and projects not only the actual things and happenings, but their subjective impact which is quite as real. Arthur Danto has yet another way of distinguishing *creations in the region of music* from material objects. The former, in his view, are "logically incombustible" in the sense that whereas all material objects can be destroyed by sufficiently intense heat, the burning of the notation of a composition will do nothing to harm the music itself.[33] But, then, are we to accept the *ideal* theory of Croce and Collingwood, which says that all works of art are, in essence, the *artist's own intuition,* which is at once (spiritual) expression too; and that what is called (overt) expression is only a secondary and practical activity? We can hardly say, yes; for the acceptance of such a view would be simply to miss the vital truth that most works of art reveal what they do by means of, or rather in terms of, their uniquely shaped *material* or *perceptual* elements. What is more, the specific character of its material not only determines (and largely delimits) the expressive power of an art, but (along with other factors) contributes to its distinctiveness. Thus, whereas on the one hand, our rhythm,

33. Nelson Goodman, *Languages of Art,* Indianapolis: Hackett, 1976, chapter III. But, one may ask, what about paintings and literary works? *They* cannot be said to be "incombustible" in this sense.

with its wordless material of mnemonic syllables, cannot tell a story or express an emotion, it is on the other hand exactly this material, comprising many Hindi letters but not in the way of (meaningful) language, which separates this art from other arts and makes it a virtual paradigm of *pure* art. Oppositely, the *art* of drama uses quite a few different materials — say, language, gestures, music, and dance. So it is infinitely capable of representation and expression, as against rhythm which can only be made *to add to* the expressiveness of some other artistic element, say, *abhinaya* in our dances. It is therefore clearly improper to underestimate the value of materials in art. Luckily, there is a kind of middle view too which seems to do justice to both aspects of art — the material and the non-sensuous or spiritual. Arthur Danto believes that "the relation of [say] a sculpture to the shaped material of which it consists is analogous to the habitation of the human body by a soul." According to this view, the non-material something which distinguishes a work of art from a mere thing "is not, as on the ideal theory, located in the artist, but in the work itself; it is not found in the human soul, but rather animates a piece of bronze or a canvas charged with pigments."[34]

We may now turn to the second meaning of "art." If art is a distinct kind of activity, it is so partly because the agent here is no ordinary person, but an individual who has trained himself in a particular way and has his own way of looking at things. This is of course common knowledge. But when we focus on this simple fact, the need is at once heightened to reckon with the *artist's* own point of view and experience in discussing questions about art. His (art-)activity, however, is distinctive not merely because he is its source, but because it can be objectively marked off from other major fields of human endeavour, say, craft, morality, science, and philosophy.

---

34. Crispin Sartwell's essay "Aesthetic Dualism and the Transfiguration of the Commonplace" in *JAAC*, Summer 1988, p. 461. This view has been called "aesthetic dualism."

Art-Craft *differences*:

1. Of all these human concerns it is craft which is necessarily related to art. Therefore, how the two *differ* has to be carefully thought out. They cannot be said to be utterly dissimilar. Both call for a considerable degree of skill. Both, again, involve the manipulation of some given material — be it stone, pigment, clay, or wood. What is more, both produce objects of value. But, and now we turn to distinguish the two, whereas a product of craft is generally important mainly because it is practically useful, a work of art is of value because it expresses or communicates a feeling or some meaning, *and is therefore meant to be contemplated rather than used.* Art is never mere craftsmanship, but craftsmanship *as harnessed to a special end*: "the creation of . . . visually, audibly, or even imaginatively perceivable forms"[35] that seem to be expressive or otherwise significant, say, by virtue of their ability to provide disinterested delight or some other kind of non-sensuous satisfaction to a knowledgeable contemplator. The difference is in fact reflected in our everyday parlance. It is usual to speak thus: "a craftsman *produces* goods, but *creates* a thing of beauty"; "a builder *erects* a house, but *creates* an edifice if the house is a real work of architecture, however modest." An artefact as such is merely a combination of material parts, or a modification of a natural object to suit human purposes. A work of art, on the other hand, is more than an "arrangement" of given things . . . something emerges from the tones or colours which was not there before," and the ground of value is here this emergent form, semblance or significance.[36]

2. Further, as he sets out to exercise his skill, a craftsman has a fairly clear idea of the details of the particular

35. S.K. Langer, *Problems of Art*, p. 111.

36. S.K. Langer, *Feeling and Form*, Routledge & Kegan Paul, 3rd Impression, 1963, p. 40.

object — say, a table — which he proposes or has been asked to produce. The method of making too is fairly prefixed; and but for very few changes that may be demanded by some unsuspected detail — say, a knot in a piece of the wood being used — the act of making itself is on the whole foreseeable. The "making" of *art* is a quite different activity. It is rarely notable for the kind of foreseeing and pre-determination that distinguish mere craftsmanship. Even the making of a film may not be regarded as the slavish execution of a prefixed script; and there is plenty of good sense in the view of Vera Chytilova,[37] a well-known contemporary Czech director, that the making of a film is not the mere illustration of its script; that the latter is only the provisional foundation of a film; and that during its (subsequent) making quite a few such changes may have to be made as are a clear departure from the script. Further, we have it on the authority of Herbert Read that Picasso rarely knew "in advance what he . . .[was] going to put on the canvas, nor . . . [would] he decide what colours to use . . . [the crucial thing here being] a renunciation of the will and a surrender to the promptings of the unconscious."[38] And should we seek a senior (Indian) classical musician's opinion on the matter, he would insist that at the moment of opening a recital what he decides (and knows he is going) to do is simply the treatment of a particular composition in a specific *rāga-tāla* setting; that, in respect of the details and disposition of the musical filling, what he knows only is that they are nowhere to be allowed to flout the demands of the specific melody and rhythm (or *rāga* and *tāla*) chosen; and that such (mere) generalities

37. Expressed in the course of an "interview" during our 12th Film Festival, January 1989.

38. W.G. Archer, *Indian and Modern Art*, George Allen & Unwin, 1959, p. 60.

relating to the order of presentation have also to be kept in mind as the precedence of *sthāyī-antarā* over *bahlāvā, baṛhat* and *taan*s, or of *vilambit* in relation to *drut* compositions. But, he would hasten to add, exactly how many times the *bandish* is to be sung (or played), which particular *taan* is to have priority over others, the precise moment of switching over to the *drut* composition, or the exact length of time for which the voice is to tarry at the *tār shadj,* — all this is quite undecided as one begins, and has to be left to the impulse of the moment. Further, there is here a positive feature which explains why the progression of *our* music cannot be predetermined in detail. Where a musician performs in the presence of some *rasika*s, he is generally quick to register their reactions; and just as the making of a painting is (in general) not the breathless execution of a prefixed plan, but a sensitive response to, and determination by, what the presently completed detail of the work itself seems to demand or suggest, so the musician — if he is not a mere craftsman — depends for the next step quite often on how exactly the immediate *svara-samūha* sounds, and also, if but occasionally, on how the *rasika*s react to the details of the ongoing music.

3. Further, the good that the arts do to us is not the same as what we gain from the crafts. The latter cater for our specific *needs,* say, for food, shelter, clothing and ornament. Builders, weavers and jewellers are therefore of obvious value to society. But the making, contemplation, and appreciation of works of art relate to our attitudes, states of being, and cognitive/affective capacities. By creating a work of art the artist gets the deep, inner delight of effective self-expression which he cannot possibly equate with any other gain. As for the *rasika*s, they too can benefit richly from contemplation of works of art. It is an admitted fact that aesthetic experience relieves tensions and checks

destructive impulses, refines perception, and "develops . . . imagination, and along with it the ability to put oneself in the place of others" which is so essential even for the maintenance of good inter-personal relations in daily life. What is more, on entering the world of art we may at the same time get closer to our fellow-beings:

> If two people listen to the same music or see the same painting, insofar as they have learned to make similar responses, they share an experience. All shared experience helps to bring people together in friendship and mutual respect. Aesthetic objects . . . represent a quintessence or distillation of certain qualities of experience, and any two people anywhere who enjoy one of these qualities will have a bond between them.[39]

Now, it is clear that if the way we have distinguished art from craft is accepted, much that is commonly classed as art may have to be called craft and vice versa. Quite a few of our Kathak dancers perform but mechanically, providing only a *laboured* exposition of rhythm. The TV serial *Nukkaḍ*, on the other hand, has been generally a *captivating* performance by a well conducted team, though merely because of this one consideration the whole genre of TV serials cannot be regarded as a new art-form. At the same time it would surely be wrong to insist that just because Kathak has for long been regarded as a major form of our classical dance, its exponents must *all* be called artistes, and that *those who participated in the serial* in question can at best be called good craftsmen, if not entertainers, just because such *presentations* have not yet come to be commonly regarded as art. Whittick is indeed right when he contends that *any* activity which aims, in the main, at the creation of a new aesthetic experience should be regarded as an art, and that the traditional list of five fine arts is a bit too narrow. Kant included landscape gardening too among the fine arts, and he is here justified. For,

---

39. M.C. Beardsley, *Aesthetics — Problems in the Philosophy of Criticism*, Harcourt, Brace & World, Inc. 1958, p. 575.

when a landscape gardener arranges trees, lawns, shrubs, flowers, water and perhaps sculpture in a park, or in the ground of a mansion, he is working primarily with aesthetic intention, and with a feeling for colour, line, mass, light and shadow, very much as a painter.[40]

ART-CRAFT RELATION

1. Though the primary aim of a craftsman is to produce articles which serve some everyday purpose, he can, if he so desires, easily invest them with beauty and some quite new decorative features, and so turn them into possible objects of aesthetic regard. Indeed, though they are obviously meant to cater for our primary needs, vessels and cloths of everyday use have always been more than mere objects of utility. In the Indian tradition specially:[41]

> There has always been interaction between arts and crafts . . . For all we know, weavers may have tried to make their fabrics more and more transparent because of the erotic fantasies of poets who tried hard to discern the form of the beloved through the drapery that covered her. The *haṁsa lakṣaṇā sāṛī* [with a border showing a row of swans] is described in Sanskrit texts and can be seen in Ajantā . . . [and] the very rich decorative patterns in grille and inlay . . . [that distinguish the tomb of Aurangzeb in Aurangabad] . . . have been adapted for fabrics and furnishings.

Yet such instances of relatedness are hardly enough ground for denying that art is not quite the same kind of activity as craft. Both sides of the matter have to be kept in mind. The *fact* that there is craft *in* every art is one thing; the *view* that art

40. Arnold Whittick, "Towards Precise Distinctions of Art and Craft", *BJA*, Winter 84, p. 51.

41. The extract that follows has been taken from Krishna Chaitanya's critical piece "A halation of beauty" in The Hindustan Times of 14.6.1987. The bracketed portions in the quote are all insertions, barring the first one.

may be generally regarded *as a* kind of craft is quite another.[42] There is nothing odd in a book's being entitled: *The Craftsmanship of Keats;* but many would join Collingwood in objecting to the view of Plato and Aristotle that poetry too is a craft.[43] No student of Hindi literature would agree that just because he appears to be much more conversant with the rules of prosody, Keshav may be regarded as a better poet than Sūrdās. Art includes craft; but it does not stop there. Craft is here used for a quite distinct end; namely, the creation of forms which are (at least) pleasing in themselves; its role here, though undeniably essential, is hence but subsidiary.

To conclude, art and craft are not only related to, but distinct from, each other. As a kind of skill, craft is present in every art. Further, motifs and images from the region of art have been freely availed of by craftsmen to beautify their own work. Yet, on the whole, the distinction holds, and is clear and overriding. Any kind of activity that aims at creating forms of intrinsic charm or significance, or any class of artefacts which are commonly expected to evoke disinterested delight may be said to be art. Craft, on the other hand, is skill exercised essentially in creating objects of utility.

Our main concern, however, is art's relation to *philosophy*, not only because the kind of aesthetics we have picked for attention is philosophical, but because, in view of the obvious fact that art is *directly attended to and enjoyed* in galleries and concert halls, the propriety of seeking to relate it to a highly *intellectual and often abstract* subject like philosophy may be easily questioned.[44]

Now there is no doubt that art is quite different from philosophy. Philosophy just cannot be done without a careful

---

42. S.K. Langer, *Feeling and Form*, p. 384.
43. R.G. Collingwood, *The Principles of Art*, Oxford: Clarendon Press, 1955 Reprint, p. 18.
44. I say (only) "*often* abstract" because existentialism and phenomenology cannot be said to be abstract.

use of language. The bulk of art, on the other hand, does not use the verbal medium, literature and vocal music[45] being the only arts that build upon words. There *are* people who would like even painting and sculpture to be regarded as *a kind of* language on the ground that, after all, works in the region of these arts also appear to "say" something. But what could this suggestion really mean? If the words, *a kind of*, are taken to suggest that art is not language *as it is commonly understood,* our insistence on the art-philosophy difference would remain unaffected. In case the words in question are taken to imply only that art too *is expressive* (more or less) like language we may not object to the emphasis on expressiveness taken quite generally; but we would surely have to reject the suggestion, in case it is actually made, that non-verbal art is expressive *in the way of language.* For, whereas in the everyday use of language, verbal meaning is detachable from the particular words which presently convey it — insofar as it can be conveyed by synonymous words from a quite different language — the meaning, or rather the *import* of a particular work of art cannot be accurately provided by any other work, for the simple reason that the distinctive perceptual elements (or "perceptua") of any work of art are integral to its overall meaning. The way in which a work of art is related to what it "says" is indeed to be clearly understood. It does not merely transmit or convey, but is *an embodied revelation of its meaning.* Art is not the mere index, but the necessary locus of its meaning. Precisely for this reason it would be patently wrong if the words "a kind of" are deleted from the proposed view we are discussing and it is categorically said that art is a language. To comprehend the meaning of written or spoken language we have to proceed in a determinate before-after order; but where what we seek to get at is the "meaning" of, say, a painting or sculpture, we are free to begin with a notice of whichever part of the work catches the eye, though of course every detail of the work must be attended to ultimately.

45. That is, all singing barring *ālāpa* of the *dhruvapad* manner.

There is a good deal more that *distinguishes* art from philosophy. The purpose of philosophy is to clarify our ideas, and to determine the truth of our views by means of analysis, discussion and argument. The process of art-making too involves a good deal of thinking and self-criticism. But the aim of such ideal activity, here, is not to clarify, refute or support a theoretical position in the way of philosophy, but to ensure better performance or to make the work better organized or more expressive or truly representational. For instance, where a Kathak danseuse prepares and rehearses for a forthcoming recital, and checks the *pace* of a particular pattern or the *sequence* of the various numbers that she proposes to include in the recital, her objective is (a) proper projection of the *form* of the pattern — so that it may neither appear flaccid nor huddled because of the excessively slow or too quick sequence of the constituent syllables (or *bol*s) — and (b) greater impact of the individual numbers achievable by so putting them in a before-after order that their distinctive character may be heightened by virtue of contrast, as of *vilambit* with *drut* or of *śṛṅgāra* with *vīra rasa* numbers. The painter too must carefully check as to which two colours, if used adjacently, would appear to go well together.

Such agreeable adjacence, of which a clear instance in our music is provided by the working of *saṁvāda*, may be called *aesthetic* consistency. It is quite different from logical consistency which is of paramount value to the philosopher. The former is the mutual agreeableness of two details of *fact* in respect of their *sensuous* character, say, look in the case of colours or sound in that of musical *svara*s. The latter (or logical consistency) is an understood accord of verbal *meaning*. In art, as already pointed out, congruence or harmony simply means that the elements of the work appear to go well together — to direct contemplation. To say that *shadj* and *madhyam* seem to belong to each other in a *rāga* like *Kedāra* is to admit the working of *aesthetic* consistency. Philosophically, on the other hand, if we object to such talk: "A is the *best* student in the class, but B is also *as good* as A," we protest simply because the meaning of the word "best" — that is, "better than *everyone else*" — prevents us from saying that the best can have an equal too. Here, our appeal is to logical consistency.

Yet it is neither possible nor desirable to keep philosophy away from art. Philosophy today is not so much a subject of study with a distinct subject-matter as a sustained and systematic attempt to clarify our ideas. Matters relating to art are in fact freely discussed by critics, educators and artistes themselves. How then can we object if philosophy offers to improve the quality of this ongoing debate? Concepts like *form, feeling* and *expression*, which occur so freely in our talk about art, are often misconstrued, and so the assistance of philosophy should only be welcome to all those who are really serious about understanding art.

In contemporary aesthetics, indeed, what we find generally dominant is analysis of theories of art — say, as form, expression, or as symbol — and of certain concepts related to or within art: for instance, the concept of the *work of art*, and the concepts of representation, illusion, intention, and meaning within the arts. This is however only the focus, not the whole ambit of present-day aesthetics which (we have seen) is visualized very widely today. It is regarded as a serious, academic and many-sided concern with *the arts*. The viewpoint of philosophy is only one of the many approaches here listed. In other words, *philosophical* aesthetics is only a form or part of aesthetics taken generally. But whatever be the kind of aesthetics, its subject of study is held to be *art*; and today the word "beauty" is often left out.

This omission, however, is not quite fair. It is true that a good deal of contemporary art cannot be said to be *beautiful* in case the word is taken to mean: "of immediate appeal to sense." But, on the other hand, it is equally true that there *are* numberless works which seem to be paradigms of beauty. Further, the beauty of nature cannot be kept out of the purview of aesthetic experience, which is freely discussed in books on aesthetics. Historically, aesthetics has always been importantly concerned with beauty: and today, specially since the appearance of Mary Mothersill's book: *Beauty Restored*,[46] aestheticians are perhaps not as averse to the concept of beauty as they were till a few years back. In India too, as we know, *saundarya* (or beauty) has always dominated thinking about art. Therefore it seems demanded that philosophical aesthetics be regarded as the philosophy of art *and beauty*.

The supplement, *and beauty*, would, on the one hand, make our understanding of aesthetics adequate to its traditional character; and, on the other hand, provide not only for the possible disjunction of works of *art* from *beauty*, but for distinct lines of enquiry demanded by the two concepts. As the philosophy of *art*, aesthetics is concerned with such specific questions as the following: the nature and definability of art; the ontological status of a work of art or the relation of art to Being; the place of art in the entire panorama of human activities, for art is a distinctively *human* phenomenon; and, above all, the meaning and truth of aesthetic discourse. And where it focuses on *beauty*, philosophical aesthetics studies such problems as the nature and effects of beauty, and analysis of the whole "hierarchy" of the concepts that are cognate to the beautiful, namely, the graceful and the pretty, the grand or the majestic, and the sublime. A discussion of this "hierarchy" would naturally come up against the question as to how or in what precise respect one concept differs from the others; and an inquiry will also be needed into "the ways in which the beautiful in its wide . . . sense is different from and . . . related to the good, the true, and finally to being itself."[47] All these lines of enquiry cannot possibly be pursued in this essay, but it would surely be of help to see, if in brief, how even the more abstract ones of these can give us some interesting ideas.

Consider, for instance, the relation of art to *Being* as Heidegger visualizes it. It is common to look on works of art

46. Oxford, Clarendon Press, 1984.

47. C.W. Nwodo's essay, "Philosophy of Art vs Aesthetics", in *BJA*, Summer 1984, pp. 200-01.

as *objects that we see in galleries and museums*. But this is only a secondary relation of art. Originally, a work of art is *a revelation of Being*. Here, we may note, *Being* is to be taken not in any transcendental (supernatural, mystical) sense, but simply as what is there historically, that is, in a specific time-place setting; and "revelation," as projection of the essential or typical *functional reality* of an object. Accordingly, Heidegger values Van Gogh's painting, *Two Shoes*, not because it is the faithful representation of a particular pair, but because it is revelatory of the pressure and distortion that the peasants' shoes generally suffer as they trudge — day in, day out — through craggy and uneven pathways straggling across the fields. The farmers themselves only use the shoes; they do not focus on the shoes' functional *career*. The painting does it — and projects the truth effectively. The point of what Heidegger here says is borne out by Van Gogh's own report on the logic of his creative effort in producing another notable work:

> I have tried hard to paint (*The Potato-Eaters*) in such a way that the spectator is immediately struck by the idea that these people, eating potatoes in the lamplight, have dug them up with the same hands with which they are now taking them out of the dish; that they are real workers . . . have literally earned their food. . . . I was not interested in creating something that somebody might think "good" or "beautiful" . . . I . . . have searched for *the ultimate pattern* and . . . it might prove to be a *real peasant picture*.[48]

As a real peasant picture, we may note, this work has a general relevance, and a whole segment of farmers' real life is captured on the canvas — "the same hands" growing potatoes, digging them up, eating them, the dim lamplight (we may add) not quite revealing the soil that still clings to the hands. All in all, it betokens the labour that precedes the humble meal. However, though the point we have just tried to make is not without sense, its relation to Being is not the only way of

48. M.E. Tralbaut, *Van Gogh — A Pictorial Biography*, London: Thames and Hudson, 1959, Italics added.

looking at art. How its *beauty* is related to the good and the true is also a fit object of philosophic enquiry. Consider, for instance, Maritain's view that "the beautiful is not a kind of truth, but a kind of good; the perception of the beautiful . . . is not so much a kind of knowledge as a kind of delight."[49] The meaning here may not be easy to seize, but a little close attention is enough to show that what Maritain here says has a ready appeal. It is of course not easy to *define* beauty, but one thing is clear. Whatever strikes us as beautiful *delights* us; we just like it and feel impelled to call it *good*. On the other hand, relating beauty to truth or knowledge is never so easy or natural; it calls for some effort, is a strain on the mind; and so is removed from that immediate appeal which is always the impact of whatever strikes us as beautiful.

Such philosophic reflection, however, is not the only discriminating way of being concerned with art. Art appreciation and art criticism are two other ways which involve both percipience and analytic thinking in varying measure. Yet they both should and *can* be distinguished from philosophical aesthetics.

> Instead of *reflecting* on the nature, significance, or reality of works of art, *art appreciation* consists largely in looking at . . . [or in some other way contemplating them] on different occasions *and in different moods*, so that one may gradually come to *enjoy and savour* everything in a work of art that is there to be enjoyed and savoured. This appreciation may involve lectures, demonstrations [*or lec-dems,* such as the ones which are organized by Delhi's own *Spicmacay*], and informal conversations with others; but it may also be *silent*, consisting only of *repeated exposure* to the works of art.[50]

The keywords in the above extract are actual and "repeated exposure" to works of art; for by focusing on these two words

---

49. Jacques Maritain, *Art and Scholasticism and the Frontiers of Poetry*, tr. J.W. Evans, University of Notre Dame Press, p. 26.

50. John Hospers, *Introductory Readings in Aesthetics*, New York: The Free Press, 1969. Italics and bracketed words added.

we can easily see what art appreciation really is. Take the case of music, for instance. Just as a child is enabled to distinguish sweet from sour taste by actual tasting, so a listener is enabled to mark off a lower note from a higher one by actually listening to the music himself. It is true that the child may learn to use the *word "sweet"* for the eatable (which really has this taste) by following its parent's habitual use of specific words for particular articles of food; but what *sweet taste* itself really is, for which the *word "taste"* is used, has to be sensed by the child on its own. Similarly, a *rasika* (or trained listener) may well try to help a tyro by saying (while pointing to a particular note): "Look! this *svara* is a little higher than the one you have just heard"; but the actual difference has to be perceived by the lay listener himself. This explains the traditional Indian emphasis on the metaphor of *tasting* in respect of art appreciation. We have to listen to music ourselves and repeatedly if we are to perceive even minuscule differences between the pitch of two adjacent notes; and this is quite as true of perceiving even the slightest changes of tempo. The Indian word for such percipience is *nigāh* or the ability to see not only the differences or changes we have just referred to, but even the slightest suggestion of transgression of the grammatical limits of a *rāga*. No amount of reading books on music can replace this personal *and repeated* contemplation of actual music. A talk on music can only *invite our attention* to specific details, segments or genres of music. Truly to see how all these actually sound, flow, or interrelate is to be marked by the listener himself. Nor does a *lec-dem* necessarily *explain why* the opening line of a song is called *sthāyī* or *when* it is to be regarded as a good specimen of its type.

Such interpreting and evaluating are the task of *art criticism* which always uses language and (unlike art appreciation) can never be "silent." What is more, if a critical write-up on a work of art — say, on a poem or painting — is successful, "it will enable the reader to see in the work . . . many features, *lines of connection, and subtleties of detail* that he did not perceive before." To illustrate the point it would be better to turn to poetry in preference to the other arts, just because works from their regions cannot be presented here. So let us consider the following lines from Shakespeare's *The Winter's Tale* (Act IV, Scene IV):

> . . . daffodils
> That come before the swallow dares and take
> The winds of March with beauty.

Here, without the expert help of a literary critic, an ordinary reader is likely to content himself with a grasp of the merely literal meaning of the words which is easy to get. Such understanding, however, cannot be the source of any delight (as distinct from merely cognitive apprehension) because there is no *obvious* charm here of impressive language or of lilting rhyme. But see now what the following critical interpretation reveals:

> As against the swallow that *dares* into the scene from afar, the daffodils just *come* or arrive on the scene gently, without any fanfare, so to say. The word *dares* supplements the image of the long-winged *migratory* bird, on the one hand; and balances it against the flowers' gentle appearance (because they only *come*), on the other — providing a kind of aesthetic relief. A swallow's meteoric streaks into the blue can easily coerce attention, but the daffodils' quiet act of just taking "the winds of March with beauty" is likely to be missed or only vaguely noticed by a passer-by; which is probably why the poet has chosen to picture it. But the real charm of the lines dawns upon the reader's mind only when he visualizes that a flower which only takes (or receives) the caressing winds cannot but lend itself to them; and that, therefore, a gentle and (so to say) unmurmuring *swaying* of the *diffodils* is the real import of the lines, though of course the charm tends to dissipate in the very course of being so accounted for, analytically. It should now be clear how (as we have said in an extract already cited before quoting Shakespeare) criticism can make us see some "lines of connection" and "subtleties of detail" that are very likely to be missed by uncritical attention.

Music criticism can also be of similar help. Take the case of a Ravi Shankar-Ali Akbar (*sitār-sarod*) *jugalbandī*, for example.

There is hardly any lover of Indian music who has not been fascinated by such music, but its inner knitwork — and so the secret of its charm — as also, if incidentally, the true aesthetic function of a *jugalbandī*, are revealed to us only by critical write-ups such as the following:

> . . . The two performers . . . try to reinforce each other's effects by matching playing in one octave with similar or simultaneous playing in the other; and by trying to articulate audibly what the partner's playing as it ends, demands by suggesting, either as continuance or as a repartee (*sawāl-jawāb*). The one reinforces, completes, or just caps with the dainty singleness of just one note, the meaning or the manner of the patterns of the other. *Sometimes it appears as if one heaves a sigh and the other lends a tear to it.*[51]

This extract, we may note, is a critic's actual reaction to a particular recital by the two maestros, though it is generally relevant to their usual playing too, as a duo. Philosophical aesthetics, on the other hand, does not *confine* itself to individual works or some select genres of art; and as a branch of philosophy, it raises and discusses the time-honoured basic questions of philosophy, in respect of art, — questions (as we have said earlier) of meaning, truth, reality, knowledge and value. It is true that neither art criticism nor philosophical aesthetics can do without language; but whereas the former only uses some concepts without worrying as to what they really mean, the latter — that is, philosophical aesthetics — takes pains to clarify these concepts at length, — concepts like the aesthetic, beauty (or aesthetic value), meaning . . ., representation; expression; . . . [and] art. . . .[52]

Such concepts, it is obvious, relate to art in general, and are not confined to any particular form of it. This indeed is what distinguishes aesthetics clearly from criticism which

---

51. S.K. Saxena, "Essentials of Hindustānī Music" in *Diogene*, 45, Paris, 1964.

52. John Hospers, *Introductory Readings in Aesthetics*, p. 2.

focuses, as a rule, on individual works of art. At the same time, aesthetics is by no means quite unrelated to criticism. The two *are* related, first, because we cannot do aesthetics until we have some critical statements to work on; and, second, because, as *metacriticism*, aesthetics becomes a natural demand of critical statements when we try to clarify what they really mean. To illustrate, were we faced with statements such as the following: "art is a symbolic expression of the forms of human feeling" (Langer), aesthetical thinking may easily begin by asking as to what exactly is meant here by: *symbol* (as against *sign* and *signal*); *expression* (as artistic, not physiognomic); and *feeling in general* as against specific, designable emotions (such as joy and sorrow). Similarly, where a critic admires a picture as one which shows a *profound sense of reality* we may naturally wonder as to what exactly the word *reality* here means.

> [It] may mean the surface appearance of things, the sense qualities that are open to immediate inspection: smells, tastes, textures. A "profound sense of reality" could then be a strong interest in sense appearance, a fascination with it, a desire to reproduce it. . . . This . . . [interpretation] fits the French impressionists, but not the . . . Gothic and Byzantine artist . . . [to whom *reality* means] a . . . supernatural world known not through sense experience but through intuition or pure reason.[53]

In other words, *aesthetics as metacriticism* is critical thinking about the concepts (and criteria) which a critic merely uses but does not himself clarify.

But, one may ask, is the *meaning* of our talk about art — that is, of the words it comprises — the only concern of philosophical aesthetics? Does it have nothing to do with our actual *experience* of contemplating art? The answer, affirming philosophy's positive interest in art contemplation, is provided by the *phenomenological* way of doing philosophical aesthetics which may now be distinguished from the *linguistic* approach.

---

53. M.C. Beardsley, *Aesthetics — Problems in the Philosophy of Criticism*, New York: Hartcourt, Brace & World Inc., 1958, p. 5.

The analytic approach, associated in particular with Bertrand Russell and the early work of Wittgenstein, maintains that analysis of language is the basis for resolution of philosophical issues. It therefore attaches great importance to clarity of meaning and protests against glib generalizations which merely ignore differences of verbal meaning and so also the diversity of facts that words signify. How these two emphases actually work is easy to illustrate:

a. Consider, for instance, the following high-sounding tribute:

> . . . The music of Lourie is an ontological music, in the Kierkegaardian style; one would also say, "existential." It is born in the singular roots of being, the nearest possible juncture of soul and spirit.[54]

Now, we cannot say anything about the truth or falsity of this compliment unless we are first somehow enabled to see what the words here used really mean. Yet this meaning is precisely what we find very difficult to determine. It would make perfect sense if someone said, "He put himself into the song." The meaning, then, would clearly be: he sang wholeheartedly. But the words that the extract cited uses make it patently unclear on the whole. The ontological is that which relates to Being; "existential," in philosophy, means "based on personal experience," "concrete" as opposed to "abstract." Up to this point we may perhaps agree to grant some meaning to the utterance; for it does make sense to suggest that music gains in quality where, instead of being an exercise in mere technique (and so "abstract") it is full of some feeling recollected (maybe) from a deeply personal experience (and is in that sense "concrete"). But the words that follow: "born . . . soul and spirit" serve only to prevent us from regarding the extract as having a determinate meaning on the whole. We may even agree to distinguish *soul* from *spirit* (as we are required to by the word *and* conjoining the two as "soul *and* spirit"), for whereas

54. E. Elton (ed.), *Aesthetics and Language*, Oxford: Basil Blackwell, 1970, p. 2.

soul may be taken as that immaterial part of man *which is believed to survive the body after death* (that is, as *ātmā*), *spirit* may be interpreted merely as *prāṇa* or that life-principle which animates the body of living things. But the words "*nearest possible juncture* of soul and spirit" posit our ability to discriminate between varying degrees of closeness between soul and spirit. Such a suggestion can only bewilder the reader.

b. Take, next, the following emphatic thesis of Clive Bell:

> The representative element in a *work of art* may or may not be harmful; *always* it is irrelevant.[55]

Now, what do the words, *a work of art*, here mean? If we take them *along with "always"* (as we are required to — mark the semi-colon which *conjoins* the two segments of the sentence) they could only mean: "*every* work of art which has a representative element." But to suggest that the representative element is always irrelevant to the aesthetic value of *every* work of art which has it (that is, the representative element) is simply to miss *the difference between the various arts*, because in some of them, as in landscape painting, the element in question is undeniably important. So the thesis in question only bespeaks an aesthetician's excessive craving for generality. Do not the characters, situations and happenings — which our epics, *Rāmāyaṇa* and *Mahābhārata represent* (in the sense of bringing clearly before the mind, or setting forth in words) — provide a rich and impressive content to them, instead of impairing their value as literary works? Does not the greatness of Michelangelo's works painted on the ceiling of Sistine Chapel depend very importantly on *the exalted character* of the subjects they *represent*? It is surely this quality and not merely the size or extent of the whole superlative effort that Goethe had in mind when he remarked: "Without having seen the Sistine Chapel no one can form an appreciable idea of what [not merely how much] one man can achieve."[56]

---

55. Clive Bell, *Art*, Grey Arrow Edition 1961, p. 36.
56. Rolf Schott, *Michelangelo*, London: Thames and Hudson, 1st edn., 1964, p. 38.

Yet, though scrupulous attention to the *language* that we use in aesthetic discourse is surely necessary to ensure clarity of meaning, it is by no means enough for a proper understanding of our *total concern with art*. The creation and contemplation of art and our non-verbal responses to it — that is, how it evokes semblances of feeling, quickens our imagination, and how it relates to our life-experience as a whole — all this has also to be taken into account. It is precisely this need which is met by the *phenomenological* approach to aesthetics. How this approach is distinctive can be easily brought out, in spite of the fact that, insofar as they both arose as a challenge to idealism, phenomenology has generally tended to work along with existentialism.

One basic emphasis of phenomenology is on the need (a) to philosophize without any presuppositions or theoretical bias, and therefore to dwell upon the phenomena of art (as experienced) without sundering their delicate tissues through analysis; and (b) to neither reduce nor elevate art to something which it is *not* in actual fact. For example, where a painting actually looks warm in its colours and vibrant in its brushwork to the contemplating eye, phenomenology would like us to just keep insisting that the work really looks so, instead of *contriving* the explanation that, insofar as what we call warmth and vibrancy (or energy, animation) in real life cannot be actually there in a picture which is literally lifeless, the qualities in question are only our subjective reaction (fictitiously) superimposed on the picture; for, so to explain the experience will be only to divide its actually felt singleness into two artificial halves. The manifest seamlessness is its truth, and the aesthetician has to hold on to it. Indeed, if even in respect of the everyday perception of an object we cannot determine the precise contribution of the percipient and mark it off from what the thing itself presents, how can we overcome this inability in the case of aesthetic experience where the focusing of attention is generally more intense and the subjective responses — comprising half-blown impulses and imaginings, all quickened by the work — far more varied than in the case of perceptions of daily life? It is not that phenomenology forbids us from registering the *details* of an aesthetic experience. What it insists on only is that our use of language here should be "illuminative" rather than disintegrative. Thought just cannot work without marking differences in its object, but it can yet avoid sundering the object's unity and regarding it as a mere aggregate of separate parts.

Phenomenology itself makes some very helpful distinctions. One of these opposes *intention* to (what it chooses to call) *intentionality*. An intention is a plan. It is more or less fixed in the sense that one is expected to stick to it generally. Further, the aim of an intention is some attainment that is *yet to come*. Intentionality, on the other hand, is one's involvement with what is present *here and now*. Now, to turn to the *creation* of art, what seizes its essential logic is *intentionality*, not *intention*. The making of a work of art is very rarely the quite slavish execution of a predetermined plan. It may well be that as he sets out to create a work of art the artist has a vague, general plan in his mind. But when creation actually begins he (as a rule) focuses on the detail just accomplished, registers *its* aesthetic demand, and then proceeds accordingly, with the result that when the work is completed it may turn out to be quite unlike its vaguely prefigured character. To conclude, it is the concept of intentionality, as against that of mere intention, which enables us to explain the *emergent* character of those works of art which are truly creative.

Finally, insofar as we have spoken of the joint working of existentialism and phenomenology, we may dwell upon and clarify two points: first, how the (combined) aesthetics of existential phenomenology can deliver some basic truths about art experience; and, secondly, how the linguistic-analytic and phenomenological approaches are both required for an adequate understanding of the facts of art and art experience. Now, as for the first point, here is one clear truth provided by existential phenomenology: a work of art (as contemplated) presents experience as unbroken or pre-judgemental. In other words, no clear distinctions are here drawn between what we feel, think or imagine, or even between what is now presented to us, and its colouring by reminiscence. As for the equal necessity of the (other) two individual approaches we are dealing with, the following example from the region of music should serve. Suppose, while listening to the basic composition (or *bandish*) of a *khyāl* recital, *as it is gently accelerated in pace* by the singer, we are struck by the sudden appearance of a kind of bloom in the *sthāyī* as it arrives sharply and designedly at the *sama,* and are therefore moved to say: "See, how well it has come to bloom!" (देखिए ! कैसी खिली है स्थायी). Now, how exactly are we to make sense of or interpret these words of acclaim? The correct answer would be that here the *right verbal understanding* can be had *only if* we make the attempt all along *in the context of actual listening,* and discriminatingly, that is, with the help of experience (if any) of repeated exposure to such music in the past. The point may be clarified as follows:

Suppose, as we make the remark in question, it is also heard by a fellow listener who has no idea of what classical music really is. How will *he* understand our words of acclamation? Naturally, he would do this (if incorrectly) in the light of *his* own everyday experience and so look on what he has heard as a mere complex of varying sound and pace, and not *as art.* He is therefore very likely to think that we made the remark (in question) just because we noticed a certain expansion or distension in the music, because in everyday parlance (as against our talk about music *as art* to which he is alien) the word खिलना commonly evokes the image of an object's unfolding itself, or gaining a little *spread* or *distension.* But such interpreting will be clearly untrue to what has actually happened. By gently forcing the pace of singing a little, the vocalist has in fact *shortened* the intervals between the *svara-samooha*s and the *mātrā*s (tonal phrases and beats) *reducing* the overall extent of the *bandish,* and thus making it and its inner linkages *more easily manifest to contemplation.* It is this increased ease of apprehension, aided of course by the literal liveliness of a slightly quicker pace, that makes the *sthāyī* appear to bloom. Of course, a major inner detail that the quickening of pace may here serve *to vivify* is the relation of the *sama* to the *way* the basic line (or *sthāyī*) attains to it. Because of the overall shortening, the preceding *svaras* now appear to be *heading for* the *sama* which therefore comes to look like the target of the passage, and so gives one the distinct impression of a little tension released, because of due attainment of what the *sthāyī* itself appears to demand, *that is, arriving at the sama*. In other words, instead of spreading out or becoming a little flaccid, the *sthāyī* which now appears to "bloom" has in fact become shorter (in musical space); and also, because of this little compression, more easily evident in its overall form and inner details. So the viewpoint of immediate and discriminating *experience* of music, or the phenomenological approach, is here essential for the right *understanding* of what the "blooming" of a *sthāyī* really means. Surely, the blooming of a flower, as the *visible* opening of its petals, is not the same as the *intelligible* bloom of a work of art's segments, occurring as improved *manifestness* of its knitwork and design. And should we decide to *speak* of the semblance (or the "blooming') evoked, we will have to be careful in our choice of words. The right words here will be: "स्थायी ज़रा सिमट गयी है" not "स्थायी ज़रा सिकुड़ गयी है!" As demanded by what we have called the linguistic-analytic approach, our speech has to be adapted precisely to the apprehended character of fact.

2
Some Basic Concepts and Distinctions

TODAY, indeed, a key requirement of philosophy of art is to be maximally careful about the meaning of words that make our aesthetic discourse. So we may devote this chapter to a discussion of some key concepts and basic distinctions that generally figure in our talk about art.

THE AESTHETIC, NON-AESTHETIC, ARTISTIC

The aesthetician distinguishes the aesthetic from the non-aesthetic, on the one hand; and from the artistic, on the other. What exactly is the ground of this distinction? One may at once feel tempted to answer that whereas aesthetic qualities relate to *works of art*, the non-aesthetic ones are qualities of *things* or of what is non-art; and it would seem plausible to say so. Terms like "expressive" and "serene" are commonly applied to works of art, say, in the region of poetry, music and painting; but nobody uses such words for articles of furniture. However, a wider look at the world around us quickly shows that such a way of distinguishing cannot hold. There is indeed plenty of *non*-art to which the adjectives we have just spoken of may be aptly applied. A human face, for instance, can easily appear to be expressive or serene in different situations. Again, a particular landscape too may seem serene to us; and even our everyday use of language, accompanied by appropriate gestures, can at times be quite expressive. In fact, there are quite a few terms which are commonly regarded as aesthetic, but are yet freely and fairly applied to both art *and non-art*. The following are some such words: nimble (or lively), cheerful, pretty, beautiful, graceful, and sublime.

A musical passage and the way a man moves about in daily life may both appear to be nimble. Again, one may speak, with equal sense, of a pretty little poem *and* of a pretty face. "Beautiful" and "graceful" too are alike usable in respect of artistic creations and human figures, and sublimity may be seen not only in an epic poem, but in a snow-clad mountain range or in the ascesis of a man like Gandhi fasting manifestly for the sake of a common good and at the risk of his own life. So the aesthetic qualities we have just adverted to cannot be said to characterize art alone. In other words, we are yet to find a clear basis of distinction between aestheic and non-aesthetic qualities.

Could it then be suggested, as Sibley does, that whereas the apprehension of aesthetic qualities requires "the exercise of taste, perceptiveness or sensitivity of aesthetic discrimination or appreciation," the non-aesthetic features (of things or even of works of art) may be noticed by "anyone with normal eyes, ears, and intelligence"? From this point of view, the following may be said to be clearly non-aesthetic terms: *square, oblong, red, green,* and *noisy*. Indeed, anyone who knows the meaning of these terms can easily judge whether a table is square or oblong; the colour of a curtain, red or green; or a crowd, rowdy or merely restive. Quite as effortlessly, we use *non*-aesthetic terms when we say that a *dohā* has but two lines; that its endings rhyme noticeably; or that a particular *taan* in music appears to go up (*āroha*) and down (*avaroha*). Aesthetic terms, on the other hand, are not so easily usable; their use calls for some prior discipline of thought or perceptual refinement. If two persons disagree as to whether a painted landscape looks *serene* or merely uncluttered, the disagreement may be due as much to differences in understanding what the word *serene* means as to inequal ability to perceive the suggestiveness of the colours used in the work. But, one may ask, what about words like "graceful," "beautiful" and "pretty"? Surely, we use them freely in everyday life; here, we (seem to) need no prior training; and, at the same time, all these words are quite as applicable to what we find in the region of art. How, then, can such terms he said to be essentially aesthetic (which they obviously are) in Sibley's view? A possible answer is that though nothing like a formal course in art appreciation is here (in daily life) necessary, a measure of aesthetic discrimination is yet quite essential. After all, however pleasing his facial features may be, a short and stocky person *with a shuffling gait, cannot* be said to be *graceful*. Nor is this term applied by us to a lofty snow-clad mountain range, though the impress of its flawless white may be direct and irresistible. Both these negations imply that the predicate in question — that is, *graceful* — is used *or avoided* thoughtfully, and not as an utterly reflex response to what is merely seen. In either case a wider context is taken into account. A pleasing face does not chime with a shuffling gait; and the sheer bigness of the mountain range prevents its overpowering white from appearing (merely) graceful. Yet, there *are* some who do not (or cannot) take care to use words that really suit the precise, apprehended character of fact, and who feel free to use a word like "cute" indiscriminately, say, to cover the small and merely pretty on the one hand, and the big and impressively beautiful on the other.

However, as Osborne points out, apparent errors or differences in the use of aesthetic words, like "beautiful" and "graceful," are not always due to one's inability to pick the right word for an object with a fairly determinate and generally accepted character. They may also arise from deep-rooted cultural differences. A word like "beauty" may *mean* a specific character to one group of people, and a quite different one to another group. Even today a bony female figure is much less likely to be accepted as "beautiful" by the generality of people in India than in the West; and a woman who is correctly called dumpy among Scandinavians will not be so labelled among

Eskimos.[1] In other words, in case we choose to go by the criterion of the relative ease (or difficulty) of apprehension, our understanding of the aesthetic-non-aesthetic distinction will remain quite indeterminate until we have also taken every cultural tradition into account, a task which may never be completed. On the other hand, no such lack of definiteness disturbs our understanding of words like "square" and "triangular." All those who know the meaning of these terms may be fairly expected to agree as to whether a table is or is not square or triangular in shape.

This simple fact can be used to suggest another way of distinguishing aesthetic qualities from non-aesthetic ones. One may proffer the view that the former — say, qualities like beauty, grace and serenity — are merely phenomenological; or that they indicate only how things *appear* to us, not what they really are in themselves; and that, on the other hand, the judgement: "This is a *square* table" means that squareness really belongs to the table and is not merely a matter of how the object appears to us. Our talk about aesthetic qualities comprises "*look* statements," and because the onlooker is here satisfied with mere appearances, such statements neither need nor receive any inter-subjective checking, say, with the aid of such quite objective norms of measurement as can be easily used in respect of (non-aesthetic) statements like,"This table weighs 5 kg." But, in spite of its plausibility, such a way of making the distinction we are seeking to determine precisely is open to the following objections:

(a) The average individual is not always satisfied with his own look-experience, and may have to check it with that of an acknowledged expert. It may be that one does not feel quite sure if the colour of his furniture truly agrees with the colour of the distemper on the wall, and so is impelled to consult an interior decorator.

---

1. H. Osborne, *The Art of Appreciation*, London: OUP, 1970, p. 64.

(b) Further, where he does not *seek* any correction he may yet need it for making his talk *acceptable to others*. Thus, if a gigantic waterfall is said to be a pretty sight by one member of a party of tourists, others may at once like to replace the word, as Coleridge once had to do irresistibly, with *sublime*. But, of course, we would do well to remember that whatever be the aesthetic term that one uses to characterize an object, the immediate appearance is *not* here regarded as the veil *of some hidden reality*.

(c) It is noteworthey that though we do not generally think of it, some restraint is also quietly exercised in our everyday experience of *non-aesthetic* qualities. Osborne clarifies the point admirably:

> Imagine that I am looking at the surface of my desk and notice in my visual field a white patch, which I then judge to be *square*. I *do not mean — or do not mean primarily* — that if I apply a measuring rod and a set square to the piece of cardboard which is the physical stimulus of my presentation, I shall find that all the lines are equal and all the angles 90 degrees. If I think about it, I will probably realize that owing to the well-known optical illusion whereby verticals look longer, comparatively, than horizontals, the piece of cardboard will not in fact measure up as a square. But when I say it is square I mean, *or mean primarily*, that this visual presentation, this bit of my present phenomenologically objective visual experience, has the property of being square. And if . . . the visual presentation looks square . . . it is square (so far as *my present* apprehension is concerned) *whatever [be] the [actual] dimensions of the cardboard*. When in ordinary life we say that something at which we are looking is square we do not mean [as an *engineer* might do] that, to the best of our judgement and after taking account of optical distortions, if the physical stimulus were measured up it would be found within prescribed limits of tolerance to have four right angles and four equal sides. We mean first and foremost something like

> this: that the visual object *gives an impression* of all-round symmetrical stability, equilibrium, poise, non-directionality, etc. [qualities which an *architect* takes into account in his building component] with the corollary that it does not appear asymmetrical, unbalanced, slender . . ., etc. All these features are implicit in the squareness that we *see.*[2]

In other words, the "look-being" or "appearance-reality" distinctions cannot be used to mark off aesthetic from non-aesthetic qualities; for, in ordinary life, whether we find (and say) that a thing is square or that it looks beautiful we are *in either case* concerned with what the thing *seems to us.* Are we then to believe that there is no reasonable way to distinguish aesthetic from non-aesthetic qualities?

Luckily, we do not have to give up. A little close attention to the second and third sets of italicized words ("or do not mean," "or do not mean primarily") in the long extract cited above (second para of *c.*) is of help. It reveals that Osborne concedes that when one apprehends a patch as being *square* the mathematical meaning of the term does *not quite* disappear from the mind of the observer. Now this can at once be used as a clue to think of a possible ground of distinction between the two kinds of qualities, aesthetic and non-aesthetic. True, when a man finds (and says) that a patch is square he is not *talking* in exact geometrical terms; but if he is asked to explain what he *means,* he will have to refer to the word's mathematical meaning; and this meaning, we may note, is widely and quite definitely understood and accepted by people. On the other hand, when one is asked what his meaning really is when he says that a painting is *expressive,* he may well reply that it expresses or projects a particular feeling; but to indicate *what a work expresses* is not really to answer the question, what it is *to be* expressive. Oppositely, "being an equilateral rectangle" is the very essence of *being* a "square." In other words, *the meaning*

---

2. H. Osborne, op. cit., pp. 59-60. All italics and words within the first two brackets are my addition.

of many[3] *non-aesthetic words can be more definitely indicated in objective and widely acceptable terms than that of words like beauty and grace.*

Perhaps a surer ground for the distinction we are presently concerned with can be had by focusing attention on our apprehension of aesthetic qualities. It seems proper to say that whereas the needed sensitiveness to *aesthetic* qualities requires an abiding and evergrowing openness on our part to what or how things directly appear to us individually, the apprehension of *non-aesthetic* qualities, as a rule, admits of — though it may not straightaway seek — *a commonly acceptable finality* because some quite objective ways or norms are available to determine their presence and character. The former calls for, or brings about a widening or refinement of our powers of apprehension, and not inoften a growing intimacy — or what has been sometimes called an "exchange of being"— with things; or, so to say, a watchful peep into their insides. The latter apprehension — that is, of non-aesthetic qualities — on the other hand, merely repeats some settled way of experience or perception; and provides at best some easy or superficial (if useful) information about things. The perception of a patch of colour as *square* is the finding of but another instance of squareness that we already know. But we cannot register the expressiveness of the music before us unless we notice the details of *this music,* and open to the *uniqueness* of the way they are *here* held as one. The point may be brought out by considering how Harold Osborne distinguishes the different kinds of aesthetic qualities.

KINDS OF AESTHETIC QUALITIES

Sensory Qualities

To begin with, there are sensory (aesthetic) qualities which are "first-order" and are revealed to perception in a single sensory mode, say, the qualities of shape. But the variety of

3. Of *many,* to be sure; but *not of all.*

real shapes clearly exceeds the number of *set words* or concepts at our disposal for speaking of such shape-qualities. The words are few, say, the following: *square, circle, cube, triangle, parallelogram*, and so on. But the actual shape-qualities that we commonly find and do not — or cannot — speak of in *geometrical* terms are far more numerous. Shapes of the following diverse kinds are indeed freely come across: "short, long, slim, straight, bent, crooked, sinuous, bulbous, bloated, pinched, spare, tapering, undulant . . . angular . . ., blunt."[4] Then, there are "shape-patterns of the human body" which we commonly characterize thus: "obese, lank, gaunt, plump, chubby, snub, flaccid." What is more, "people who attend to the shapes of pots and other artefacts, animal and plant forms, become aware of innumerable recurring shapes and characteristics of shapes *for which they have no words . . .*"[5] Yet, such shapes are clearly real; *they* do not become subjective simply because *we* have no words to describe them. However, and this is important, there is always a risk of their being ignored. We all tend to ignore qualities which lie outside our personal vocabulary. So the average man has to make a special effort to *notice* and dwell upon the numberless shape-qualities that are found in the region of nature and man-made things, that is, works of art and other artefacts. The aesthetic merit of a whole painting may not bear

> *any direct* relation to our aesthetic valuation of its contained shapes. We are . . . [no longer] tempted to praise a painting if the women in it are slender and sinuous or to condemn it if they are ugly and obese. Nevertheless we cannot apprise a painting at all unless we have seen it, noticed and attended to the sensory *shapes and patterns* upon which the whole superstructure rests.[6]

Inter-sensory Qualities

The complexity of art appreciation also arises from the fact

4. H. Osborne, *The Art of Appreciation*, p. 61.
5. Ibid., p. 62. Italics added.
6. Ibid., p. 65. Emphases mine.

that the perceptual qualities we here come across often involve more than one sensory mode, because of which they may be called *inter-sensory*. Music affects us through the *ear*; sculpture, architecture and dance cater, in the main, to the *eye*; and literature charms us by means of words which have to be *understood*. Yet, works in the region of many of these *diverse* arts may *all* appear to be *gay*: music because of its easy rhythm and brevity of compass, as in the case of a *drut gat* or *khyāl bandish*; a painting, by virtue of its colours; a dance-number projecting *holī* revelry, not merely because of its thematic content, but because the abandon of its nimble rhythm and its *aṅg-bhāva* can all be easily sensed; and a poem, like Herrick's "Delight in Disorder," on account of its not too tight rhyme and the pleasing casualness of the details of dress and bearing it projects, as follows:

> A lawn about the shoulders thrown
> Into a fine distraction:
> An erring lace, which here and there
> Enthrals the crimson stomacher:
> A cuff neglectful, and thereby
> Ribbands to flow confusedly
> A winning wave (deserving note)
> In the tempestuous petticoat:
> A careless shoestring, in whose tie
> I see a wild civility:
> Do more bewitch me, than when art
> Is too precise in every part.

In this context, however, two points have to be borne in mind:

(a) First, though a common term may be used for works in diverse arts, the "commonness" does not in any way lessen the need to attend to the *individual* character of the works. Thus, to turn once again to the instance of the quality we have just discussed, whereas the "gaiety" of a painting is revealed to visual notice, in a music composition the same quality is "seen" by trained listening which here means not merely the right perception of the euphonic character of the *svaras*, but the *ideally apprehended* meaning of the text — in case the composition is a song — *and* of the evenness and cyclic character of the rhythm. The training demanded for perception of "gaiety" in the two cases is very different. What is more, in the region of one and the same art — say, music — a person who is sensitive to vocal finenesses may be relatively obtuse in respect of rhythmic subtleties. Indeed, a *rasika* cannot afford to be complacent with his ability to appreciate art; instead, he must take care to keep himself ever willing to be led into new ways of perceiving and imagining, by contemplation of fresh works of art that may come his way.

(b) Second, the "gaiety" *of the dance-number* (we have referred to) cannot be reduced to any one quality that may be there in its elements. One who is not trained to see dance as art may well be able to register the occasional (impersonated) look of mischief in the dancer's eyes, the seeming bustle of the number, or the frolicsome meaning of the song being danced, and yet remain unaware of the overall *gaiety of the number itself*. The integral perception requires not merely a (facile) sensitiveness to elements just distinguished, but an openness to such subtle details of inner integration as the wilful skipping of a beat by the danseuse where the look of mischief enlivens her eye or the gentle *descent* of a musical phrase exactly when "Rādhā," as projected in dance, *coyly withdraws* from a loving embrace. The quality of "gaiety" in art — like the other inter-sensory qualities indicated by terms such as the following: pretty, dainty, elegant, stately, decorative — is indeed a tertiary quality "attaching to fairly high level sensory configurations, but not attributable to the elements from which these configurations are composed."[7]

7. H. Osborne, *The Art of Appreciation*, p. 66. It would here be apt if I also cited the following: "Aesthetic qualities are sometimes regarded as a sub-class of "tertiary" properties — properties, that

Emotional or expressive qualities

Inter-sensory qualities can be expressive quite easily. In fact, where we use such terms as "serene" and "stately" it is often difficult to decide whether they are being employed to denote inter-sensory *descriptive* qualities merely or also with some *expressive* implication. Where we want to state our reaction to, say, a real landscape as painted by Vermeer or Cezanne we may indeed have to oscillate between two alternative sets of words, say, the following: "How serene it *looks*" and "How well it *expresses* the serenity of the place." And where we find a person *stately* in his figure and bearing, our meaning may simply be that dignity is *manifest* in the very way he carries himself or answers a question with poise and patience.

What is, however, more relevant to our present purpose is another kind of difficulty — a difficulty relating not merely to the choice of the right kind of words for what is nonetheless clearly seen, but to the very perception of a subtle kind of expressiveness in art. Where art is clearly representational, as in the *nṛtya* part of our classical dances, the expression of emotion is often physiognomic or through "bodily and visible signs — in particular by the set of their features, posture, {gesture} . . . and so on."[8] Qualities which distinguish expression of this kind — commonly called *aṅg-bhāva* in the discourse of Kathak dance — are quite easy to identify. "They are almost universally recognizable and immediate in their appeal. Consider, for example . . . the dignity and power of Michelangelo's *Moses*,[9] the tenderness of the gesture of the man's hand in Rodin's *The Kiss*,[10] the warm radiance of . . . Renoir's sculptures of women,[11] (and) the erotic appeal of an Indian

is, which are dependent on or emergent from configurations of primary and secondary properties of things." Ibid., p. 59.

8. H. Osborne, *The Art of Appreciation*, p. 70.

9. Ibid., p. 71.

10. Ibid.

11. Ibid.

apsarā . . .. "[12] But the expressiveness that belongs *to a whole work of non-representational art, and primarily in virtue of its formal and structural features,* is much more difficult to register. That a *bhajan* in Rāga Bhairava expresses devout feeling may be quite easy to see, say, because of the following: the very meaning of the text, the morning time when this *rāga* is commonly sung (or played), and its known character as a vehicle of *bhakti.* But the ability to discern similar expressiveness in an exposition of the same *rāga* in the wordless, free-of-*tāla,* unbounded and leisurely built-up form of *ālāpa* is not given to many. Generally, however, it is not difficult to *understand* how expressiveness can belong to merely formal features, as distinguished from the representational or verbal content of a work of art. The wayward manner in which a tiny tot is often seen to walk does not *say* anything, but it is identifiably expressive of a carefree state of mind. Here, however, the identification is done on the basis of a feature of life and experience with which we are all familiar, and requires no special training. In the case of our concern with an art, on the other hand, we need a good deal of knowledge (of the character) of its technical elements, and a long period of getting used to *perceiving* the variety that this character admits of, before we can come to "see" the expressiveness of the very form or formal features of a work. What is more, this perceiving often reveals qualities for which we have no special words, but which yet appear to be clearly there *in* the work. In the region of our rhythm, for instance, a particular *bol* — or a syllable *sans* meaning — expresses *flightiness* if it is made to mark a point *between* two adjacent beats or *mātrās* moving at a (nimble) pace. The quality in question emerges because the syllable occurs at a (normally) *unmarked* point in the *laya*-flow. In other words, it arises from the deviant way it is *related to* the grammatical (or beat-marked) character of the aesthetic pace (or *laya*); and insofar as an untrained listener cannot perceive this relation, because he has not yet quite learnt to register the beats as evenly held apart, the aesthetically

12. H. Osborne, *The Art of Appreciation,* p. 71.

evoked *flightiness* will be wholly missed by him. The *rasika*, on the other hand, may at once call such a syllable उचटता हुआ (or flighty) delightedly.

But, be it noted, such words are not a part of the technical vocabulary of rhythm comprising words like खाली (*khālī*), भरी (*bharī*), सम (*sama*), विषम (*visham*), मात्रा (*mātrā*); they are taken from everyday discourse. Yet the listener will not be able to see what exactly they mean *in the region of rhythm* unless he takes pains to train his ear and understanding to perceive the basic structure of this art.

It would here be relevant to add that the expressive character of not only an individual syllable, but of a whole composition, be it rhythmic or melodic, may depend on its being sung, danced or played *at a particular pace*. It is a common experience of *rasika*s in the region of Hindustānī *sangeet* — that is, of those who are initiated into the subtleties of our vocal/instrumental music and dance — that if a *sthāyī* (the first line of the song) is sung or a rhythmic pattern played (at the *tablā*) or danced (by a Kathak) at even a minimally slower pace than the (aesthetically) proper one, the composition will fail to exhibit what Langer has called "livingness," or would appear quite cold or spiritless; (ठंडा, बेजान) and that the moment the performer is able to correct himself, and to pick the proper pace for the composition, it would come to bloom, so to say (खिल जायगा). The *lay* contemplator may well be able to register, in a general way, the greater overall liveliness of the second presentation, but he will not be able to see *how* exactly the blooming in question has come to pass. *Strange though it may seem to abstract thought, the flowering — which literally means* "developing" *to full maturity — is here due to the greater inner* "compactness" *of the composition because of a relatively quicker pace.*

Formal Qualities

These qualities may either belong to *whole* works of art, and be denoted by such terms as: *unity, balance, integration, harmony* and *proportion*; or to line, texture and other non-representational *elements* of art, in which case we use words like the following: *wavy, firm, frenzied, smooth, luminous, and pulpy*. But however apt be the use of any one of these terms in respect of some specific details of a work of art, the exact perceptual character of the quality denoted is never quite captured in words, and the needed supplement or corrective is always provided by percipience at work. The Taj is a picture of symmetrical balance; and so may be a good composition too — a *sthāyī or a gat* — set to *drut (teen) tāla*, if not so irresistibly as the architectural marvel. But whereas in our contemplation of the Taj, the basis of the felt equality (or sameness) of the two "halves" is an ideal vertical running across a direct presentation, in the case of the music composition it is merely a point, or the *khali*-beat, in a floating rhythmic round.[13] Again, because (as ordinarily used), words like "pulpy" and "luminous" denote qualities that tickle (respectively) the senses of touch and sight, and not the ear, one has got to turn from mere language to actual music to see what is really meant when we speak of the "pulpy luminosity" of the *akāra*, say, of the late Ustad Bade Ghulam Ali Khan.

In fine, it is essentially because they make growing demands on our percipience that aesthetic qualities differ from the non-aesthetic ones.

AESTHETIC AND NON-AESTHETIC QUALITIES

Yet the two kinds of qualities freely go together. A painting which is expressive of sadness (an aesthetic feature) must have some dimensions too, and these are clearly non-aesthetic. As "tertiary," aesthetic qualities, like the *recessive* or *vibrant* look of colour in a painting, may well be dependent on the picture's formal organization; and so they may fairly be said to be a little removed from the actual extension of, and the colours used in,

---

13. I here feel impelled to express my agreement with Osborne's remark "that some formal qualities, such as dynamic symmetry in . . . the complex rhythmic combinations of some Indian music, can be apprehended by *most* people only through feeling." *The Art of Appreciation*, p. 109. Italics added.

the work. But, indirect though it be, some relation *is* there between all these qualities. Though not entirely, the aesthetic qualities here mentioned are produced by proper *superposition and juxtaposition*. But, it is obvious, neither of these devices would be possible were the canvas not extended.

But what exactly is the nature of this relation? It is not logical, we may say, but only perceptual. The proposition: "He is a bachelor" entails "He is unmarried." But no such (necessary) relation is there between "*being* linear" (a non-aesthetic quality) and the aesthetic property of "*appearing firm.*" A line may suggest tension in one painting; and the quite different effect of repose in another. Everything depends not only on its own precise look — may be firm and diagonal, wavy, or vertical and fine — but on how it is put along with the other elements of the painting; and, in some measure, on how the entire complex is viewed by the onlooker.[14] That all aesthetic features are "related" to *some* non-aesthetic features may well be agreed. But we cannot say that *select* aesthetic features are tied to some *specific* non-aestheic ones. When critics invite our attention to the colours and multiplicity of figures in a painting, their intention is not to convince us staightaway that (therefore) it *is* a good painting and that we should quietly accept their judgement, but only to help us to so look at the non-aesthetic features that the aesthetic ones may be revealed to *our* personal attention. In any case, if the evidence of actual efforts to relate the aesthetic to the non-aesthetic in art is kept in mind, none of the following attempts to relate the two (that is) aesthetic (A) to non-aesthetic (NA) features can be said to be logically compelling:

(a) "This expressive (A) painting employs a new colour-combination (NA). In quite a few other expressive

---

14. It is important to remember that what one "sees" in a work of art depends vitally — though of course not entirely — on what kind of a person the contemplator is. This is indeed why traditional Indian aesthetics puts so much emphasis on the role of a *rasika* in aesthetic experience.

works too we find the same kind of novelty. So *all* expressive paintings may be said to *use* new colour-combinations."

Here, it may at once be pointed out that a mere look at works like Edward Munch's *The Scream* is enough to expose the falsity of such argument. This well-known work *is* expressive *without* using any colour scheme, conventional or new.

(b) Figures in expressive art are literally complete. The figure projected in this work is not in fact complete. So it is not — and it cannot be — expressive.

Here, again, the argument can be easily refuted by pointing to the evidence of fact. One has only to think of Auguste Rodin's incomplete sculptures. When he felt certain that he had been able to capture the requisite expression, Rodin would often leave some "limbs" of the work incomplete; and this would neither detract from the work's aesthetic impact nor drive away buyers.

A clear reason why such (arbitrarily) prefixed ways of relating the two kinds of properties, A and NA (as put in a and b) cannot hold is that "being expressive" (or striking) really means "appearing" so to someone; and that a work's seeming to be such and such depends upon *how it is (to be) looked at* — a factor which varies greatly with different works and their observers. Even if we take "presupposing" in a relatively broad sense, as in the following:

> 'X marries Y' presupposes (because of a certain legal requirement) that X and Y are not both male or female,

it would not serve our purpose. Any set requirements, like good drawing and proper use of colours — or, in the case of music, right handling of the *rāga-tāla* framework — may be met, and yet the resulting work may utterly fail to deserve the epithet, *expressive*. The work has in fact to *appear* so to us before we can say it *is* expressive.

To conclude: by means of mere thinking, and without

extending meticulous attention to the individual work — that is, to its details of structure — we cannot decide, or even roughly anticipate, which non-aesthetic qualities may be confidently expected to produce some select aesthetic qualities. The relation in question is rather to be *found* than to be merely thought about.

THE AESTHETIC AND THE ARTISTIC

The artistic is not so subject to the need to "appear." Yet it is not merely different from, but bears a vital relation to, the aesthetic. This can be easily explained. The original meaning of *aesthetic* is "relating to perception by the senses." But the word is also freely used to signify: "relating to the having of a sense of "beauty", "tasteful", and "relating to aesthetics." The word "artistic"on the other hand, only means "relating to art, or to skill in art." In other words, the "aesthetic" includes, but is not confined to the "artistic." Hence we see again that, in spite of being related, the two concepts are *distinct*.

However, the *relation* between the two is also fairly obvious. Take the case of a poem. If it is properly structured, it will be said to have the artistic value of being well *formed*. But, to be sure, the *details* of its inner integration may not be manifest at once, or to everyone. As a rule, they have to be carefully noticed before one can truly say that they cohere. This is indeed a clear ground for distinguishing a work of art from everyday objects. Whatever is pleasing in things — say, the perfectly oblong shape or the smooth, shiny surface of a table — is perceived without any strain on our apprehending powers. But the value of a poem as art is importantly due to the cohesive disposition of its words and word-bound images, and of pauses, verbal sound and sense; and this inner interlinking has to be discerned by the trained reader. He must adopt the right kind of attitude, which would here be a patient attempt to get into the spirit of the entire work, and to provide the requisite supplement of meaning where, in the poem's "zones of indeterminacy," such a filling is *demanded*, but *not quite clearly provided* by their context. This process has been called "concretion" by Roman Ingarden. And it goes without saying that when the coherent quality of the poem has been *thus* realized, the resulting experience will be no mere thought of a complex unity, but at once a kind of felt commitment to it, a self-opening to what the poem says or signifies, and an impulse to remain so attuned for a while. Therefore, artistic values may be said to call for a changeover into aesthetic ones. They press for self-completion in the aesthetic; and they not only help, but flower in *tādātmya*.

But some artistic values may be easily seen, that is, without any strain on our attention. Thus, we all readily notice and admire the living-flesh-like quality of the marble in some of Robin's sculptures; and it *is* an artistic excellence because it signifies skill in making art, or in handling the material used. This thought of a (relative) ease of perception in some cases can indeed be used to heighten the *distinction* between artistic and aesthetic values. Thus, the fluent, up-and-down movement of music; the clear and flowing quality of lines in painting; and the highly polished, or "living" quality of the material in some sculptures — these easily noticeable qualities are all *artistic*. On the other hand, the cyclic, self-gathering quality of a *bandish* (or composition in music); the balancing of onward and regressive lines in a painting, so that attention is ensured for every part of the work; and the *undisturbing* incompleteness of some of Robin's sculptures — these have all to be regarded as *aesthetic*, for none of them is accessible to untrained or casual attention. Qualities of the second set are, of course, not disjoined from the work; they are "of art" and in this sense artistic *as well*; but they are not merely artistic, but aesthetic. Aesthetic values are a needed self-completion of the artistic.

FORM AND CONTENT

There is yet another pair of terms which deserves our attention: *form* and *content*. These are also everyday words in our talk *about* art; but here, *in* the region of art, their meaning is different. So we have to determine their *basic aesthetic* meaning

— that is, a meaning which may be relevant to works of art taken *generally* — by distinguishing it from what they signify in day-to-day talk.

Form

Now, to begin with "form," such accepted meanings of the word as are more or less relevant to our purpose may be listed as follows:

(a) The shape or configuration of something as distinct from its colour, texture, etc.

(b) A fixed mode of artistic expression in literary, musical or other artistic works, such as the sonnet and the epic forms in poetry, or the forms of *khyāl*, *dhruvapad* and *dhamār* in music.

(c) Style, arrangement or design in the arts, aiming at a pleasing or otherwise effective result, and considered as opposed — and so not quite without some reference — to content.

The third meaning is the one we are looking for. We could indeed truly say:

> By form is simply meant *arrangement* or order; and by content whatever that happens to be, that is arranged or ordered.[15]

But we cannot merely ignore the first two meanings of "form," for they too are relevant to art, if in imperfect measure; and we have to argue why they cannot be regarded as the *basic* aesthetic meaning of "form."

(A) The first of these, that is, form as shape, is of course freely used in everyday parlance. It is thus common to hear people say: " I need an oval, not a round table for this room." The reference in such talk is to shape alone. No mention is made of the table's colour or size. We

15. C.J. Duccase: *The Philosophy of Art*, New York: Dover Publications, Inc., 1966, p. 202.

abstract *shape* for attention from the object in its wholeness. "Form," thus used, is therefore an absractable concept; and, in the example we have taken, it means a *geometrical shape*.

Now, in this everyday sense, the word "form" is also used in our talk about art. Where we use it with regard to *parts* or *elements* of a work it may mean mere shape, as in the following:

> But the secret of Guernica's romantic impact is found neither in its classic architectural symmetry, nor in its symbolism, but in the inner character of its *forms*.[16]

Even where one speaks of *complete* works or of a whole style of art, an implicit reference to shape may be freely present. Thus, see the following:

> The Kandarīya Mahādva temple (Khajurāho) is "one of the finest examples of *curvilinear* building construction."[17]
>
> This twin-towered temple (Bṛhadīśvara temple, Tanjore, tenth-eleventh centuries) is perhaps the most imposing example of *pyramidical* form.[18]
>
> The artists of Ajantā frescoes handled the *circular* composition with incredible subtlety.[19]

Yet, though all these instances relating to the art of architecture look on form as shape, it does not seem possible to regard geometrical (or abstractable) shape as the *basic aesthetic* meaning of "form." Shape or form in *this* sense is indeed not usable about art taken generally. Nobody acclaims a poem's *form* as being perfectly square or semi-circular. Nor do we speak of it (a poem's form) without giving some thought to what

---

16. Osborne, *The Art of Appreciation*, p. 267.
17. *The Oriental World* (Landmarks of the World's Art), London: Paul Hamlyn, 1967, p. 65. My emphasis.
18. Ibid., p. 59. Emphasis added.
19. Ibid., p.46. My italics.

it contains, its word-bound images that make and project a rich and unified meaning. Here, it is clear, form is not a matter of abstractable shape. Further, though we do speak of the *shakl* (or shape) of our rhythmic patterns, what we really mean is the varying inner disposition of their syllabic filling.[20]

(B) In the sense of a sub-type too, "form" is commonly used in the context of individual arts. Thus, *dhruvapad* and *khyāl* are two major forms of Hindustānī (or north Indian) vocal music, as are *still life* and *portraiture* in the region of painting. *But terms such as these are confined* to *particular arts*. It is of course quite proper to speak of *portrait* painting. We also have a kind of art that is called *portrait sculpture*. But no *poem* is as such a portrait, a *dhruvapad*, or a still life picture, though the movement of its (blank) verse may well seem to have the majesty of a *dhruvapad*, and though it may well be *about* the daffodils, or a telling *portrayal* of a little girl's innocence as to the difference between life and death (The reference here is to two very appealing poems of Wordsworth: *I wandered lonely as a cloud* and *We are Seven*). Therefore, fixed *modes* of artistic expression too cannot be regarded as the basic (or generally relevant) aesthetic meaning of *form*.

(C) This takes us to the third meaning. We may put it thus:

> Form is such an *arrangement* of whatever is there in a work of art that the whole (work) may be able to elicit and hold for a while (or/and repeatedly draw) the attention of a *rasika* or knowledgeable contemplator.

The key ideas which call for some individual comment here are: inner integration; form in its aspect of impact or effectiveness; perception of form (by the *rasika*); and form *as against content*. But as we set out to develop these points we

20. The reference here is to changes of *laya*, or of चलन and to what is called बोलों का भराव.

must remember that the "arrangement" here spoken of need not be a matter of *conscious* effort alone. The following words of Herbert Read are here noteworthy:

> The later pictures of Picasso . . . [presenting] a strangely distorted female form; heads incomprehensively interlocked or dislocated . . . ; gigantic sculptural forms built up with misshapen bones . . . cannot be rationally explained without some theory of the *unconscious* origin of imagery. In the state in which he admittedly paints these pictures Picasso is . . . in the condition . . . perhaps . . . of self-hypnosis . . .. To will is not enough. "The genius of poetry", wrote Keats, "must work out its own salvation in a man . . .. That which is creative must create itself![21]

What is however easier to accept is the view that so far as the inner *ordering* of details is concerned, it is generally done intentionally, if (more or less) effortlessly, and can therefore be made out by an attentive onlooker. In the case of painting, a common way to organize the various figures in the same work is to make one of them appear central by so regulating the looks of the other figures that the onlooker's eye is easily led to the focal figure at once or eventually.[22] Thus, in *The Sistine Madonna* by Raphael,[23] whereas the contrast between "the Christ Child's serious expression . . ." (or) "his unchildlike gaze" expressing "his divinity" and "the *putti* below"*may have to be pointed out* to the ordinary viewer, nobody can miss the effective organization of looks. The central figure in this work is the Queen of Heaven descending "from the clouds as the curtains are drawn back" *and* openly holding the holy child; and the

21. Cited from W.G. Archers's *India and Modern Art,* George Allen & Unwin, 1959, pp. 60-61. Italics mine.

22. In poetry, it is obvious, this ordering is done very differently. See, in this context, my detailed analysis of Wordsworth's poem: "*I wandered Lonely as a Cloud,*" in *Hindustani Sangeet and a Philosopher of Art,* New Delhi: D.K. Printworld (P) Ltd., 2001, pp. 44-46.

23. Also known as "The Madonna of Sixtus", this work is reproduced in Osborne's *The Art of Appreciation,* p. 233.

two together become and remain the target of our notice because whereas the venerable figure on its right, Pope Sixtus II, looks directly at it, the downward gaze of the Virgin (on its left) not only takes our eye towards the cherubs below but carries it back once again to the focal region because they themselves are looking upwards.

The same simple device is at work in Leonardo Da Vinci's *The Virgin of the Rocks.*[24] The Mother's look here is visibly sweet. But if the sweetness does not appear to be merely sensory, it is partly because of the effect of sombre rocks and colouring. They appear opposed to, and so heighten by contrast, the spiritual look of the lit-up faces. However, this is not the only source of relief. The look of light itself is here made to vary. Thus whereas the facial glow is warm and radiant, the patches of outer light appear frozen and cold. The integration of gestures is even more obvious. The looks are all so co-ordinated that the baby Jesus remains the onlooker's focus. It is true that the holy child himself, as he curls his baby fingers in blessing, *looks at* his playmate (St.) John, but the look is readily *returned* by the latter, in open and directed obeisance.

It must however be forthwith added that form as inner integration is not necessarily the *projection* of details. The requirement only is that the content of the work should not seem divided or broken. Consider, for instance, an impressionistic work, say, Cezanne's landscape: *Chestnut Trees at Jas De Bouffan.*[25] Here it is the elimination of details which makes for the "simplification of form," so that "a true effect (is conveyed) in the briefest possible language." Trees, buildings, mountains and fields are all here drawn with the sculptor's emphasis on solidity and indifference to detail; and though the overall luminosity is a mark of impressionism, what strikes one here is the "austere, epigrammatic" abstraction of form

24. Reproduced in *Great Painters and Great Paintings*, Pleasantville, Montreal, Sydney: The Reader's Digest Association, 1965, p. 57.

25. *World Famous Paintings*, Compiled by A. Bury and C.R. Cammell, London: The New Educational Press, 1958, facing p. 64.

which is very far removed from the luxuriance of details that marks the landscapes of Constable or Turner.[26] Even the form of our music, we may note, cannot be said to be *articulate* everywhere. Langer takes the epithet to mean clarity of notes in the midst of their linkages; but the *svara*s in a long and languid *mīṇḍ* (or glide) do not *appear* as distinct accents, though they *can* of course all be distinguished by a trained listener.

Indeed, apart from the quality of an overall coherence of a work's content, perhaps nothing else can be fixed as the essential requirement of artistic form. The ways of inner ordering can vary infinitely. In the Ajantā frescoes the link between one group of figures and the next is achieved by means of some subsidiary figures, just as in relief it is the half-tones that provide the transition from light to shade.[27] As for the accordance of looks which we have emphasized in the context of painting, it may be found in sculpture too. Thus, in "the Descent of the Ganges," a relief at Mamallapuram, the focal point of the entire composition is provided by the river in the guise of serpent men. But it is made to appear central by means of a compositional device. All those who are seen in postures of prayer and meditation — and all animals as well — appear to move towards, to look at or to pay homage to the river. It is "these converging movements which give the composition an overall unity."[28] This does not however mean that the details do not matter. Care has been taken, for instance, to see that the Brāhmaṇas, who are commonly believed to be the most peace-loving of men, appear to simply wait at the river's edge. What is more, as required by their function in life, they carry vases to be filled with holy water, and are seen to worship the river with due devotion. A much easier way to heighten the centrality of a figure in sculpture is to oppose it to smaller ones. Thus, in a stele (in the Pāla style)

---

26. *World Famous Paintings*, p. 64.
27. *The Oriental World*, p. 46. A fresco is a very durable kind of wall painting using water colours on wet plaster.
28. Ibid., p. 50.

depicting the Buddhist divinity Tārā, the female counterpart of the Bodhisattva Avalokiteśvara,"is placed against (the) stele with a rounded top . . . (and) the smaller scale rendering of her supporters (on her either side) accentuates the importance of the central figure."[29]

But, we may note, artistic form operates as intergration of details not only in the case of a work showing *many* figures, but even in that of a sculptured representation of but *one* figure. This is easily borne out by a comparative study of Boticelli's painting, *The Birth of Venus,*[30] *and* a Pārvatī *bronze* from southern India now housed in the Metropolitan, New York.[31] In *The Birth of Venus* the goddess is made to appear focal by putting her in the centre of the picture and by making the other three figures look at or towards her. But there is no striking integration of two hands with each other; nor is her gaze — visibly frontal — made to go with her hands, though they do appear to be related mutually as a vertical. In the sculpture, on the other hand, where Pārvati is the sole figure, integration can only be immanent; and it indeed is so. The look links the visage, slightly turned towards the right, directly with the *mudrā* of the right hand; and this hand makes a perfect diagonal with the left one, so that the eye is enabled to survey the whole figure up to knees in one effortless look. The facility, we may note, arises in part from a subtle use of *tribhaṅgī,* which is gently spread over the

---

29. *The Oriental World,* p. 47. A stele is an upright stone slab or column decorated with figures or inscriptions.

30. Reproduced in the following:

    (a) *World Famous Paintings,* p. 32.

    (b) *Great Painters and Great Paintings,* p. 55.

    (c) W. Gaunt: *A Companion to Painting,* London: Thames and Hudson, 1967, p. 156.

    This work projects Venus, the goddess of love and beauty, in the way of classical allegory.

31. The reference here is to the tenth century Choḷa bronze in the Metropolitan Museum of Art, New York.

whole figure. The first flexion is provided by the slight tilt (towards the right) of the face and the right breast; the second by the left hip; and the third by the almost imperceptible bend of the right knee which is a little heightened by the straight, almost stiff, positioning of the left leg. Be it noted also that whereas the upper body is nude and holds the eye by virtue of its very figural quality, the same end is served in respect of the legs by folds of the drapery and the parallel hang of the left hand which saves the left leg from utter neglect by the onlooker. It is also important to see how the work is a subtle blend of representation and some built-in embellishment. The figure *represents* a female; but the *tribhaṅgī* which distinguishes it is at once an implicit *ornament*.

Nor is architecture deficient in devices that make for overall unity. Take, for instance, our better known temples, that is, those of Koṇārk and Khajurāho. In the Kandarīya Mahādeva temple (Khajurāho) the main sanctuary is capped by a huge tower, decorated by tiers of turrets which grow smaller as they move upwards. These turrets are miniature *shikhara*s (or उरूशिखर – *urushikhar*). They surround the main *shikhar*, the *mūlmañjari*, of which they fall visibly short, heightening its loftiness; and in so doing they serve a purpose which is visual and also perhaps ideal. They lend some extra impetus to the upward movement of the eye, and may be taken to symbolize the surpassing quality of life's spiritual end.

In respect of sheer formal excellence, however, the Taj Mahal is our pre-eminent architectural marvel. It is a paradigm of symmetrical balance, perhaps a little more so than, say, Raphael's *Madonna di San Sisto*. Raphel's creation is a work of classical balance which requires equal measures on each side of a central figure. It also ideally displays balancing elements from top to bottom, producing the visual effect of a pair of scales. In the case of the Taj, however, the balancing is not only of similars, but of opposites. The vertical is opposed to, and seems demanded by, the arched; and the lean is similarly related to the voluminous. The big, central dome is really the focus of many smaller domes, two of them being adjacent, and the others, capping the minarets, a little away. They heighten its bigness by *contrast*. This principle is also used a little subtly. Whereas the central dome is continuous with what supports it, the other domes cap a vertical ventilation of space; and this opposition heightens the imposing *compactness* of the central dome. The terrace as such has nothing to detract attention from the structure it supports. The eye is dominated by the upper part; and therefore, though it does literally rest on the terrace, the structure appears to be just put gently on the terrace rather than rooted securely in it. The overall design is very easy on the eye, so easy indeed that the whole work appears as originally single; and, as an immediate reaction, one admires its sheer shapeliness, instead of wondering how its different parts might have been put together, or how much labour and time must have gone into its making.[32] We seize the work's form instantaneously.

PERCEPTION OF FORM

In such cases the perception of form is intuitive — in the sense that it is not the result of any analytic thinking. Nor does it seem to call for any prior training on the onlooker's part. But in other cases, such as when a music lover listens to a swinging *madhya laya* composition in *tritāla*, the form may of course be registered pretty quickly, but *not without* the aid of discriminating attention (or निगाह - *nigāh*) which is itself the result of past experience of attending concerts of classical music. The same may be said about the perception of a passing *disfigurement* of form in the case of a rhythmic — say, a solo *tablā* — recital. Here, when the drummer sets out to weave a subtle pattern after the *ṭhekā*'s basic pace has been set (or "established"), the slightest suggestion of an unwanted change of pace — which is at once some (felt) deviation of an occurrent form — may be forthwith sensed by the listener as a slight,

32. The Taj is the product of twenty-two years' labour, involving twenty thousand masons.

but painful jab (so to say), provided his own sense of *laya* has become duly refined as a result of repeated communion with rhythmic recitals in the past. In any case, the perception of *artistic form*[33] is not a state of just getting excited over such mere details as fluent speed, the pleasing *āroha-avaroha* sweep of a *taan*, the vibrant brushwork of a van Gogh landscape, or the overall pathos of a poem. It is rather the awareness that some diverse parts or elements make a compellingly winsome unity. Such *awareness* may be more or less immediate, but the subsequent *analysis* of form is never so quick. Even where the "object" is so small and simple as a *tritāla madhya laya ṭhekā*, the understanding of the disposition of its content — or, say, of its segments (or *vibhāgs*) of flow in relation to its *bols* — may call for a measure of discriminating attention, though after years of recurring listening the notice of such details becomes quite effortless.

Where the form of a work of art in fact takes effect, instead of being merely talked about or analysed, it may (as a whole) be said to be significant, expressive, living or articulate. These are indeed some important characterizations of artistic form and they all call for some individual comment.

DIFFERENT VIEWS OF FORM

Form as significant

The view that art is a significant form first receives emphasis in the writings of Clive Bell and Roger Fry. What Bell means by this concept is, in his own words, as follows:

> Lines and colours combined in a particular way, certain forms and relations of forms, stir our aesthetic emotions. These relations and combinations of lines and colours, these aesthetically moving forms, I call "significant form"; and "significant form" is the one quality common to our works of visual art.[34]

33. Here, I mean the whole art work's form, as against the particular forms that may be present or descernible in it.

34 Clive Bell: *Art*, Grey Arrow Edition, 1961, p. 23.

In other words, if a painting is art, it is so because it is such a combination of lines and colours that it moves us in a particular way. Bell adds that being thus moved is the only true way to recognize that something is a work of art; and that a person's own reaction to what he *himself* sees in art — that is, its "significant" combination of lines and colours — is alone the proper beginning of his concern with the aesthetic. Mere acceptance of what the art critics say will not do.

It is easy to see why Bell speaks of lines along with colours and form. Lines and colours are inseparable.[35] It is impossible to find or imagine a line without colour. Nor is the coupling of colour with form unwarranted. Every relation of colours must in fact have a form. Some may however suspect that in all such talk *cotnent* is merely left out. But Bell would rejoin that lines and content go together. "You cannot imagine a boundary line without any content, or a content without a boundary line."[36]

But what shall we say of *representational* content ?[37] Does not the value of quite a few paintings depend also on their fidelity to what they are about, or represent? Here, a part of Bell's anwer runs as follows:

> Let no one imagine that representation is bad in itself; a realistic form may be as significant, in its place as part of the

---

35. However, Bell's own language here is questionable. He insists that "you cannot *conceive* a colourless line." (Ibid., p. 26. Emphasis added). But "conceive" really means "to think"; and a line *is* thinkable apart from colour. In *defining* a line as a length without breadth, do we at all speak or think of colour? Bell should speak (instead) of the impossibility of *imagining* or *finding* a line without colour.

36. Ibid., p. 26.

37. Here it is important to remember that all content is not representational. A painting which has no figures or identifiable shapes, but is only an effective combination of colours, cannot be called contentless — there *is* something present *in* it; only it does not refer to anything outside the work itself. So the content is here *not* representational.

> design, as an abstract. But if a representative form has value, it is as form, not as representation. The representative element in a work of art may or may not be harmful; always it is irrelevant. For, to appreciate a work of art we need bring with us nothing from life, no knowledge of its ideas and affairs . . . nothing but a sense of form and colour and a knowledge of three-dimensional space.[38]

Finally, if it be asked as to what it really is to be moved by the combination of lines and colours in a painting, Bell would offer the following answer:

> Art transports us from the world of man's activity to a world of aesthetic exaltation. For a moment we are shut off from human interests; our anticipations and memories are arrested; we are lifted above the stream of life.[39]

Fry, we may add, not only agrees with all this, but goes a step further. Quite unlike Bell, he insists on applying the concept of significant form even to literature. The greatness of a tragedy, he believes, arises from the vivid sense of the inevitablity *of the way* in which the events appear to unfold themselves. Another emphasis which distinguishes Fry is his view that it is the imaginative mode, as opposed to our instinctive reaction to things, which governs the creator and spectator of art.

Let us now see if and how far Bell's view is defensible. Where he says that "to appreciate a work of art we need to bring with us *nothing* from life . . . but a sense of form and a knowledge of three-dimensional space," the "nothing . . . but" may be questioned. But the hint that is here given about the value of the integrating tendencies of perception itself cannot be ignored, for it has the clear support of Gestalt psychology. Nor can we deny that where it is present, the representational element has to subserve the requirements of overall form. This is so even in ancient specimens of the potter's art. Thus, in

38. Bell, *Art*, pp. 36, 37.

39. Ibid., p. 36.

Terracotta Amphora[40] (about 550-525 BCE) which is signed by Taleides as potter and shows Theseus attacking the Minotaur Greek — the figures represented are all made to wear a gentle stoop so that it may accord with the overall look (of the vase's form) which is not of mere containment, but of enclosure. Further, the theory in question seems to rightly suggest that a work of art's form is not an empty shell, a mere (separable) container, but a whole *formed* object. See, here, the following from Langer:

> . . . An abstract concept that may be exemplified in various instances . . . this is a legitimate and widespread meaning of "form." But . . . when Bell and Fry . . . spoke of "significant form" . . . they meant a visible individual form produced by the interaction of colours, lines, surfaces, lights and shadows or whatever entered into a specific work. They used the word in the sense of something formed, as sometimes wonderful figures of soft colour and melting contours are formed by clouds, or . . . as a pot is made out of clay.[41]

One must also admit that the theory in question is justified, if not entirely, in emphasizing the value of the work of art *itself*. The welcome suggestion here is that such questions as what precise intention (of the artist) it expresses, or what things it represents may well be quite irrelevant to the work's aesthetic value. In literary theory too today, we may note, the autonomy of the work is freely emphasized.[42] Some artists also subscribe to this view. Thus Focillon contends that:

---

40. Reproduced in *Art Treasures of the Metropolitan*, Harry N. Abrams, New York: INC Publishers, 1st edn., 1952, p. 39 (Plate 29).

41. Langer, *Problems of Art*, p. 128.

42. An early instance of this emphasis is to be found in A.C. Bradley's essay, "Poetry for Poetry's Sake" in his *Oxford Lectures on Poetry*, MacMillan, Papermac, 1970 rpt., pp. 3-27.

    A much later work, *The Verbal Icon* (by W.K. Wimsatt Jr. and Beardsley), Noonday Press, 2nd edn., 1980 contains an essay, "The Intentional Fallacy" (pp. 3-18) which is a reasoned attempt to maintain that the value of a poem is to be judged without raising the question as to what the poet's own intention was.

> Whereas an image implies the representation of an object, and a sign signifies an object, form signifies only *itself*.[43]

He even suggests that art history may well be written entirely as a succession of isolable shapes or patterns. Nor are art critics slow to see the superior value of form. Thus, in a letter on poetry to Roger Fry, G. Lowes Dickinson says:

> All the essential aesthetic quality has to do with pure form. . . in a proportion as poetry becomes more intense the content is entirely remade by form and has no separate value at all.[44]

Finally, there is in fact a good deal of art which is free from representation. Painting and architecture are often quite so. If it be contended that a church made by the architect should after all seem to be like an actual church, the formalist's reply would be that the demand in such cases is as much for conformity *in design*, as for sameness of look. And it is indeed generally true that today the highly perceptive devotees of visual arts respond mainly to form rather than to content. But, and with this we turn to protest against the theory under review, is it proper to say, as Bell openly does, that the representative element is *always* irrelevant? Here, we have to answer in the negative, for one just cannot ignore the following facts of art appreciation:

We "see" distance in painting by judging the superposition and comparative size *of objects*. And this necessarily involves their identification, and so *a reference to the outer world*. The artist too has to remember what *in fact* admits of distance and what is not so open. Thus, in painting recessiveness Chirico builds upon horizons, not upon façades. Even in two-dimensional compositions, the break-up of surface into units depends on our recognition of suggested objects — no less than on the formal tendencies that are inherent in perception — for integrating

---

43. Cited fron F.E. Sparshott's *The Structure of Aesthetics*, University of Toronto Press and Routledge & Kegan Paul, 1963, p. 341.

44. Ibid., pp. 348-49.

details. And where a picture shows action, the balance achieved arises as much from the intensity and direction of the depicted, identifiable movements as from the opposing masses of mere colour. Facial expressions, directions of glance and the meaning of grimaces — all objects of everyday experience — are often vital elements in a formal composition.

Parker is indeed right in insisting that "the supreme works of art . . . contain all the four types of values": design, values of line and colour, plastic and spatial values,[45] and values that are distinctly spiritual. He adds that formalists like Bell have no right to single out but one element, the form, and to fix it as the essence of art. The element of representation is grossly undervalued by Bell. As Ducasse rightly insists, representation of dramatic entities is often a powerful source of significance in painting. It may well make sense to contend, as Bell and Fry do, that narration is really the way of literature; and that, insofar as no art may be expected to try what is naturally better suited to the powers of another art, painting should eschew narration and confine itself to the rendition of significant form. But Duccase would here say that the kind of representation — that is, *visual* — which is so open to painting, is quite outside the ambit of literature; and that pictorial narration should therefore remain a vital concern of painting.

Finally, when we turn to the literary arts, it becomes even more difficult to defend Bell's exaggerated emphasis on form and belittlement of the value of representational content. In poetry formal excellence may come from the balance of opposing ideas, and these are here meant by words, and so understood in the light of our experience of life.[46] Two good instances would here be the following:

45. De Witt Parker: *The Analysis of Art*, New Haven, Yale University Press, 1926, pp. 96-7.

46. In the region of English poetry an apt illustration is here provided by the following lines from Wordsworth's well-known sonnet:

> The world is too much with us: *late* and *soon*,
> *Getting and spending*, we lay waste our powers,

a. राम सौं *बड़ो* है कौन, मो सौं कौन *छोटो*
राम सौं *खरो* है कौन, मो सौं कौन *खोटो*
(Tulsīdāsa in *Vinaya Patrikā*)

b. *ऊंचे* पानी न टिके, *नीचे* ही ढहराय
नीचा है सो *भर पिये*, ऊंचा *प्यासा* जाय। (Kabīr)

Here, in the case of both the couplets cited above, balance is provided by pairs of words (all duly underlined), which oppose each other in respect of meaning, *and which have all to be understood in the light of our experience of daily life*. Reference to life (or representation) is even more essential for novels and plays. Form in a novel depends substantially on the balance of incidents; and dramatic form is, in part, a matter of shaping action, and of consistency in respect of portraying character. All this would remain unrealized should the context of life be somehow utterly left out of consideration. Bell himself realizes that the concept of "significant form" is inapplicable to literary arts which make a class of their own.

Form as expressive

Yet, in spite of all that may be said against it, the concept of significant form *is* important in a way that Bell perhaps did not visualize. The word *significance is* commonly taken to be synonymous with meaning; and *meaning, rather than* beauty, is today regarded by many as the key aesthetic concept. On the other hand, what Bell's view misses is the possibility that art can be significant *in the sense of being worth considering* because of qualities that are quite different from the possible evocativeness of a happy combination of lines and colours. Art has been very freely acclaimed because of its potential for *expressing* what the everyday use of language cannot articulate with equal effectiveness, and also because of its organic or deeply integrated quality. Of all those modern aestheticians who speak of artistic form as necessarily expressive Susanne Langer is perhaps the

---

Little we see in Nature that is ours;
We have given our hearts away, a sordid boon . . ."
(Italics added).

most consistent and singular, if not unchallengeable. She even ventures to suggest that the problem of expressive form is pivotal to aesthetics.[47] What such form really is may be put thus, in her own words:

> An expressive form is any perceptible or imaginable whole that exhibits relationships of parts, or points, or even qualities or aspects within the whole, so that it may be taken to represent some other whole whose elements have analogous relations. The reason for using such a form . . . is usually that the thing it represents is not perceivable or easily imaginable. We cannot see the earth as an object. We let a map or a globe express the relationships of places on the earth, and think about the earth by means of it.[48]

What this passage means may be brought out as follows:

(a) As an expressive form, a work of art may be essentially a perceptible whole — as in the case of music and the visual arts — or an imaginable one, as in the case of a poem or play. The net point here is that what enables us to seize the expressiveness of artistic form, taken generally, is the exercise of percipience and imaginative sympathy.

(b) Further, the adjective *expressive* is noteworthy. The verb *express* is generally taken to mean, *to press out*, or to externalize some inner content, as when we speak of expressing our thoughts or feelings in terms of language. What is thus expressed is taken to be, in a way, loosened from its original locus. On the other hand, when we are struck by the innocence *in* a child's face, the quality remains precisely where it is; and the words, "the face is express*ive* of innocence," will be a closer approximation to the apprehended character of fact than "the face express*es* innocence," because the latter way, I repeat, would be untrue to the (firmly)

47. Langer, *Problems of Art*, p. 149.

48. Ibid., p. 22.

embodied character of the quality in question. Similarly, when we choose to speak of a work of art as an express*ive* form we remain maximally true to *the indissoluble unity of what a work of art is and what it expresses to direct contemplation*. A simple example should make the point clear. The sadness that we may see in a piece of music is surely inseparable from the droop of its melodic phrases and from the subtly and gently regulated rise and fall of its tonal volume.

(c) Finally, artistic expression is very different from the way we commonly express our emotions in daily life. When a man gets very angry he may well turn red in the face and clench his fists. But he does not intentionally adapt these bodily changes to the provocative situation; they occur automatically. The artist, on the other hand, has to actively organize his material so that he may be able to express what he wishes to. In other words, expressiveness in art is a matter of weaving deft and intimate relations between the materials used, say, words in the case of poetry, and notes and beats in the case of music.

Form as organic

This leads us to consider another way in which artistic form may be said to be significant or of exceptional value, namely, *form as organic*. What this concept means simply is that the elements of a work of art are deeply integrated so as to make for the total work's expressiveness; that, within the ambit of the whole, none of them can be said to have an independent value; and that therefore it is impossible to determine exactly *how much* they individually contribute to the work's overall import or expressiveness. Langer clarifies the point by means of an interesting analogy:

> The import of a work of art is its "life," which, like actual life, is an indivisible phenomenon. Who could say, how much of an organism's life is in the lungs, how much in the legs or

> how much more life would be added to us if we were given a lively tail to wave? The Art symbol is a single symbol, and its import is not compounded of partial symbolic values.[49]

Now, ignoring for the moment the question if it is at all proper to regard a work of art as a symbol, the meaning of the above extract may be put quite simply. Just as one cannot indicate exactly *how much* life is contributed by a particular bodily organ to the life of the total organism, so it is impossible to fix the precise amount of meaning that the individual elements may be said to provide to a work's overall import.

The argument seems plausible, but one may doubt if it is quite fairly put. Meaning is not a quantity, and therefore the words, *how much*, do not go well with it. Our questions, here, have to be rather put as follows. What or how (or in what way), *not how much*, does an element contribute to the meaning (or expressiveness) of the total work? And if they are so put, the questions can surely be answered, may be differently by different interpreters. What follows directly from the emphasis that the elements of a work of art are deeply interwoven only is that its unity has to be unknit with care — that is, with maximum regard for the context of the detail that we focus on; and that if we are able to proceed thus, the final and not quite anticipated meaning which may dawn upon our minds will delight us with the very suddenness and obliquity of the way it emerges.[50] Further, because it will come as a sequal to our thinking and imaginative sympathy, it will strike us as *our finding*, rather than as a mere reception by us of a readymade meaning, and so will add to our relish. All this is very clearly borne out by what has already been done in our "critical appreciation" of some lines from Shakespeare's *The Winter's Tale*.[51] I may add that even *non*-dramatic poetry provides ample

---

49. Langer, *Problems of Art*, p. 135.

50. Many will here be reminded of what has been called *chamatkṛti* in traditional thinking on the concept of *dhwani*.

51. Act 4, Scene IV.

illustrations of the point that I am here trying to make.[52]

Form as articulate

The view that the form of a WoA is no mere juxtaposition of parts does not, however, mean that their individual character is necessarily rubbed out in the work's cohesive unity. It may indeed be contended that the form of quite a few works of art is articulate, or that they are "compositions which are not produced by mere mixture, like a new colour made by mixing paints but . . . [are] *articulated,* i.e., . . . their internal structure is given to our perception . . . [music, for example is] an articulate form.[53]

Now, what *is* said here is true even of that genre of literature where form can be specially intense, namely, poetry; for the *meaning of individual words* — and how it contributes to, and is itself modified by its context in the poem — can well be indicated fairly clearly, if variously. But such distinguishing hardly seems possible in the case of an impressionistic painting where (immediate) fuzziness, rather than (subsequent) clarity of outlines is an express feature, and *where form may appear to be fused* with colour.[54] Nor is articulateness a *necessary* and *pervasive* feature of music. It is certainly an important mark of *khyāl-gāyakī* which is noted for its variety of *taans*, the constituent notes of which are required to appear distinct without of course hampering the run of the pattern. But where, during the course of *ālāpa*, a *vīṇā*-player or a *dhruvapad*-singer avails of a *mīṇḍ* (glide) traversing three or four notes, none of them *appears* to be self-existent, though all of them may be registered in idea, and can even be identified, if required, by a discriminating listener (or *rasika*), by way of *saragam* or recitation of note-names.

52. See, here, the sixth chapter of this work.

53. Langer, *Feeling and Form*, pp. 30-31.

54. Louise Dudley and Austin Faricy, *The Humanities*, 3rd edn., revised by Louise Dudley, McGraw Hill Book Co., 1960, p. 113. Throughout this para and the following one, I have followed ch. IV of the work referred to.

FORM AND ALLIED CONCEPTS

A work of art is as much a case of making, if not of the same kind, as an article of furniture; and, to speak quite generally, whatever a man makes, be it a work of art or an object of everyday use, it is not only produced out of something, but in *accordance with* some plan, however general or tentative it be. Further, when the object is completed it appears as a unity of some distinct — or distinguish*able* — and, more or less, essential parts. Now, any substance out of which something is or may be made is generally called *material*. The plan which determines, may be quite loosely, the making of the object is its *design*; and the parts or components which seem essential for the wholeness of the object are called its *elements*. Finally, the way in which these elemetns combine to heighten each other's character or charm, as in the case of a work of art, is called *form* in the basic aesthetic sense. Therefore, to clearly bring out the meaning of (artistic) *form* we have to distinguish it from the allied concepts of *material, medium, elements* and *design* or structure.

The first two of these can also be distinguished. Wood is a carpenter's material; it is out of wood that he *makes* articles of furniture. *Medium* signifies the means by which an artist *expresses* what he wishes to. Here, in the region of art, it is *also* the stuff of which he fashions his artistic creations. A carpenter is not said to express or communicate anything; he merely *makes* things of daily use. The substance that he uses, wood, is just *material* only. On the other hand, where a sculptor avails of wood, the material is used not for the sake of making a thing of daily use, but a work of art which is only meant for contemplation. Here the wood, as turned into a piece of sculpture, expresses the artist's way of looking at something, or visualizing a situation or a state of experience. So, in the context of art, the material used is at once a medium too.

Medium

(a) There is yet another way in which we can reflect on the concept of (artistic) *medium*. The word can be used in two distinct senses. The first is: any intervening means, instrument or agency *through which* some end is attained. In this sense a *sitār* or *sarod* is the medium of the music which it produces, because the music is made available to us through the particular instrument. The second meaning of "medium" is: any enveloping substance *in which* a thing (or being) lives or exists or becomes significant. It is in this sense that water may be said to be the medium of marine life; and oil or water colour, the medium of the pictures of a painter who works in these media, and revels in exploring their aesthetic potential. It is important to note that in *this* (second) sense the medium is very much present *in* the work as its material, quite unlike water which merely envelops, though it also sustains, marine life. Further, from the viewpoint of the immanence of medium in the work, neither the painter's brush nor a musician's instrument can be said to be the medium of the art which they serve to produce, simply because neither of them appears as a part of the work created by means of them. At best, they can be called material as mere equipment *for* the making of art, not material as the medium *of* works of art. To conclude, the medium of an art is its essential material which is also present in the works created by its being used artistically. Clearly, there can be no art without medium; but there *is* plenty of art without subject and purpose. Further, every art has its own category of materials to serve as means of creating expressive or significant forms.

(b) For *architecture* the most important materials in use today are structural steel and reinforced concrete. But some other materials — like glass, aluminium, linoleum, plastics and rubber — have also gained wide acceptance. Steel and reinforced concrete are both strong and light. They are good for any kind of construction, but the type that distinguishes their use is known as *skeleton* construction. In such construction thin but very strong beams of steel or reinforced concrete make the framework which supports the whole building. The steel rods are added because concrete alone can stand only weight, not strain or tension. For *sculpture* the two mediums that are most freely used are stone and metal. As it appears *in* the completed sculpture, the stone can look so smooth that one may be tempted to run one's hand over its surface, and to even suppose, in case the work in question represents (say) a feminine figure, that if he could touch the "skin," he would find it soft and pliable. As for metal, the one most commonly used is bronze. But though both stone and bronze are common mediums of sculpture, the processes used in turning them into works of art are quite different. "Stone statues are made by cutting away the stone until only the intended figures are left. Metal statues, on the other hand, are first modelled in wax; the sculptor builds up the figure he wants, and then has it cast in bronze."[55] The rich colour of bronze, and its smooth texture which can easily reflect light, make this metal an excellent medium for sculpture. What is more, because bronze is light in weight, a figure made of it can support itself in even such positions as cannot be achieved in stone. However, wood, terracotta (or "baked earth") and ivory are also important mediums for sculpture, though the last two of these are not very freely used today. Wood is relatively cheap, and easy to get and cut. What is more, it can be very well polished and coloured, and so invested with an even, shining surface. Further, if a sculpture in wood is skillfully made, the grain of the medium can show itself and thereby heighten the effect of the whole work. This is clearly seen in the two well-known works of Henry Moore:

55. Louise Dudley and Austin Faricy, *The Humanities*, op. cit., p. 114.

Reclining Figure and *Two Forms*.[56] Terracotta, used mostly in pottery, is made by firing clay. Modern sculptors are making use of some other mediums as well, such as cast stone, wrought iron, aluminum, glass and steel.

(c) The medium of *traditional* painting is not marked by such variety. In fact, the entire art of painting may be regarded as essentially[57] the application of coloured pigments to a flat surface, usually canvas, paper, wood or plaster. But, of course, insofar as they are originally dry, colours have to be mixed with something to be spread on a surface. This substance, commonly a fluid, is called the *vehicle*. In oil painting the vehicle is oil; in water colour paintings, water. Oil is probably the most commonly used medium of painting today. It remains moist for a long time, enabling the artist to work over what he is doing, and to make the necessary changes *today* in what he might have painted *yesterday*. When pigments mixed *with water* are applied to wet plaster on a wall, the work which results is called *fresco* painting. As the colour dries and soaks in the plaster, the picture becomes a part of the wall. Michelangelo's frescoes on the ceiling of Sistine Chapel are the best known examples of such painting.

Pigment, however, is not the only medium of the arts that are classed as painting. It is *not* the medium of mosaic, stained glass and tapestry; yet all these arts are generally regarded as painting. In mosaic, a picture is made by conjoining small pieces of coloured glass or stone which are commonly square in shape. The stained glass window is also a kind of patchwork. But here what is held together, by bands of lead, is coloured glass in small pieces. Tapestries are fabrics comprising hand-woven designs.

56. *The Humanities*, p. 114.

57. Though surely not entirely, as indicated in the very next para.

Drawing provides yet another medium in which pictures may be seen. In the (other) sense of an instrument, the *medium* here used may either be a pencil, pen or silverpoint. "Silverpoint [is] drawing with a gold or silver wire on a specially prepared paper . . ."[58] Prints, woodcuts, etching and lithography are other known mediums of painting.

(d) The chief mediums of *music* are well known. They are pure or meaningless, but not undifferentiated *sounds*, and *laya* or aesthetic pace. Sounds which bear meanings, or words, are the distinctive material of literature. It is true that in our classical singing too language is freely used. But words are just not there in instrumental music and (*dhrupad*-related) *ālāpa*; and even in the region of *khyāl*-singing many of those maestros who represent the traditional *gharānā*s give but scant attention to the use of words. So language cannot be regarded as the *distinctive* medium of music. What is here essential is sounds as making a scale. *Laya* too is an indispensable element of our music. There is no classical music in India without *rāga*; but a *rāga* itself cannot be there without a *more or less leisurely* projection of the *vādī-saṁvādī* relation. Further, barring *mārvā*, every *rāga* calls for a *restful* treatment of the tonic. It may here be pointed out that if aesthetic duration and pure sound are regarded as the essence of *music*, our rhythm would also be covered by the word, for our entire rhythmic system is nothing but a knitwork of meaningless sounds regulated in respect of pace. What lends added point to this suggestion is the fact that, in the case of all Indian music, the drum that provides rhythmic accompaniment has to be carefully attuned to some specific note in the musical scale.

In its other sense of instrument or agency, *medium* may be taken to mean the whole variety of our musical instruments.

58. *The Humanities*, p. 131.

They are commonly put under three classes: percussion, wind, and string. What is here important to note is that the aesthetic purpose of an instrument and the character of the music it produces are alike, in a measure, determined by its structure. Thus, whereas the *tānpūrā* — which is quite without frets and is tuned only with some key notes of the *rāga* chosen by the musician — provides only a helpful drone, the *sitār*, with its many frets and sympathetic strings, is admirably suited to produce a very rich filigree of *svaras*, so to say, and of varying design, pace and tonal filling. As distinguished from this most important medium (or instrument) of classical Hindustānī *instrumental* music, the *sāraṅgī*, because of its very tone, is admirably suited to "accompany" classical singing in north India. Yet it would be wrong to believe that no other musical instrument can serve the same purpose. South Indian *violinists* are commonly seen to provide excellent "accompaniment" to Carnatic vocalists; and they are surely quite as capable of producing intricate patterns as the *sāraṅgī*-players of north India. Again, the *vīṇā* is, in general, more capable of providing deeply impressive and virtually seamless *ālāpa* than either *sitār* or *sarod*. On the other hand, *sitār* and *sarod* are much better vehicles of *drut gatkārī*[59] than the *vīṇā*.

Aesthetic requirements may even necessitate some structural modification of an instrument. Thus, it was with a view to providing more tuneful "accompaniment" to *sitār* and *sarod* music, which charms not so much by its work in the *mandra* regions as by its use of *madhya* and *taar saptaks*, that the older *tablā*, with a broad face, had to be abandoned in favour of what is called, छोटे मुंह की पुड़ी just because this *puṛī* — or skinny covering of the right drum — can be attuned to notes which

59. *Gatkārī* means playing of the basic *gat* — that is, the opening rhythmically organized musical line — as also of tonal and rhythmic patterns by way of relieving the essentially unchanging appearance of the *gat*. Where it follows the *vilambit* (adagio) idiom, it is (as a rule) prefaced with three other phases of playing, namely, *ālāpa*, *joṛh*, and *jhālā*.

are higher in pitch. More or less similarly, rhythm as marked by the big one-piece drum, *pakhāwaj*, is a better accompaniment for the depth and stateliness of *dhruvapad* and *dhamār* than the two-piece *tablā*.

As for literature, its essential medium is obviously language, though in its use of various metres and alliterative sounds, it may well be said to avail of rhythm and sweet sounds, and so of a measure of music too. It is indeed its adroit employment of words that makes it eminently capable of exercising all those functions which have been ascribed to art by literary critics and aestheticians, namely, *representation* of things, situations and happenings, portrayal of human character, *expression* of thoughts and feelings, and even that intense *embodiment* of meaning in artistic medium which makes the two virtually inseparable. However, unlike many works of architecture, quite a few paintings — and a considerable amount of music, rhythm and dance — the appeal of literarature is *confined* to those who know the language used in the work.

It is precisely with a view to securing *wider* appeal that some artistes are compelled to use quite a few different mediums, and so to produce a work of "combined" art. The theatre and dance are obvious examples of such art. The first of these is the writing and production of plays in general; and the second comprises what we in India call *nṛtta* and *nṛtya*. The theatre employs *language* in the form of dialogue; *abhinaya* in the expression of thought and feeling; and also, quite often, specially designed costumes, lighting, and music. It is because of its integrated use of so many diverse mediums of expression and exceptional evocative power that Indian tradition has given to drama a pre-eminent place among the arts. Of dance, taken generally, the emphasis is, of course, on rhythmic bodily movement; but costume, lighting and music are also freely used here. The movements that go to make a dance may be roughly divided into two classes: movements within the body, such as those of the eyes, arms, or torso, *at* a limited part of the dance floor; and movement *from one place to another*, such as stepping or jumping. There is yet another twofold division which is distinctive of *Indian classical dances*, and which we have already referred to. They are all alike distinguishable into two kinds: *nṛtta* and *nṛtya*. *Nṛtta* is "pure" dance in the sense that it only creates varying designs in rhythm, and does not tell stories, depict situations or express emotions. *Nṛtya*, on the other hand, is frankly representational or/and expressive in purpose. What we call *abhinaya* is a feature of *nṛtya*, not of *nṛtta*, though the two can, of course, be easily combined in a single number. In its aspect of expressiveness, the art of dance may be said to be very direct in its impact. Quite a few of the thematic intra-forms[60] of Kathak, and of course its display of pure footwork (or *tatkār*), are presented in such a way that they seem to be addressed *to* the audience, instead of just being danced *in* their presence. The full seizure of their aesthetic character and impact, however, depends on the degree of refinement of the onlooker's percipience and aesthetic sense. Opera and cinema may also be classed as "combined" arts. An opera is a play set to music. As a medium, it employs all the arts of the threatre. Further, here the characters have to sing their parts; and, what is more, group singing and dancing are also often used. Opera may therefore be said to combine some of the greatest mediums of all art: music, action, story and spectacle. It is not only the most complex, but perhaps also the most difficult of all artistic mediums. Here the demands on the performers are indeed quite heavy.

Elements

For *aesthetic theory* too, the art of opera presents a difficulty. We commonly speak of the following three as essential elements of art taken generally: *aesthetic surface, design or structure* and *form*. But what would the first of these, or *aesthetic surface*, precisely mean in the context of opera? The problem will

60. For reasons which make me speak of Kathak numbers as *intra-forms* rather than as items, see my essay: "Kathak: Some Terms and Distinctions," *Sangeet Natak*, no. 51, January–March, 1979; pp. 5-14.

become obvious as we turn to see what the three elements of art, just distinguished (and italicized) exactly signify.

(a) The concept of *aesthetic surface* was brought into prominence by D.W. Prall. It signifies such *sensuous* elements of works of art as are usually more easily grasped than the other elements. Some clear examples of aesthetic surface may be listed thus: the hard white marble of a statue; the loftiness of a temple; the curvature of lines used in a painting; the mellowness of a seasoned singer's voice; the *mukhavilās* and the fluidity of the movements of a graceful danseuse, or her figural shapelines, or liquidity of eyes, and the alternating softness and intensity of her footfalls (or *padchāps*). Whatever be the art in which it is found, aesthetic surface is only an immediate source of appeal, and the man who cares for the work of art in its wholeness has got to go beyond mere aesthetic surface if he wishes to seize the essential import of the work in question. Yet it is undeniable that the pleasure derived from attention to aesthetic surface is effortless. Do we ever have to *try* to be charmed by the manifest sweetness of a singer's voice or of a *tablā* quite correctly attuned to the tonic of the singer?

Exactly how much is covered by the meaning of aesthetic surface is, however, not easy to determine. Sensible qualities such as the ones listed above, qualitative relations like the alternation of a leisurely pace with brief and sudden spurts in a rhythmic pattern, and the relation of disposition in space — say, the diagonal positioning of two figures in a painting — may be safely put under the concept in question. But what about the representational elements in a work of art? At this point, aestheticians are divided. Some contend that these elements take our attention beyond or away from the content directly presented to perception, and so away also from aesthetic surface, as Prall regards it;

others deny this, and maintain that the presentational elements may only make for the *immediate* recognition of the precise character or identity of what is presented to attention in a work of art, and so do not at all take us away from the work itself.

(b) Another important element of art is *design*. It is indeed not uncommon for an artist to begin a particular work with a specific kind of design in mind, a design which can often be referred to in isolation from the other details of the work, and sometimes — as in the regions of painting and architecture — in geometrical terms. We indeed freely speak of the different kinds of balances. Raphel's well-known work: *Madonna di San Sisto* (Gallery, Dresden) is a good example of classical balance. Such balance requires, almost in the manner of a pair of scales, equal measures on each side of a central figure or object.[61] Yet another good example of such balance is provided by Leonardo da Vinci's *The Last Supper*. Here, Christ is placed in the exact middle with two groups of three apostles on either side. Such an obvious use of mathematical equality could have made the entire composition appear a little stiff and lifeless, had it not been for the relief provided by the graceful and mobile postures of the apostles. What is more, in this case "the doubling of objects on either side of a central figure not only gives the main subject [some extra] importance but contributes the peace, symmetry and solemnity appropriate to religious feeling and decorum."[62]

---

61. H.R. Poore, *Composition in Art*, The Oak Tree Press, 1967, p. 6.

62. W. Gaunt, *A Companion to Painting*, Thomas and Hudson, 1967, p. 142. It may here be added that this particular painting is a good instance of what may be called the *radial plan* of organization in the visual arts. In this plan the lines of the pictures form radii "which meet at a point in the centre." Here, in this picture, "all the lines of the ceiling and walls, as well as the hands and faces of the twelve disciples, point to the head of Christ. Leonardo puts his point of focus directly in the centre of the picture." *The Humanities*, p. 273.

A distinction is also often made between horizontal (or lateral) and vertical balance. The former kind of balance is specially important for a landscape painting, because it makes for extended perspective. Some paintings employ a circular plan. Here, an apt illustration would be the well-known work of Henri Matisse, entitled *Dance.*[63] Compostitions may also be based on a diagonal plan. We see this very clearly in the picture, *Raising of the Cross* by Rubens — a work which is very clearly expressive of dynamic movement.[64] Michaelangelo's *The Creation of Adam*[65] is a typical example of a very effective use of (a semblance of) the curvilinear (or "S") form. Such a design imparts movements and life, which is the essence of the subject of the work referred to. In the region of our classical dance, the *tribhaṅgī*, which is so obvious in the basic Oḍissī posture, suggests movement without of course letting the danseuse really move. The posture is indeed a clear index of the art of dance where movement reigns supreme. In the region of our classical vocal *ālāpa* the formal excellence known as *dagar* (डगार) is a fair example of curvilinear movement, though here this movement is literal, and not merely suggested as in the case of the *tribhaṅgī*. Another geometrical kind of design which is usable in art is the oval one. It is quite clearly present in Vincent Van Gogh's *The Potato Eaters.*[66] As for the pyramidal design, it has been effectively used in quite a few of our temples.

(c) Design, however, is not a single entity. As it appears in a work of visual art, it itself comprises quite a few

---

63. *A Companion to Painting*, op. cit., p. 162; picture no. 142.
64. Ibid., p. 35; picture no. 26.
65. *The Humanities*, p. 58; also p. 103. *The Paintings of Michel Angelo*, Thames and Hudson, 1965.
66. M.E. Tralbaut, *Van Gogh*, Thames and Hudson, 1959, p. 55.

elements, namely: line, colour, texture, value, volume, and perspective.

The simplest and the most fundamental or widely used means of creating visual art is the line. If we ask a child to draw an object, he will first try to out*line* it. Lines, however, are not merely a necessary element, but also suggest movement. They always appear to be moving, and we tend to follow them, with our fingers or with our eyes. Colour is not originally possessed of this dynamic quality, though it *can* be made to appear vibrant, as van Gogh does it with his typical brushwork. However, to speak of the dynamic quality of a line is not to say everything about what it can suggest in a visual work of art, and some important distinctions have to be made. Lines may be straight or curved. Straight lines, again, may be horizontal, vertical, or diagonal. The essential suggestion of a horizontal line is relaxation or quiet. In Rembrandt's etching, *Three Trees*, for example, tranquility is suggested essentially by the long line of the horizon.[67] The vertical line can also be a line of rest, but here the stillness is one of poise or balance, and not of relaxation. Chimneys and towers, which employ the vertical, do not seem to be relaxed; rather, they seem to be making their way up and to hold themselves in that position. The diagonal is manifestly a line of action or tension. In the painting, *The Uprising*, by Daumier, the sense of the onward march of people is evoked not only by diagonal disposition of the other figures before and behind the leader, but also, and importantly, by the upraised arm of the leader which makes a clear diagonal.[68]

Curved lines can also appear to be dynamic; but they never look stiff; they even lend a pliant look to the object which employs them. Incidentally, as in the case of music, whereas a quick curve appears to be light and gay, a slower one seems to be restful and contemplative. It is here important to note that

67. *A Companion to Painting*, op. cit., p. 166.

68. Ibid., p. 160.

however conducive they may be to a suggestion of grace, curved lines need a relief or the steadying effect of adjacent straight lines; otherwise, they tend to betoken disorder or instability. Thus in Van Gogh's picture, *La Berceuse* (*Mme Roulin Rocking the Cradle*), the abundant use of curves is relieved by the straight supports for the arms of the chair.

Another element of the visual arts is colour. Its value in the art of painting is well known. But colour can contribute to the appeal of sculpture and architecture as well. In these two arts the colour of the material itself is an important factor, be it the creamy whiteness of marble or ivory, or the rich brown of poished bronze or wood.

But to speak of colour in this general way is hardly enough; and here, again, some distinctions have to be made. Colours differ in hue, value, and intensity or brightness. *Hue* is that quality which enables us to distinguish one colour from another. The three primary hues are red, blue, and yellow. All the other colours can be made from them. The *value* of colour is the quality by means of which we distinguish the shades of a single colour as light, dark, or medium. *Intensity* is the vividness of a colour. Two colours may be both red, and equally dark: yet one may be richer or clearer that the other. From the viewpoint of expressiveness, however, the more important distinction is the one between *warm* and *cool* colours. Perhaps because of their association in everyday experience with trees, grass and sky — all of which are credited with a cooling or soothing effect — green and blue are commonly regarded as *cool* colours. In works of visual art — of painting, in particular — these colours suggest quiet and serenity, and also (at times) recession or retreat. On the other hand, yellow, red and orange are *warm* colours, perhaps because of their association with warm objects like the blazing sun, glowing coal, and fire. These colours, that is, the *warm* ones, always seem closer than the *cool* colours; this is why they are called *advancing* colours. If a red and a blue circle are placed side by side, the red one would seem closer to the spectator than the blue one. In a complete work of art, however, no colour is seen exactly as it itself is. Its closeness to other colours necessarily makes it seem a little different from its own independent look. To illustrate, if a patch of red colour is put beside another one of violet, the latter will appear more like blue than what it itself is.

A more interesting detail of art contemplation relates to *texture* which is another important element of art. Texture is commonly perceived by touch, as when we feel the difference between the roughness of tweed and the smoothness of serge. But, as the tactful feel of objects becomes a familiar content of our everyday experience, texture comes to be sensed by the eye too, and quite without actual touch. Here it may seem to us that we have run our hands over the marble (of a piece of sculpture) even though we do not touch the work at all. In the region of painting where a work is only to be *seen*, the term *texture* relates to the representation of skin, cloth, jewels, metals and furniture, etc. In a still life painting — which represents lifeless (and everyday) objects like flowers, fruits and vegetables — what is of basic importance is obviously not the subject as such, but texture, colour and organization. Chardin's *Bowl of Plums*,[69] for instance, is distinguished by its projection of the texture of plums and the pitcher, along with other effects of the play of light on the pitcher and the plums.

Yet another art element which determines the charm of both painting and architecture is *value* which signifies the relative degree of light and dark. In painting it generally remains fixed. Dark or lit up areas, or shadows remain as they are made by the painter; they do not change with — because they are not generally exposed to — variations in the source of light or in the passage of day. But in architecture and sculpture the values can easily change with variations in light. A distinctive charm of the cathedral of Notre Dame in Paris lies in the play of lights and shadows on the subtly regulated carvings of the façade. It is precisely with an eye to this aesthetic possibility that an architect often makes a model of the building he

69. *A Companion to Painting*, op. cit., p. 174.

proposes to design; he essays to foresee the precise effects of the shadows as far as he can.

It is, however, in relief sculpture that value acquires a *special* significance. This is so primarily because in most cases the design can be clearly seen mainly in the shadow cast. These shadows are deep — and the lines, bold and distinct — where the relief is high. Further, because of bolder projection, the figures here are almost in the round. In low relief, on the other hand, where the figures are only slightly raised from the background, the shadows are less deep; and the lines, quite delicate.

To turn now to volume, it is obviously that quality which makes us realize that the object before us possesses not merely length and breadth, but thickness as well. Where we depend on vision alone, volume is perceived in two main ways: by noting the shapes or outlines of objects, *and* by means of surface lights and shadows. This is so probably because in daily life too things are seen to have solid shapes, *and* to cast shadows. A shadow, again, is known as such because of its contrast with light. Therefore, where he wishes to create a semblance of volume, the artist too has to use clear outlines *and* shadow-light contrast, though any one of these elements may be *more* effectively used in some works than in others. Thus, whereas in Michelangelo's *Cumaean Siby*[70] both the ways we have distinguished are employed with equal effect, in Rembrandt's *An Old Woman Cutting Her Nails* the suggestion of volume is achieved almost entirely through shadows.[71] But a skilful use of lines alone can also create the same effect, that is, of solidity. Japanese painters have been able to do this admirably. They believe that shadows are but fleeting appearances; and that only the permanent should be represented in painting. In the region of classical Indian music too volume can appear not merely in the original width of a vocalist's *akāra* or in its skilful regulation during singing, nor even merely in the deeper *mandra*

70. *A Companion to Painting*, p. 180.

71. Ibid., p. 181.

tones of an instrument, say, the *vīṇā*, but also, and importantly, in the use of long and relatively leisurely use of curves which often seem *to encompass an unseen filling*. How, otherwise could *ālāpa* of the *dhruvapad* manner which does not use any words, appear so full of depth?

However, quite unlike painting and architecture, music cannot ordinarily be credited with that art element which is called *perspective*, and which means the representation of objects in space, with effects of solidity and distance, so that we are enabled to make distinctions of "before or in front of" and "behind or beyond." Architecture uses *actual* space, whereas painting creates a mere semblance of it. The interior of a building — in which we can move about and which can readily impress us with its spaciousness — is real, enclosed space; and its exterior too is something that we can actually walk up to. In a painting, on the other hand, the distance that we may seem to see cannot in fact be traversed. It is only virtual, not real distance.

But perspective can be linear or aerial. Linear perspective is indicated by the direction of lines and the comparative size of objects. When we stand on the tract of a railroad and follow the lines with our eyes, they seem to rise, meet, and fade in the distance. Similarly, though all the minarets of Taj Mahal are equally tall, the ones that are seen to be *behind* those that are in front seem to be smaller in height. Aerial perspective is created by the device of making objects lighter in colour and indistinct in outline as they approach the horizon. Thus in Monet's *Waterloo Bridge* the buildings on the horizon are so hazy as to be hardly visible, and therefore seem to be quite remote from the bridge.

Monet, incidentally, is an impressionist painter; and if, unlike the Renaissance artistes — such as Raphael, Perugino and Van Eyck — he is indifferent to the clarity and exactness of perspective lines, it is simply because of the avowed credo of the movement which he leads — that is, the belief that the essential concern of the painter is with the momentary appearance of objects, and with colour. There is, however, one more reason why the painter of today is not particular about the exact representation of perspective. He argues that if the camera — which is, after all, a mere machine — can reproduce perspective lines accurately, why should the *creative* art of painting work for the same end? Be that as it may, it is a fact that the painter of today feels free to change or falsify exact perspective for the sake of a more effective projection of his basic idea. For instance, in Chirico's *Melancholy and Mystery of a Street*,[72] the normal rules of a truthful perspective are clearly ignored, the white and remoter part of the work being as clearly and firmly outlined as the black portion which is closer to us. This deviation from the normal practice of a painter is resorted to just for the sake of a more coercive expression of the idea that the carefree play of the little girl with the hoop is quite out of tune with, and so heightens by contrast, the dark and ominous character of the world in which she plays.

Perspective, we have said, is not an element of music. But this widely acclaimed art is distinguished by quite a few other elements which are just not there in any other art. These essential elements of music are: rhythm, tempo, dynamics, timbre, melody, and harmony. If it here be objected as to why we have not included *rāga* in this list, our answer could be that though it is admittedly of great importance in the entire classical music of India, a *rāga* is, after all, a melodic wholeness and is therefore not really left out by our list which does include *melody*.

Rhythm is just as important for our music as *rāga*. Our word for rhythm is *tāla*. *Tāla* is *laya* (or aesthetic pace) as measured and identified with the help of beats and *bol*s (or mnemonic syallables or their tufts); and in its basic sense of regulated flow or movement, rhythm may be said to be a most essential element of music, for all music is a going forward, or a turning back — some ascent or descent — or both; but necessarily some

72. *A Companion to Painting*, op. cit., p. 191.

movement. A single *svara*, however sweet it be, becomes an element of the art of music only when it is embraced in a melodic flow at a particular pace. But, be it noted, our rhythm is a blend of the accented and the unaccented; and the off-beat is important in every cycle, and even central in seven-beat cycles. Tempo is the actual speed of music. In India we commonly distinguish it as *vilambit*, *madhya*, *drut* and *atidrut*. The word *dynamics* signifies the varying degree of force and sonority which music may assume, from as soft as possible to the maximally loud, though never (in principle) unpleasantly so. Sonority in music is not mere softness or loudness as such, but the *actively controlled quality* of sound in music. The point can be easily seen in the light of the formal graces in which our music abounds. *A murki* and a *mīṇḍ* may be equally soft, but the two surely strike the ear quite differently. The one appears light, pretty and frolicsome; the other impresses us with its sweep and seamlessness. Timbre, on the other hand, is the original peculiar quality of a sound produced by a musical instrument or a singer. Each voice and each instrument, indeed, has its own characteristic *timbre* or tone colour. Thus, in musical parlance, when we wish to appreciate how a properly tuned *tablā* or *tānpūrā* sounds we often say: "इसकी बोल-चाल अच्छी है." Not merely does the same *svara* produced by a *sitār* and a *sāraṅgī* sound different in the two cases, but the difference may be manifest even if both the instruments attended to are *sitār*s.

Melody is a tune, an arrangement of tones in the before-after order. A tone, as opposed to unpleasing sounds which we call noises, is an agreeable sound produced by a *regular* series of vibrations. What enables us to distinguish a tone or a whole tune as *higher* or *lower* is *pitch*. There can be no melody without a *pitch*. A tune must appear to go up and down.

At this point, however, a question may be readily put. There is a free use of up-and-down movement, or *āroha* and *avaroha*, even in *ālāpa* of the *dhruvapad* manner. How is, then, a tune different from *ālāpa*? The answer is, however, easy. A tune is pretty short in extent; it has a fairly obvious setting in a particular *tāla*, and a look of self-completeness; and so we can easily hold or encompass it in attention as a distinct object, and may even be able to repeat it. *Ālāpa*, on the other hand, is a vast and gradually built-up expanse of melody. It is impossible to repeat a full-length exposition of *ālāpa*. The artist himself cannot do it from memory. And as for the individual phrases (or *svara-samoohas*) that go to make the whole fabric of *ālāpa*, however irresistible be their intrinsic appeal, they are always looked upon as paving the way to what is to come, and never as complete in themselves. What is more, these constituents of *ālāpa* are clearly not set in any rhythmic cycle. What here determines the ordering of notes and tonal phrases, and so provides *form* to *ālāpa*, is the individual vocalist's attitude to the *rāga* being presented and his aesthetic sense; and the content is *svaras* and their linkages, all regulated in terms of both abidance at specific notes and pace of passages that interlink them.

FORM AND CONTENT[73] IN ART

The way we have just spolen of *ālāpa* makes it clear that *form* and *content* do not exclude each other. Tonal phrases are surely ways of *forming* music; but they are by no means vacuous, and all alike have some *svaras* as their *content*. Every work of art must have both a *form* and some *content*. But two notes of caution may here be sounded. First, we have to guard ourselves against the everyday way of talking about *content*. When we think of clothes as the content of a box we assume that the content — that is, the clothes — can be taken out without causing any harm to the container or the box. Such thinking is plainly irrelevant to a work of art. If we could somehow take away its filling of words from a poem, the poem itself would disappear. And what would a melody be without its *svaras*? Secondly, as is implied in the question we have just put, the

73. My treatment of these two concepts is largely based on W.E. Kennick's essay in *Art and Philosophy*, ed. Sidney Hook, New York University Press, 1966.

form of a WoA is no mere container. It has rather to be taken as the unique interrelatedness of the aesthetically treated details or elements it comprises. Indeed, the *form* and *content* of a WoA do not exclude each other. At the same time, in spite of their obvious relevance to art, the two do not exhaust all that can be said about a work of art. When we say: "This poem is an ode," we obviously say something about the poem, but nothing about its "form" *in the basic aestheticc sense of the word.* Similarly, the statement: "This statue has so much of bronze," does not really touch the (aesthetic) "content" of the statue, though it does say something relevant about the *material* used by the sculptor in making the work.

Yet, *the tint or texture* of the bronze may well be said to be a part of the (aesthetic) content of the statue, insofar as they can both easily become object of aesthetic appreciation. Therefore, instead of characterizing it as "*whatever* is there in a work of art as organized in a particular way," we may say that *content* signifies what is there in a work of art *and is a possible object of aesthetic appreciation*. It may here also be added that *all* aesthetic appreciation does not refer to the *organization* of a WoA. Thus, when we admire *a* note in a melody as being intensely tuneful or grammatically and aesthetically significant[74] we say nothing explicitly about the structure of the melody. Similarly, it is easy to see the difference (and the relation) between form *as shape* and form *as arrangement*. In quite a few cases the (overall) form of a painting is mainly the arrangement of many individual forms or shapes.

"Content" too has to be distinguished from *subject-matter*. Alliterative sounds may well be a part of a poem's *content*; for one *can* admire them. But, to be sure, they are not a part of the poem's subject-matter. Every WoA has some "content," but not necessarily a subject-matter. Except in the case of thematic orchestral compositions, instrumental music has no subject-matter, tones and beats being only its material. *Subject-matter,*

---

74. The *Gandhār of Rāga Darbārī*, for instance.

again, is (in many cases) different from the mere *subject* of a work. The subject is (often) the mere topic of a work. Thus, the ethereal friendship of Rādhā and Kṛṣṇa is the *subject* of many of our *nṛtya* numbers in dance; it is *what they are generally about*. On the other hand, the details of the individual items in terms of which this theme is portrayed — details like Rādhā as waiting, fretting when Kṛṣṇa fails to turn up on time, Kṛṣṇa's persuasive efforts to appease her, and finally their dancing happily together as one — are all here parts of the subject-matter which we often see presented by the way of *abhinaya*, in the main. Sometimes, however, the *subject* and *subject-matter* of a WoA may denote the same thing. Thus, in the case of a still life painting, entitled *Flowers*, flowers in the vase are also the subject-matter of the work. It may here be added that the semantic point of view also admits of this possible identity. The common dictionary meanings of the word "subject" are: topic, a *theme, that which is treated or handled*. Yet, for purposes of thinking it is generally needful to heighten the *difference* between the two concepts. A WoA may have a subject, but no subject-matter. Brancusi's "Bird in Space" is a case in point.

The fact, however, is that even the form-content distinction has been rejected by some, as by Weitz. He contends that there is no difference between the form and content of a WoA; that the content of a WoA is *all* that is there in it — "all the elements, expressive characteristics and the *relations* that obtain among them"; and that, insofar as form in art is also commonly taken to mean a work's overall *relatedness*, it is wrong to oppose form to content.

Now, one may ask, why exactly does Weitz deny the distinction which seems so obvious? Perhaps it is because of the capacity of statements about content to "absorb" or include references to relations among content. Thus, one may speak as follows in respect of a painting: "This picture *contains a woman in a yellow blouse pouring milk from a jug sharply silhouetted against a brightly lighted wall.*" But we may forthwith point out that even here the form-content distinction persists. "Being silhouetted against" is a relation, a matter of form. What is so silhouetted — the jug and wall — are parts of content.

At the same time, in interpreting "form" as a matter of internal relations we should not forget that the character of elements, which are obviously a part of the work's content, may itself determine the relations vitally. Thus if in the rhythmic aspect of our music, the *sama* (or the focal beat) is reached with immaculate sharpness and in a well-designed way, the whole pattern may appear to bloom.

In passing, we may also mark the difference between form-statements — that is, those that speak of relatedness — which are aesthetic and those which are not so. "A is to the right of B"; "this colour contrasts with that." Statements such as these are non-aesthetic, or simply factual. On the other hand, the following: "A and B are *awkardly* arranged"; and "The colour contrast, here, is *subtle*" are both clearly aesthetic, because a little evaluative. But to speak quite generally, relations (which presuppose plurality) are important as necessary conditions of such formal properties as unity, harmony, and coherence. A single colour or unmodulated tone cannot be said to be *harmonious*, — except, of course, in relation to the adjacent ones.

SOME AESTHETIC PREDICATES

There are some terms, however, which are more commonly used for expressing our reactions to whole works of art and to the beautiful in nature. These are called aesthetic predicates. Care is needed to use them properly, if only because they cannot all be distinguished quite clearly.

Different words come to the mind when we look at art and nature. An actual landscape and a painting (say, by Vermeer[75]) may both seem to be *serene*. A well sung lullaby can

75. I have here the following in mind: "Every painting of Vermeer's is bathed in . . . serenity. . . . There is no violence in his work, of thought or action. There is an eternal stillness, of music that dies on the echo, of the mind entranced by a message of love, of

be easily *sweet* and *soothing*.[76] The Taj, on the other hand, is an object of wondrous beauty; and *vīṇā* music or *ālāpa* of the *dhruvapad* kind can attain to *sublimity*. Of all such predicates the better known ones are *graceful, beautiful* and *sublime*; and the one that leads the field is undoubtedly *beauty*. Because of its very pre-eminence *beauty* calls for fuller attention than the other predicates, and so we may turn to it last of all for leisurely treatment. Incidental references to it will however be necessary from the very outset.

The Sublime

The predicates *graceful* and *beautiful* are applicable to both human figures and movements. On the other hand, sublimity is found, if only occasionally, in art and nature. Because of the manifest loftiness of his *motives* a person's conduct too can at times appear sublime. But merely on the basis of this one instance from the subjective aspect of life we cannot accept the unusual view, put forth by Croce, that the sublime is not an aesthetic, but merely a psychological concept. This particular concept is fairly prominent in the aesthetics of Winckelmann, Burke, Kant and Hegel; and, what is more, it is possible to be fairly definite about the nature of the objects that can appear sublime. At the same time we cannot blink the fact that though it was certainly popular in the eighteenth century, the concept of the sublime is but "peripheral to contemporary aesthetics."[77] Philosophers today are generally indifferent to the reality of the transcendent; and therefore in their aesthetics as well, the sublime appears but rarely, in the form of occasional articles in journals.

---

fingers that gently guide a thread of lace, of a tiny pearl suspended in delicate scales . . ." Sir Herbert Read's "Critical Appreciation" in *Vermeer* (The Masters, 2), Paulton, Nr. Bristol: Knowledge Publications, Purnell & Sons Ltd., 1965, p. 6.

76. Such as the well-known following one: नन्ही कली सोने चली, हवा धीरे आना sung by Geeta Dutt in the film *Sujātā*.

77. Rudolf Makkreel: "Imagination and Temporality in Kant's Theory of the Sublime," *JAAC*, Spring 1984, p. 303.

Contemporary Western poetic theory too focuses mainly on questions of technique. Yet, it is essential to add, literary *criticism* today is by no means wholly indifferent to the sublime,[78] and as for art activity in India, it is surely not quite lacking in instances of sublimity. The *Kāmāyanī* of Jai Shankar Prasad is here a clear instance;[79] and the vast stretches and the moving depths that may sometimes be sensed in *ālāpa* on the *vīṇā* (or in *pure* singing which prefaces the *dhruvapad* song)[80] are closer to the sublime than to the merely sweet and impressive. Further, the concept of sublime is also of help in understanding the development of modernist aesthetics. "There is, in fact, a direct chain of influence from Burke's treatise [*Philosophical Enquiry*],[81] by way of Kant and the Schlegel brothers, through Mme. de Stael to the French Symbolists . . . whose theories in many respects form the foundation of modernist poetics."[82] Nor is every writer on contemporary art indifferent to the sublime. Consider, for instance, the following from an essay on architecture:

> Nothing in nature is more sublime than centred space . . . Its power tends to lead [the architect] to iconic and conventional symbolizations. The rolling roof of Le Corbusier's Chapel of Notre Dame du Haut . . . at Ronchamp, which twists up as if in agony and sweeping appeal, suggests ultimate concern; the dim flickering luminosity of the perfectly balanced interior of Saarinen's Chapel of M.I.T. suggests reverence;

---

78. Thus see A.C. Bradley's essay on the Sublime, in his *Oxford Lectures on Poetry*, pp. 37-65.

79. I think here specially of Dr Nagendra's essay, "Kāmāyanī kā Mahākāvyatva", in *Adhunik Hindi Samīkshā*, Sahitya Akademi, 1980.

80. A *dhruvapad song* has words and is set to a rhythm-cycle. But in the *dhruvapad* form of our vocal music, this song is preceded by *ālāpa* which may be called "pure" because it is free from admixture with words and beat-measured rhythm.

81. The major eighteenth century English treatise on the Sublime which had a profound impact on the aesthetics of Romanticism.

82. Karl Elise Lokke: "The Role of Sublimity in the Development of Modernist Aesthetics" *JAAC*. Summer 1982, p. 421.

> and the fresh radiant simplicity of Matisse's Chapel of the Rosary . . . at Vence suggests peace . . ..[83]

Our main purpose, however, is to see what is meant by the sublime in aesthetics. To begin with, it may at once be said that the concept in question signifies "objects" that are possessed of surpassing *greatness* and *are capable of* exciting in us some distinctive feelings and attitudes, specially the following: astonishment, rapture, awe, and (maybe) even self-abasement.[84] Greatness, in this context, surely includes, but is by no means identical with bigness of extent or size. Further, the four subjective marks we have listed need not be actually manifest in, but simply go with the sublime as a mere potentiality. What is sublime *can*, but does not always actually evoke the reactions that distinguish an *experience* of sublimity. Specially in the case of the non-visual arts like literature and music, the fact whether one feels only enraptured, or even overawed by the "object" contemplated, would depend also — and importantly — on the trained and adjustable capacity of one's own apprehending powers. So it would perhaps be better to say that, in general, objects *come to appear* sublime rather than that they *are* sublime.

Yet there are some occasions when the experience of sublimity is virtually immediate and irresistible. Consider, for instance, the case of a sunrise as seen from the Vivekananda Rock Memorial, or of a sunset as it appears to us from the Gandhi Mandapam in Kanyākumārī, where India's southern tip merges into the seas. The unending expanse of water provided by the meeting of the three seas overwhelms the onlooker because of its sheer immensity, though after this initial check or rebuff, as Kant would put it, the very bounds of one's own being feel a little stretched, making for an experience that is wondrous, very deeply satisfying, and one of an *uplifting* communion, so to say, with the outer spectacle. The feelings of

83. "Architecture and Sublimity" in F. David Martin's *Art and the Religious Experience: The "Language" of the Sacred*, Bucknell University Press, Lewisburg, 1972, p. 256.

84. A.C. Bradley's essay, p. 37.

awe, or wonder touched with reverence — and rapture, because of the glorious play of colour and light — are here everybody's experience, though the feeling of reverence with a touch of felt humility is likely to be deeper in the case of those onlookers whose attitude to nature and life tends to be religious. But perhaps neither the physical bigness of the object nor the onlooker's actual religiousness can be said to be *essential* for an experience of sublimity. The "old black-throated sparrow" that perished in the "heroic" attempt to save its young one from the open jaws of Tourgeneiff's "huge" dog[85] would have perhaps evoked reverence in one and all, because of its "passionate outburst of . . . love" which seemed to be "verily stronger than death and the terror of death." Here, what is expected to give rise to the impression of sublimity is clearly *not bigness of size, but the greatness of self-effacing love.* Indeed, as A.C. Bradley insists, "it is not in the quality alone, but in the quantity of the quality, that the sublimity lies."[86]

Where *this* constituent of the sublime is present, considerations of aesthetic *form* may wholly cease to matter. As illustration, one may here give a brief account of Gandhi's last rites at the ground which is now known as Rājghāt. It was then a huge and unkempt, uneven ground. Nor was the vast seething mass of humanity, present on the occasion, standing or seated according to any plan, though we were all alike quiet, if not quite motionless. Then, as the bier moved towards the crematory ground, accompanied by chanting of appropriate texts from various scriptures, we not only felt subdued by the sense of an overwhelming catastrophe, but for a while raised aloft beyond mere grieving to *an intense and soulful absorption* in thoughts of Gandhi's lifelong and self-effacing, epic adherence to the way of love in opposing evil — a communion which at once seemed to touch the hidden good in us all, and to make for an experience that was at once deeply moving and sad, and yet a moment of felt ennoblement. Here, if anywhere, it

85. A.C. Bradley's essay, p. 44.

86. Ibid.

should be easy to see the truth of Kant's emphasis that, as opposed to the beautiful, the sublime can go along with an utter absence of form.

On occasions such as the one just alluded to, no conscious feeling of self-abasement may be there, though one may well feel overwhelmed by the object's surpassing loftiness. But in experience that is patently religious, and in poems which give vent to such experience, the feeling in question may well be manifest, occurring as a reflex of the devotee's intense sense of His surpassing glory and goodness. The mainspring, indeed, of the sublime in religious poetry is extolment or exaltation of God. What evokes (or accompanies) the focusing of one's mind and heart on His attributes may however vary. Hegel believes that it is the religious mind's insistence on the ultimate nullity of *the world of objective fact* which throws His greatness and eternity into bolder relief; and that the thought that *we* are (yet) made in the image of *such* a God makes us exult in our spiritual nature as we experience the sublimity of, say, a Psalm in the Old Testament. But, one may contend, the *attributes of God* may be seen to be of superlative value also if we turn to them with the faith that they will surely relieve us from our measureless lowliness and depravity. After all, a devotee does not merely contemplate the attributes of God, but leans on to them as sources of relief with a feeling of serene assurance which Hegel's view simply misses. As illustration, the following opening of a hymn of Tulsīdās may well be cited as a paradigm of sublimity in religious poetry:

तू दयाल, दीन हौं, तू दाता, हौं भिखारी
हौं प्रसिद्ध पातकी, तू पापपुंज हारी . . .

Here, we may note, the soulful utterance of the thought that He is the great redeemer can at once be a moment of self-steadying. To *think* of an attribute of God is one thing; *to feel and use it* in prayer, is quite another.

It is important to note that in the lines just cited there is no elevation of style, and that the feeling of sublimity arises only when the reader is able to visualize the surpassing fervour and intimacy of the devotee-deity relation which this paean of prayerful petition and praise expresses so directly. What makes the poet pine for relief (as an आर्तभक्त) is no mere pinch of an intractable adversity, but the utter ineradicableness of his own sinfulness; and his reliance on God's redemptive power (पापपुंज हारी) is quite uncalculating, because it is simply an act of implicit faith. *The experience is sublime insofar as the attitudes it comprises recalcitrate all measuring. In religious poetry, generally, sublimity is more a matter of feeling, inner attitudes and experience than a reflex of concern with impressive objects.*

Yet it would be wrong to believe that sublimity is confined to the religious part of human life. Under the plastic stress of poetic treatment even those contents of subjective life can come to acquire the quality in question as appear but commonplace to the average man. In Jai Shankar Prasad's *Kāmāyanī*, for instance, even *vāsanā* and *lajjā* acquire a touch of sublimity because they are projected not as items of an individual's psychology, *but as pervasive determinants of the whole of human life, personality and experience*. Thus, see the following:

"विश्व में जो सरल सुन्दर हो विभूति महान,
सभी मेरी हैं, सभी करती रहें प्रतिदान।
यही तो, मै ज्वलित बाड़व वह्नि नित्य अशांत,
सिन्धु लहरों सा करें करें शीतल मुझे सब शांत।।"[87]

— वासना

उज्जवल वरदान चेतना का
सौन्दर्य जिसे सब कहते हैं,
जिसमें अनन्त अभिलाषा के
सपने सब जगते रहते हैं।
मैं उसी चपल की धात्री हूँ।
गौरव महिमा हूँ सिखलाती

87. Jaishankar Prasad, *Kāmāyanī*, Bharati Bhandar, Allahabad: Leader Press, 14th edn., Saṁvat 2026, p. 93.

ठोकर जो लगने वाली है
उसको धीरे से समझाती . . .
मैं रति की प्रतिकृति लज्जा हूँ,
मैं शालीनता सिखाती हूँ
मतवाली सुन्दरता पग मैं
नूपुर सी लिपट मनाती हूँ।[88]

— लज्जा

On the other hand, where the subject-matter is already possessed of "high seriousness" and where its treatment is all along meticulous, sublimity arises quite naturally. The frescoes of Michelangelo are a perfect instance here. The themes represented are from the Bible and the representation is distinguished by largeness of extent and fidelity to detail which are both awe-inspiring.

Here, however, a question is possible. Where the sensuous charm of the object is as unmistakable as its bigness of size, as in the case of Taj Mahal, could we not say that *its beauty* is sublime? In other words, it may be that sublimity is not as independent a quality of art as we have made it appear, but just a higher form of beauty. The answer, it is obvious, would depend on our conception of beauty. In its widest, if imprecise, sense the beautiful may be said to be that *which draws us to itself*, not always instantaneously maybe, but always without the conscious use of a prefixed principle or criterion. But if such a view of beauty is accepted, the beautiful will appear *to include* the sublime on the one hand, and the pretty on the other; for our experience is, in either case, one of felt closeness with the given.

Now, *beauty* is doubtless a comprehensive concept. Yet it is by no means amorphous. We *can* distinguish it easily *from* the true and the good. A description is *true* if it corresponds with the fact it describes; but no such (thought of) correspondence is involved when we find a flower or rainbow *beautiful*. Again,

88. Jaishankar Prasad, *Kāmāyanī*, pp. 110-11.

when we approve of an action as good, we do so only because we perceive, more or less readily, that it squares with a moral principle. No such reference to a principle or norm is involved when we *find* an object beautiful; though, *after* the experience, as we set out *to understand why* the object seemed beautiful to us, thinking of some aesthetic principle[89] may well become unavoidable. Above all, whereas it is our everyday experience that we are more or less apart from — if not quite opposed to — what yet strikes us as undeniably good or true, a thing which appears beautiful to us invariably throws a kind of spell on us. Now, as we have already said, a felt immediacy of appeal may characterize our experience not only when we find an object *beautiful*, but also when we find it *sublime*. So it is not as easy to distinguish *the beautiful* from the sublime as it is to mark it off from the true and the good. Luckily, however, if we focus attention on the essential features of *the sublime* which is *not an object of everyday experience, and also bear in mind the wide variety of objects that appear beautiful* to us, the following differences may be drawn between the two, largely in the way of Kant:

(a) Whatever is beautiful is perceived as having a form. Our senses or imagination are able to seize it as a more or less well-defined totality. Sublimity, on the other hand, can be experienced even in respect of an object which appears quite limitless to us. A lofty, snow-clad mountain range can with ease appear sublime to us even though we may not be able to see where it begins and where it ends. The object of sublimity may not in fact be immeasur*able*, but when it seems sublime it is always unmeasur*ed*.

---

89. This qualification is necessary. The *full* beauty of a poem may be seized *after* we have spent quite some time on unravelling the inner integration of its details — say, partly in accordance with the principle of sound-sense harmony; and the beauty of a great man's character too may be revealed to us, convincingly, only as a sequel to the realization that the details of his life are all organized around the pursuit of a single noble end.

(b) This is why the sublime does not please us at the very first touch of attention. Directly, it seems to overwhelm us, by being a bit too great for our powers of perception or imagination, or for our customary attitudes and sense of values. It is only a little later — that is, when our own being has somehow been able to stretch or steady itself inwardly — that we come to experience a deeply satisfying and even elevating delight. As Winckelmann pointed out, when the sea appears sublime to us it is not a simple experience; rather, the mind here feels, first, a little depressed and "then recovers itself more strongly" to experience a kind of delight that makes us feel better *and bigger*, though it would be too much to say that whatever seems sublime necessarily generates in us *the consciousness of an infinite or absolute Reality*.

(c) Details or elements which are ugly in themselves can more easily find a place in the sublime than in the beautiful. A long and lofty mountain range may well be marked by grey tops and yawning crevices which are all in themselves unwelcome to the eye. But instead of detracting from it, they may only contribute to the sublime look of the total range, arising from its sheer extent and height. On the other hand, there is a good deal of the beautiful in art which just cannot brook any ugly details. To take a simple instance from our classical music, it is just impossible for a beautiful *bandish* to have any *svara* which is even minimally off-key.

On the other hand, it would be wrong to suppose that the sublime is patently *incompatible with* sensuous charm. The truth rather is that *ālāpa* (in music) which may begin to seem sublime after moments of initial build-up must also be winsome to the ear all along. Nor is any ugly looking detail to be found in the sublimity of a large rainbow overarching the heavens or of a gorgeous sunset over the tranquil waters that seem to stretch endlessly towards the horizon. Indeed, the sublime can appeal to us not only by straining the ambit of our senses, but by appealing to them; and so fear cannot be said to be a *necessary* feature of our experience of the sublime. The philosophic detachment of a Socrates as he approaches his end, and the starry heavens at the dead of night can both appear sublime to us; but, though they may well impress us greatly, and even appear elevating as we contemplate them, they cannot be said to generate any real fear.

(d) But, of course, whereas our experience of beauty is on the whole tranquil, though not merely playful, the feel of sublimity is in every case a serious and stirring one, making heavier demands on our apprehending powers than the contemplation of beauty. Yet, the sublime is *not utterly* different from the beautiful. There are at least two features that the two may be said to share. In either case the agreeable feeling is quite independent of the thought that the object is somehow useful to us. Nor is the feeling in question (as utterly non-utilitarian) a part of our everyday experience. Indeed, whether the object seems sublime *or* simply beautiful, the joy we experience is (in either case) impersonal, share*able* and disinterested in principle.

THE CONCEPT OF DISINTERESTEDNESS

What *distinterestedness* means has, however, to be thought out with care. The word cannot obviously be taken in a wholly negative sense, that is, as meaning utter lack of interest. The fact rather is that whether the object of attention is natural beauty or an interesting work of art we like to dwell upon it, and often also to turn to it more than once. Our delight here is "disinterested"only in the positive sense of being impartial. It is not based on any "personal" conditions to which . . . (one's) . . . subjective self might alone be a party.[90] To illustrate, if a

90. Kant, *The Critique of Judgment*, tr. J.C. Meredith, Oxford: Clarendon Press, 1964 rpt. p. 51.

man takes delight in a music composition simply (or mainly) *because it is his own work*, his response will not be truly aesthetic. It would be disinterested (or aesthetic) only if he feels charmed, say, by the structure of the composition itself.

Further, the delight of beauty may be said to be disinterested or without interest if "interest" is taken to mean "the delight which we have been designed to communicate and confirm";[91] and it is indeed "the most powerful and general assumption of contemporary aesthetics and practical art criticism . . . that works of art are to be valued . . . at least in part by "autonomus aesthetic standards."[92]

What is more, the concept of disinterestedness is related to that of *fine art*. The point may be brought out by citing the following words of Osborne:

> In the past, . . . works of art were made for a purpose; and like all other artefacts they were valued for the excellence of their workmanship and their efficiency in serving the purpose for which they were intended — as vehicles or promoters of social values, for their moral values, their didactic uses, and so on. The concept of "fine arts" [on the other hand] was based on the idea of a class of artefacts constructed solely[93] or primarily for the purpose of being contemplated aesthetically.

Such contemplation, it is obvious, is not at all determined by the question if the object is in some way useful to us. A work of art is of course no mere nothing. But at the same time it is not "real" in the way of things which serve some purpose *and are meant to be used for practical ends*. In other words, one could make a distinction between the world of real existence — or of everyday, useful things — and the world of aesthetic existence where the works

---

91. *The Critique of Judgment*, op. cit., p. 42. Italics added.

92. Ibid., p. 44.

93. H. Osborne: *Aesthetics and Art Theory — An Historical Introduction*, New York: E.P. Dutton and Co., Inc. 1970, p. 158. Also see pp. 154-58, generally.

are only meant to be contemplated, and not to be used. By making such a distinction we are not only able to avoid relegating works of art to the realm of pure nothingness, but also to preserve their otherness from everyday objects.

It indeed seems reasonable to take the disinterestedness of *beauty* (or artistic significance) as indifference to *utility*. The difference between these two concepts is clear. Whatever is useful (or good for something) implies the concept of an end. Our experience of beauty does not do so. When we say that a knife is good we mean that it is good for or can serve, say, the purpose of quick and clean cutting. On the other hand, when we determine that an object has (pure) beauty, we can do so without the explicit use of the concept of the object, that is, without a clear notion of its perfection, or of what is ought to be or to do.

This idea of freedom from determination by concepts, we may note,[94] is of greater help in realizing the measure of truth in Kant's emphasis on the disinterestedness of our experience of beauty than his *categorical assertion* that such experience (of disinterestedness) has nothing to do with the consideration of real existence. For the assertion in question looks suspect in the context of Kant's own views on pleasure. The point may be brought out as follows:

> It is true that Kant distinguishes the beautiful from both the agreeable and the good; and that the way he distinguishes the three concepts is, on the whole, fair. The agreeable feeling which follows the relief of an everyday need like hunger is experienced as a kind of gratification or *self*-indulgence. On the other hand, where we admire a man because he has acted rightly in the teeth of some temptation, the feeling, though again quite positive, is one of esteem or *respect* for *his* conduct. So the merely agreeable is different from the good. But (and this is where we tend to move away from Kant) the difference would persist even if the action approved is one's own.

94. Following Paul Guyer's essay, "Disinterestedness and Desire in Kant's Aesthetics" in *JAAC*, Summer 1978, pp. 449-60.

> Feeling happy because one has (in fact) been able to act according to a moral principle is a quite different experience from the felt gratification of a bodily need.

It is indeed easy to see the difference between "to act as one *ought to*" and "to get what one *in fact* needs." The impact of beauty is of yet another kind. It is neither the pleasure of self-indulgence nor a feeling of rational approval. The beautiful simply pleases us.[95] We may of course feel drawn by it; but this is here the consequence of the object's own character and not of the pre-existence in us of any inclination or material need for it. Yet, and this is what is here noteworthy, whether it is caused by an object's physiological effect on the senses, or by its subsumption under a concept of the good or the useful, or even by its power to bring about that mutual accord of imagination and understanding which, according to Kant, distinguishes an experience of beauty, the feeling of pleasure, (he believes) may be *generally* regarded as

> the consciousness of the causality of a representation in respect of the state of the subject as one tending to *preserve a continuance* of that state.[96]

But if, like "objects" that we find agreeable to sense or acceptable to our sense of moral value, even objects of beauty tend to prolong the pleasure that they give us, does it not mean that when we experience the delight of beauty we experience the *desire* that this delight and the representation which is causing it may both continue to really *exist*? Here, one can only say, yes. But then how can we accept Kant's insistence that our pleasure in the beautiful is quite disinterested or free from determination by the desire for *existence*? Paul Guyer suggests that it can here be of help to avail of a definition of interest which Kant proposes in the Critique of Practical Reason. Here (in the second Critique) he thinks of interest not as itself a feeling of pleasure, but as rather a kind of concept of an object,

---

95. Kant, *The Critique of Judgment*, p. 49.

96. Ibid., p. 61.

as an "incentive of the will so far as it is presented *by reason.*" To illustrate, if a man thinks of buying some chairs and tables he may be said to be *interested* in the sense of being motivated by the *concepts* of these articles of furniture; and, to be sure, here he may not at all be interested in the perceptual qualities of any present chair. It is precisely in this sense of being interested that our experience of beauty is not "interested" or *is dis*interested. The mere classification of an object as a rose surely does not give us any pleasure in its beauty.

One can see a good deal more of value in Kant's thinking on art and beauty. Some of his emphases and distinctions are indeed striking. He insists that in arts like painting and sculpture the *design* is the essential thing; and that, where it does not directly enter into the structure of the beautiful, ornamentation is mere finery, a mere distraction from beauty. At the same time, the way his thought develops in *The Critique of Judgement* clearly shows that he is by no means indifferent to the value of *content* in art. Here he appears to be mindful of the fact that, unlike wallpapers which are merely decorative, a work of *artistic* genius is posessed of quite a few aspects which admit of separate attention, and "to each of which corresponds a distinctive dimension of value":[97] formal, moral, spiritual and psychological.

Nor can we ignore the distinction which Kant draws between free and dependent beauty:

> There are two kinds of beauty: free beauty . . . or beauty which is merely dependent. The first presupposes no concept of what the object should be; the second does presuppose such a concept and, with it, an answering perfection of the object. Those of the first kind are said to be (self-subsisting) beauties of this thing or that thing; the other kind of beauty, being attached to a concept (conditioned beauty), is ascribed to objects which come under the concept of a particular end.[98]

97. Paul Guyer's essay, op. cit., p. 457.

98. Geoffrey Scarre's essay, "Kant on Free and Dependent Beauty", in *BJA*, vol. 21, no. 4, Autumn 1981, fn. 10, p. 362.

To go by some of his own illustrations of this difference, beauty is quite *free* in flowers and creepers as we find them in nature. Here we admire the beautiful *without* at all raising the question as to what the object looked at *should be*. Other clear examples of "free" beauty, in Kant's view, are: quite a few birds — say, those with coloured plumage and beaks,[99] decorative patterns[100] or foliage; *designs* for framework or wallpapers which are not supposed to mean or represent anything; and all music which is not set to words.[101] In all such cases, it is clear, as we register the object's charm, no thought is given to its function or possible utility. On the other hand, works of art which *represent* something — say, men, horses and buildings — have all to be regarded as cases of dependent beauty. Such beauty "presupposes a concept of the end that defines what the thing has to be, and consequently a concept of its perfection."[102] Here, as we admire the beauty of the given, the thought of its utility or function can easily come to the mind and temper our judgement. Thus, when we speak of the beauty of a horse our utterance may well be (partly) determined by the consideration that this particular animal is good enough for the purpose of running, as horses are expected to be. Similarly, when we are delighted by the look of a temple our reaction may well be coloured by the practical consideration that, as a temple is required to be, the structure in question is capacious enough to hold the throng of devotees on sacred days.

Yet, even in the context of Kant's own aesthetics, the concept of dependent beauty at once raises a question. As we know, it is his considered view that judgements of beauty are determined by feeling and *not by concepts*:

---

99. Kant, *The Critique of Judgment*, p. 72.

100. As distinguish *alpanās* of various kinds in Indian homes.

101. Nor even to beat-measured rhythm, we may add. I am here thinking of *ālāpa* of the *dhruvapad*-singer.

102. Kant, *The Critique of Judgment*, p. 73.

> The *beautiful* is that which, apart from a concept, pleases universally.[103]
>
> The judgement is called aesthetic for the very reason that its determining ground cannot be a concept, but is rather the feeling (or the internal sense) of the concert in the play of the mental powers as a thing only capable of being felt.[104]

If this is so, how are we to interpret his own view, already cited, that dependent *beauty* is (yet) "attached to a concept"? Are we to suppose that whereas free beauty is, according to him, independent of concepts, dependent beauty is beauty *because* it is grounded in a concept? To say *yes* to this question would be clearly untenable, because of what it would imply; and why it would really be so can be brought out as follows. If a warrior is said to have dependent beauty because his appearance seems well adapted to his function of fighting, it would follow that the more ferocious he looks the more beautiful should he be said to be. But there is nothing in Kant's writing to show that "he would accede to the (absurd) view that an ugly brute of a warrior has beauty of any sort."[105] In fact, he appears unable to accept this view. Thus, see his own following words:

> . . . Here is one whose rugged features might be softened and given a more pleasing aspect, only he has got to be a man, or is, perhaps, a warrior that has to have a warlike appearance.[106]

"[In such cases] we cannot help reviewing . . . also in respect of the sensation in the Subject."[107] Taking all these (quoted) words together, we may say, that, according to Kant, though the appearance of a warrior has to be such that he may look suited to the fuction of fighting, it should not be such that it may look

103. Kant, *The Critique of Judgment*, p. 60.

104. Ibid., p. 71.

105. Geoffrey Scarre's essay, p. 353.

106. Kant, *The Critique of Judgment*, p. 73. Italics added.

107. Ibid., p. 74. Italics added.

offensive to the eye; and that only then will the appearance in question be said to be a case of dependent *beauty*. At the same time, if an object is known to have a function, our concern for its aspect of *free* beauty has to be kept in check. The warrior in question cannot be invested with features of free beauty to such an extent that his function as a warrior may be eclipsed. Here, again, some of Kant's own words may be cited with advantage:

> Much might be added to a building that would immediately please the eye, were it not intended for a church. A figure might be beautified with all manner of flourishes and light but regular lines, as is done by the New Zealanders with their tattooing, were we dealing with anything but the figure of a human being.[108]

The suggestion here clearly is that "when we mean to judge something aesthetically, we should look at it not only from the point of view of its free beauty, but should also ask ourselves whether it is fitting that an object of its type should possess whatever features make it beautiful."[109] Kant is here trying to set a standard of *decorum*. The tattooing such as we find on a New Zealander may be very fine, but it is *not right* for a *human* being to be painted that way. A house may well be good to look at, but it should not be so at the expense of its provision for comfortable living.

Here, if in passing, it is important to note that Kant's treatment of aesthetics is all along infused with ethical concern. In his view, our passion for the beautiful in art should not be allowed to override our practical interests wantonly. This is a basic emphasis in his view of dependent beauty.

Kant on two kinds of sublimity

However, even in respect of sublimity, Kant distinguishes two kinds: mathematical and dynamical. The former, according to him, is the *absolutely great*, that is, that which is felt to be

108. Kant, *The Critique of Judgment*, p. 73.

109. Geoffrey Scarre's article, pp. 357-58.

incomparably great without the use of any measure. The real locus of *such* greatness, he adds, is not any outer object, but our inner being. Both these points have to be clarified. We may do it thus:

It is obvious that if a lofty mountain range appears absolutely great (*or mathematically sublime*) to us, the impression does not result from any conscious comparing of the range with the magnitude of *other* objects. Nor do we here use any *unit* of measurement. In other words, the estimation of magnitude is here non-conceptual or *aesthetic*. Such (*non-relational*) greatness is never an object of our *everyday* experience. Here, in daily life, the magnitude sensed "is always [implicitly] based on comparison."[110] But if this is so, if nothing in physical reality is the locus of the (*mathematically*) *sublime*, could it be said to reside somehow in our inner being? Kant's answer here is related to his whole conception of the role of our apprehending powers in experiencing things as beautiful *or sublime*. We may briefly put it as follows:

Even where we are faced with an object of very great magnitude, imagination tries to take in the whole representation in one single intuition, but "there is an upper bound to its capacity," and so it feels strained.[111] On the other hand, as it eludes the grasp of imagination, the object appears to be infinite. Indeed, nature "is sublime in such of its phenomena as in their intuition convey the idea of their infinity."[112] Reason, however, cannot be content with this negative idea of mere unboundedness. Its nature is to seek a completed totality. Imagination fails to provide for this need, also because it cannot shake off its tendency to move ever onward from what is given to what is greater or bigger.[113] But by this very failure it serves

110. Kant, *The Critique of Judgment*, p. 95.

111. Monroe C. Beardsley: *Aesthetics from Classical Greece to the Present*, The MacMillan Co., 1966, p. 219.

112. *The Critique of Judgment*, p. 103.

113. Absolute totality of an endless progression is obviously impossible. Ibid., p. 104.

a purpose. It makes us realize, and feel happy in the awareness that we possess a faculty which is supersensible.[114] We here grow "alive to the . . . supersensible side of our being";[115] and it is this awareness of "a faculty of mind transcending eve y standard of sense," and not any other object, which is the real seat of sublime feeling. The point may be clarified in the light of our actual experience.

Quite apart from the question as to which of our faculties are here involved and how, an experience of sublimity may be said to have three clear features. First, the object may be not only vast, but ill-defined, even unattractive to the eye. Secondly, the experience itself is yet (in the end) a deeply satisfying one, though not without some initial unrest. Thirdly, in spite (or rather because) of the felt discomfort which it initially produces by stretching our apprehending powers, the experience culminates in making us feel elevated above the thing which first appeared a bit too big or great for us. So Kant seems to be right in suggesting that because of their inherent lack of charm, "shapeless mountain masses towering one above the other in wild disorder . . . or the dark tempestuous ocean" cannot *in themselves* be said to be sublime.[116] It is also true that we try, but fail to embrace the whole range of the sea or the mountain in a single look; and that, initally, this makes us feel a little subdued, uncomfortable. But what finally makes the total experience deeply stirring, and not merely restful like an experience of pure beauty,[117] is the fact that, if not at once, we also experience a sudden upsurge of power within and a widening (so to say) of the very bounds of our being;[118] and

---

114. Kant, *The Critique of Judgment*, pp. 97-8.

115. Ibid., p. 106.

116. Ibid., p. 104.

117. Ibid., p. 94.

118. See here the following: "[Whereas] the beautiful is directly attended with a feeling of the furtherance of life . . . the feeling of the sublime is a pleasure that . . . arises indirectly, being brought

are thereby not only enabled to stand up to the extent (or might) of the object, but also feel elevated to a very satisfying sense of being self-subsistent and quite beyond the reach or grasp of the merely physical. Such a feeling of freedom cannot obviously be had in our everyday life; but it becomes easier to secure if the mind is already equipped with ideas of freedom from sense and of accordance with our essential nature as spirit.[119] All this is borne out by Kant's own following words:

> . . . The sublime . . . cannot (really) be contained in any sensuous form, but rather concerns ideas of reason, which although no adequate presentation of them is possible, may be excited and called into the mind by that very inadequacy itself which does admit of sensuous presentation . . . One must have stored one's mind in advance with a rich stock of ideas, if an . . . intuition [say, of the storm-tossed ocean which in itself only looks horrible] is to raise it to the pitch of a feeling which is itself sublime — sublime because the mind has been incited to abandon sensibility, and employ itself upon an idea involving higher finality.[120]

Such a felt elevation of being, according to Kant, also distinguishes our experience of the dynamically sublime. But the two kinds, he adds, show some clear differences as well. An impression of mathematical sublimity is evoked by objects which appear to be

---

about by the feeling of a momentary check to the vital forces followed at once by a discharge all the more powerful." Kant, *The Critique of Judgment*, p. 91.

119. Such ideas, according to Kant, are related to Reason. See, here, his following words: "It is . . . for us a law [of Reason], which goes to make us what we are, that we should esteem as small in comparison with ideas of reason everything which for us is great in nature as an object of sense; and that which makes us alive to the supersensible side of our being harmonizes with that law." Ibid., p. 106.

120. Ibid., p. 92. I hasten to point out that the instance of sublimity referred to by words within the second bracket relates to its *dynamical* kind. But everything else that I say in this section is about mathematical sublimity, in the main.

infinite *or boundless in extent*. Dynamical sublimity, on the other hand, arises when we are faced with such aspects of (or happenings in) Nature as seem to teem with *intense activity and destructive power*. Everything in "raw nature" that is of vast magnitude can be an object of the first kind; and as for instances of the second kind, Kant cites the following:

> Bold, overhanging, and, as it were, threatening rocks, thunder-clouds piled up the vault of heaven, borne along with flashes and peals, volcanoes in all their violence of destruction, hurricanes leaving desolation in their track, the boundless ocean rising with rebellious force, the high waterfall of some mightly river, and the like . . ..[121]

By way of a fuller account of what the dynamically sublime is and of how it arises, Kant makes the following points:

(a) Both Man and Nature have their individual *might*. Both are capable of overcoming limits or obstacles. But in an experience of dynamical sublimity, though we of course see and acknowledge the might of Nature, we do *not* let it have any dominion *over us*.[122]

(b) The *object* here certainly looks frightening. Yet *we* are not afraid of it. The point may be brought out by considering a detail of the religious man's relation to God. He believes that God is all-powerful; he can also imagine that it would be useless were he to try to resist God's laws or authority; and so he may regard Him, quite objectively, as a power to be feared. But because he himself does not seek to flout His commandments, God's fearfulness (as thought of) is no cause of *felt* anxiety to the individual in question. In the same way, when a storm-tossed ocean appears sublime to a man he *recognizes* that the object is fearful, but does not himself *feel* afraid of it, if he is so positioned that he does not have to resist its might.

121. Kant, *The Critique of Judgment*, p. 110.

122. "Might . . . is termed *dominion* if it is also superior to the resistance of that which itself possesses might." Ibid., p. 109.

(c) Were he to *feel* afraid in such a situation, the man facing it would simply flee the place. In the instance in question, on the other hand, the observer stays where he is, contemplating the ocean, and finding it "all the more attractive for its fearfulness," assuming of course (we repeat) that his "own position is secure."[123] What is more, in case his experience attains to sublime feeling, the person involved comes to "discover within . . . [himself an uncommon] power of resistance, which gives (him) *courage* to be able to measure . . . [up to] the seeming omnipotence of nature."[124]

Here, however, two questions may be put. First, how is the newly found power here truly one of *courage* if there is no actual threat to one's own security, as when we survey the ocean from the safe inside of a solid structure of stone or concrete? Secondly, how exactly is this power uncommon?

Now, Kant's answer to both these questions would be that though *in the case envisaged* the sceptical wonder may well seem to be plausible, quite apart from this particular situation — and in life taken generally — the courage in question yet admits of "development and exercise"; that such exercise "is left to us and remains an obligation";[125] and that, as fully developed, it is seen as the superlative ability to face, fearlessly, the threat that the forces of nature may pose to one's property, health or even life *in the steadfast pursuit of "our highest principles,"* as when a man leaps into the turbulent sea to save his friend from drowning.[126] It is of course not very common to show such courage and to experience the sublimity which its exercise involves. But the truth that the satisfaction which is here felt arises from becoming at one with the essential (or spiritual) part of our nature as human beings is borne out by the fact that the display of such courage

123. *The Critique of Judgment*, pp. 110-11.

124. Ibid., p. 111.

125. Ibid., p. 112.

126. Ibid., p. 111. (Here, however, the illustration is mine, not Kant's).

is readily acclaimed *by one and all.* Here, again, we may turn to some of Kant's own words:

> What is it that, even to the savage, is the object of the greatest admiration? It is a man who is undaunted, who knows no fear, and who, therefore, does not give way to danger, but sets manfully to work with full deliberation.[127]

To conclude, nature is dynamically sublime not directly in respect of any of its given properties or features, but if and when it makes one rise to the consciousness of an inner power to refuse to be cowed down by the visible might and tumult of Nature, or by the threats that its forces may pose to one's safety in the pursuit of ideals. "Sublimity . . . does not reside in any of the things of nature, but only in our mind. . . ."[128] [Where it is dynamical] "the irresistibility of the might of nature [not only] forces upon us the recognition of our physical helplessness as beings of nature, but at the same time reveals a faculty of estimating ourselves as independent of nature, and discovers a pre-eminence above nature that is the foundation of a self-preservation of quite another kind from that which may be assailed . . . by external nature." A man's spirit may remain quite unbent even when his body gives in to the fury of nature. It is in moments such as these that we are blessed with an experience of the dynamically sublime.[129]

The graceful

Utterly opposed to objects which strike us as dynamically sublime are those which we call graceful. "Grace" and "graceful" are everyday words, and we use them in various contexts. Thus, we speak of a graceful figure or bearing; and just as freely of a graceful player, runner or dancer. We admire the person who is graceful in defeat, and the ageing head of a

---

127. Kant, *The Critique of Judgment*, p. 112.

128. Ibid., p. 114.

129. Ibid., p. 111.

family who has learnt to grow old *gracefully*. Finally, men of faith are often seen to acknowledge the working of *God's grace* in their lives.

Now, all these instances of the graceful betoken a measure of acclaim or approval. The approbation may be mild, as when we find the gait of a passer-by graceful, or quite deeply and inwardly affirmed, as when a devotee feels quickened with gratitude on "seeing" the hand of God's grace in his own suddenly heightened power to withstand a catastrophe. And in all cases of this kind no such detail is seen as could appear to ruffle the overall appeal. This is generally true even of works of art. For instance, in the paintings of Botticelli — who is known for his deft employment of *graceful*, wavy lines — perhaps no human figure is seen to wear an overweening frown;[130] and that, conversely, a movement that is required to look graceful during the course of an "illustrated" talk on our classical dances will fail to strike us as such *if* its projection in a running number is marred by even the slightest deviation from the basic pace. The noteworthy point here is that, though it is occasionally a mere *detail* that is said to be graceful, it is here always seen as an accent in, or as even the focus of a wider, if dimly apprehended unity. To take yet another illustration, now from the game of cricket for a change, even as a young prodigy Azharuddin was a fluent stroke-player; and quite a few of his strokes could well be said to be graceful because his eye-on-the-ball stance, nimble footwork, and deft use of the wrists — all seemed to be *effortlessly* adapted to the end of despatching the ball to the ropes, and so graceful. But whenever, during the *telecast* of such stroke-making, Azhar's face — which always somehow wore a harassed grin — was *projected on the* screen,

---

130. It is true that a slightly furrowed forehead and knitted eyebrows are to be seen in Botticelli's fresco (112 x 152 cm.), *St. Augustine in his Cell*. But the overall look of the face is not one of anger. I may add that, in this artist's works, drapery, tresses and the representation of human figure, are all distinguished by the use of winsome, flowing lines.

we would find it difficult to call the stroke a graceful one. Indeed, if a movement is to appear graceful it should not only itself be marked by a seeming ease, economy, and inner accord of turns and twists, but be *free from counteracting suggestions in the setting in which it occurs*. Even in religious life the experience of His grace generally comes as the sense of a sudden, yet *tailored* help as a sequel to a spell of sweet, because soulful praying.

To turn again to our everyday life, an overall *look* of effortlessness, inner accord of parts and a measure of manifest relish (where an agent is involved) are common requisites of grace. Where these essentials are missing, even a due reaching of the goal will not make for an impression of grace. We may cite, in this context, the case of Emil Zatopek,[131] the legendary long distance Czech runner. His style of running appeared to be rather loose and shuffling. Many of the movements he made did not *appear* to be required by the goal of winning. But the runner himself explained it all in a way that made sense. He tossed about his limbs, he argued, because he wanted to divide the strain of running over the whole body. We may accept the explanation, but it could not cancel the actual, immediate look, and one had to agree with the following:

> Zatopek . . . was *not an aesthetically attractive runner* because so much of his movement *seemed* irrelevant to the ideal of the most direct accomplishment of the task.[132]

The complaint, here, is directed at the seeming irrelevance of some details of the means *to the basic aim*. Yet, as Cordner contends, grace cannot be taken to be necessarily linked to

---

131. Emil Zatopek, born 1922, winner of the 5000 and 10,000 metres' races and the Marathon at the 1952 Olympic Games in Helsinki, the Capital of Finland.

132. D. Best, "The Aesthetic in Sport", *BJA* 14 (1974), cited in Cordner's essay, "Grace and Functionality" in *BJA*, vol. 24, no. 4, Autunm 1984, p. 302. Italics added.

functionality. He invites our attention[133] to the following lines in Milton's Paradise Lost:

> Grace was in all her steps, heaven in her eye,
> In every gesture dignity and love . . .

This description (by Adam) of "her" (or Eve's) grace is not related to any end. Cordner contends that "her" grace is rather a matter of all that is "manifested in her being," namely, "heaven," "dignity" and "love." But, one may rejoin, though the lines cited surely say something *about* (feminine) grace, they themselves can hardly be regarded as a sample of grace *in poetry*. They do not seem to be relaxed in structure; and, in respect of semantic idiom they have the stiffness of emphatic statement. By contrast, the following lines cited by A.C. Bradley appear to be a better example of the same quality, though he himself used them for a quite different purpose.[134]

> The air
> Nimbly and sweetly recommends itself
> Unto our gentle senses . . .
> The heaven's breath
> Smells wooingly here.

The uneven length of the lines gives them a carefree look. A touch of abandon is provided also by the very *profusion* of apt qualifying words (see: *nimbly, sweetly, gentle, wooingly*) and the interplay of their individual meanings. It is the *movement* of the breeze which is nimble, and not really the act of its recommending itself to our senses. But the word *sweetly* works in two directions, preventing (on the one hand) the *air* from appearing too strong, and providing (on the other hand) a lightness to its impact on us, so that no violence is done to our *gentle* senses of touch and smell *which, as a rule, merely receive and do not look for anything*. The suggestion that the experience is, by and large, one of inhaling the sweet and inviting feel of

133. Cordner, *Grace and Functionality*, op. cit., p. 303.

134. A.C. Bradley, *Oxford Lectures on Poetry*, p. 51.

the gentle and freely flowing breeze (see: *wooingly, breath, heaven's*) is crystallized by the last two lines. But what is noteworthy here is not so much the net verbal meaning of the lines, which is by no means uncommon and is easy to follow, but *the free and graceful way the lines seem to move* and dispose themselves, and the manner in which the meaning shapes itself, quite without any air of studied care. It is this effortlessness of *the way* poetic meaning arises which is here graceful, though the extract as a merely verbal whole may not be so called appropriately. However, the *way* we interpret the lines may not actually look *graceful* if we do not also visualize and so feel, if but in idea, the experience put in words. Grace is here the sensed elegance of form or movement; and outside the spheres of manners and religious experience, it is essentially a quality of what is seen or visualized. This is why lines that run as under may be regarded as a paradigm of grace in poetry:

मुअत्तर मुअत्तर, ख़रामा ख़रामा
नसीम आ रही है कि वो आ रहे हैं

Smelling sweet all along, and at a leisurely pace, what is it that
is seen to approach, the caressing breeze or the beloved himself?

But, of course, the moment we put the meaning thus the magic of the poetic lines disappears. The meaning here, we may note, is merely pleasing; it is not by no means deep or subtle. Indeed, where the real import or meaning of its lines grows difficult to realize, a poem may at once lose its initial look of grace, even if their easy pace persists. Mark, for instance, *the passage of thought from the first two couplets (of Jigar) to the third one*, all abstracted from the selfsame *ghazal*:

1. हम दुआ दें औ तुम कोसो
   अपनी अपनी ज़ुबान है प्यारे

2. हम तो तुम को ख़ुदा समझते हैं
   अपना अपना ख़्याल है प्यारे

3. तुझमें मुझमें तो कोई फर्क़ नहीं
   इश्क क्यों दरम्यां है प्यारे

However, even in the first two couplets, we may note, the run of poetic sentiment is not quite free, insofar as it is *made to end* at the *same* word. On the other hand, the following lines from the Hindi poet, Nirala, are quite as free from this constraint of similitude, and quite as evocative of a look of a free, self-regulating run of words and imagery *as the Shakespearean lines* we commented on a little earlier. (The air . . . wooingly free); and so may well be said to be a picture of grace in poetic expression:

"विजत-वन-वल्लरी पर
सोती थी सुहाग-भरी
स्नेह-स्वप्न-मग्न, अमल-कोमल-तनु तरूणी
जुही की कली
दृग बन्द किये-शिथिल-पत्रांक में"

However, the graceful *in art* is no mere ease or freedom of flow, actual or virtual. It must also tickle the eye, the ear, or our fancy. Happily, this requirement is duly met by the lines just cited; but let us see how:

As upon the poet's own view, the main determinant here is *pravāha* or flow of the words built on.[135] It is of course no mere ebullience, but whichever manner it avails of is demanded by, and is a direct aid to the run, *and so also to that semblance of release* (from all contrived ending) which may be said to distinguish *mukta chanda*. I say so not so much because of the alliterative *va* (व) sound which opens the first three words *and so favours a run of attention as against its focusing*, but because of the number of hyphens (between whole words) that distinguish not only the first three lines, but even the fourth one — a device by means of which the next word appears to take over the

---

135. See here, Nirala's own following words: "केवल प्रवाह कवित छन्द सा-जान पड़ता है। कहीं कहीं अक्षर आप-ही-आप आ जाते हैं। मुक्त-छन्द का समर्थक उसका प्रवाह ही है। वही उसे छन्द सिद्ध करता है, और उसका नियम-राहित्य उसकी मुक्ति। . . . यहाँ 'सोती थी सुहाग-भरी' आठ अक्षरों का एक छन्द आप-ही-आप बन गया है।" Surya Kant Tripathi Nirala's essay, "Parimala kī Bhūkmikā" in *Adhunik Hindi Samīkshā*, ed. Nirmala Jain and Prem Shankar, New Delhi: Sahitya Akademi, 1985, p. 63.

baton of meaning, so to say, before the first one has quite delivered it; *and also* because of the coupling of some half letters with undivided ones — a formal fineness which quietly makes for a look of nimbleness. Yet, we may note, the flow is not on the whole avid or impetuous. For, partly because of their freer use of *dīrgha mātrā* (see *वल्लरी, सोती, भरी, जुही, कली*), the second and the fourth lines appear to gently relieve the more *or* less expansive quality (respectively) of the third and first lines. In the final line, though the word शिथिल means "loose" or "relaxed," the very way it is placed — with a pause on its either side — makes it appear as a source of equipoise, so that the looseness in question is to be taken not as a symptom of fatigue (so to say) but as an index of utter freedom from care (see: दृग बन्द किए) which is indeed how, in the realm of imagination, the bud may be said to feel as it nestles at a mere point of the leaf (*patrāṅka*) *which, in a way, embraces it* (see: here the meaningful में). It is *this* evocative quality of the words: पत्रांक में which prompts the poet, probably, to avoid the alternative: पल्लव पर, though these (alternative) words would have been literally truer to how exactly the little bud is perched. It is only when we see the whole final image — *of a sweet and secure self-abandonment to a loving embrace* — in the mind's eye that *the run of sound and sense* appears as a graceful element of poetic beauty, instead of remaining what it may seem to the casual eye, that is, mere literal passage.

Be it noted that we have been using the predicate, *graceful*, only in respect of the *element* of flow (or प्रवाह) in poetry, not in relation to a whole poem. It is indeed not common to use the predicate in question to characterize a WoA taken as a whole, barring dance recitals where *figural movement* dominates. What the two words here italicized mean is an important requirement of grace. This is why the predicate in question is quite usable in respect of dancing, but not with reference to music and rhythmic recitals which do not include any human form as a part of their content, though they surely abound (respectively) in virtual movement as ascent and descent of *svaras* or as occurrent sequences of rhythmic syllables.

To conclude, the chief locus of grace as a cognate of beauty is movement which may be actual or merely apparent. A curve *suggests* movement or flow. So it is common and fair to speak of a curvaceous human figure as graceful where no counteracting elements disturb the eye. Where, on the other hand, movement is *actually* present, our use of the predicate would mean that the movement looks seamless, free from jerks, effortless, easy to follow, *and* pleasing to the eye even in the context of what includes or surrounds it.

The Unique

The everyday meanings of the word *unique* are: sole, without a like, pre-eminent. But if it be asked as to what the uniqueness of a WoA means, different answers may be given. Some of these, put forth by philosophers, appear clearly odd when viewed in relation to the critics' talk about art. Yet, as we know, it is precisely in the field of art criticism that aesthetic predicates are generally used, and more or less thoughtfully. So we cannot quietly accept every *philosophical* account of the unique, and have to look into the matter carefully.

What a layman can mean by calling a WoA unique is easy to see. If a lover of Hindustānī music feels captivated by a *khyāl* recital, but is unable to put his reaction properly in words, he may signal his inability by merely exclaiming: "I have never heard anything like it before. It was just unique!" This inability may arise not only from ignorace of concepts relating to the different aspects or technique of music, such as *bandish* and *baṛhat*, but from lack of training in *describing the perceived* as such. The critic, on the other hand, is not (supposed to be) thus handicapped; and when he calls a work of art — say, a music recital — *unique*, he surely has something determinate in mind. His meaning here may either be that the WoA is so original — in respect of style or structure (or both) — that no traditional categories can be used to describe it; or that, though it conforms (on the whole) to a conventional form of music — say, *vilambit khyāl* — it is yet distinguished by the pre-eminent excellence of the way it uses and projects the different elements of this kind of singing. In the former case, we are required (by the critic) to believe that the recital in question is to be judged "by its own standards"; and in the latter, that it is the best specimen of the art-form it represents. In either case, his meaning would be clear. That we may not yet accept his final view is quite another matter.

What is, on the other hand, quite difficult to understand is the view (of some philosophers) that uniqueness is the intrinsic distinctness of a work, or that *every* WoA is unique. The practising critic would hesitate to speak thus. His task is rather to actively *distinguish* the work which appears unique to him from others; but if *every* WoA is quietly taken to be "unique", no one of them would be actually distinguished. Yet the sweeping view in question has in fact been voiced by the following: the Romantic critics; philosophers like Dewey, Santayana, Croce, Prall; quite a few literary critics; and two contemporary authors of note, Margaret Macdonald and Stuart Hampshire. The arguments they have put forth are roughly as under:

(a) Why should the view in question appear odd to us at all? Do we ever feel lost for meaning when an antique-collector speaks thus: "*Each* piece of furniture in this collection is unique"?

The argument, however, does not prove the intended point. A work of art is not a mere curio. A curio is an article which is valued only for its rarity or unusualness. That it may also delight us is a quite secondary matter. Nor are we generally impelled or expected to unravel the *structure* of a curio. A WoA, contrarily, makes us happy quite freely, or at least refines percipience; and it admits of and triggers analysis by the knowledgeable. Further, the effort to classify it — say, from the viewpoints of medium and style — is usually an immediate moment in reacting to it knowledgeably. But to classify a WoA is once to see its similarity to other members of the class. So, a WoA cannot be said to be *unique* like a curio, that is, as just being quite different from others.

(b) However, the philosopher may rejoin by protesting that a WoA art cannot be classified or defined without a prior notice of its uniqueness. We can of course say that it is the only one of its kind, but we cannot say what *its kind* is except by focusing on the particular work itself. If it be contended at this point that just because its faithful reproductions are quite possible, a WoA cannot be fairly said to be unique, those who are wedded to the (categorical) uniqueness theory could easily reply that even where it is quite faithful, a reproduction only repeats, but does nothing to nullify the aesthetic uniqueness of the original. If a man just goes on repeating, accurately but glibly, the maxim, "virtue is its own reward," how is the unique value of the original utterance undone?

(c) The Romantic critics — say, Wordsworth, Hazlitt, and Coleridge — argue for the uniqueness of WoAs, specially poems, in their own way. They believe that poetry is in essence a confession of *individual feeling*. No poem, if it is a genuine one, follows a formula. It is rather expressive of a poet's own manner of how he reacts to a particular experience as directly felt.

It is to easy to see, however, that this view cannot apply to every kind of art. There is a good deal of art which is admired only for its structural excellence, clarity, sweetness, and fluency; and which neither seeks nor appears to express feelings. A considerable amount of our instrumental music bears witness to this truth. And even if we choose to confine ourselves to poetry, the expressionist view may be easily questioned. Poems which may be (plausibly)[136] said to express the poet's

136. But not truly; for a quite direct expression of feeling, like an

own feelings directly are autobiographical lyrics. But what shall we say of our epics like *Rāmāyaṇa* and *Mahābhārata*? Their content of representation, narratives, and even philosophical wisdom is a bit too substantial, well thought out, and organized to permit their being regarded as a mere spill-over, so to say, of individual feeling. Yet they do not have many parallels. We cannot, therefore, accept the view that the basis of uniqueness in art is the mere peculiarity of *individual* feelings expressed in the work.

(d) A much better way to argue for the uniqueness of a WoA is provided by those who subscribe to the Autonomy Theory — that is, art for art's sake — *in its weaker form*. They believe that every work of art is unique in the sense than no existing set of rules is really *enough* for determining the excellence of any particular work of art. A critical judgement cannot be deductively established by reference to a first principle. We cannot, for example, be content with the following kind of arguing:

> All good art is properly organized and expressive.
> This is a work which is possessed of both these qualities.
> So, it *is* good as a work of art.

It is easy to see how such thinking is suspect. A classical vocal recital may be both expressive and well-knit, but if it deviates, off and on, from the acknowledged grammatical character of the *rāga* being presented, it cannot be said to be unique in the approbatory sense, though it may well be regarded as an amusing oddity. So, the Autonomy Theory (in its weaker form) surely appears to make sense.

(e) Its stronger form, however, is clearly open to question.

---

exclamation of wonder or an angry shout, is not a WoA. As a rule, a WoA is the result of actively controlled and in some way organized use of materials, and therefore not really a matter of *direct* expression.

It says that every work of art is unique in the sense that, if it is good, it is so only because of its own character, *and never because of what it shares with other works*. Acceptance of this view would at once make the critic's task clearly impossible. The critic just cannot proceed without using words like expression, structure, and form, *none of which is confined to features of any single WoA*. Further, he has to argue as to why he regards a WoA good or bad, but no argument is possible if he is prevented from using *rules* like the requirement that a work of art must be *cohesive* on the inside. But words like *cohesion* or *coherence* all alike relate to art in general.

At this point, however, we may well be opposed. Stuart Hampshire, for instance, argues as follows:

> It makes sense to seek for rules and general methods of solution *only* where there are problems that have to be faced, as in the region of morality. An action is necessarily the choice of a way to act, and it has to be right, or to accord with some principle of conduct. Otherwise, its consequences may harm the individual or society. So here one may well be forced to take the help of rules of conduct which represent the wisdom of generations of men. But a work of art is not expected to solve any pressing problem. Therefore, here it does not make sense to speak of rules and criteria. Instead, the critic should discuss the work on its own merits alone. "He need not look elsewhere, and to possible alternatives in making his judgement. On the contrary, his purpose is to lead people not to look elsewhere, but to look here, at precisely this unique object; not to see the object as one of a kind, but only to see it as individual and unrepeatable."[137]

This argument, however, can be easily questioned. There *are* rules for mixing colours, rules of counterpoint,

---

137. Stuart Hampshire's essay, "Logic and Appreciation" in *Aesthetics and Language*, Oxford: Basil Blackwell, 1970, p. 165.

principles of composition; and these are all intended, and are often actually seen, to help the artist in solving his problems relating to the making of a particular WoA. One may of course here point out that dependence on set rules *alone* does not make for excellence in art. But this negative emphasis holds also in respect of conduct. Mere awareness of principles of morality is hardly ever enough for right action at a particular moment. The specific demands of the situation have to be taken into account, and the individual's own ability to interpret and use the rules properly is also a vital factor. His will power and discrimination are here of paramount value. Nor is it right to say that rules are necessary to deal with only those problems which are unavoidable. When a nation is not actually at war, no one is *compelled* to take due steps for meeting an air raid; but if a mock air raid and the safety measures against it are yet rehearsed simply as a preparatory measure, some rules have got to be followed. The mere absence of a problem is no warrant for random behaviour.

Further, it is too sweeping to say that art is never a solution to any unavoidable problem. The apt expression of a deeply moving experience may well be an urgent problem for a sensitive man; and if he knows the poetic craft, the creation of a poem may here be the only way for him to regain his peace of mind.

Finally, as we have already argued, if he is not to refer to anything which the work itself does not directly provide, how can the critic at all draw our attention to its artistic features? By putting one's finger on them, through spotlights or exclamations, *or by using language*? Surely, one has got to use words. The critic must speak of *balance*, or of *vibrant* or *recessive* (colours); of *form* and *perspective*; or of adroitness in blending the verbal with the melodic, say, in the case of music. But all these words (put in italics) have a general meaning, and as such are usable in respect of many works other than the present one. As for criteria, do we not often use the principle of sound-sense harmony in assessing the value, if in part, of both a poem and a piece of vocal music?

(f) Yet another way of arguing for the essential uniqueness of a WoA is to insist on the fact that there just cannot be any substitute for it.[138] May not a lover of music insist on retaining long-playing records of *both* Bade Ghulam Ali and Amir Khan, just because one cannot take the place of the other?

But here, we may answer, everything would depend on what exactly is meant by "not being substitutable." If the meaning is that *no* work of art is exactly similar to another, we are told nothing *distinctive* about any work, because they are *all* said to be dissimilar mutually. Nor would this sweeping negative suggestion say anything *artistic* about any work. Even a pebble must ever remain distinct from another, if only because of their occupying different parts of space. If, on the other hand, the meaning of "not being substitutable" is: "one cannot serve the purpose of the other," substitution would appear to be fairly *possible*. If a particular record of Bade Ghulam Ali Khan's music is seen to provide an adequate idea of his *gāyākī* in all its richness, and if that particular L.P. is no longer available, the same purpose may be fairly well served by listening to three or four *other* records of his music.

(g) So far we have discussed the question of a WoA's uniqueness primarily in relation to the critic and to works of art in general. But the matter may be looked at also from the viewpoints of what a work of art does,

138. Here, I have in mind the view of Margaret Macdonald. See her essay, "Arguments used in Criticism of the Arts" in *Aesthetics and Language*, p. 125.

and how it is made. Thus, Susanne Langer would like to say that all works of art are unique because, quite unlike the discursive use of language, they are presentational (if symbolic) expressions of our felt life. And L.A. Reid may be taken to emphasize the uniqueness of all works of art — as against all other "made-to-a-plan" objects — by suggesting that in the region of art the net character or significance of a work is always "emergent," never pre-fixed or (quite) preconceived; *and* that this "meaning" (or significance) is here inseparable from the work's perceptual elements.

Now, a detailed discussion of these theories cannot be attempted here. But their basic defects can certainly be pointed out. As for Langer's theory, it should suffice to say that it is as sweeping to regard all art as expressive as to hold that imitation is the essence of all art. And Reid's theory makes little sense in respect of the literary arts where the perceptual elements, emphasized by the concept of embodiment, cannot be said to dominate.[139]

To conclude, it does not seem posssible to hold that *every* work of art is unique. But if *some* works may be said to be so, as is certainly possible, what is it that makes *them* unique? In other words, how are we to explain the uniqueness of those works which are already admitted to have this quality?

A common explanation here could be that a WoA is unique because of its distinctive *structure*. The assumption here obviously is that a difference in *structure* produces an *aesthetic difference*. But is this necessarily true? Let us see:

To begin with, what is an aesthetic difference? It is, we may say, a difference of aesthetic *content*. This content may, in turn, be taken to mean "the set of all aesthetic *attributes* belonging or attaching to the work."[140] As we explain "aesthetic

139. Fuller attention to these important theories will be given later in this work, — in chapter 5, to be precise.

140. Jerrold Levinson, "Aesthetic Uniqueness", *JAAC*, Summer 1980, p. 435. Throughout this para I am indebted to this essay.

content" thus, what is there *in* the work — say, the subject-matter in the case of a literary work of art — is of course not left out; but it is to be taken in its aspect of appearing, say, cohesive, balanced, or expressive generally. The general term, *attributes,* is also to be taken with care, that is, not only as an attribute *of* (something), but as *itself* in its being as quality — say, as a detail's looking graceful or as gracefulness *itself.* Further, an attribute may either relate to a whole WoA or to a part of it. Some common instances of aesthetic attributes are unity, tightness, garishness and febrility.[141] Every such attribute is necessarily perceivable. So are the non-aesthetic ones, like redness and weight. Yet the two kinds of attributes are different too. Non-aesthetic attributes are, by and large, the same for different percipients; but the aesthetic ones can easily vary. What is garish for one man may only be cheerful for another. It is, we may note, the non-aesthetic attributes that relate to the elements of structure. These elements are chiefly the following: "line, shape, colour, texture, shadow, tempo, pitch, rhythm, timbre, word order, rhyme, height, width, etc."[142] All this is common knowledge. But the trouble is that during the actual process of creation, every artist builds upon these elements in his own way. So the question, if structual differences actually make for aesthetic ones, cannot be decided abstractly.

Could we then suggest that in calling a WoA unique what is meant simply is that it is *great* art? Here too, it seems, we cannot at once say *yes*. For, whereas we freely speak of great art *quite generally*, bearing the whole *class* of masterpieces in mind, nobody talks about unique art in the same way. What is more, were *uniqueness* merely a *shared* property like greatness,

141. That is, the suggestion that the work has been feverishly made. This quality is manifest in some works of van Gogh. In our classical (*khyāl*) music it is seen where the singing of *taans* is not only nimble but torrential, caring little for the occasional, but essential return to *sthāyī*, the very first line of the song.

142. Jerrold Levinson's essay, p. 437.

how could it be taken to mean *singularity* which it clearly does? We may not deny that a *masterpiece* can well be *unique* as well. But what the two concepts mean is not really identical. An artist's masterpiece is *his outstanding* achievement as seen in relation to *his* own other works. But in the meaning of uniqueness no such reference to an artist's own works is clearly involved. One cannot therefore agree with those who tend to identify greatness with uniqueness in art.

We may consider, in this context, a detail of Margaret Macdonald's explanation of uniqueness in art. Whereas two tennis players or two roses, she argues, may well *tie for* the first place, two works of art can never do so. "It seems logically impossible that there should be *twin* masterpieces in art. Works of art are (in this sense) unique."[143]

But this view too is not beyond question. It may be true that the criteria for judging works of art cannot be so clear cut as those for grading roses, or for picking a player for *man-of-the-match award* in a game of cricket where *two* men are sometimes so honoured for exceptional performance in the *same* match. Yet it is by no means improper or meaningless to say that Oedipus and King Lear are the two greatest tragedies;[144] or that Shakespeare, Goethe and Kalidas are the world's greatest dramatists, and that we *cannot* decide as to which one of them has the edge over the others.

We may note that where *such* judgements are made by knowledgeable critics after careful thinking, the acknowledged inability arises from intense awareness of the fullness of qualities in each of the acclaimed artistes; and that they are all marked off from other artistes — and so are said to be unique

---

143. Margaret Macdonald's essay, "Arguments used in Criticism of the Arts" in *Aesthetics and Language*, p. 125.

144. Indeed, if the impact of both *Abhijñānaśākuntalam* and *King Lear* on an authentic *rasika* is overwhelming, and if he just cannot decide as to which of the two is greater, what will he say except that *both* are masterpieces?

— because of some *positive* excellences. These excellences may relate to some *detail* of technique or to the *overall* vision and manner of the whole work. Thus, the singing of the late Ustad Aman Ali Khan may be called *unique* because of its deft employment of patterns of note-names (*sargams*); and that of the late Ustad Bade Ghulam Ali Khan *singular*, because of its unmatched balancing (in *taans*) of clarity (or *dānā*) of notes with an amazing nimbleness, *and* quite without any adverse effect on the pulpy and luminous quality of his *akāra*. In the region of Western art quite a few works have been similarly acclaimed. See, for instance, the following from Roger Fry's comments on Van Gogh's *Sunflowers*:

> (It is) a harmony based almost entirely upon yellows . . . *Such a use of yellow is rare in European art.*[145]

The work of Auguste Rodin, the sculptor, is *unique* because of two clear features: the exceptional value of patina (or colour) of his bronzes to their overall aesthetic charm, and the self completing appearance of his "partial" figures for the the viewer. It was a noteworthy detail of his practice that the moment a sculpture was able to capture a "completeness of spirit," some parts of the body were dispensed with.[146]

But the uniqueness of a WoA comes closer to greatness where it shows exceptional relevance to some basic human interest, along with freshness and power in respect of both vision and skill of execution. However, these qualities which tend to make the work a unique embodiment of artistic values are not easy to register, and indeed it is often quite long before they are duly noticed and acknowledged. The uniqueness of a work, therefore, cannot be generally regarded as an obvious, or given property. Much here depends on our aesthetic sensibilities which may take time in acquiring the requisite refinement. Today, *in a sense that is specific*, Picasso's *Guernica* is

145. Cited by L.A. Reid in his book: *Meaning in the Arts*, George Allen & Unwin, 1969, p. 23. Italics added.

146. Albert Elsen (ed.): *Auguste Rodin*, Prentice-Hall, 1965, pp. 3, 4, 8.

regarded as "the *first* historical picture painted for men consciously in the act of making their own history."[147] But early critical reaction to it was not all positive. Some, in fact, accused it of being deficient in compositional values; and almost a quarter of a century elapsed before the following reversal of adverse judgements could appear in print:

> . . . This is no historical painting to divert the spectator. Nothing separates us from the women screaming in terror as death falls senselessly from the sky. We find ourselves caught between the noble horse struck down and the bull, a brutal force of darkness. We are not just being told a story. No divine power is there to relieve us. The calamity is ours, experienced under a sun made by human hands. *Guernica* . . . is the mirror image of a world of atrocity and bestiality from which it is man's duty to emerge."[148]

To conclude, a work of art is unique if it employs old materials in a new way, or builds on a theme that is wholly new or so far unavailed of. If it is so utterly new that it seems to be quite different from all other art (say, paintings) that we so far have, it may be said to be the only one of its kind, and has to be judged on its own, whereupon it enlarges the critic's sensibility, and may even enrich his critical apparatus. And if it conforms to a conventional form, but has all the major excellences of this form in a pre-eminent degree, it has to be regarded as the best of its kind. In either case, it may be duly called unique.

The Perspicuous and the Poignant

A treatment of aesthetic predicates does not commonly include the perspicuous and the poignant. But these two predicates are very relevant to aesthetic interest. However, such interest itself calls for a word of comment.

It is a basic thrust of aesthetic appreciation today that we try to like such objects aesthetically as are not in themselves or obviously likeable. It is no longer believed that aesthetic interest

147. Pierre Daix: *Picasso*, London: Thames and Hudson, 1965, p. 166.

148. Ibid.

is a kind of peculiar interest that we take and can take only in some class of specially pleasing or "sweet" objects. Generally, of course, it is things with a striking *sensory* quality or structure that interest us aesthetically. But the *ideal* structure of a novel or a play can also give us contemplative pleasure. What is more, aesthetic interest is today taken to be (in a sense) latent in all other interests. Indeed, whatever be the object of our concern, and whether our attempt be to understand it or to deal with it practically, it is always open to us to be interested merely in the character of the object or activity, quite regardless of the question if it really exists or if it could in any way be useful to us. At any moment, an organism with a sufficient measure of "dispensible energy" can swing over into a mood which we call "disinterested" and which lacks involvement with reality and usefulness.[149] The aesthetic attitude is, so to say, "consciousness itself, in its purest, least instrumental self-activity and self-enjoyment."[150] This attitude is typical of our early childhood, but it is by no means irrecoverably lost to us, grown-ups. Even in our adult years, when we are not preoccupied with life's routine activites, it is possible to feel lost in the play of the season's first raindrops on the window-sill, and naturally quite without any thought as to how it is going to help us. Now, what facilitates recourse to this attitude, if in part, is the presence of perspicuity and poignancy in the object.

The main, acknowledged meanings of *perspicuous* are: lucid, crystal clear, shining, transparent, easily understood. The word *poignant*, on the other hand, means: touching, moving, painful, penetrating. But in the context of aesthetics — that is, from the viewpoint of contemplation of art and beauty — perspicuity means that there is given to consciousness a presence which is not only clearly projected,

> but which also involves a certain stationariness or arrest. [Here] one's vision revolves and moves within a relatively

149. J.N. Findlay's essay, "The Perspicuous and the Poignant" in *Aesthetics*, ed. Harold Osborne, OUP, 1972, p. 95.

150. Ibid., pp. 95-96.

> restricted orbit and does not attempt to go beyond it, nor to explore those connections which place one's object in the real world.[151]

The mind here dwells simply upon the character of the given itself, and is indifferent to its context and (even) actual existence. Perspicuity, so regarded, "is in fact nothing beyond a loving, lingering prolongation of our orientation to one object . . . (or to) whatever is illuminated in one such orientation. . . . In *aesthetic perspicuity* our conscious focus rests upon something, plays over it, so that what is played over is brought home to us more notably than in more cursive experience."[152]

It is important to see how this quality is *not* tied down to actual existence. The object which is perspicuous is either merely "intended" or actually "given"; but in either case it is not a thing simply as it itself is. It may be given in one way to one subject, and quite differently to another. Indeed, what is perspicuous to one man may not be so to another. The point is that whereas the object as it is in actual existence cannot highlight itself, the way it is given to consciousness admits of varying accentuation of some features and indifference to others. What is more, as the object gains perspicuity, its own actual features may come to be overlaid with "others that do not coincide with anything real, which either relate what stands before us to standards and models . . . in our own mind, or which simply represent illusion or mistake."[153] Thus, in the case of the instance (of rain drops) we took a little earlier, the total experience may easily get tinged and vivified with some memory of our childhood playfulness. And quite as possibly, a *clear and emphatic, but perfectly sensible* expression of disagreement with *one's own views* may strike one as violent opposition simply because one has cherished them for long and a bit too fondly. But whatever be the object, if it is to look

---

151. J.N. Findlay's essay, op. cit., p. 97.

152. Ibid., pp. 98-99.

153. Ibid., p. 99.

perspicuous, all its features have to appear as going well together. Consider, for instance, the following counsel of faith, "Cast thy troubles on the Lord; *that* anchor holds."

Here, the meaning is clear. It is simply an advice to depend on Him alone in crises; and the image it evokes, of troubled waters and casting anchor, accord with each other perfectly. What is more, the demonstrative *that*, which implies a little *steadfast* attention, buttresses the idea that faith never fails to work.

As for poignancy, in the context of aesthetic interest it is to be taken simply as the quality of being sharp and penetrating in effect, maybe as a little sad too, but without being acutely painful. The point may be clarified with the help of a case where poignancy goes along with perspicuity. When one returns to one's old school building after years of being away from it, the look is surely eager and may pause at every detail of the structure, making at once for perspicuity; but it is also likely to be tinged with a little sadness at the thought of a link that was once alive and vibrant, but is no longer so. And to turn to art, say, the art of poetry, the following well known couplet of the Urdu poet, Mīr, may be said to provide a perfect instance of the joint presence of the qualities in question:

पत्ता पत्ता, बूटा बूटा, हाल हमारा जाने है
जाने न जाने, गुल ही न जाने, बाग़ तो सारा जाने है

The lines are quite without any verbal ambiguity; and a very easy seizure of the hint that *gul* here stands for the beloved — and the surrounding verdure, for the wide, open world (or people in general) — at once evokes the moving image of love that is widely acknowledged, but is yet quite unrequited by the one who really matters. Every lover of Urdu poetry knows how the mind cannot help riveting not only on the import of this couplet, but on its verbal structure. The energy or impulse that makes for continued and fascinated dwelling on the aesthetic object is a requisite for sensing both perspicuity and poignancy.

Now, the way we have looked at these two qualities relates, pretty closely, to both aesthetic interest and experience. How exactly this is so may be brought out as follows:

(a) Aesthetic consciousness is of course an *absorbed interest in some object*. But this is not what makes it distinctive; for, focusing of attention on the "object" is very much there also when we follow an intricate philosophical argument or try to repair a delicate, broken article that is dear to us. What makes aesthetic interest different from all other interests is that the play of consciousness here, though surely directed to an object, is yet quite free from those constraints to which our common ways of being concerned with things are subject, say, the consideration as to whether the object really exists or how it can help us in life. In other words, consciousness here revels in its own play upon the object's intrinsic character. We *all naturally* rejoice in such an exercise of our faculties. This is what lends both necessity and universality to aesthetic satisfaction, and makes it a "higher-order" delight.

(b) To consider the matter from the side of objects, it is clear that they do not in themselves have any aesthetic character. They *come to acquire* it, as and when they are presented perspicuously and poignantly.

(c) As something which comes to appear, aesthetic character is indeed largely determined by subjective attitudes which vary from person to person. That which is a bit too intricate, and so repulsive for untrained attention, may only be invitingly rich, and so come to appear both perspicuous and poignant to a genuine *rasika*.[154]

---

154. Differences in aesthetic response to the same work of art can also arise from differences in age, sex, and temperament of those who attend to the work. This should become quite clear to the reader when he goes through the sixth chapter of this book.

(d) Does this mean that the object's own character is here of *no* consequence? Not at all. It matters, but only as a facilitating factor, not as a necessitating cause. The sight of the waters of a lake, now utterly tranquil, where one *has seen* a boat capsize with quite a few crying children, or a sudden encounter with an old friend after years of forced separation because of our country's partition — objects such as these naturally make for a tarrying of attention on what faces one presently, and also for both perspicuity and poignancy as some sad reminiscing. But, and this is here the crux of the matter, should this dwelling on the object be somehow hampered — say, by a man's insistent preoccupation with *his own worries* — the objects in question *will not effectively make for what they only tend to facilitate*. Where there is some actual inner discord in the object itself — say, if in a literary work the presence of ornate and repetitive expression is quite out of tune with its trivial theme — or if an everyday object, say, a part of the house that we daily pass through, has lost all appeal because of long habituation, it becomes very difficult to experience perspicuity and poignancy.

Greatness in Art

The quality which is regarded as the hallmark of consummate artistic achievement is however neither perspicuity nor poignancy, but *greatness*. Generally speaking, a great *human being* is one who is credited with some outstanding talent and accomplishment, and is therefore widely and highly respected and admired. In respect of human endeavour, achievements, and objects — be they artistic creations or parts of the natural world — greatness signifies exceptional attainments or quantity, intensity or value or sheer extension. Thus, we freely and rightly ascribe greatness to the following: Buddha, Jesus, and Gandhi, as poineering upholders of ethico-religious values; Gandhi's *Salt Satyagraha*, as an epic exercise in non-violent opposition; Kālidās, Shakespeare, Goethe, and Picasso, as artistes of surpassing excellence; Winston Churchill, as an exceptionally courageous prime minister; and the Himalayas as one of the world's loftiest mountain ranges.

Our concern, however, is with *works of art*; and here, it is obvious, there are some exceptional features — such as skill in handling the material or means of art-making, and the ability to provide definite occasions for contemplative and disinterested delight — which have to be given special regard. At the same time, there are certain other features — such as *sheer* bigness of size or extent that make us speak of some bridges and wars as great — which may have to be *underplayed* in the context of art. Richardson's *Clarissa Harlowe* is a bigger, but surely not a better novel than *A Tale of Two Cities* by Dickens. At the same time, bigness is not necessarily opposed to artistic value. Our epics, *Rāmāyaṇa* and *Mahābhārata*, are by no means puny in extent; but they are admittedly great as literary works.

Yet, if we ascribe greatness to these epics, as we surely do, it is not merely because of their size, but essentially because of their concern with some essentials of human life, *and* because this concern includes a sensible vivification of norms of righteous human conduct, as against the forces of evil. Attachment, lust, jealousy and greed are all here at play in the lives of eminent personages; and they call for — and heighten the value of — lives and messages of sanity, wisdom and moral steadfastness. It can of course be contended, as Beardsley has done, that perhape "nobody has ever given any plausible reasons for the Didactic Theory of literature which may be taken to say that in order to be "great," a literary work must contain not only true, but profoundly true, theses"; [155] but a simple and effective rejoinder does seem to be possible here. Works of art are meant for contemplation by human beings; and if, besides giving us disinterested delight — say, by virtue of their *poetic skill* — *they also set up some norms of human conduct, and bring out their value convincingly* for a whole human life of felicity, this additional

155. M.C. Beardsley: *Problems in the Philosophy of Criticism*, New York: Harcourt, Brace & World, Inc., 1958, pp. 426-27.

extra-aesthetic function cannot be taken as necessarily a drain on the aesthetic value of the works. The *Rāmāyaṇa* is noted for its poetic qualities; it even lends itself to uncomplicated singing. Further, it has also served as a manual of life for countless generations of men and women in India. Yet no one has ever complained of a clash between its didactic and purely literary aspects.

However, this is not to suggest that a *clear* didactic vein is just *indispensable* for greatness in art. The Taj does not deliver any sermons, but it is surely a marvel of architectural beauty. To turn now to another masterpiece of visual art, Picasso's *Guernica*, what is it that makes for its irresistible greatness? It is true that the canvas is huge — measuring 25 ft 8 inches by 11 ft 6 inches. But what makes it a work of surpassing significance is its sheer expressiveness. Picasso's own words *and* an extract from Roger Garaudy's critical write-up on the work may here be cited with advantage:

> The war in Spain is the battle of reaction against the people, against liberty. . . . In the painting on which I am now at work, which I shall call *Guernica* — and in all my recent works — I am very clearly expressing my horror at the military caste which has plunged Spain into a sea of suffering and death."[156]
>
> — Picasso

> It is not true that such works are unintelligible to the masses. Such art is inaccessible only to those who feel they must decipher each figure and its meaning as though it were a riddle, and having done so, proceed to write trivial literature. . . . It would be an odd conception of art, underestimating human intelligence, to claim that . . . only the most superficial realism . . . [is] within the reach of popular taste.[157] — Garaudy

Taking the two extracts together, we may say that the greatness of *Guernica* lies in its immensely powerful expression of basic human horror and revulsion — say, at an orgy of senseless violence.

156. Pierre Daix, *Picasso*, London: Thames and Hudson, 1965, p. 166.

157. Ibid., p. 167.

Michelangelo's claim to greatness has beeen explained, quite generally, as follows:

> In content and in form, in piercing intensity of feeling, and striking beauty of mass and line, in sublimity of imagination and newness of vision, even in delicacy of colour . . . few professional painters in the history of art can remotely approach him.[158]

His titanic genius, rightly called *terribilita*, is matched only by his contemporary and rival, Leonardo da Vinci. What he has depicted on the vast ceiling of the Sistine Chapel, namely, *Last Judgement* — is of course enormous in size. But what makes *his art* attain to surpassing greatness in his ability to paint the human form in such an exalted manner — say with such power and dignity[159] — that his treatment of Biblical themes acquires a semblance of God's own creative prowess. This is almost universally and immediately recognizable in his *Moses*.[160]

It is in this context relevant to add that so unremitting is Michelangelo's focus on the human body that, generally, he not only omits halos, but wings even where he paints angels. This becomes intelligible in the light of his views that physical beauty is a manifestation of the divine, and that it is "only their greater power and their startling beauty that distinguish the angels from ordinary mortals."[161]

However, *impersonal* and exalted themes like "Souls Ascending to Heaven" and the "Creation of Sun, Moon and Plants" or "The Separation of Light from Darkness," which find favour with Michelangelo, cannot be said to be *essential* prerequisites of greatness in art. The excellence in question can appear even where art becomes a *singularly powerful*

158. Frederick Hart, *The Paintings of Michelangelo*, Thames and Hudson, 1965, p. 101.
159. H. Osborne, *The Art of Appreciation*, p. 71.
160. Cf. W. Gaunt, *A Companion to Painting*, Thames and Hudson, 1967, p. 101.
161. Frederick Hart, *The Paintings of Michelangelo*, p. 134.

"objectivization of *subjective* content into universally comprehensible and lasting symbols, i.e. a non-verbal image which communicates a meaning not verbally expressible."[162] As illustration, one may here refer to Edward Munch's *The Scream* which eventually provided a climax to the group of works which he entitled *The Frieze of Life*. The entire group is a unique, psychologically obsessive drama in paint; and *The Scream* — painted in mixed media of oil, pastel and casein on cardboard (91 x 73.5 cm) — provides a poignant climax to it all. Actuated by the faith that what "alone gives art a deeper meaning is the painter's depiction of *his own* deepest emotions, his sorrows and joys . . . his heart's blood,"[163] *The Scream* may be said to express, in a very singular way, *the artist's own "fear of being incorporated into the environment*."[164] And the meaning, here, is by no means difficult to seize; the work's own features say it all:

> The sexless, emasculated figure of *The Scream* loses itself in the environment, as its skull-like face and twisting torso takes on the *art nouveau* curvature of the landscape rather than retaining human form.[165]

Individual psychology is a far cry from the basic impulses, emotions, and attitudes that *the whole of humanity* shares. Yet these common ingredients of life can also serve as quite apt material for great art. The point is borne out by *Kāmāyanī* to which we have already alluded earlier. The poet here builds upon such shared elements of human experience as worry, hope, faith and desire; and he not only focuses on their individual character and varying involvement in how we react to them in life, but even locates their apt analogues in nature. Thus, see the following:

a. धीरे-धीरे हिम-आच्छादन
हटने लगा धरातल से

162. Reinhold Heller, *Munch — The Scream*, The Penguin Press, 1973, p. 89.

163. Ibid., p. 23.

164. Ibid., p. 89.

165. Ibid., p. 90.

जगीं वन्स्पतियाँ अलसाई
मुख धोती शीतल जल से
— आशा[166]

b. जीवन! जीवन! की पुकार है
खेल रहा है शीतल दाह
किस के चरणों में नत होता
नव प्रभात का शुभ उत्साह
— आशा[167]

Here, hope is pictured as that which quickens life in both nature and human beings, *and* as the quiet impulse that makes for the dawn of tireless commitment to righteous (or शुभ) ends.[168]

So the content or subject of a great work of art is not rigidly fixed. It varies from artist to artist. Perhaps only the following may be said to be invariable marks or determinants of greatness in art: freshness, intensity, and largeness of vision; original and skilful execution, so as to make for a powerful and wide-ranging, if not immediate, impact; and acquirement of undimmed acclaim from generations of critics and *rasika*s. A great work of art is surely that which has stood the test of time.

Some thought may now also be given to those features which *cannot* be said to be indispensable for greatness in art. Literal completeness is one of these. *Hyperion* of Keats is a great poem, though it lacks a clear finish. We may say the same of quite a few sculptures of Rodin. Nor can mere consistency or orderliness be said to characterize every great work. In the ceiling of Sistine Chapel, Michelangelo has changed the scale of figures in mid-passage, so to say. Strict consisteney is more likely to be there in small works than in bigger ones. The greatest artists — Homer, Shakespeare, Michelangelo, and Tolstoy — have all given us works that are full of problematic

166. Jai Shankar Prasad, *Kāmāyanī*, p. 31.

167. Ibid., p. 35.

168. Ibid.

features. Distinctness of parts, clear grouping and definite axes are of course necessary features of a well-ordered whole, and

> this canon excludes the intricate, the unstable, the scattered, the broken, in composition; yet such qualities may belong to a whole in which we *can* discern regularities if we are disposed to them by another aesthetic. In the modern compositions with random elements and relations, as in the works of Mondrian and the early Kandinsky . . . [there] are many correspondences of form: the elements may all be rectilinear, of one colour or restricted set of colours, and set on a pronounced common plane; however scattered they appear, these elements are a recognizable family of shapes with an obvious kinship.[169]

Beauty

The most popular aesthetic predicate is however *beauty*. It is a word of everyday discourse. The word *cute* too is very freely used, but it is not employed in our talk about works of art. On the other hand, the concept of beauty is of interest to students of aesthetics not only because of the part it has played in traditional art theories of both India and the West, but because of the *aestheticians'* own changing attitude towards the concept.

Philosophic reflection on beauty is of course as old as the Dialogues of Plato. According to the Laws, Phaedrus, Symposium, and Ion, the highest art is inspired by a direct vision of the pure, eternal forms of Beauty, Truth, Goodness, and the like. In the story of the soul's gradual progress as narrated by Diotima in the *Symposium*, the determining principle of the ascent is the desire for the beautiful, and the steps make a series of growing release from the merely physical. One begins by falling in love, say, with a beautiful young man; and then, if the search continues, with ever more abstract manifestations of beauty until the form of Beauty itself is revealed as an object of love. It is noteworthy that, according

---

169. H. Osborne: *Theory of Beauty: An Introduction to Aesthetics*, New York: Philosophical Library, p. 7. Italics and bracketed word added.

to Plato, *beauty awakens love*, a view which is quite unlike Santayana's credo that *love discovers beauty.*

However, even in our day aesthetics has been freely "discussed as a branch of critical philosophy, whose function is to expose and co-ordinate the valid principles which underlie all genuine judgements of *the beauty* of *things called beautiful*." At the same time aestheticians have also felt the need to recast the question, "What is beauty?," as "What is aesthetic value?" on the ground that the word "beauty" does not really cover all the arts. For instance, "one speaks of a beautiful painting or symphony, but not usually of a beautiful drama or novel."[170] Philosophers such as C.I. Lewis, Dewey and Monroe Beardsley believe that "beauty" is "a less perspicuous appellation than . . . "aesthetic value."[171] Nelson Goodman's argument is easier to follow. He points out that "many of the best pictures" are "in the most obvious sense ugly."[172] Passmore clarifies the point as follows:

> We would not feel quite comfortable if we called the etchings of Goya or the engravings of Hogarth beautiful . . . "Beauty" is always nice, always soothing; it is what the bourgeois pays the artist for. . . . In more professional circles, it is the refuge of the metaphysician finding a home for art in his harmonious universe, attempting to subdue its ferocity, its revelations of deep-seated conflict.[173]

More recently, however, Mary Mothersill has tried to show in her book, *Beauty Restored* (1984), that the concept of beauty is still quite relevant to aesthetics; and it is interesting to follow the way she argues for this view:

---

170. John Hospers, *Introductory Readings in Aesthetics*, The Free Press, 1969, p. 11.

171. Mary Mothersill, *Beauty Restored*, Oxford: Clarendon Press, 1986 rpt., p. 248.

172. Ibid., p. 269.

173. J.A. Passmore's essay: "The Dreariness of Aesthetics" in W. Elton, (ed.) *Aesthetics and Language*, Oxford: Blackwell, 1954, p. 50.

> It is of course possible to object to the *word*, beauty; one may replace it, as has in fact been done, with "aesthetic value." But it is impossible to find or visualize a way of life where the *concept* (of beauty) has no application, that is, "one in which nothing either is or is taken to be beautiful."[174] The concept in question is indispensable because of a fact which is "central to our way of life," that is, our ability to regard widely various items as beautiful.[175] Indeed a person who is quite without this capacity — that is, to whom nothing is ever beautiful — can hardly be called normal.

Further, if "beauty" is not a standing concept, we should be able to get along without it in the region of aesthetic *theory*. Attempts and (recommendations) have of course been made in this direction, both today and in the past. But do they succeed? Let us see, bearing it in mind that our tendency to use the word "beauty" in respect of quite diverse objects — such as flowers and creepers, articles of daily use, works of art, and the human figure — is natural, and cannot be set aside.

(a) To begin with Hegel and Croce, they believe that art is expression; and, further, that expression itself is beauty. But, we may at once ask, if beauty is identified, and so taken to be replaceable with expression, what shall we say of the beauties of Nature which is not generally credited with *expression* as the word is ordinarily understood? Are we to proffer the awkward suggestion, as the philosophers we have mentioned are compelled to do, that "the beauties of nature are "as-it-were beauties," so called by analogy or figure of speech?"[176]

(b) Collingwood goes a step further. He not only accepts the identification of art with expression, and of expression with beauty, but argues as follows to show

---

174. Mary Mothersill, *Beauty Restored*, p. 275.

175. Ibid., p. 277.

176. Cf. Ibid., p. 250.

that the Greek view does not really regard beauty as a necessary attribute of art:

> The Beauty of anything is, for . . . [Plato], that in it which compels us to admire and desire it; *to Kalon* is the proper object of *eros*, love. The theory of beauty is thus, in Plato, connected not with the theory of poetry or any other art, but primarily with the theory of sexual love; secondly, with the theory of morals as that for the sake of which we can act when action is at its highest potency . . . and thirdly, with the theory of knowledge, as that which lures us onward in the path of philosophy, the quest for truth. To call a thing beautiful in Greek, whether ordinary or philosophical Greek, is simply to call it admirable or excellent or desirable. A poem or painting may certainly receive the epithet, but only by the same kind of right as a boot or any other simple artefact. The sandals of Hermes, for example, are regularly called beautiful by Homer, not because they are conceived as elegantly designed or decorated, but because they are conceived as jolly good sandals which enable him to fly as well as walk."[177]

Here, it is obvious, two distinct points are made: first, that *Kalos* is not tied down to the arts; and, second, that if beauty is found to distinguish a work of art it is, so to say, only as an accident. Now, we may accept the first point; for it was only during the Renaissance that the concept of fine art — or of art that is *necessarily beautiful* — made a definite appearance. But the second point must be rejected, for the poems of Homer are, *for Plato*, clear and undisputed instances of beauty.[178] What is more, insofar as Plato uses it to cover "such disparate items as youths and maidens . . . horses (and) lyres. . . . " *Kalos* may be taken as almost a synonym for our word

177. R.G. Collingwood, *The Principles of Art*, OUP, 1963, p. 38.

178. In Ion, we may note, Socrates speaks of Homer as "the best and most divine of all" poets. E. Hamilton and H. Cairns: *The Collected Dialogues of Plato*, Bollingen Series LXXI, Princeton University Press, 7th printing 1973, p. 216.

"beauty" which is just as widely used.[179]

(c) At this point, however, another similar objection may be made to Mary Mothersill's advocacy of *beauty*. Kristeller, for instance, contends that *Kalos* was never neatly or consistently distinguished from the morally good; and that "when Plato discusses beauty in the *Symposium* and the *Phaedrus*, he is speaking not merely of the physical beauty of human persons, but also of beautiful habits of the soul, and beautiful cognitions."[180] However, this only shows that Plato could not bring out the distinct status of beauty — indeed he is not quite clear about the relation of the Form "Beauty" to the Form "Good"; and that therefore the task of "undertaking a philosophical study of *the beautiful*" still remains important for aesthetic theory.[181]

(d) Wittgenstein is said to have pointed out that often "in real life, when aesthetic judgements are made, aesthetic adjectives such as "beautiful," "fine," etc. hardly play any [meaningful] role, and that a man who just feels moved by some tender music — and exclaims, "How beautiful!" — but "can't remember the simplest tunes, doesn't know when the bass comes in, etc." cannot be credited with any understanding of what beauty in respect of music means, "any more than we call a dog musical it it wags its tail when music is played."

Now, here too, Mary Mothersill's rejoinder appears to make sense. It may be put thus, in brief; and partly as supported by some instances of our own:

"Taste that is ignorant or undiscriminating is not anaesthesia."[182] What is more, even a reaction which appears to

---

179. Mary Mothersill, *Beauty Restored*, p. 251.

180. Ibid., p. 252.

181. Ibid., p. 252.

182. Ibid., p. 258.

be merely reflex may be found to register a quality which is really there in the object. Thus, lay listeners who cannot be credited with *any* knowledge of classical music, have sometimes been seen *to gape at* — and so to *rightly* register without, of course, being able to account for — the *wondrous* depth and expansiveness of *ālāpa* of the *dhruvapad* manner.[183] And if those who have never consciously *reflected* on symmetry in architecture are yet seen to react with an exclamation of wonder and delight on seeing the Taj for the first time, is the reaction to be dismissed as wholly non-aesthetic, say, like the reflex shudder of fright evoked by a bang? Even if they are inarticulate, instant and intense reactions may not be quite without value. Indeed, "unless at *some* stage we had just gaped and said, "How marvellous!" how could we be led to develop a cultivated taste?"[184] Yet another point has to be borne in mind. Where people share a common interest, or are engaged in the same kind of activity, even casual talk tends to move around a particular concept; and, instead of being explicitly mentioned, this concept may yet be assumed as an implicit point of reference. Thus, when *teachers* speak of a heavy workload and of the quality of *work*, it goes without saying that they are talking about *academic* work. Similarly, when lay listeners openly acclaim a recital when it ends, with the words, "How wonderful," a more or less definite conception of musical beauty as consistent tunefulness may be implicit in their exclamatory acclaim.

(e) Yet another objection to the view that *beauty* may be regarded as an independent aesthetic concept has been put forth by Lewis who prefers "aesthetic value" to "beauty." He takes pains to argue that in respect of the quality of experience there is no notable distinction . . . between the innocent value found in a little red wagon and the cultivated value one may find in a sonnet or a

183. Here, I speak in the light of my own experience as a music critic.

184. Mary Mothersill, *Beauty Restored*, p. 258.

> Grecian urn . . . [and that though] the symphony and the sonnet may be . . . justly ranked higher in the scale of comparative value . . . [because of] their character as enduring, cultivated . . . it is the same scale of goodness to which they all belong."[185]

Now, it is not easy to see how the experience of taking delight in a little red wagon *and* in a sonnet are essentially similar in quality; for if — as may be safely assumed — the overall character of an experience depends on how and how much it enables us to feel, think, and imagine, the contemplation of a good poem must be said to differ clearly in quality from the experience of taking delight in a mere wagon which surely does not quicken our fancy as powerfully as a good sonnet can. The point that may here be pressed, however, is that if the wagon and the sonnet belong to the same scale of goodness, how is their value to be characterized generally? Shall we say that these "objects" are (alike?) good or true, or that they are both objects of beauty? To pick the word "good" here would be only to miss the requisite emphasis that both "objects" please us because of their form, *and not* because they exemplify some ideal or virtue in the way of a very good act, nor even because they are serviceable like everyday objects. As for the epithet "true," it is obviously irrelvant to the way we *commonly* look at the "objects" in question. We can only say: *both* objects are *beautiful*; but the moment we say so we lend point to Mary Mothersill's contention that the concept of beauty may be regarded as a distinct and standing concept[186] in the "scale of goodness" (which Lewis speaks of) because it can apply to objects of the most diverse kinds.

It should now be easier to reflect as to what *beauty* may be taken to mean quite generally:

> To begin with, items of *any* sort may be beautiful. It is common to speak of beautiful vases and flowers, maidens and poems;

---

185. Mary Mothersill, *Beauty Restored*, p. 260.

186. Ibid., p. 261.

> but it is by no means meaningless to use the predicate for an original idea which radiates new and promising ways of looking at a problem, or even for a disciplined character or the precis of a long passage, by way of acclaiming their integrated, rounded quality. Predicates like "pretty" and "graceful" are hardly so widely applicable. Indeed, no one would think of using them in respect of the Taj or Milton's *Paradise Lost*. On the other hand, it would not be a gross abuse of the term, *beautiful*, if we used it in respect of a lofty epic poem. However, the point that we are seeking to prove is not that other aesthetic predicates are unnecessary, but only that the word beautiful applies to a much greater variety of items than any other predicate. "Aesthetic value" may be all right in respect of the arts; but, as Beardsley interprets it — that is, in terms of formal unity, or completeness and coherence — it seems irrelevant to landscapes, and not quite fitting to charming human figures.

Yet, though the range of *beauty* is unlimited, its character as a good is quite definite. Mary Mothersill puts the point admirably:

> To be beautiful is a blessing in itself and a social asset. From infancy on, the personally attractive receive preferential treatment. [This may seem to be unfair; for,] like health and intelligence, beauty is a natural gift, [and so] we deserve no credit for it. If so, it is a cosmic unfairness . . . Given the unequal distribution, it seems not unreasonable, other things being equal, to prefer the beautiful to the plain . . . That beauty is *a good* is [also] shown by the fact that [in] contexts of deliberation and choice it counts as a plus if it counts at all . . . [and, of course,] nothing could be unworthy of choice simply in virtue of being beautiful. On the other hand, beauty [as we commonly understand it] is *not the greatest* good, and sometimes [as in passing a judicial sentence on a beautiful murderess] it doesn't count at all.[187]

Further, beauty attracts us, gives us pleasure, and inclines us to dwell upon, and love the object of beauty. One also desires

187. Mary Mothersill, *Beauty Restored*, p. 262. Italics and bracketed words added.

it. But the object to which we ascribe beauty is not necessarily other than the self. It is common knowledge that "to believe *oneself* beautiful is a cause of pleasure; to *be* beautiful is to give pleasure *to others*. . . . It is also a pleasure to produce something beautiful."[188] This manifold relatedness of beauty to pleasure is indeed quite obvious. But can we say the same about the relation of a beautiful object to its tendency to evoke love in us? In respect of beautiful human figures our answer may well be a confident *yes*. But what about, say, a beautiful novel? Surely one does not ordinarily speak of *falling in love with a novel*, though it would be quite sensible to speak thus: "this novel has fascinated me, and I would love to read it again and again." Similarly, when a man is characterized as a lover of nature, what is suggested is not that the person in question has fallen in love with nature, but only that he has become specially sensitive to its charms.

However, a crucial question remains. It may be agreed that when we find a thing beautiful we are pleased by it. But can we say that *every* object or activity that gives us pleasure is to be regarded beautiful? Obviously not. There are certain pleasures which are relatively mindless — such as sunbathing or a hot bath or a cold shower;[189] and which are certainly enjoyed, but without being regarded as experiences of beauty. What then are the distinguishing marks, if any, of the pleasure *of the beautiful*? The following brief suggestions may here be made by way of outlining an answer, on the basis of the views of Kant and Mary Mothersill:

The pleasure *of beauty* is that which arises from the very apprehension of the object itself. This apprehension is, on the one hand, not an *express* interpretation or evaluation of the object; but, on the other hand, it is yet a definite grasp of the object *as an individual*, and not the perception of a mere "context

---

188. Mary Mothersill, *Beauty Restored*, p. 271, Italics added. (Our words here are: आकर्षक, सुखद, रमणीय, and कमनीय.)

189. Ibid., p. 278.

[or diffused state] of pleasure."[190] Sensations of bodily welfare may well give pleasure to a healthy man; but they can hardly be called "beautiful," though the appellation is quite fairly used when one looks at *a* sunlit lawn on a chilly morning, and exclaims: "Beautiful weather!" Similarly, though the *feeling* that follows a talk well delivered and happily received is distinctly pleasant, it is only with reference *to the talk regarded as a wholeness* that the speaker feels like saying: "It went on *beautifully.*" Indeed, it is the lucid and rhythmic quality *of the talk* that he may love to recall subsequently in moments of vacancy. More or less similarly, where a sudden, insightful suggestion is said to be beautiful, the object of acclaim is regarded as a *singleness* of clues for understanding and fruitful enquiry, or for helpful conduct.

What is more, it is the apprehension of the object *itself,* and not the thought of its being related to things and concerns of life — or of its accordance with any norms of reality, correctness or utility — that produces the distinctive pleasure of beauty. This is the point in Kant's well-known insistence that beauty "pleases without a concept." But if no *concept* — that is, no thought of features that may be common to things found beautiful — is here involved, is the experience of beauty a wholly *mindless* pleasure? The question may be answered as follows:

Kant's words that we just picked for mention do not convey his complete meaning. The full sentence they have been taken from runs thus:

> The judgement of taste determines the object independently of concepts, *in respect of delight and of the predicate of beauty.*[191]

The meaning obviously is that *so far as a thing's being experienced as beautiful and (therefore) delightful* is concerned, *it does not depend*

---

190. *Beauty Restored*, p. 324.

191. Kant, *The Critique of Judgment*, tr. J.C. Meredith, Oxford: Clarendon Press, 1964 rpt., pp. 59-60. Italics added.

on the object's being referred, presently and explicitly, to any concept as a norm. What is here surely *not* suggested is that no concept is at all involved *in our total experience* of the object. After all, some concepts are involved in the very recognition of flowers and foliage (*as such*) which Kant cites as paradigmatic sources of the delight of beauty.[192] What is more, as Mothersill rightly points out, to assert that the experience of such delight is not *determined by* any concept is to say nothing about what such unfettered experience *internally* is. It is wrong to suppose that

> by drawing the *conceptual* boundaries of the beautiful one is directly or indirectly describing what it is like *to find* something beautiful . . . Definitions are like maps in that while they indicate borders, rivers and roads, and are . . . a help in getting around, they do not conjure up a landscape for the imagination; they are not travelogues.[193]

Even generally, perhaps no pleasure can be said to be wholly mindless. "Pleasure *is* a 'heed concept.'" If someone feels pleased on receiving a news, he must be able to say what the news *is*;[194] and as for feeling delighted by the beauty of art, the experience necessarily involves some awareness of what the work contains or signifies. Paying attention to the work is necessary, but not quite enough: one has to *grasp* what it has to offer.

> To be appreciated, music must [not only] be listened to but also heard [discriminatingly]; paintings must be looked at but also seen [perceptively]; poems, not only read but understood.[195]

In the end, we may give some careful thought to a possible question we have so far only hinted. How is the word

192. Kant, *The Critique of Judgment*, p. 46.

193. Mary Mothersill, *Beauty Restored*, p. 320. Here, only the second italics is original.

194. Ibid., p. 281.

195. Ibid., p. 324.

"beautiful" applicable, if at all, to works which are widely acclaimed as art but are not good to look at? The question may be answered thus:

Consider, to begin with, the best known work of Picasso: *Guernica*. True, no *layman* would call it beautiful, because none of its principal figures — namely, the bull, the frightened horse, the vulnerable woman, the child holding a symbol of hope in an outstretched hand — can be said to tickle the eye. But if merely because of this *Guernica* is labelled ugly, and denied the predicate, *beautiful*, the judgement would relate to the work regarded *as a mere appearance to the untrained eye*. On the other hand, if the significance of the work as art is duly registered by intelligence, the shapes of unusual angularity and ferocity — or, to put it more precisely, "angularity itself turned into the equivalent of ferocity"[196] — would appear to be admirably expressive of Picasso's emotional reaction of anguish and indignation to the Spanish Civil War, *and in this sense beautiful*. Even generally, it is neither meaningless nor an abuse of language to say of a particular author that in some select passages he has expressed himself beautifully.

It may here be added that in respect of a work of art that is commonly acknowledged as a good one but which does not readily appeal to the eye, men of culture do not summarily say: "This is an ugly work." They prefer to say: "It does not tickle our eyes, but may yet be a good work in the view of connoisseurs of art." It is indeed both necessary and proper to distinguish between a work's superficial or immediate look and its latent aesthetic significance.

---

196. H. Osborne: *The Art of Appreciation*, p. 263.

3

The Aesthetic Attitude, Experience, and Point of View

As *rasikas* or as laymen, how we characterize the appearance of things that we feel drawn towards should now be clear. But there are some other contexts too which give meaning to the word *aesthetic*. These are: our *attitude* to the objects in question, our distinctive *experience* of them as objects of beauty or significance, and the *viewpoint* we adopt in adjudging them as such.

THE AESTHETIC ATTITUDE[1]

Now, to begin with the aesthetic attitude, two distinct questions may be discussed in relation to it. What do we generally mean by the aesthetic attitude? And is this attitude really a *distinct* one?

A fairly sensible answer to the first question is provided by Stolnitz:

---

1. A different discussion of this topic, and one which deals with *some more recent thinking* in this context than is covered in the present chapter is provided by the essay, "The Aesthetic Attitude", in my book: *Aesthetical Essays*, Chanakya Publications, Delhi, 1981, pp. 3-34. It is an organized presentation of the debate that took place on my paper, The Aesthetic Attitude, appearing in different issues of *Philosophy East and West* (28, no. 1, January 1978, "Reply to my Critics", 29, no. 2, April 1979; and "The Aesthetic Attitude: Reply to some New Criticisms", April 1980.

> The aesthetic attitude is the attitude of *disinterested* and *sympathetic* attention to, *and contemplation of any object of awareness* whatever *for its own sake alone.*[2]

Now, why the word, *disinterested*, cannot be taken in a purely negative sense has already been argued. Positively, the word may be taken to mean that when our attitude to the object is truly aesthetic, our attention is not only close, but impartial, like that of the judge who carefully attends to every detail of what is presented to him, without any prefixed bias for or against any party or plea. If I attend a dramatic play only (or mainly) because the central character in it is a friend of mine, my attitude cannot be called aesthetic, because the play as such is not the object of my attention here, and I am likely to slur over, instead of carefully attending to such parts of the play as do not project the role of my friend. The same may be said of my purchasing a painting just because its acquisition is expected to raise *my* status in the eyes of others. Indeed, where a man's attitude is really disinterested his attention is not at all disturbed by the conscious thought as to how he is going to be helped or harmed by it; here the object itself is the focus of attention. Such severance of an object from our practical needs (and fears) has been called *distancing* by Bullough. The concept is important. Following Bullough, some aestheticians have even regarded it as an aesthetic principle;[3] and it has been an object of aesthetic enquiry for quite some time.[4]

So we may give a little careful attention to what Bullough says in his well-known essay on the subject.[5] This is necessary

---

2. J. Stolnitz's essay, "The Aesthetic Attitude", in *Introductory Readings in Aesthetics*, ed. J. Hospers, The Free Press, New York (PB) 1969, p. 19. Italics added.
3. See, for instance, Sheila Dawson's essay: "Distancing as an Aesthetic Principle", *Australasian Journal of Philosophy*, vol. 39, 1961, 155-74.
4. Kingsley Price, "The Truth About Psychical Distance", *JAAC*, Summer 1977, 411-23.
5. Edward Bullough, "Psychical Distance" in Melvin Rader's *A Modern Book of Esthetics*, 5th edn., Holt, Rinehart & Winston, 347-62.

also because, though the concept of psychical distance is freely talked about, *the full extent* of its meaning — and its value for the creation and appreciation of art — as outlined in the essay in question, are not always realized. Its *essential* meaning is of course quite clear. It is simply an emphasis on the truth that where we attend to WoA (work of art) properly, though we are surely so close to it as to be able to notice its details and seize its essential significance, often in the light of our own past experience and training, we do not yet become so "personal" in our concern with the work that *it* may recede into the background, and our attention may come to dwell upon some segment of *our* own past experience, or on *our* feelings of joy or sadness that may be evoked by the work being contemplated.

The concept in question, we may note, is not so odd as it may appear to be, though the "distance" we *commonly* talk about is a feature of the space that we *see* all around us, and is therefore not *psychical*. The truth yet is that what Bullough means by psychical distance is often seen to mark our everyday experience. Thus, when we look at the rainbow and take delight in doing so, the likeable feeling is of course quite real, but what we *attend to* is the rainbow before us, and not *our feeling*, from which we may therefore be said to be *distanced* at the moment. The rainbow before us is so clearly the focus of attention, and is of such an unusual character that we find it natural to look *at* it, and to keep so directed for a while, instead of turning to our own present feelings. If, on the other hand, what we find agreeable is only *the day's weather*, we think essentially of the pleasant sensations it produces in *our* body, and not of the character of the weather itself as indicated in the weather report. In other words, what Bullough calls psychical distance is helped by the object's *actual remoteness in space and unusualness or exceptional quality*. This is why, in his discussion of the concept in question, such additional factors — and *the ways or instances of incorporating them in art* — are also taken note of.

Bullough's essay begins by indicating what psychical distance is *not*. He is obviously right in distinguishing it from both *actual spatial* distance which separates things and places in our everyday world and the *represented spatial* distance which has been such a common feature of landscape paintings in general. We explore distance in real life by moving about freely in the space around us. In psychical distance, on the other hand, such movement is just not thought of, because the remoteness here is only ideal, a distancing of *the self* from "its (own) affections";[6] and no visible stretch of ground is there before or around us. How psychical distance differs from (pictorially) *represented* — or, as Susanne Langer would say, "virtual" — distance is just as easy to see. Separation *of the self from its own needs and fears* is obviously not the same thing as the distance we may see *in a work of art before us*. Putting it roughly, whereas the former is subjective, the latter is objective, a feature of the work itself. Nor can psychical distance be confused with remoteness in time which distinguishes the imaginal mode. Where a story opens with the words: "Once upon a time there was a kindly king" what is "distanced" from our present reality is the *imagined* king, the subject of our story. In psychical distance, on the other hand, the subject that is kept apart from its own affections is no imaginary event or character, but the actual experiencing self.

Positively, if we bear in mind all the major points that Bullough makes in his article being discussed, the essential, if not the full, meaning of psychical distance may be put as follows:

> It is such an aesthetically desirable (and actively regulated) remoteness of the self (of the onlooker/reader/listener, or of the artist himself) from its own interests (/needs, fears, and past individual experiences) while contemplating an object (or an objective situation) that the phenomenal character of what is attended to, be it merely perceptual or emotional too, is (a) perceived quite without distraction, though not of course

6. Edward Bullough, "Psychical Distance" in Melvin Rader's *A Modern Book of Esthetics*, 5th edn., Holt, Rinehart & Winston p. 348.

> without the requisite measure of sympathy and insight, and (b) so comes to be invested with unusual clarity, and perhaps a little charm as well.

The key ideas implicit in the above may now be listed, so as to permit some individual attention to them:

1. Psychical distance is the attitude of *not* caring for one's own interests, life and past experiences in the act of attending to an object.
2. It is aesthetically desirable, because it lends clarity and charm to the look of the object;
3. and also makes for a better appreciation of the emotional/expressive, and not merely sensory qualities of the object.
4. Yet it is not quite impersonal; for the object is judged *in the light of, though not for the sake of merely dwelling upon* one's past experience.
5. Such a way of looking at *art* does not come to us easily. It has to be brought about and carefully kept up, for the risk is always there of identifying oneself too closely with, *or* being a little too indifferent to, the emotional or expressive qualities of the object.

1,2. Now, for the sake of understanding the first two points, we may consider a possible situation visualized by Bullough himself:[7]

> Imagine a fog at sea: for most people it is an experience of acute unpleasantness . . . physical annoyance . . . [and] fears of invisible dangers . . . [But if] for the moment [we ignore] . . . *its danger and practical unpleasantness*, just as every one in the enjoyment of a mountain-climb disregards its physical labour and its danger . . .; direct the attention to the features

7. Here, and in the paragraphs that follow, the numbering has been done not in the proper serial order, but with the purpose of indicating which of the five key ideas just listed is being picked for fuller comment.

> "objectively" constitutingthe phenomenon — the veil surrounding [us] with an opaqueness as of transparent milk . . .; note the curious creamy smoothness of the water . . . , and, above all, the strange solitude and remoteness from the world, as it can be found only on the highest mountain tops . . . the experience may acquire . . . a flavour of such *concentrated poignancy and delight* as to contrast sharply with the blind and distempered anxiety of its other aspects. This contrast, often emerging with startling suddenness, is like a momentary switching on of . . . a brighter light, illuminating the outlook upon perhaps the most ordinary and familiar objects . . . [as we sometimes experience] in instants of dire extremity, when our practical interest snaps like a wire from sheer overtension, and we watch the consummation of some impending catastrophe with the marvelling unconcern of a mere spectator.[8]

The essence of what Bullough here means may be brought out by considering a parallel provided by Hospers. When a man is in fact involved in a shipwreck, he just *does* all that he possibly can to save himself. It is presently impossible for him to lavish leisurely attention on the details of the sinking. If, on the other hand, he happens to watch a film on the happening at some later date, he is free to let his attention tarry serenely at the details, and may even feel impressed and fascinated by the wavy turbulence and the ship's final lurch. Here, it is clealy the *absence* of worry about his personal safety that enables the onlooker to contemplate the (represented) scene *fairly attentively*

8. Bullough, "Psychical Distance", pp. 347-48. Italics added. As an illustration of what is said towards the close of this passage, reference may be made to a remarkable incident in the life of Thomas Edison. When a fire broke out in his plant, destroying "all the packing compounds, celluloid for records, film and other inflammable goods" and, at the age of sixty-seven, he saw all his assets going up in smoke, the great inventor just shouted at his son in perfect detachment: "Where's Mom? Go get her. Tell her to get her friends. They'll never see a fire like this again." Charles Edison: "The Electric Thomas Edison" in *Great Lives Great Deeds*, The Reader's Digest, 1965, p. 224.

and even restfully. Bullough distinguishes the two states of the experiencing self as the negative and positive aspects of psychical distance. The negative aspect is by no means unimportant. Bullough in fact insists that "contemplation" becomes possible only by means of psychical distance which puts the self "out of gear with [its own] practical needs and ends";[9] and may add that this is exactly what makes psychical distance "aesthetically desirable" or even necessary.

3. However, Bullough adds, we should not suppose that the attitude of "distancing" is *utterly* impersonal. Perhaps a man's attitudes can never be quite independent of what he is. Even the scientist has a personal, passionate interest in the pursuit of Truth; such pursuit is in fact *his* own chosen way to exercise his uniquely trained faculties, and to feel rewarded thereby. But, at the same time, he is (in principle) ever careful to see that his perception of the meaning and character of some additional facts he may hit upon is not influenced by his *set views or theories* or by his desire for facile success. The average individual, on the other hand, even where he has "distanced" his perception of what faces him from the thought as to how it can benefit or harm him, cannot help judging an additional object (that he may chance upon) as agreeable, or odd and unlikable, essentially on the pattern of his reactions to similar facts in everyday life. Thus, when he witnesses a dramatic presentation of Rāma wailing for the abducted Sītā, he tends to be sympathetic; and where what he sees on the stage is a Dushyanta appearing quite oblivious of his love for Shakuntalā (once deeply cherished and even avowed) he may react with a little sorrow, surprise or even irritation. But if, as is necessary for contemplating art *as art*, his attitude is duly "distanced," in neither case will he feel impelled *to resort to the same kind of overt behaviour* — say, consoling the aggrieved "person," be it hero or the heroine — as he would, were he to face similar situations in real life. Nor would he allow his attention to turn away from the play and to luxuriate in reminiscence of parallel

9. Bullough, "Psychical Distance", p. 349.

experiences, if any, of unhappiness in love in his own life. This is what Bullough means when he speaks thus:

> Distance . . . describes [not the] impersonal, purely intellectually interested relation [which distinguishes the scientist's attitude to his work, but] a personal relation, *often highly emotionally coloured*, . . . [though of a peculiar character]. Its peculiarity lies [in the fact that] . . . it has been cleared of the practical, concrete nature of its appeal, without, however, losing its original constitution . . . [Thus] . . . events and characters of the drama . . . appeal to us like persons and incidents of normal experience, except that *that* side of their appeal, which would usually affect us in a directly personal manner, is held in abeyance. . . . The proverbial unsophisticated yokel whose chivalrous interference in the play on behalf of the hapless heroine can only be prevented by impressing upon him that "they are only pretending" is not the ideal type of theatrical audience. . . . [Similarly, where a perfomance of Othello is being seen by a man] who believes that he has cause to be jealous about his wife [if the concordance of] the feelings and experiences of Othello with his own [makes] him acutely conscious of his own jealousy [the *object of contemplation will no longer be] Othello apparently betrayed by Desdemona, but himslf in an analogous* [and actual] *situation with his own wife*. This reversal of perspective [from the properly aesthetic to the merely practical] is the consequence of the *loss* of Distance.[10]

4. It should now be clear how, in the act of "distancing" as Bullough conceives of it, the contemplator is related to the "feeling" in the object. The relation is certainly not one of indifference. Bullough, in fact, emphasizes what has been called *sahṛdayatā* in our traditional thinking on the arts.[11] He believes

10. Bullough, "Psychical Distance", 350-51. Italics added.

11. According to the traditional Indian view, the ideal reader of poetry not only possesses a general artistic aptitude which is required for the appreciation of all art, but is "one of similar heart" . . . [that is] a person whose insight into the nature of poetry is, in point of depth, next only to that of the poet. Hiriyanna: *Art Experience*, Mysore: Kavyalaya Publishers, p. 41.

that the more exactly the "*feelings* and experiences"[12] of a dramatic character coincide with the contemplator's own, "the more perfectly" should the latter be able to appreciate "the situation, conduct and character" of the former.[13] But, he hastens to add, appreciating the "object" in the light of one's own past experience is not the same as allowing it to serve as a mere reminder, or as just an impulse to wallow in the (emotional) experiences, of one's own past life. In other words, though in "distancing" (as involved in the aesthetic attitude) one *is* required to vibrate in "personal" sympathy to the "feeling" in the object, a concurrent effort must also be there *to see the "feeling" all along as located in the object*, and to check it from diverting one's attention from the object to one's own past. This is why, whenever we seek to define *the aesthetic attitude*, it must always be borne in mind that, howsoever determinate be the attributes ascribed to it, it is not a readymade link, as it were — which is simply to be put and just allowed to work on its own — between the subject and the object, but such an orientation, more or less deliberate, of the subject, as is always a precarious mean between overmuch closeness to, and excessive remoteness from the object, and which has therefore *to be kept* duly balanced with a degree of effort.

It would here be relevant to add that what Bullough essentially means by "distancing" is not the same as what is implied by the cry for "dehumanization" in art, or for that ideal of purposely moving "away from the 'human' object" or "lived (or human) reality)" which has been said to mark "the indubitable presence in the world of a new aesthetic sensibility."[14] This new (or new fangled?) ideal pleads for the maximum possible severance of *art-making from our familiar reality*; it requires us

12. Bullough's essay, Italics added, p. 351.

13. Bullough's essay, p. 351.

14. Jośe Ortega Y. Gasset, "The Dehumanization of Art" in M. Rader's *A Modern Book of Esthetics*, Italics added, p. 368.

> not [merely] to paint something . . . [quite] different from a man, a house, or a mountain, but to paint a man with the least possible semblance of a man, a house which preserves of its nature only what is strictly necessary for us to witness its metamorphosis, a cone which miraculously springs forth from what was previously a mountain. Aesthetic pleasure for the new artist emanates from the *victory over the 'human'*: for that reason it is necessary in each case to make concrete such victory and to show the strangled victim.[15]

The "distance" which Bullough *emphasizes* is, on the other hand, a freeing of the self from its own hopes and fears as it contemplates an (art-)object, *not* from attention to the humanly expressive in the object contemplated. He, in fact, insists that the proper way to look at art is to be duly sympathetic to the manifestly human (or emotional) element in art.[16]

Here, by way of clarifying this emphasis, some relevant remarks of Harold Osborne may be summarized, partly because they will be of help to us later in understanding how exactly the attention involved in the aesthetic attitude is "sympathetic":

The *disinterestedness* of the aesthetic attitude is commonly taken to mean that it makes for a clearer awareness of the object's *sensory* features alone. It is not realized that — because of the absence of practical, everyday kind of interest — the *emotional or expressive* qualities of what is contemplated are also here more vividly perceived. A simple example should here serve. During the course of a walk, the sight of a *threatening*

15. Bullough's essay, p. 369.

16. See here the following:

    a. "Distance . . . describes a *personal* relation, often highly emotionally coloured." Bullough: "Psychical Distance", p. 350.

    b. "The success and intensity [of an art-work's] appeal [may be said] to stand in direct proportion to the completeness with which it corresponds with our intelletual and emotional peculiarities . . ." — Ibid.

sky may well make us think of things that can shelter us from imminent rain, say, the nearby house of a friend or an umbrella. But if the same sight catches the eye when we are seated securely within a building — that is, when there is no sense of practical urgency — our attention will remain focused on the menacing look of the presentation itself and will naturally not be distracted by any thought of safety measures. In the routine of daily life, detachment from practical interest is but *occasional*, as when in a moment of willed disengagement from the disturbing character of a crowded and uproarious meeting, a man may just unbolt a window and take a look at the quiet open outside. But in art contemplation the detachment in question is the *norm*. Here, we are not faced with any problem of real life; and this freedom, along with the work's own such arresting features, as are generally familiar to men, enables us to savour also the work's *emotional* qualities more vividly than we generally can in the everyday world where we have to respond to them, more or less directly, in terms of practical adjustments.

Sensitiveness to the emotional/expressive character *of things themselves* is indeed a special gift of "distancing" as involved in the aesthetic attitude. Its uniqueness as an attitude cannot be said to lie in the fact that the attention it involves is *selective*, for this quality is a feature of attention in *all* our attitudes. It is the quite different quality of *disinterestedness* which makes the way of aesthetic regard distinctive. And this can be easily explained. Where our concern with things is practical, we look upon them as mere means to realize some purpose. Thus, in daily life, a knife is regarded as simply a tool for cutting things; we hardly ever let our look linger over its shape. The scientific record of the character of things is also quite abstractive. It is an effort to leave out not merely how things *affect us*, but also the *look of emotion or expression in things themselves. It is not the scientist, but the poet who can find the moon looking lovelorn*. The aesthetic attitude does not of course *focus* on the feelings that a thing may evoke *in us*; but, precisely because of this avoidance of self-referent attention, it enables us to see the emotive look *of the object itself* more clearly than is possible in daily life where our primary concern is to deal with things, or to adapt ourselves in relation to them without undue delay. In exercising aesthetic percipience a person is not merely indifferent to the question, how the object can be *useful* to him, but also to the way it may affect *him*. In other words, he is freed from both practical and emotional involvement with self; and this directly makes for fuller attention to — and a satisfying contemplation of — the emotional look *of the object itself*.[17]

We may further note that the detachment or disinterestedness which makes for a clear perception of a WoA's *emotional qualities* is also helped by the fact that "however intimately we project ourselves into . . . [the work], realizing imaginatively the emotional implications of the situations it presents, we always remain *residually* aware [if effortlessly] that we are in the presence of a fiction and that we are contemplating something which is unreal."[18] (This is why when we recall an aesthetic experience of even a highly emotional character — say, the experience of having been greatly moved, even overwhelmed, by the singing of a *bhajan* by Omkarnath Thakur or Kumar Gandharva — we do *not* look upon the devoutness contemplated as a quality *of our own* praying, or as an influence as directly conducive to the growth of our personal religiousness as the soulful moments of our own prayers in real life can sometimes be).[19] Even our most powerful aesthetic experiences are always somewhat "framed" in the sense that they are never taken to be directly continuous with the real world or with the history of our personal lives. To "see" sadness in music is not the same thing as being saddened by an unfortunate turn of events in daily life.

---

17. Osborne, *The Art of Appreciation*, O.U.P., 1970, p. 87. Italics added.
18. Ibid., p. 77. Words within brackets and the italics are all my addition.
19. This illustration is mine, not that of Osborne whose views I am here summarizing: hence the brackets.

Finally, following Osborne again, some thought may be given to the way in which feelings become specific *under the impact of the aesthetic attitude.* This is not to suggest that emotional perceiving is not a feature of our everyday life. The truth rather is that "whenever we become aware of something as . . . ominous, . . . touching, reassuring, stimulating, disgusting, delightful, thrilling . . . disturbing, we are *perceiving emotionally.*"[20] But here, in everyday life, "the perceived is *not* held aloof from the percipient and his concerns . . . but is apprehended in its relation to the precipient, in terms of the significance it bears for him as a part of a total situation fraught with emotional meaning for him."[21] To illustrate, if a fierce dog appears sinister to me, and I feel vaguely anxious, it may be because the animal is moving about freely, and so poses a threat to my safety. If the same dog is quickly tethered by its owner, it would cease to appear so sinister to me. On the other hand, if, when it is at large, the dog begins to bark at me, my anxiety may develop into definite fear. This indeed is how the basic moods of feeling — such as anxiety and calm, elation and dejection — assume the form of specific emotions *because of the overall character of, or as a sequel to some change in, the objective situation.*

But the aesthetic attitude, as directed to a WoA, concretizes a feeling quite differently. Here, we are obviously not subject to the stress of any real life situation. We are free to attend to what meets the ear or the eye in the work of art — that is, to its sensory qualities — and to the way they are put together in that particular work. We are therefore also enabled to perceive *its emotional or expressive* quality as effortlessely as sadness in a living face; and what is more, with greater clarity and definiteness, because of its skilfully controlled projection in artistic terms, *and so in utter freedom from varying determination by the flux of circumstance.*

---

20. Osborne, *The Art of Appreciation*, p. 74.

21. Ibid.

Psychical distance is, however, necessary not only for the proper appreciation, but for the very making of art. This is what Bullough means by saying that "distance" is a factor in all art.[22] But at the same time he also openly insists that "what is . . . both in appreciation *and production* most desirable is the utmost *decrease* of Distance without its [utter] disappearance."[23] How does he argue for this emphasis which appears to infect his thinking with a clear self-discrepancy? We may answer the question as follows, by taking a wider look at Bullough's view.

a. He believes that an intensely personal experience is very good material for the artist, for he is so close to it and knows it through and through. But, on the other hand, this closeness cannot be allowed to remain absolute *if the experience in question is to emerge in terms of a work of art*. To accomplish this end the artist must, so to say, extricate himself from the experience, and look at it as an object. Only then can he give it the consciously controlled and organized treatment that all art-making requires. Artists are indeed distinguished by their ability to so distance their "most personal affections, whether ideas, percepts or emotions" that they become "aesthetically appreciable."[24] It may here be added, in passing, that perhaps we are all possessed of this ability, if in a lesser measure. (Thus, if one is being treated for a chronic pain by a homoeopath, and if the doctor insists on being provided with a clear account of the character of the pain — say, whether it is a kind of continual dull heaviness or an occasional occurrence of stitches or throbs — the patient may well find it possible, with a little effort, to "look" at the pain, so to say, as an object, and to describe it satisfactorily).[25]

---

22. Bullough, "Psychical Distance", p. 349.

23. Ibid., p. 351. Italics added.

24. Ibid., p. 352.

25. Once again, the example given is mine, not Bullough's; hence the brackets.

b. However, if an experience is of such a nature that it just recalcitrates "distancing," it will not lend itself easily to artistic treatment. This is why whereas what is seen or heard is freely found fit for art-making, gustatory sensations are unhelpful as art material. Why the arts of the ear and the eye dominate should now be easy to see. (This, however, is not exactly the reason why, in ancient India, the ear and the eye where regarded as the main aesthetic senses. Bharata's view is that the aesthetic is, in principle, *shareable*; and that insofar as what is seen or/ and heard — say, a play — can be contemplated by many people at the same time, only the ear and the eye can claim to be called "aesthetic" senses).

c. But if in a WoA which is both seen *and heard* — say, in a recital of classical Indian dance where the ear too may be fed richly on the sounds of rhythmic and vocal accompaniment — there are passages which project a theme of love or pathetic tenderness (*śṛṅgāra* or *karuṇa*) in a manner which is *too close to life, and quite without stylization*, the *rasika* will tend to turn to his own experience of a similar emotional hue; the requisite "distance" of the self from its own affections will tend to disappear; and the aesthetic attitude will be replaced by the practical idiom of a merely personal reverie.

d. However, if the same themes are presented by the dancer in a *way* which is clearly *different* from how we behave in life when we are *in fact* gripped by love or pathetic feeling — say, in terms of elaborate music and bodily movement and gestures which appear to be consciously controlled and are *made to go well* with the song and the rhythm — psychical distance will remain, and so will the aesthetic attitude. Incidentally, it is common knowledge that no *rasika* ever looks on a well-planned Rādhā-Kṛṣṇa *śṛṅgāra rasa* number as an echo of his own love life.[26]

---

26. This reference to Indian dance is also mine, not Bullough's.

Indeed,

> every kind of visibly intentional arrangement or unification must, by the mere fact of its presence, enforce Distance, by distinguishing the object from the confused, disjointed, and scattered forms of actual experience.[27]

In the region of *every* art the purpose of distancing us (from our own reactions in daily life) is achieved by so integrating the elements of the work that the latter comes to strike us as a far more cohesive unity than anything that we experience in real life. This is not to suggest that our everyday experience or conduct shows no *inner* unity at all. The truth rather is that our daily behaviour is, also generally, a blend of quite diverse elements. Thus, where we wish to emphasize a particular *idea*, the *pace* of our utterance may slacken, and our voice grow deeper noticeably, along with a duly expressive *hand gesture*. But, though the elements of a man's own behaviour are often so adapted *to each other*, and without too much effort, the total action may not be quite at one *with the context or environment*. The very thought which is sought to be emphasized may arise from an improper reading of what the other person says; and the utterance may lose in general effect simply because its elements do not get the notice they demand, maybe in virture of some noise or commotion in the room. On the other hand, where we watch a classical dance — say, a Kathak number of the expressional kind (that is, *nṛtya*) — the setting in which it is presented (that is, a patiently listening audience) only favours its unimpeded continuance. What is more, the images or ideas which make the substance of the number itself receive such a rich, articulate yet seamless projection through a skilful integration of diverse factors — say, appropriate make-up and costume, the dancer's own gestures, and helpful singing by the vocal accompanist

---

27. Bullough: "Psychical Distance", p. 360.

— that the number alone becomes and remains the object of *rasikas*' attention. Here, even the drumming can be carefully adapted to the needs of dance. For instance, the rhythm itself can (be made to) appear *to bounce* where the danseuse seeks to project the image of Kṛṣṇa (as a child) *playing with a ball* — a detail which generally distinguishes the number known as *Kāliyamardana*. Further, in such cases, a congenial prefactory context, which enables the *rasika* to get properly disposed towards the number, is provided by the compere's opening remarks. The result is that the number as danced appears so insulated from our actual everyday life and so cohesive internally that it not only quickly elicits, but holds our attention, and does not allow us to turn to *our own* present feelings or past experiences, *thus at once making for psychical distance.* The details of the way in which a WoA is organized, of course, vary greatly in accordance with the individual idioms of the different arts. But the end aimed at is always one: "unification of presentment." This end is achieved by availing of

> such qualities as symmetry, opposition, proportion, balance, rhythmical distribution of parts, light arrangements, in fact all so-called "formal" features, [or] "composition" in the widest sense.[28]

Such qualities, of course, make it easy for us to attend to the work *as a whole*; but they also serve to mark it off from the content of our everyday experience.

e. All arts provide some clear instances of how controlled presentation (or intentional arrangement) makes for the requisite measure of psychical distance. Framing in the case of paintings, and stage setting — along with music and even poetic dialogue in the presentation of plays — alike serve to isolate what is here presented to the

28. Bullough's essay, p. 360.

eye and the ear from our everyday experience, and to make it appear as a distinct object before us. These are indeed the usual ways to minimize the risk of our regarding the artistic presentation, and the thoughts and feelings it may project, as a part of *our own* everyday life and experience. In the region of sculpture, lack of colour is an obvious feature which separates the work from everyday objects. Further, the use of pedestals literally takes the WoA a little away from us, and makes it easy for us to contemplate it as an object. This "is evident to anyone who has experienced the *oppressively crowded sensation* of moving in a room among life-size statues *placed directly upon the floor*."[29] Contemplation of a work of art involves looking *at* (or attending *to*) the work for quite a while. So a measure of the work's actual remoteness from us in space is also of definite help here.

f. Scope for intentional arrangement or composition is, however, greater in the region of music and architecture where there is generally no constraint of representing any given object or happening.[30] Here, incidentally, in the context of music a detail of difference may be noted between the viewpoint of the artist and that of the *rasikas*. The *musician* gets easily "distanced" from the world by the very character of his material. *Svaras* as arranged in a scale are very different from the random sounds and noises of the everyday world; and the beats of rhythm, which are actively set and increased or decreased in pace by the singer and the drummer, are also quite unlike the monotonous ticks of a clock by which we regulate our daily living. On the other hand, the *rasika* is released from the hold of reality by the euphonious and integrated quality of the music

29. Bullough's essay, p. 360, Italics added.

30. Ibid., p. 361.

presented to him.[31] It is true that in watching the playing of a maestro like Ustad Wilayat Khan many of us marvel at the nimbleness with which his fingers play at the frets of his *sitār*. Yet such a superficial, if admiring, notice of the artist's own skill is hardly a part of the *rasikas*' discriminating openness to the artistic form of music which should here be the real object of attention. Similarly, where what is presented is a solo *tablā* recital, what the more knowledgeable among the listeners admire is not so much the drummer's obvious capacity for fluent playing as *the undimmed form or shapeliness of the patterns even at quicker speed*, a quality which cannot be manifest to one and all. It is such aesthetic qualities that *endear* the playing to the true *rasika* and provide an occasion for the exercise of *his own percipience*, thereby preventing the risk of both over-distancing and under-distancing.

The same may be said of our responses to vocal *ālāpa* of *dhruvapad* manner. Here, though the *singer's own* dexterity in presenting occasional spells of *gamak* — which have to be noticeably deep yet quite without a trace of effort or awkwardness — can also elicit applause, the aesthetic features *of the music itself* which make *ālāpa* so highly valued as a distinct musical genre are suggestions of contemplativeness, serenity and sheer expanse which we experience very rarely in the everyday world which is a bit "too much with us."[32]

g. Melody and rhythm lend themselves quite easily to varying aesthetic treatment just because they are not tied down to anything in the world of things, persons and situations. As we noted earlier, their very material is "distanced" from the world. Yet it would be wrong

---

31. From here onwards, I may add, till the end of this point, what is stated is my own argument, and no extract from Bullough's essay.

32. The reference here is to Wordsworth's poem, "The world is too much with us."

to suppose that the content of characters and happenings is necessarily hostile to "composition and technical finish." The truth rather is that if it is exceptional and exalted, a theme can be easily open to intentional arrangement. It is common knowledge that "heroic conceptions lend themselves better to verse than to prose." Here, a good illustration is provided by our own folklore. Whereas the valorous deeds of आल्हा (*ālhā*) and ऊदल (*ūdal*) are set to poetry and music, the stories of तोता-मैना (*totā-mainā*) are narrated in simple prose. Bullough points out that

> monumental statues require . . . more elaboration of setting and artificiality of pose than impressionistic stautettes . . .; [and that] an ecclesiastical subject is painted with a degree of symmetrical arrangement which would be ridiculous in a Dutch interior.[33]

A fuller illustration of Bullough's view that "distancing" becomes easier when intentional arrangement is made to work upon themes of an uncommon or elevated quality — and that this, in turn, can lend a deeply satisfying character to such situations and happenings as only cause pain or disgust in real life — is provided by the art of tragic drama. If our attitude to it is truly aesthetic or duly "distanced" — that is, if we do not allow a sad situation in a dramatic presentation to become a mere stimulus to prolonged dwelling upon a similar experience of our own in the past — a good tragedy does not appear sad in the same immediate or personal way in which a mishap in real life does. Here, the content is "distanced" from real life by its very unusualness. The situations, the characters, and the way they talk and behave, are all out of the ordinary, and are more clearly projected than their rough parallels in real life. The characters, in particular, are distinguished by a manifest "consistency of direction, a fervour of ideality and a persistence and driving force which is far above the capacities of average

---

33. Bullough's essay, "Psychical Distance," p. 361.

men."[34] To illustrate, the way in which an old ailing father in real life may express his chagrin at his own children's indifference towards him is not at all the same as the ornate and exalted manner in which King Lear explodes at his daughter's ingratitude:

> Hear, nature, hear; dear goddess, hear
> Suspend thy purpose if thou didst intend
> To make this creature fruitful;
> Into her womb convey sterility;
> Dry up in her the organs of increase;
> . . . If she must teem,
> Create her child of spleen, that it may live
> And be a thwart disnatur'd torment to her;
> Let it stamp wrinkles in her brow of youth;
> With cadent tears fret channels in her cheeks
> . . .; that she may feel
> How sharper than a serpent's tooth it is
> To have a thankless child! — Away, away.

However, quite apart from the exceptional quality of artistic content and skill of intentional arrangement, the kind of "distancing" which Bullough emphasizes at the outset of his essay is that which is demanded by the very nature of art making, and is present even where art is "subjective." Lyrical poetry is indeed subjective in the sense that *what* it gives utterance to is some intense emotional experience of the poet himself, but *how* this expression is here brought about, or the manner of utterance, is not subjective in the same sense in which an involuntary spilling of feeling, or an exclamation is. Lyrical poetry is not "a direct statement of a wish or belief" or "a cry of passion."[35] The poet has to extricate, so to say, the emotion that he wishes to project as art from the jumble of his personal experience, and to look at or contemplate it, so that he may be able to determine as to how best to express it in artistic form.

Finally, it is "distancing" as implicit in the very act of

---

34. Bullough's essay, p. 359.

35. Ibid., p. 349.

"looking at" (or contemplation) which explains how "the whole sensual side . . . (of art) is purified, spiritualized" and relieved of "the grossly personal and practical elements."[36] *Svaras*, for the classical musician, are no mere separate, if agreeable sounds; he visualizes them as located differently in the scale; as opening, enlivening, or climaxing a melodic passage; and as investing the passage with a distinct euphonic, decorative or expressive character. The *rasika* too notices *all this*, and does not merely hear the notes alone. What is presented to the ear both demands and assists discrimination; it is looked at in relation to the *rāga* being presented; and may even be perceived as expressive of a particular feeling.

It should now be clear, as we turn anew to the definition proposed by Stolnitz, that its emphases on "contemplation" and attending to the object "for its own sake alone" are traceable to Bullough's concept of psychical distance. But, one may ask, does "distancing" stand for a separate act at all? Or, is it just another way to emphasize the obvious truth that where our attitude is aesthetic, it is the object, not the self, which occupies the focus or our consciousness? These are indeed the questions which determine the following protest of Dickie:[37]

> In Bullough's view the jealous husband at the Othello performance is "under-distanced." On the other hand, a spectator who is concerned only with how the play is presented by the stage manager — say, with matters relating to arrangements on the stage and lighting from the wings and above — is "over-distanced," because he does not get into the inside of the play at all. But these are both simply cases of lack of attention to the play as such. Does then the requirement of due "distancing" only mean that we should give close attention to the play? If yes, why cant't we put the matter directly in these simple words? Why should we invent and speak of a new process of "distancing"? "To introduce

---

36. Bullough's essay, p. 361.

37. Here, I am referring to his essay, "The Myth of the Aesthetic Attitude" in *Introductory Readings in Aesthetics*, ed. John Hospers, pp. 28-44.

> the technical terms [like] "distance" . . . [and any others] . . . does nothing but send us chasing after phantom acts and states of consciousness.[38]

The protest, however, can be easily met. Dickie contends that it is improper to use the terms "to distance" and "being distanced" as if they referred "to *special* kinds of acts and states of consciousness."[39] But an admitted meaning of the word *special* is "exceptional" or "uncommon," specially in respect of some excellence; *and in this sense* "psychical distance," *as Bullough conceives of it,* is certainly "special."

Consider, here, his own following words:

> The working of Distance is. . . not simple, but highly complex. It has a *negative,* inhibitory aspect — the cutting-out of the practical side of things and of our practical attitude to them — and a *positive* side — the elaboration of the experience on the new basis created by the inhibitory action of Distance.[40]

Now, it is *by no means common* for us to suspend our practical concern with things, *and* thereby to see in them a richness and beauty that may well be there. Fry is indeed right when he says that under the stress of our everyday life "we learn to see only so much as is needful for our purposes."[41] Therefore, if the suspension of our practical concerns — along with the dawn of a richer awareness — happens only occasionally, it must be said to be a "special" occurrence. Yet there is no reason to doubt *the felt reality* of the suspension in question or of the gain in experience which results therefrom. In contemplating a work

38. George Dickie, "The Myth of the Aesthetic Attitude", p. 30.
39. Ibid.
40. Edward Bullough's essay, "Psychical Distance", p. 348.
41. "With an admirable economy we learn to see only so much as is needful for our purposes . . . just enough to recognize each object or person . . ." Cited from Roger Fry's *Vision and Design* (pp. 24-25) by John Hospers in his essay, "The Esthetic Attitude" in Melvin Rader's *A Modern Book of Esthetics,* Holt, Rinehhart and Windton, Inc., 4th edn., 1935, p. 397.

of art as such, even where attention is drawn with effortless ease by the work's own arresting quality, because of the very thought of what one has set out to do, one has often to try to prevent attention from being diverted — say, by a seeming lack of colour or determinateness in the work — towards one's everyday, practical concerns; and to focus it on the work being attended to. "Distancing" *has to be done*, and its use as a verb is therefore legitimate. Nor is "being distanced" a meaningless use of words. Becoming free from the yoke of daily concerns is not a "phantom state of consciousness," but a positive experience, *a kind of feeling released, a lightening of self*; and where it occurs as a moment in attending to a work of art, the object is naturally perceived more clearly, because of a free exercise of percipience. Nor are "under-distancing"and "over-distancing" mere metaphors. The former is our common *problem* where we contemplate a work of intense human appeal; and the latter (or "overdistancing") may persist, for example, so long as a *rasika* at a music concert feels undecided as to what precise *rāga* is being presented by a vocalist who revels in presenting *aprachalit* (or rare, not well-known) melody-modes.

To conclude, the concept of psychical distance is by no means arbitrary. However, because our main concern at present is with the aesthetic attitude, we may resume our attempt to see what the key words in the definition we have picked for attention mean, and whether this meaning is defensible.

Now, to begin with the first of these words, it may be noted that though Dickie, Fisher and some others have strongly criticized the concept of disinterestedness, they themselves admit that it has withstood these attacks and continues to be used by quite a few aestheticians.[42] But, of course, everything here depends upon what the concept in question may be taken to mean. Here, once again, Kant's view may be cited with advantage:

---

42. Geroge Dickie, "Reconsiderations 6", *JAAC*, XLII (Fall, 1983) pp. 84-85, John Fisher's review of Wolterstroff's *Art in Action*, *JAAC*, XXXIX (Winter, 1980), p. 209.

> One must not be in the least prepossessed in favour of the real existence of the thing, but must preserve complete indifference in this respect, in order to play the part of judge in matters of taste.[43]

This does not however mean that the existence of *art objects* is of no consequence to us. We all have a practical interest in their continued existence and proper maintenance, for many of us would love to go to them repeatedly for the delight, and deeper awareness of the world's beauty that they can provide. The point only is that, as Osborne rightly puts it,

> *within the process of appreciation itself*, while we are aesthetically intent on the object, considerations of its real existence are irrelevant. Aesthetic contemplation is concerned with the object as presented, with the appearance.[44]

To Stolnitz, however, the *disinterestedness* of the aesthetic attitude means rather that "we do not look at the object out of any ulterior purpose which it may serve."[45] Now, this is indeed the sense in which the word in question is commonly used; and, as we have already noted earlier, this meaning of the word has been preferred by many in the context of the good life. Yet, in respect of the aesthetic attitude, this interpretation of *disinterestedness* has been questioned by Hospers. His protest may be put thus:

> It has been freely maintained that where one's attitude is disinterested, one savours the experience of perceiving the landscape itself, instead of "using the perceptual object as a means to some futher end."[46] But it is doubtful if in such cases we really perceive the object for its own sake, *rather than for the sake of the delight such attention may give us*. Indeed, would anyone continue to attend to the object if such attention

---

43. Cited, from Kant's: *Critique of Judgment*, by Harold Osborne, in his *The Art of Appreciation*, p. 33.

44. Osborne, *The Art of Appreciation*, p. 33. Italics added.

45. Stolnitz, *The Aesthetics Attitude*, p. 20.

46. John Hospers, "The Esthetic Attitude", p. 397.

> ceases to give joy? Further, whereas it is perfectly proper to speak of *judging* in a disinterested (or impartial) way, it makes little sense to so speak of *perceiving*.[47]

Now, to the first part of the protest of Hospers our answer could run thus:

There *are* situations where the object is so irresistibly beautiful and such an immediate source of delight that because of this very *feeling*, though not as disjoined from the object's own fascinating look, one may be effortlessly induced to keep looking at what is presented to the eye. This is what happened to Wordsworth when his eye suddenly fell on "a crowd, a host of golden daffodils";[48] and such a gripping experience is repeated even today as our very first look lands on the Taj Mahal. But such occasions are few and far between, and where the object is a WoA, in most cases *we* have to try to focus attention on it, putting everything else aside, so to say, for the moment. Indeed, as a way of looking at things, *the aesthetic attitude is far more frequently actively adopted by us than merely elicited by the object*. What is more, the intentional effort recurs and may even be felt as a kind of active gathering of self when we seek to repair to the object after some momentary distraction. It may be added that quite a few works of modern art have no immediate appeal for the eye, and that one has to probe for their artistic significance through a wilful focusing of attention and exercise of percipience.

As for the question if it is proper to speak of *perceiving* disinterestedly — that is, impartially — our answer may simply be that the word *disinteresed* also means "not influenced by private feelings or considerations"; and that, as already brought out, the aesthetic attitude is disinterested in the sense of being unrelated to personal, practical needs.

---

47. John Hospers' essay, p. 399.

48. These words occur in Wordsworth's well-known poem: "I wandered lonely as a cloud".

Goerge Dickie's protest is more elaborate, and we may put it clealy, as follows, before we turn to examine it:

> To speak of *disinterested* attention (to the arts) would make sense only if our attention here can sometimes be said to be *interested*. But the so-called "interested" ways of looking at the arts — whether it be the playgoer who likes a dramatic performance because *his* daughter has a key role therein (personal satisfaction); or the director of the play gloating over the way *he* has been able to solve the technical problems relating to the presentation of the play (intellectual satisfaction); or the moralist who is pleased because the play is likely to have a salutary healthy effect on young minds — "are not really cases of interested *attention* to the play, but just different ways of being distracted from the play."[49] In other words, there is nothing like interested (or basically self-centred) *attention*. But if this is so, the concept of *dis*interested attention also become meaningless. The fact (in Dickie's view) is that, though it is of course possible for us to be more or less attentive to art, to attend to it for different reasons, and also to be distracted from it in a variety of ways,[50] the way to (positively) attend to art is only one; and that is neither "interested" nor "disinterested," but simply close attention. The critic too "differs from other percipients only in the motives and intentions and not in the way he attends to art."[51] "It can make sense to speak . . . of listening disinterestedly to music only if it makes sense to speak of listening interestedly to music . . . [or] "with an ulterior purpose". . . [Now, *a*.] suppose Jones listens to a piece of music for the purpose of being able to analyse and describe it in an examination the next day, and Smith listens to the same with no such ulterior purpose . . . certainly . . . Jones has an ulterior purpose and Smith does not, but this does not mean Jones' listening differs from Smith's . . . . [*b*.] *There is only one way to listen to* [or to attend *to*] *music*, although the listening may be more or less attentive and there may be a

49. George Dickie, "Myth of the Aesthetic Attitude", 33. My italics.

50. Ibid., p. 32.

51. Ibid., p. 39.

variety of motives, intentions and reasons for doing so . . ..[52]

Let us now see if what is said in the above is defensible, by focusing first on the point distinguished (by us) as *a*. It is obvious that if the listening of Jones is done with an eye to preparing for an examination, it will also at once be an impulsion to find apt words for reporting on what strikes his ear. It will also probably involve a more or less explicit use of criteria for determining the technical and aesthetic correctness of the different passages or facets of the music in question. The listening of Smith, on the other hand, though it may well be discriminating, will neither be so analytic nor necessarily touched with the desire to find suitable language, because he is listening to the music for its own sake, and is simply enjoying it. What is more, the listening *feels differently* in the two cases. In the case of Jones, it is marked by *a sense of effort* to distinguish, interpret and analyse what is heard; and in the latter, it is just an act of happy self-abandonment, not quite undiscriminating to be sure, but yet just a *restful* mirroring of the form and flow of music. If this difference is not one of kind, how else shall we characterize it? *Listening with a view to verbalizing what is heard is surely quite unlike the relish of music in a state of wise passivity.* To turn now to *b.* — namely, the *view* that "there is *only one way* to listen to music, although the listening may be more or less attentive" and determined by a "variety of intentions and reasons" — a close look at the very way it is phrased (mark the second group of words within inverted commas) reveals that it fails to make the intended point. But first let us note a distinction. Attention can of course be close and unremitting; but without abjuring this character, it can also be *more or less comprehensive*. Now, these differences in the span of attention actually given to an ongoing piece of music are almost inevitable. They arise because of differences in what exactly the listeners are individually interested in. If the listener is himself a *tablā*-player, he will care more for the rhythmic aspect of the recital than for anything else in it. In case he is an

52. George Dickie's essay, p. 32.

aesthetician, he will tend to focus on the music's expressiveness and formed quality. A regular music critic is of course expected to be much more comprehensive in his attention to the music he has to write on; but because of his penchant for melody *or* rhythm — *or* in virtue of his habitual indifference to the musician's needed skill in switching over from one *rāga* to another, definitely but without any jerk or abruptness — even he may not be able to do justice to *all* that the recital has to offer. But, be it noted, whichever aspect of music is (or has to be) picked for notice, attention can be very close and almost unremitting in every case. *So, closeness or acuity is not everything about attention; its range or span is as much a fact.* As we have already said, this span is determined by the listener's individual tastes and motives which can vary greatly; and it is this variety which makes for different *kinds* of attention at work. The attention of a musicologist who generally cares more for the grammatically correct treatment of *rāga* and *tāla* is very different to that of an authentic *rasika* who just lets the music seep into his being, and does not allow his effortless notice of the character of *rāga* and *tāla* — and other technical details — to ruffle the unity of relish.

A *rasika*, though he certainly registers quite a few of the niceties of the music presented to him, does not do so *for the sake of analytic* reporting or even understanding; and this is a part of Stolnitz's meaning when he says that the aesthetic attitude is disinterested in the sense that it does not aim at *any* purpose at all. In this sense, indeed, the attitude of a *rasika*, as he listens to music, is in fact *dis*interested; it is in fact accessible to all those who know and love music, and its distinct reality is brought out by its contrast with the many other ways of listening to music which are determined by one's own subjective tilts and purposes.

The *dis*interested quality of the aesthetic attitude may also be taken to mean that attention is here "intrinsic" or "*in*transitive." But, at this point, a question may be readily put. Does it make sense to speak of, say, reading a literary work of art *transitively*? Vivas say, yes, and cites some instances of such reading. One of these is the perusal of a poem "as diagnostic evidence of the another's neuroses."[53] But Dickie protests that

> this is a case of [merely] using information gleaned from a poem to make inferences about its author rather than attending to a poem. If anything can be said to be attended to here it is the author's neuroses [at least they are being thought about]. This kind of case is perhaps best thought of as a rather special way of getting distracted from a poem. . . . Such "biographical" distractions . . . may turn into whole careers. . . . [Only] certain "informational" aspects of a poem [are here attended to]. . . . It is at best a case of attending to certain features of a poem and ignoring others.[54]

Now, one sees in this extract the strain of an improper emphasis and a rather awkward use of language. The passage opens by suggesting that making inferences about its author is no attention to the poem (at all). But this is clearly wrong. How can one draw the inferences in question without attending to the poem? Dickie himself is forced to see and temper the exaggeration in his opening emphasis; and he concedes, as the passage ends, that "certain features of a poem" *are* here attended to. Further, if a scholar makes it his lifelong business (his "whole career") to discover the poet in his poems, how can this commitment be spoken of as a mere "distraction"? It is rather a matter of *resolving to look at them with an ulterior purpose or from a particular point of view*. It is really a case of *interested* attention.

Two other protests of Dickie may here be dealt with. Both alike seek to show how the concept of disinterestedness is harmful to aesthetic theory.

a. The first of these is a protest against Stolnitz's view of associations or aesthetic relevance which runs as follows:

> . . . Whether an association is aesthetic depends on

53. George Dickie, "Myth of the Aesthetic Attitude", p. 34.

54. Ibid., p. 35.

> whether it is compatible with the attitude of "disinterested attention." If the association re-enforces the focusing of attention upon the object, by "fusing" with the object and thereby giving it added "life and significance," it is genuinely aesthetic. If, however, it arrogates attention to itself and away from the object, it undermines the aesthetic attitude.[55]

Stolnitz illustrates the point of this view by referring to the possible responses of "two students" to the following lines from a poem:

> Between the erect and solemn trees
> I will go down upon my knees;
> I shall not find this day
> So meet a place to pray.

On reading these lines, one of the students in question (it may be) is led to think of a "rugby forward running"; the other one may react with the image of a cathedral. The first image, Stolnitz contends, cannot be aesthetically relevant (or an aesthetic association), for it only takes attention away from the poem; but the second (the cathedral image), he insists, is aesthetic or aesthetically relevant because it is "congruous with both the verbal meaning of the poem and the emotion and mood it expresses. It does not divert attention away from the poem."

Dickie here protests that the criterion which Stolnitz "actually uses is congruousness with the meaning of the poem, . . . [and that this] is quite independent of the notion of disinterestedness."[56] Now, everything here would turn on how Stolnitz interprets the "disinterested" attitude. This is how he actually does it:

> It means that we *do not* look at the object out of concern for any ulterior purpose which it may serve. . .. Our

55. Stolnitz, *The Aesthetic Attitude*, p. 37.

56. George Dickie, "Myth of the Aesthetic Attitude", p. 38.

> interest *comes to rest upon the object alone.*[57]

A close look at the above at once makes it clear that Dickie is able to make his protest only by ignoring the second (positive) emphasis in the above. For, if being "disinterested" (also) means *caring for the object alone,* and if (as in the case in question) the object is a poem, what could this "caring" mean except being guided by the *meaning* of the poem? So, congruousness with the meaning of the poem is in fact demanded by, instead of being independent of, the notion of disinterestedness *as fully understood.*

b. But does not the "attitude theory" exaggerate the independence of the aeshetic? Does it not appear to suggest that aeshetic value is *always* independent, say, of morality? Dickie thinks, it does; and his protest here begins by inviting our attention to the following words of Stolnitz:

> Any of us might reject a novel because it seems to conflict with *our* moral beliefs. . . . When we do so. . . . we have *not* read the book aesthetically, for we have interposed moral . . . responses *of our own* which are alien to it. This disrupts the aesthetic attitude. . . . To maintain [this] attitude, we must follow the lead of the object and respond in concert with it.[58]

Further, Dickie readily proceeds to oppose "this conception of the aesthetic attitude [because it] functions to hold the moral . . . and . . . aesthetic aspects of the work of art firmly apart."[59] Here he first makes an approving mention of David Pole's thesis " that the moral vision which a work of art may embody is aesthetically significant";[60] and ends by stating his own position as follows:

---

57. Stolnitz, *The Aesthetic Attitude*, p. 20.
58. Dickie, "Myth of the Aesthetic Attitude," p. 41.
59. Ibid.
60. Ibid.

> My concern . . . is simply to insist that a work's moral vision is a part of the work and that therefore a critic can *legitimately* describe and evaluate it. I would *call* any defect or merit which a critic can legitimately point out an aesthetic defect or merit, but what we call it does not matter.[61]

Let us now attend to the details of Dickie's protest:

That a work may embody a moral vision; and that, as is true of quite a few poems, novels and plays, this vision may be "an essential part" of the work, — all this is clearly admissible. We may also agree, quite generally, that a critic can describe and evaluate *whatever* is there in the work as a part of its content. But, one may ask, can we allow the critic to deal with the work's content *in any way* he likes? We cannot say, *yes*. Whatever it may precisely be, the way has to be the proper (or legitimate) one. Dickie too speaks of what the critic can point out or "describe and evaluate" *legitimately* or/as a merit of right. But the critic's rights also put him under an obligation; he must look at WoAs aesthetically. But what is this way of aesthetic concern? How are we to deal aesthetically with the moral vision which appears (where it does) as a part of the work? In the absence of any answer here from Dickie himself, we may proffer the common, if negative, reply that the concern in question does not consist in checking the "vision" with *our own moral views from the outside*. It may be noted that it is only this *external* moral checking — the interposition of "moral" . . . responses *of our own* which are alien to it (or the work) — to which Stolnitz objects in his words picked by Dickie for comment. He does not deny that a moral vision may be a part of, and so conduce to the aesthetic value of other details of the work's content, say, by being congruous with them. What he insists on, we conclude, is not a categorial separation of morality from the aesthetic,[62] but a subordination of the aesthetic to moral beliefs *of the man who contemplates the work*.

---

61. George Dickie, "The Myth of the Aesthetic Attitude", p. 43.

62. Stolnitz, *The Aesthetic Attitude*, p. 41.

Stolnitz, we may note, is just as emphatic about the distinctness or autonomy of the aesthetic attitude from the way we look at WoA *critically*. He believes that the critical attitude is opposed to the aesthetic; that "whenever criticism obtrudes, it reduces aesthetic interest"; and that though it is of course necessary to attend to a work of art as acutely as one possibly can during the course of aesthetic experience itself, we must not "analyse, [and] measure [the object of attention] in terms of value-criteria."

However, this emphasis too is unacceptable to Dickie. He protests that the (aesthetic-critical) opposition envisaged by Stolnitz is not in fact true. Recalling his own experience of preparing for a panel discussion of some films, he remarks that making notes on their various aspects once actually enhanced his appreciation of the films. There is hardly any "significant difference," he adds, between attending to a work "perceptively and acutely" — a requirement which Stolnitz himself admits as being necessary for appreciation — and searching for reasons which make such appreciation aesthetically credible. Nor need we suppose — as (in Dickie's view) Stolnitz appears to do — that making notes on that which is contemplated leaves us with much less time for its "enjoyment." For, "finding a reason is [here] an achievement, like winning [not running] a race"; it does not take time. It is instantaneous like a sudden insight. Surely, we hardly take any time in "seeing" that a note is off key or on key; or in marking that an actor has mispronounced a particular word.[63]

Now, to this particular protest, we would rejoin thus:

Everything here depends on what meaning we give to the keywords say, *criticism* and *aesthetic* interest. The "criticism" which Stolnitz regards as being hostile to aesthetic interest is analysis and *measurement in respect of value-criteria*. Dickie thinks that such critical assessment (or the finding for reasons) is not

---

63. George Dickie, "The Myth of the Aesthetic Attitude," p. 40.

significantly different from perceptive and acute attention to a work. But the truth is that the two are fairly distinct.

Consider, in this context, the case of listening (knowledgeably) to some classical Indian singing. It would be called perceptive and acute if the listener has not missed even the slightest deviation from *sur* and *tāla*, and has also been alive, all along, to niceties or structure and style, say, the power and fluency of *taan*s coupled with perfect inner clarity (that is दाना or discreteness) of their constituent notes, or the seemingly self-complet*ing* design of the first line of the song (*sthāyī*). The perception of such details is indeed almost immediate where the critic is knowledgeable and attentive. But these are mere material for "critical" analysis and "measurement in respect of value criteria," not explicit criticism or in themselves "reasons" for the final evaluation of the music. The ultimate critical write-up calls for a proper placement and viewing of these details in the economy of the whole; and, maybe, also in the light of such overriding criteria of theory as might have been pushed into momentary oblivion as a direct reflex of the focusing of notice brought about by the gripping quality of what meets the ear. Thus, when the recital is over and the critic sets out to prepare his write-up for the press, he may have to reflect that the fluent and *vigorous taan*s, impeccable though they all looked in themselves, were (in this case) not quite warranted, neither by the *gentle* import of the text of the song, which means that they violated the principle of sound-sense harmony; nor by the aesthetic *demand* of the *rāga* (say, *pūrīya*) that a semblance of tender emotion (in this case, *viyoga śṛṅgāra*) be duly evoked; and that, though the *sthāyī* and *taan*s were all in themselves properly designed, the breathless torrent of (so many) *taan*s tended to eclipse the *sthāyī*, so that, instead of appearing as figures *against a steadfast background*, they semed to be a mere melodic assortment detracting from, rather than adding to, the overall *lucidity* of the recital. In such critical thinking, the value-criterion is coherence of the whole; and assessment of this kind is by no means instantaneously accomplished. The "finding" of such reasons for the grading of a music recital is an attempt *to think out and formulate* one's reactions, and *no mere discovery of attentive perception.* Were the direct findings of keen listening the same as giving reasons, it would not have been necessary for the critic (which it surely is) to assess the details of the music heard from the viewpoint of the concepts and principles of music as he understands them; but such an explicit assessment of aesthetic value is, as we know, a truly vital need of criticism.

And as for making notes on the work being attended to, whether or not it impairs aesthetic interest would depend on how exactly this noting is done. If, for instance, what is sought to be recorded is the manner of movement by which a note is (in the end) daintily touched, a quick *line* on the paper, ending with the mere mention of the note-name, may not ruffle listening noticeably; but if the same is written out *in orderly language,* the loss will not be negligible. Be that as it may, the risk is always there, in the case of occurrent arts in particular, that the moment attention shifts from listening to careful noting, the very next accent of beauty may be utterly missed or very weakly registered. If aesthetic interest or experience be taken to mean "rapt attention . . . [to] an *object's* immanent meanings and values *in their full presentational immediacy,*"[64] the critical attitude, in its express form (which we have taken care to distinguish) truly seems opposed to the aesthetic attitude.

Here, incidentally, we at once get a clue to see what could be meant by the next keyword, *sympathetic,* in the definition we have been discussing. The aesthetic attitude is sympathetic not in the sense that we are already biased in favour of the object as we turn to attend to it, but only insofar as, instead of looking at it in relation *to our* needs and set expectations, we give the *object* a chance to reveal its *own* significance to us. Where a complainant gets a sympathetic hearing from the judge, the latter only follows with due attention and patience the narration of the grievance; he is not already predisposed in favour of

64. Stolnitz, *The Aesthetic Attitude*, p. 34.

the plaintiff. The actual ability to give the object a chance is, however, not merely a matter of immediate resolve; it is, in a vital way, the result of past traninng as well. To attend to a painting as art is not only to look at it closely, but also discriminatingly; and discriminating perception or (what is admired as) percipience (or निगाह) in relation to art, is the result of long and repeated communion with WoAs in the past. This means that though, as the definition in question insists, *anything* that we are aware of can become an object of the aesthetic attitude, not *anyone* can adopt the aesthetic attitude towards a work instantaneously. On the other hand, a present decision of the will is also, in a measure, important. But this decision is simply the self-effort to remain open-minded in the sense that, though no one is expected to approach a work of art with a vacant mind — that is, in utter ignorance of the individual character and technique of the art to which the work in question relates — he must all along try to refrain from the insistence that every work must faithfully meet his own criteria of artistic worth. What is here needed is watchful openness to the work's own significance. Be it noted that because "aesthetic attention is alert and vigorous," the word *contemplation* is more helpful for defining the aesthetic attitude than the simpler word "perception."[65] However, this emphasis is by no means enough for the purpose. The truth about the attitude in question is that, where it is really at work in relation to a work of art, the individual involved does not only himself direct his close and undivided attention at the object facing him, but throughout remains willing to let his own perception and imagination be directed into new and unsuspected ways of functioning *by the work's own significance*. This is why the word, *contemplation*, has to be supplemented with *sympathetic* which means flowing in concert with or following the lead of the work before us.

An example may here be taken to illustrate the point. Suppose a keen and knowledgeable music listener, who has frequently heard the singing of some of the bygone *ustāds*,

---

65. Stolnitz, *The Aesthetic Attitude*, p. 23.

gets his first chance to attend a concert by Kumar Gandharva, a maestro of recent years. As he gets set to listen, we may further suppose, the *rasika* is already equipped with his own idea of what good *sthāyī-bharnā* is. Now, the moment the recital begins, and our *rasika* finds that the present singing of the opening *vilambit sthāyī* does not use the traditional device of *kan bharnā* — that is, the filling of those spaces in the first line, which are not covered by words, with drawn-out passages of pure (or wordless) *akāra* — he may feel tempted to underrate the present singing because it does not square with *his own* conception of how a *sthāyī* is to be made to look duly unbroken. But if he is "sympathetic," that is, if he decides to be a little patient, and to look for some other way in which the present musical utterance may be trying to create a semblance of singleness — say, by making the vocal volume swell and subside in such a way that the look of feeling thus evoked by the phrases may quietly *follow* them, *and so bridge (for contemplation) the recesses that in fact keep them open* — the listener's *attitude* will be truly aesthetic or one of sympathetic contemplation; and also its own improving exercise. *Indeed, somewhat like the adoption of a sympathetic attitude towards our fellow-beings, every exercise of the aesthetic attitude in respect of works of art puts an edge on our ability to seize fresh occasions for perception of value.*

At this point it is necessary to add, if only because percipience is often taken to mean keen attention to an object's *individual* features alone, that the aesthetic attitude is one of sympathetic attention not only to a work's *details*, but to their *relatedness, or to the work's* overall structure as well; and that this has to be so because the same emotional quality may be projected variously in different works and art traditions, by virture of the use of dissimilar *structural* devices. As Osborne rightly points out, "the serenity of a Raphael Madonna is not the serenity of a Khmer Buddha . . . [and] the eroticism of Indian *apsarās* differs from the eroticism of a Boucher."[66]

---

66. Osborne, *The Art of Appreciation*, p. 88.

In other words, the expressive character of WoA is, as a rule, inseparable from its individual structure. Hence, the need to repair to the work of art itself, as distinguished from its subsequent description or analysis, is repeatedly felt. This is so also because though the same words may in practice be applied to both our states of mind and works of art, the precise character indicated in the two cases may in truth differ greatly. Take, for example, the word "cheerful." It may be used not only for an individual's present mood, but for a melody. But whereas in the first case the quality in question may arise from a little fall in temperature producing pleasing changes in coenaesthesis which may show up in a beaming countenance, in the latter case it is the nimble rhythm, and so an easy-to-follow form — along with the requisite overall sweetness, of course — which makes the melody look a little *cheerful*.

However, the structural details and unique expressiveness of an artistic creation are not always readily accessible. As in the case of going through a work of literary art — say, a poem — one has often to try to get behind or beyond the obvious meaning of the art elements, here the collocations of words and word-bound images; to comprehend the total vision or experience that they embody; to register its true *affective* quality, which is what the art theorists of ancient India mean by insisting that a fit reader of poetry is *sa-hṛdaya* or "one of similar heart";[67] and so to finally seize the work's essential import. In other words, a work of literary art has its own inner, "virtual" world of characters, feeling, thought and imagery — all alike "impersonal creations" of the artist; and the contemplator must, so today, enter into, and dwell within this inner realm of the work if he is to unravel it from the inside, instead of skimming its mere exterior. Such an intimate and (so to say) multi-track concern with the object is what sympathetic contemplation here means. The act of following "the lead of the object and . . . [responding] in concert with it" which Stolnitz emphasizes[68] is

67. Hiriyanna, *Art Experience*, p. 18.

68. Stolnitz, *The Aesthetic Attitude*, p. 21.

no automatic confluence of two separate streams, but an intense, yet discerning absorption of the self in what is presented to attention; it is at once both *anupraveśa* and *tādātmya*. *Tādātmya* is no mere coincidence of two inert points; rather, it is such a living oneness of discernment and the object's self-revelation of meaning that whatever is extraneous to this active interchange is wholly shut out, and the contemplator's overall feeling is not merely one of expanding[69] and quintessential "seeing," but of repose, not as mere absence of activity, but as the reflex of an experience that is satisfying in itself and does not "pine for what is not." It is in virture of this, and not merely because attention is here free from restriction by practical interests, that contemplation can at once be *viśrānti* (or composure).[70] What is more, because of perfect attunement with the object, the feeling is also one of delight.

This, incidentally, is a detail which Stolnitz seems to slur over. He does not *expressly* consider the question as to how it really *feels* to adopt, or to be *in* the aesthetic attitude. Yet some answer to this question is *implicit* in his emphasis that what one here does is to give sympathetic and disinterested attention to the object *for its own sake alone*. For, if our contemplation of an object is quite undisturbed by any question *about* it — say, of reality, meaning or value — and if no everyday worry or pressure distracts our present attention to it, will not our unruffled interest in the object *feel restful* as well? It is precisely this feeling which is emphasized by *viśrānti* in the Indian view of the aesthetic attitude. "*Viśrānti* denotes both the fact of being [discriminatingly] absorbed in the aesthetic object, and the sensation of pleasure *sui generis* which accompanies that state of consciousness."[71]

---

69. Hiriyanna rightly points out that contemplation is here "a progressive appreciation of the aesthetic object," *Art Experience*, p. 23.

70. Cf. Ibid., p. 15.

71. R. Gnoli, *The Aesthetic Experience according to Abhinavagupta*, p. 56, footnote, (c). The bracketed word is my addition. It is demanded

However, it is possible to make some other objections as well to Stolnitz's conception of the aesthetic attitude. They arise as we turn to the following (as yet unheeded) words in his definition: "any object of awareness whatever," and "for its own sake alone." Is there any warrant for believing, one may ask, that the attitude in question can be adopted with regard to *any* (or every) object of awareness? Obviously, we cannot at once say, *yes*; for nobody has in fact successfully tried to adopt this attitude with regard to (literally) *everything* that is there. We have to be guarded in our answer; we can only say that no limit may be drawn to the number of possible objects of the aesthetic attitude. The truth indeed is that the works of a great artist can enable us to see some intrinsic charm in the very appearance of commonplace objects, like fruits and half-broken furniture in an ill-kept room. Again, as in the everyday work of professional tea tasters and chefs, even the taste of a drink or article of food can become, if only for a moment, an object of the aesthetic attitude if it is registered with care, and in utter isolation from the practical impulse to appease one's appetite.

However, the *taste* of a drink or article of food does not require us to seek access to its maker, though *we* may sometimes like to do so. But a work of art is different. Quite unlike a taste, it is often full of meaning; and this meaning, we may say, is what has been put into it by the artist. Could we then say that when we adopt the aesthetic attitude, in quite a few cases we attend to the work of art not for its own sake alone, but for the ulterior purpose of getting at the artist's intention behind the work? This plausible question, we suggest, could be answered as follows, quite in accordance with what we have said about *intransitive* attention:

> Where our attitude is aesthetic, it is the *object* which occupies the focus of attention. To get at its meaning, it may be necessary for us to ascertain what its ceator, the artist, has tried to emobody in it; but where the artist's intention is in

---

by the other Indian emphasis that in aesthetic experience the self is *not wholly* lost.

fact taken into account, our interest is not in the intention as such, but only insofar as it is revealed in, and so can help us appreciate the work itself a little better; which means that where we take the artist's intention into account, our attention is (in principle) still exercised, ultimately, for the sake of the object alone. Artists themselves seem to favour what we here say. When, for example, van Gogh states his intention behind his work, *The Potato Eaters,* his aim is clearly to help us see what to look for in the painting itself:

> I have tried hard to paint in such a way that the spectator is immediately struck by the idea that these people, eating potatoes in the lamp light, dug them up with the same hands with which they are now taking them out of the dish; that they are real workers; that they have literally earned their food. I wanted the picture to show a completely different kind of life from the one we educated people live. I was not interested in creating something that somebody might think "good" or "beautiful." The colour they are painted in . . . is like the colour of a very dusty potato, unpeeled, of course.[72]

We may agree that to contemplate an object "sympathetically" is to give it a chance to *reveal* its significance. But this is no mere mirroring of the object in a quite unprepared mind. To attend is at once *to get set* to receive impressions of the chosen object, the character of which is perhaps always visualized beforehand, if quite generally and often, more or less, incorrectly. Be that as it may, this is unquestionable that where what is attended to is a work of art the revelation of its true character is helped by an appropriate anticipatory attitude. Otherwise, we may look for something in a work of art that is not meant to be there. To illustrate, we incur the risk of underrating quite a few works of van Gogh as lacking in visual charm if we turn to them without taking note of his own express purpose in art-making, say, incarnating truth instead of merely titillating the eye:

---

72. M.E. Tralbaut, *Van Gogh: A Pictorial Biography,* Thames and Hudson, 1959, pp. 47, 49. (The artist's own remarks at this point have already been cited in Ch.I).

> . . . Fully aware [as I am] . . . of the importance of truth . . . I want my pictures of peasant-women to be real peasant-women, and my whores to have the true whore look.[73]

In other words, though the aesthetic attitude takes care not to insist that the object must conform, somehow and entirely, to prefixed criteria, it cannot, at the same time, refrain from looking for some determinate excellence, though of course in accordance with some foreknowledge of the object's own intrinsic or intended character.

Objects of attention, however, vary greatly in what they are or appear to be. This is why the aesthetic attitude requires us to perform quite different acts in relation to dissimilar objects. Where the object is a painting, one has to *look at* the arrangement it provides of lines, colours, volumes and masses; but where it is an ongoing solo *tablā* recital, we have to mark the occurrent design and clarity of syllables, and are often impelled to *visualize* the ones that are to follow. But if that is so, can we properly speak of *the* aesthetic attitude? In other words, is there something common to the various adoptions of (the) aesthetic attitude? And is this common factor enough to distinguish (the) aesthetic attitude from the other, better known attitudes? Both these questions may be answered in the affirmative, say, as follows:

Its freedom from thoughts of utility and reality of the object is enough to distinguish the aesthetic attitude from our practical, everyday concern with *things*. In day-to-day living objects interest us *primarily* because they serve some purpose, and not because of anything *in* them; and this is why we seek to possess and use them, and are rarely content with a mere look at them. Indifference to the thought of practical *usefulness* may, of course, also be there when we contemplate the *moral* quality of a noble action. Such moments gratify us because they make us feel elevated by appealing to our own sense of values. But, at the same time, howsoever good it be, a real action as

73. M.E. Tralbaut, *Van Gogh: A Pictorial Biography*, p. 58.

visualized is never quite free from the thought of its practicability. This unavoidable referring of the "object" to actual life, we have seen, is *not* a feature of the aesthetic attitude. In fact, even where the object is a part of given reality — and not a creation of the artist's own imagination — if our attitude to it is aesthetic, the object is quietly put away, so to say, from the world of our practical concerms. Thus, though the rainbow which delights us (because of what it itself is) *is* a happening in the world in which we live and move about, we do not regard it as related to us in the same way as things of daily use generally are.

Nor is it difficult to mark off the aesthetic attitude from the intellectual attitude. Our attitude is *intellectual* when we exercise the rational powers of the mind, as in interpreting, defending or refuting a theory, or in following or examining an argument. It is so also when we interpret and evaluate a work of art. In all such cases we actively distinguish the details of the object and try to *understand how* they are related; follow the laws of logic; and resort to the use of language, sometimes as implicit speech. But no such operation of the mind is necessary for the aesthetic attitude. What is more, whereas the aesthetic attitude is one of close and continual attention to the given, and its generally *perceptual* character, the intellectual attitude not only permits, but (as a rule) demands a measure of abstraction from the object's given wholeness and reality. Indian aesthetics provides us with one more distinction. The aesthetic and the *saintly* attitudes are similar insofar as both are free from the desire *to acquire and hold on* to objects (*kāma*) and allied activity (*karman*); but whereas *avidyā* — which is the main determinant of practical activity, interest, and attachment — persists (if not quite openly) in the aesthetic attitude, the saint is utterly free from it; and so the way he looks at, and lives and behaves in the world is marked by *abiding* detachment.[74] If a poet's heart leaps up at the mere sight of a rainbow in the sky, his attitude may be truly aesthetic; but if, like Wordsworth

74. This is cetainly true in respect of saints like Kabir.

again, he also *longs for* an abidance of the capacity to revel in the glories of Nature, his attitude will cease to be aesthetic and become merely practical.

Finally, the question whether we can fairly speak of *the* aesthetic attitude may be decided by considering some other settled ways of looking at life, things and people. The sympathetic attitude requires us to behave *differently* towards the needy, depending upon their *individual* requirements. The victim of an accident may have to be given first aid; a stranded child, escorted to its parents; and a poor but brilliant examinee may need a little money to clear some outstanding college dues. But this variety of the actual courses of action to be taken does not prevent us from saying that the attitude will be, in every case, sympathetic. It is therefore hardly proper to demur in speaking of *the* aesthetic attitude simply because it requires us, say, to *listen* in the case of music, and to *move around* the object a little in case it is a piece of sculpture. It may here be contended that, ordinarily, we speak of the need to adopt *a* (not *the*) sympathetic attitude, say, in dealing with erring youngsters; and that therefore the case for *the* sympathetic attitude is yet to be proved. But at this point we may shift our ground and rejoin that, in respect of any activity which is fairly determinate in character and is widely shared, it is common to speak of *the* attitude that is appropriate to it. Indeed, we freely speak of *the* scientific, philosophical, or commercial attitude. Therefore, insofar as our concern with art is as much a distinct and determinate part of life as our concern with trade and commerce or with science and philosophy, it would be perfectly fair if the *rasika* and the artist spoke of *the* aesthetic attitude, as indeed they freely do.

We may, in the end, consider a question to which we have not given any explicit attention so far. What is contemplation really? The question has been ably answered by Osborne[75] whose view on the matter may therefore be here outlined:

---

75. Osborne, *The Art of Appreciation*, p. 360.

> Contemplation means that we hold the aesthetic object in the centre of awareness and continue to attend to it discriminatinagly. However, we not merely concentrate attention *on* it, but become so engrossed *in* it that for the time being we cease to look upon it as a mere object that is opposed to, and so is distinct from us. As contemplation proceeds in delighted awareness, the details of the art work, as they relate to the whole, become clearer to us. This clear awareness of the parts "is a precondition of apprehending the total configuration," and it "does not disappear in the awareness of the whole." The moment we *cease* to feel like expanding in our apprehension of the aesthetic object — by way of a fuller realization of the character of the parts or of the whole — contemplation in the aesthetic mode may be said to have terminated. Then we are either . . . a little bored with the work . . . or we may occupy attention with theoretical analysis or the accumulation of extrinsic information about it — which in turn may (though it need not) lead to further percipience and renewed contemplation.

It may be noted, in passing, that while agreeing with the dual point emphasized in the above account of contemplation — namely, that a clear perception of the parts is necessary for apprehendion of the work's whole form, and that the latter does nothing to undo the former — Indian aesthetics also "distinguishes between the process of contemplation and its culmination in supreme insight."[76] The critic, we are told,

> [is not straight away] transported to the peak of . . . repose. Leading up to it are the diverse impressions he is receiving from different angles, almost simultaneously. His imaginative sensibility helps him in reception while his intellect is at work all along sorting them out. When the intellect and the imagination slide into the margin, his heart is moved to an intense aesthetic state of repose which is an end in itself.[77]

---

76. K. Krishnamoorthy's essay, "Traditional Indian Aesthetics in Theory and Practice" in *Indian Aesthetics and Art Activity*, Shimla: Indian Institute of Advanced Study, 1968, p. 53.

77. Ibid.

AESTHETIC EXPERIENCE

Where the aesthetic attitude is duly adopted, specially in respect of works of art or objects of nature, the experience it facilitates is called aesthetic. Quite generally, indeed, aesthetic experience may be said to signify the distinctive character and content of our experience when we register the beauty and/or significance *of nature or art*. It is also commonly regarded as a state of intense absorption in the contemplation of the object, and of delight or (at least) deep satisfaction, if not all along the course of the experience. How it differs from the other main kinds of human experience is easy to see. Moral experience is largely confined to everyday life. It is of course not impossible to receive moral impulses from contemplation of *Nature*. But this is not very common; only some sensitive souls like Wordsworth and Sūrdās, or some profoundly religious individuals can do it.[78] Intellectual experience too can relate to Nature, as when a *scientist* seeks to probe its mysteries. But, as one who is wedded to the pursuit of Truth, he is not primarily concerned with the beauteous aspect of Nature. His main tools are observation, reasoning, theorizing, and openness to modification of conclusions already reached in the light of fresh findings. In other words, a scientist's attitude to things and happenings is essentially intellectual.

It is noteworthy that in the present age aesthetic experience is not the conern of aestheticians alone. Even psychologists are finding it useful to study children's responses to works of art.

---

78. Wordsworth is convinced that contemplation of nature can deliver moral messages, if not explicity. See, here, his following lines:

    One impulse from a vernal wood
    May teach you more of Man
    Of moral evil and of good
    Than all the sages can

    As for Sūrdās, see here the following from his bhajan which opens with the words: वृक्षन से मति ले, मन तू: and proceeds as follows:

    धूप सहत अपने सिर ऊपर, औरों को छांह करेत
    जो वा ऊपर पथर चलावे, वाही को फल देत

They believe it helps them in understanding a child's overall development. Some philosophers go a step further. They find it necessary to look at aesthetic experience in the wider context of human evolution taken generally. They are struck by the fact that "the *experience* of art is as important to a bio-evolutionary view as the *making* of art,"[79] and that, taken quite generally, "aesthetic experience . . . is universal, fundamental, and necessary to man."[80] Therefore, they plead for an enlargement of aesthetic categories and principles, so that the art of quite diverse cultures may be duly attended to. This is indeed a genuine need, because some Western views of art, like the one which has given us the slogan: "art for the sake of art," seem irrelevant not only to primitive art, but to the bulk of India's traditional artistic riches.

The philosophers *of art* (or aestheticians) put even greater emphasis on aesthetic experience. Some, like Clive Bell and Pepita Haezrahi, maintain that such experience alone is the true starting-point of *aesthetics*. Others insist that *talk about art* is meaningful only if it is somehow based on aesthetic experience.[81] What is more, the very attempt to *define* art is often so grounded. Consider, for instance, the following unequivocal views:

a. "A work of art is an artefact which under standard conditions provides its percipients with aesthetic experience."[82]

b. "An artwork is *either* an arrangement of conditions intended to be capable of affording an experience with

---

79. Ellen Dissanayake, "Aesthetic Experience and Human Evolution" in *JAAC*, Winter 82, p. 150.

80. Ibid., p. 152.

81. George Schlesinger's view cited by D.J. Dempster in his essay, "Aesthetic Experience and Psychological Definitions of Art" in *JAAC*, Winter 1985, p. 155.

82. Monroe Beardsley's essay, "Redefining Art" in *The Aesthetic Point of View*, eds. M.J. Wren and D.M. Callen, 1982.

marked aesthetic character *or* (incidentally) an arrangement belonging to a class or type of arrangements that is typically intended to have this capacity."[83]

But if it is so central to aesthetics, the need for a careful account of the nature of aesthetic experience should be obvious. Indeed, it is; but besides bringing out its own positive nature, we have to distinguish it from such related concepts as aesthetic *attitude* and aesthetic *perception*. For the sake of added clarity, aesthetic *perception* may itself be marked from *aesthetic appreciation* and *art appreciation*.

Now, to begin with the aesthetic attitude, its *relation* with aesthetic experience is easy to see. Just as one's sympathetic *attitude* for a needy brother not only runs along with, but serves as a pre-condition of the *experience* of compassion for the other, so the aesthetic attitude not only facilitates the rise of an aesthetic experience, but is all along implicit in the experience as its vital determinant. An attitude is a way in which, as a matter of habit or by present conscious choice, we regard and react to people, things and happenings in determinate ways. It cannot be taken as a way of directing and controlling our perception *alone*,[84] in case the word "perception" is equated with *sense*-experience. We are of course not bound to so restrict the meaning of the word; "discernment" is in fact an equally acceptable sense of "perception." But neither meaning of the word would cover the simple case of adopting an *indifferent* attitude towards a person or happening. Perhaps the word "regard" would be a better choice here; for, to be indifferent to an object is clearly to *regard* it as being of no concern to us. The *aesthetic* attitude, on the other hand, is one of positive and wilful attention. As already pointed out earliter, it does not merely happen to us; generally, we have to make an active

83. Monroe Beardsley's essay.

84. I have here in mind the way "attitude" is interpreted by J. Stolnitz in his *Aesthetics and the Philosophy of Criticism*, Boston, 1970, p. 32.

effort to adopt it, except of course in those rare cases where an exceptionally beautiful building or a sweet and tender musical passage may elicit our aesthetic attitude automatically. But even where the many features of an object are vivid and irresistible, and if — as when we register the serenity of a vast and uncluttered landscape — we have only to open our eyes to it, a little effort *is* needed *to keep* ourselves available to the given, and to ward off distractions. Generally, we get set to look for what the object has to offer, or to let it affect us, and so the aesthetic attitude directly makes for some (aesthetic) experience of the object's own details or significance. Yet the (aesthetic) attitude is not as such *identical* with the experience it leads to or generates. "Though admittedly important, it is just a condition that precedes and underruns aesthetic experience. Such experience is a far richer state of consciousness than the aesthetic attitude which not only facilitates but is included in the experience."[85] As a readiness to open to an aesthetic experience, the aesthetic *attitude* can at best be marked by a measure of *quiet, if happy* expectancy; an aesthetic *experience*, on the other hand, can be easily *rapturous*.

Yet, the attitude is important. As an inclination to care only for what is there in the object itself — and to be indifferent to all questions of its reality and utility — it makes for a deeper appreciation of the character of the given than is otherwise possible. *Where it is aided by past training and experience*, a clear awareness of the WoA's details — and of the linkages that hold these details as one — may be called *percipience*, or the exercise of discriminating attention (or निगाह). Where its object is a work of art, aesthetic experience is very freely an exercise in percipience, without being limited to it. Indeed, except in the case of literary arts, a clear notice of perceptual details is always the starting-point of our aesthetic concern with a work. Yet, percipience as such does not cover all the features of aesthetic experience, or its many felt movements, such as the

85. Kingsley Price in his essay: "What makes an Experience Aesthetic", *BJA*, vol. 19, 1979, p. 140.

sense of flowing along with or following the course of, say, a piece of music, or the exchange of being, so to say, between an onlooker and the resplendent beauty of the sunrise which he contemplates and which may not only ravish his whole being with wonder and delight, but may itself reveal fascinating details of varying luminance. Aesthetic *experience* is indeed quite often a very rich mass of various elements, such as the following: cohering sensations, feeling and fancy; half-blown impulses to visualize what may come next; a moment or two of felt uneasiness at the thought that the aesthetic promise of a detail or segment has perhaps not been fully brought out;[86] and some palpable emotion which may press for overt acclaim. So it is impossible to identify aesthetic experience with mere *perception*. Nor does this word directly provide for the self-completing feel of an aesthetic experience where the "object" — say, a poem or a dance recital — is itself a manifest wholeness with a definite opening and end, *and* shows an ascent to a finale, all so clearly that the entire experience seems to jut out of the run of humdrum life. In such cases, to perceive is at once to *undergo* an experience, and the distinct individuality of the experience as recalled is better conveyed by the pithy "quite an experience" than by the words: "clear and vivid perception" that we use for what is merely sensed readily.

There are two other concepts from which *aesthetic experience* has to be carefully distinguished: apprecation *of art* and *aesthetic* appreciation. The second one is obviously richer in meaning, for it covers the beauty of nature as well. As for the word, *appreciation*, what it means today in the context of our talk about art is different from its usual dictionary meaning, namely, the act of estimating a thing at its true *worth*. The current aesthetic meaning of the word is *not evaluative*; it is rather closer to the following: "perception, specially of delicate impressions or

86. I am thinking here of moments when, during the course of musical listening, we feel that a single *svara* — say, the *tār ṣaḍja* — has not been duly "fed", or that the *sthāyī* has not been firmly "established."

distinctions." However, a measure of feeling is also often covered by what the word means, as when we talk of arranging lectures on art *appreciation* for school children. Here, it is obvious we expect the young not only to understand, but *to enjoy* what is presented to them. But as thus regarded, appreciation *of art* (we repeat) cannot be regarded as being the same as *aesthetic* appreciation which covers our concern with nature too, and not only with art. In most cases, appreciation of a work *of art* requires us to *understand* what the work signifies, besides reacting to its beauty. But where we register the beauty of nature untouched by human hands the question of *understanding* what we see just does not arise. Futher, in the context of art, appreciation is *a skill which can be cultivated*. To the beautiful in nature, on the other hand, even little children respond happily — and spontaneously. They are not trained to do it; yet they surely cannot be said to slur over the details of what they see.

Our present concern, however, is with works of art; and it is with reference to them that we have to see how percipience is related to aesthetic experience. The following general remarks seem relevant here:

1. If percipience, or minute *cognitive* awareness of the object's own character, is an *essential* precondition (or constituent) of aesthetic experience, we cannot obviously accept the view that what *distinguishes* such experience is simply the *sensory pleasure* it so often provides. In other words, we have to reject aesthetic hedonism, or the view that aesthetic experience is essentially a kind of *enjoyment*. In the past, however, this view had a pretty long run of currency in the West. Our fine arts of today were simply "pleasure-giving crafts" to the ancient Greeks. Further, a nineteenth-century writer, Sir William Hamilton, was so bold as to suggest that the study named "aesthetics" could better be called "apolaustics," that is, the science of what pleases. More recently, the philosopher William James explained aesthetic emotion as merely a simple, primary and immediate *pleasure* that we take in harmonious combinations of certain lines and masses, colours and sounds.

Kant's view is however different, and more in consonance with contemporary thought. He does not deny the reality of aesthetic *pleasure*, but instead of regarding such pleasure as itself the essence of aesthetic experience, he believes that this pleasure is not the *bas*ic thing here because it itself arises from the free exercise of our cognitive faculties in the contemplation of an object. Indeed, what seems to be crucial to aesthetic experience of art is "the free and unimpeded exercise of our powers of awareness upon an object adapted to give them full play, stretching them to capacity and sustaining them in enhanced activity."[87] That such an exercise may *give rise to* pleasure is of course quite possible. We may also agree that the pleasure we take in distinguishing and relating details — say, during the course of listening to some music — facilitates the continued focusing of attention on the art object. But the pleasure, here, is but subsidiary. It is merely a consequence of close and trained perception of what is there in the work, though when it has come into being, it also serves to keep the experience alive. What a person has to do here, in the main, is to focus attention on the work of art. He may well feel happy in doing so; but what he consciously attends to is the work, not the feeling, though when the experience is over he may well be able to speak of it as an enjoyable experience. It is however important to note what exactly it is that makes a WoA enjoyable. As Osborne rightly points out, the pleasure here arises from "the free and successful exercise of a *skilled faculty* excited to a condition of exceptional alertness," and is quite different from the sensuous pleasure of, say, smelling a rose which requires no prior training. In the case of inhaling a sweet smell a man's attention is generally divided: it is partly directed to the *smell*, and partly to *the pleasure* he is experiencing. But if he here puts himself in the state of aesthetic percipience he will "become aware as never before of the precise quality of the odour," and the awareness *of the pleasure* it is giving *him* will recede. It is obviously a different attitude that brings about the change.

---

87. H. Osborne, *The Art of Appreciation*, pp. 40-41.

The "aesthetic attitude is indeed one which carries attention and awareness out upon the . . . [mental or intentional object] of experience away from inner feeling and subjective affect."[88]

It may be noted, in passing, that the hedonistic view of aesthetic experience never found favour in ancient India. *Rasa* has of course been spoken of as a kind of "tasting," but this tasting was explained as the direct grasp of the very essence of the aesthetic object by a *rasika* who is not a mere layman but has *trained* himself for the job and meets quite a few requirements of the proper way to contemplate art. Interestingly, these requirements include the inheritance of helpful *saṁskāra*s from previous births. Turning to the present, it is obvious that the hedonistic view is simply not relevant to great works of art. We surely do not value the *Gītāñjalī* of Tagore, Prasad's *Kāmāyanī*, Picasso's *Guernica* and Goya's *Disasters of War* because they tickle the senses!

It would here be relevant to give thought to the word *enjoyment* specially because in our talk about aesthetic experience it is not always distinguished from *pleasure*. Consider, in this context, the following statements both relating to dancing:

a. "I certainly *enjoyed her dance recital* last evening."
b. "I was *pleased at the confident way* she danced yesterday."

Both, it is true, express some agreeable feeling; and so, from this point of view, enjoyment may be said to be a kind of pleasure. But whereas *a.* clearly implies that some *sustained attention* was paid to the inner details of the course of the dance, *b.* seems to say that only the confident bearing or look of the danseuse was *casually noticed* and found agreeable. We lavish both attention and interest on what we *enjoy*. But this is not necessarily true of whatever pleases us, and so we cannot be said to enjoy everything that we find pleasing. It is quite proper to say: "I *enjoyed* watching the match." But if it is won by my team, I will simply say, "I am *pleased* at the result," *not* "I have *enjoyed* the result."

88. H. Osborne, *The Art of Appreciation*, p. 42.

Enjoying a thing is to enter into it, so to say; and to explore its inside in a spirit of happy abandon quite without forcing it to deliver what *we* want it to, and quietly following, instead, the lead of the object's own details. A WoA has a far richer inside than the most seductive taste or smell, and the way to *enjoy* it is not merly to look *at* its details individually, but to dwell within the vision that its structure incarnates.[89]

This should not, however, be taken to suggest that the charms of sense do not play any part in aesthetic experience. They do, if not equally or necessarily in every case of art contemplation. Our actual experience of art surely does not support Kant's categorical view that "the sensuous appeal of fine tone in music and the delightfulness of colour in painting" — though they may well serve to draw the attention of a man of uncultivated taste — contribute nothing to a work's excellence *as art*; that the pleasure they may generate is not a part of true aesthetic appreciation; and that what alone matters in the case of painting is design, and in that of music, composition. Kant said so because in his day people generally thought of colour as a mere ornamental adjunct to painting. They did not realize, what is today quite common knowledge, that colour may itself be made a vital determinant of form in visual art. As for music, neither our theory of it nor the practice of most of its better known (classical) exponents in contemporary India warrant the view, ascribed to Tagore by Ananda Coomaraswamy, that: "our master singers *never take the least trouble* to make their voice and manner attractive . . . [and that] those [members] of the audience whose senses have to be satisfied *as well* are held to be beneath the notice of any self-respecting artist.[90] In our ancient works on music, the very basic unit of melody, the *svara*, is defined as *svameva rājate* or

89. The reference here is to what Osborne says in his *The Art of Appreciation*, on p. 45.

90. This is clearly an extreme accusation; why I say so has been argued on the next page.

"the beautiful in itself." Further, the focal relation in a *rāga* — which is the overruling (melodic) form of all composition in the region of our classical music — is called *saṁvāda*, that is, consonance or auditive *appeal* of two notes when they are played as a succession or together. Further, at least three of the better known classical vocalists of modern India — namely, Bade Ghulam Ali Khan, Omkarnath Thakur and D.V. Paluskar — were admired as much for the sweetness of their voices as for their artistic competence. Above all, however susceptible a *rasika* may be to excellences of method, structure or improvization, any note which is even minimally off-key is bound to ruffle his relish of the ongoing music, and where a *rāga*-form is distinguished by the use of two adjacent shades of the same *svara* — say, *madhyam* in *Kedār* or *nishād* in *miāṅ kī malhār* — it is the norm of sheer agreeableness to the ear, and no grammatical canon which favours their singing (or playing) in terms of a gentle glide rather than by way of a flitting indication of the shades in question as two *distinct*, if adjacent *svara*s.

Yet, though in the winsome way just visualized the two notes do not seem *separate* from each other, the *rasika* never fails to distinguish them. Now as the power which both *distinguishes and relates*, thinking is indeed freely at play in aesthetic contemplation of works of art.

Thus, as we listen to a classical music recital, it is the analytic and integrative activity of thought which enables us to see that the *rāga* being presented is *bhūpālī* not *deskār*, because though the two *rāga*s build upon the same *svara*s, the way some specific ones of them are noticeably integrated in the two cases is not the same. The dual movement of thought — that is, its ability to integrate what it also distinguishes — is perhaps easier to trace in our concern with a poem. As its overall form with its inner import begins to dawn upon the mind, the lines that must first be dealt with one by one — pretty often in the way of explicit analysis, as when we try to pick that one meaning of a word which is most fitting to the context, or to see how one word-bound image heightens the effect of another through supplementation or contrast — tend to get so pressed together into a unified image or insightful affect that the whole comes to look as a direct presentation to the mind's eye in the way of a souvenir.

Yet every kind of thinking is not a feature of aesthetic experience. What distinguishes such experience is indeed no dealing with mere concepts, but thinking which is all along grounded in attention to perceived or visualized details. This again accounts for the essentially presentational nature of aesthetic experience, as also for the vital role that percipience here plays. Aesthetic experience is in every case a concentration of attention on the object before us (a.); and therefore also an abstention from of the tendency to move away from it by way of the thought as to how it could be of use in daily life *or how it relates to what we already know about things of its kind* (b.). Both aspects of the matter, (a) and (b), may be brought out by citing what Pepita Haezrahi has to say about the aesthetic and non-aesthetic ways of noticing a very simple happening in nature, namely, the fall of a leaf in autumn:

> Our leaf falls. It detaches itself with a little plopping sound from its place high up in the tree. It is red and golden. It plunges straight down through the tree and then hesitates and hovers for a while just below the lowest branches. The sun catches it and it glitters with mist and dew. It now descends in a leisurely arc and lingers for another moment before it finally settles on the ground. . . . The red and golden tints of the leaf, the graceful form of the arc described by its descent fill the whole of your consciousness, fill your soul to the brim. It is as though you existed in order to gaze at this leaf falling and if you had other preoccupations and other purposes you have forgotten them. You do not know how long this lasts, it may only be an instant, but there is a quality of timelessness, a quality of eternity about it. You have had an aesthetic experience.[91]

91. Pepita Haezrahi, *The Contemplative Activity*, George Allen and Unwin, 1954, p. 31.

Much more frequently, however, mainly because of the stress of their dominant everyday interests, people would look at "the leaf" quite differently. Thus,

> a farmer on seeing the leaf fall might mark the arc it describes in its descent, deduce from this the direction of the wind, the imminence of rain and hurry off to do whatever farmers do when rain is imminent. A botanist may observe the leaf, think that it is falling rather earlier in the year than usual, pick it up and examine its capillaries, look for signs of disease or causes for the weakening of the tissues, and so on. A sensitive soul, on seeing the leaf fall, may be induced to reflect on the transcience of worldly glory, the uncertainty of human nature and generally indulge in sad musings.[92]

Such ways of non-aesthetic concern, be it noted, are all alike attempts to relate the occurrence to "things outside itself." He who regards the leaf attended to as a mere symbol of transcience misses "its individuality and particularity; [for] *any* falling leaf is . . . (such) a symbol . . ., not just this one."[93] In so looking at the leaf, percipience is clearly sacrificed. If a reference to the class to which "the leaf" belongs *is directly there in the immediate recognition of the leaf*, the requistic clarity, and so also the aesthetic character of the experience, will of course not suffer. But if one begins *to wonder* as to what class the leaf could possibly belong to, or to *explain* how it illustrates the characteristics of its class, our aesthetic experience will either weaken or be quite replaced by intellectual experience. Similarly, if on seeing the leaf fall, a man — who did not have the leisure to notice its perceptual details — is readily induced to reflect on the transient character of all that is there, the total experience would be merely a kind of pessimistic reverie, and not an aesthetic experience. On the other hand, if the sensitive eye of a poet keeps riveting on the droop and the faded tint of a flower, and if a thought of the overall impermanence of things

---

92. Pepita Haezrahi, *The Contemplative Activity*, George Allen and Unwin, 1954, p. 31.

93. Ibid., p. 33.

so arises in his consciosness that *the flower itself* comes to look sad, the aesthetic quality of the experience may well be enriched.

This fusion of look and feeling is by no means rare. The truth indeed is that, unlike abstract thinking, our everyday experience does not easily permit an absolute *severance* of thought or feeling from perception, though any one of these may *dominate* a particular experience. It therefore seems improper to insist, as Haezrahi does, that "emotions have no place either in the act of aesthetic perception or as elements of the aesthetic appearance of the object . . . [and that] the aesthetic perception is essentially non-emotional."[94] In cases like watching a leaf fall, *the element of feeling* may be negligible as compared to that of perceptual vividness. But one may wonder if even here it is utterly absent. If, as Haezrahi herself visualizes, "the red and golden tints of the leaf" and "the graceful form of the arc described by its descent," "fill [our] soul to the brim" and if all our "other preoccupations and purposes" are presently thrown into oblivion, what can it possibly mean except that we here *feel* rapt *and delighted* or at least deeply satisfied?

We cannot, however, quietly ignore the arguments that Haezrahi advances in support of her view. The more important of these are as follows:

a. The essence of aesthetic experience is perceptual clarity, and it is this clarity which stands to suffer when we attend to our own emotions. So, these emotions must here be kept out.[95]

But to this we can easily rejoin that one can experience a measure of emotion without *attending to it*. When we converse happily with friends we surely feel happy, but the object of attention is our talk with friends, not the feeling as such. And, what is more, a measure of subdued delight may even make for clearer perception. Thus if, after years of being away from

94. Pepita Haezrahi, *The Contemplative Activity*, George Allen and Unwin, 1954, pp. 33-34.

95. Ibid., p. 34.

it, "an old student" happens to return to his primary school building, he is very likely to feel a gladness that only makes for lingering attention to every detail of the building.

b. Aesthetic experience admits of an infinite amount of variety and intricacy. Emotions, on the other hand, "are in themselves far less differentiated and diverse, far more general in tenor than sense-impressions, their possible combinations and patterns are far less numerous."[96] So, sense-impressions are far better material for aesthetic experience than emotions. To allow "the careful shape of the aesthetic perception into a formless unarticulated flow of emotion, is . . . a serious spiritual loss."[97]

Now, if the need for clear perception is also kept in mind, the point of the above argument could be simply put thus: emotions do not lend themselves to the intelligible richness, variety and form that aesthetic experience demands. But one may fairly doubt if such a view is warranted by the evidence of fact or even by aesthetic theory if, as would only be proper, it is taken to cover the traditional Indian views of art as well. The variety that is a mark of sense-experience is of course unquestionable, and it is easily explained by the fact that the world's content is so rich and various. But if things and happenings are so many and so diverse, not only the way we perceive them, but *even our feeling-reactions to them can vary infinitely;* and they really do. *Hope, for instance, may be zealous and confident, as it generally is in the case of a team of champions riding the crest of a wave; or humble and serene, as in religious faith; or a mere flicker, say, where the life of an ailing friend appears to hang by a thread. Joy and grief are just as open to diversity. A young man's exuberance on winning a prize in sports is very far removed from a thinker's quiet relish of a subtle distinction just made; and so is the present moment of a parent's cutting bereavement, from the wan memory of a bygone farewell.*

---

96. Pepita Haezrahi, *The Contemplative Activity*, George Allen and Unwin, 1954, p. 34.

97. Ibid.

Aestheticians have not been slow to mark such differences. Susanne Langer, for instance, has even drawn attention to the gentle, likeable stress of chasing an elusive thought or of just having a big idea[98] that presses to be worked out. What is more, she also rightly highlights the fact that quite a few common features run through, and lend a kind of sizeable form to, the opposite emotions of sorrow and joy, say, their poignancy or "forms of growth and . . . attenuation, flowing and stowing."[99] In dealing with the problem of expression of emotion in music, Albert Gehring distinguishes the varying linkages of (say) hope and joy, with conation:

> . . . surgings to and fro, obstructed efforts, precipitate advances, victorious emergencies, expectations, hesitations.[100]

Bharata is perhaps even more detailed in his understanding of emotional life. He not only identifies the major moods of emotional exaltation (or the *rasa*s)[101] which it is the business of dramatic poetry to evoke, but even distinguishes the abiding emotional basis (or *sthāyībhāva*) of every *rasa*; and, what is more, the 33 transient emotions (*vyabhichārī bhāva*s) which provide to the experienced course of a *rasa* its palpitaing filling, and to the *rasika*, some marks which — along with the eight, clearly listed *sāttvika bhāva*s that are all identifiable signs of the real presence of some emotion — enable him to identify a *rasa* and to be sure that its expression is authentic. It may here be added that in respect of the single emotion of love (*kāma*) Bharata distinguishes as many as ten forms or expressions which may be listed as follows: *abhilāshā* (yearning), *arthachintā* (anxiety or uncertainty as to the return or fulfilment of love), *anusmṛti* (remembrance), *guṇakīrtana* (joyous dwelling on the loved one's

---

98. S.K. Langer, *Feeling and Form*, p. 22.

99. Ibid., p. 27.

100. Albert Gehring's words cited by Langer in *Mind: An Essay on Human Feeling*, vol. 1, p. 83.

101. My English translation of *rasa* here follows that of Prof. Hiriyanna. See his *Art Experience*, p. 38.

qualities), *udvega* (excitement or discomposure), *vilāpa* (weeping), *unmāda* (delirium), *vyādhi* (sickness), *jaḍatā* (stupor), and *maraṇa* (dying). What is more, even such a simple emotion as mirth or amusement is distinguished in terms of six kinds of laughter: *smitam* (a gentle smile, not revealing any teeth, but as expressed in an enlivenment of the eyes and cheeks), *hāsitam* (a smile revealing some teeth, along with a more noticeable opening of eyes and expansion of cheeks), *vihāsitam* (laughter which is marked by a slight narrowing of the eyes and cheeks, a gentle sound, and a reddening of the face with happiness), *upahāsitam* (as seen in a slight puff of the nostrils, constriction of the forehead and the sideways quality of look), *apahāsitam* (accompanied by tears, and a shaking of the forehead and shoulder), and *atihāsitam* (or uncontrolled laughter accompanied by a filling of the eyes with tears, pressing of the ribs with hands, and an involuntary utterance of unpleasant sounds).

As for the relation of a complete art work to specific emotions, it is manifest in quite a few of the masterpieces. To illustrate,

> it is a situation of love that is dramatized by Kālidās in his famous play, *Shākuntalam;* and in the case of the equally famous play of Bhavabhūti, the *Uttara-rāmacharita,* which treats of the desertion of Sītā by her royal husband, it is one of deep pathos.[102]

Nor is the projection of affective states confined to literature. In our classical dances — in the Bharata-Nāṭyam style, for instance — the tyro is trained in the skill of making quite a few diverse suggestions by means of varying movement and position of pupils in the eyes. In the face of these details of art-theory and artistic treatment or expression, it would clearly be odd to insist, as Haezrahi does, that though sense-impressions or perceptual forms may have emotional overtones "in aesthetic perception these emotional charges are . . . disregarded . . . as irrelvant to the formation of the aesthetic

102. M. Hiriyanna, *Art Experience*, p. 34.

object."[103] Where music is pathetic and yearning, as it can easily be in an effective treatment of *rāga Jogiyā* or *Sohnī*, how is it possible, we may ask, to pick only the heard sound for attention, and to leave out the emotion with which it appears to be charged? And as we register the impact of a painting depicting, say, "the Descent from the Cross" or Pieta, how can we manage to "see" only the shapes and not the feeling writ all over the work? Again, in the region of drama, if an actor only imitates the physical marks of an emotion without working up the requisite suggestion of the emotion *as directly felt*, attention to it will only make us feel amused.

Finally, in case a *rasika* in fact gets touched with the emotion projected in a play — not a little because of his *tādātmya* or imaginative self-identification with (the essence of) what he sees on the stage — the experience may yet be easily saved from becoming "a formless, unarticulated flow of emotion" by the almost absolute control exercised by the aesthetic object or presentation which is focused on and which is surely not itself a shapeless mass or flow.

Speaking quite generally — that is, apart from what Haezrahi has to say on the matter — the protest that aesthetic experience is merely a matter of perceptual clarity and does not involve any emotion, calls for pointed attention to its two negative emphases: first, that we do not experience any emotion *ourselves* when we have an aesthetic experience; and second, that we do not "see" or perceive any emotion or emotional quality *in the object* which evokes the experience in question.

Now, the first of these cannot be accepted categorically. To be sure, the sadness that we *see* in the music may not steal into us and make us feel sad ourselves. To identify an emotional quality *in what is attended to* is one thing; to experience or feel it *oneself* is quite another. What is more, in the case of listening to music which looks sad, it is even possible for us to feel *happy* at the adroit way in which the suggestion of pathetic feeling — which may only be demanded by the very nature of the *rāga*

103. Pepita Haezrahi, *The Contemplative Activity*, p. 33.

being rendered — is evoked by the musician at work. But, while admitting all this, can we blink the fact that the approbatory feeling itself is some emotion, and that it is clearly a part of the total experience? The truth indeed is that even where what we admire in works of art is, in the main, some formal excellence — such as the paradigmatic sight of symmetical balance in Taj Mahal — and not the "presence" of any *emotion*, if the object is able to elicit and hold our admiring notice we may well experience the *delight* of self-forgetfulness in what captivates the eye.

As for the second emphasis of the view in question, it is clearly untrue to fact. We do freely find music sad or gay, and the landscape awesome or serene. Here, however, one can raise an objection too. As we commonly regard it, an emotion is a state of actual experience. Its normal locus is a living human being, not a lifeless object. How, then, can we explain the (seeming) presence of emotion — say, sadness or gaiety — in objects of nature or in music or painting? Some answer to this question is (sought to be) provided by the theory of empathy. According to the dominant form of this theory, we tend to identify ourselves imaginatively with the object of perception, and in so doing ascribe to it "feelings and emotions which *we* should ourselves experience if we were in its place." But take a simple instance. Suppose it appears to us that *the sky* looks angry. Clearly, it would be odd to explain this "look" by saying that "we imagine that we would ourselves feel angry were we put in place of the sky." Indeed, with our inalienable sense of being bound to a body with definite limits, how could we identify ourselves with the sky, so seamless and seemingly infinte? Further, in quite a few cases we may be said to identify the distinctive "look" of an object *not by putting ourselves in its place but by opposing ourselves to it*. Thus, as Osborne points out, it could be said that we perceive "the soaring of a spire, the buoyancy of a bird . . . *by contrast with* a sense of our own earth-bound heaviness."[104]

104. Osborne, *The Art of Appreciation*, p. 81, italics added.

Consider, again, the case of a cartoonist at work. Suppose he is drawing a human face and we are watching the act. Now, if the completed face turns out to be a beaming one, we should be easily able to identify it as a face that radiates joy almost as soon as drawing completes itself. Here, there is hardly any gap of time between the moment of the work's completion and our perception of the feeling in it, and so no room at all for the alleged *process* of self-identification with the object. Even quite apart from this, it would look odd to suggest that though we are here all along aware of a figure taking shape through the movement of *a mere line being drawn and controlled by a person before our eyes*, we yet find it possible to abruptly *identify ourselves* with the completed face, and read *our* joy into it. No such feeling is already there in us before the full face appears, and so cannot be read into the emerging face. The truth in fact is that when the drawing completes itself, as an outer event under our very eyes, the joy that appears in the face is at once seen and believed to be *there in the object we are looking at*. It would be clearly untrue to say that we here put ourselves in place of the "face and ascribe to it a feeling of our own." The Gestalt school of psychology rightly insists that "the emotional qualities which we ascribe to things . . . are not due to unconscious process of *association, inference* or projection but are immediately apprehended as observed qualitites of the presentation itself." A bloodhound is known to be ferocious, and a person may be widely regarded as a jolly fellow; that is, neither, we may say, has any past history of moroseness. Yet if they come to wear a worebegone expression it may well be readily identified as such *in either case*. Clearly, no process *of association* is here at work in our apprehension of the "sadness" facing us. Nor do we infer *the presence of a mental state behind everything that impresses us as alert or weary*. Even the ringing of a telephone bell, almost at once when the needed number has been dialled, may strike us as quick or prompt; and similarly the leisurely floating of tar may look weary. The following words of Rudolf Arnheim may here be cited, partly because of their relevance to the larger question of expression in art:

> . . . Expression is an inherent characteristic of perceptual patterns . . . its manifestations in the human figure are but a special case of a more general phenomenon. . . . A weeping willow does not look sad because it looks like a sad person. It is more adequate to say that since the shape, direction and flexibility of willow branches convey the expression of passive hanging, a comparison with the structurally similar state of mind that we call sadness imposes itself secondarily. The columns of a temple do not [appear to] strive upward and carry the weight of the roof so dramatically because we put ourselves in their place, but because their location, proportion, and shape are carefully chosen in such a way that their image contains the desired expression. Only because and when this is so, are we enabled to "sympathize" with the columns, if we so desire. An inappropriately designed temple resists all empathy.[105]

It is the object's own present character which really counts in aesthetic experience. Its satisfying quality is in no way related to the question as to how the object has come to be what it is. Generally, its history is of little concern to the average onlooker, though it may well be of vital relevance to art critics and historians or (where the object is a rainbow) to students of physics. Osborne puts the point fairly:

> The *intellectual* interest in knowing all that can be known *about* a work of art is ancillary to, but is not identical with the *aesthetic* interest. The two interests are related but distinct. A historian can get by passably with small powers of appreciation and a connoisseur need have little historical knowledge, though he would be rash to belittle the help that can accrue from historical orientation in *some* cases.[106]

Tagore speaks in a similar vain:

> The poem no doubt comes from the person who produced it.

---

105. Rudolf Arhneim's words cited by Osborne in *The Art of Appreciation*, p. 82.

106. H. Osborne, *The Art of Appreciation*, pp. 28-29 All emphases added, barring the second one.

> But directly a poem is fashioned, it is free from its genesis; it minimizes its history and emphasizes its independence. . . . This is true of all creation. A dewdrop has no filial memory of its parentage.[107]

On the subjective side too, as Paul Weiss puts it, an aesthetic experience is "all . . . here and now," and is therefore quite different from the greater part of our everyday experience. Ordinarly, we live in such a way that the future and the past enter into our perceptions and attitudes not only when we consciously set goals to be realized or make an effort to recall an old, childhood incident, but unuspectedly. Thus, when in a particular situation we are hopeful or apprehensive, our present attitude is determined by the thought of something that *might happen* to us; and when we are surprised or disappointed our experience owes its character, in part, to what we *have been* used to or expecting. A regret is feeling sorry for what *has happened*. Confidence relates to tasks that may have *to be* done. In other words, our normal tenor of lite is far from being a state of equipoise and neutrality; it is always more or less tilted towards a specific way of perceiving because of what we have been or have experienced and what we expect to do, to become, or to get. *It is precisely from such a tilt or "disposal-towards" that aesthetic experience releases us*. Such experience is indeed distinguished by "serenity and detachment" or is felt as *svātma parāmarśa, svātma viśrānti* (or self-referent or complete, and so restful) because it is *vītavighma* or free from disturbance by a sense of incompleteness or restlessness that are such a feature of our daily lives.[108] This indeed is partly why our thinkers of old have likened aesthetic experience to the bliss of realizing *Brahman* or the ultimate Reality.

But, one may ask, in the course of aesthetic experience itself,

---

107. Rabindranath Tagore, "The Religion of an Artist" in *Angel of Surplus*, ed. Sisir Kumar Ghosh, Visva-Bharati, 1978, p. 16.

108. All the words that here appear in italics are freely used by our traditional aestheticians to characterize the experience of *rasa*.

do we not often look forward to what is to come, as when we follow the build-up of a climax while reading a play or an ascending melodic phrase which appears to press for consummation at the *tāra ṣaḍja*? And if we do, how are we here free from determination by the future? To this, it is clear, we cannot say "no"; but we may also readily point to something that provides some answer. Whereas in everyday life our present perception *of* matters (situations) is coloured by *our* habits, attitudes and expectations, in the region of art-experience it is the *work's own character* as it has taken shape so far which determines how we look ahead at it now. Again, it is *its* promise or aesthetic demands at the present moment which evoke in us expectations as to what it may offer next for contemplation. Even in the case of those works of art which do not *prescribe* any before-after order to contemplation, such as paintings, sculptures and beautiful buildings, how we perceive an immediate detail of the work, and how our attention is to move on are alike determined not by our effort alone, but how we react to the character of the given, assuming of course that our attitude is truly aesthetic.

In aesthetic experience of art, however, not only is *our* attitude disinterested, but the WoA too is, so to say, framed variously, so as to look quite different from everyday objects. Both these ideas call for some comment.

Artists themselves are seen to employ such devices as they enable a work to draw and hold attention. The commonest of these is the framing of pictures. On the other hand, when we see a play or film, the work's segregation for aesthetic attention is made quite easy by the fact that the place where we are seated, or the auditorium, is all dark, and that our look is directed towards the lighted screen or stage where alone "things" are visible. Attention to music needs no such devices. Its very basic material, comprising *svara*s and cyclic rhythm, is (in the main) different from the sounds and passages of daily life; and, what is more, it is so presented as a compact form of intrinsic charm — or as a *bandish* — that it easily becomes and remains the focus of attention and does not easily permit it to wander. But much, of course, also depends on the contemplator himself. Of the many qualifications that make one an authentic *rasika*, a vital one (according to the traditional Indian view) is one's ability and readiness to attend to the object keenly, *yet impartially*.

However, quite apart from the question as to what determinants — subjective and objective — are here at work in our concern with the object, the important thing is the quality of attention extended; it has to be both non-conceptual and non-abstractive.

First, we do not here conceptualize or think discursively about the object. To illustrate, where we experience a flower aesthetically we attend only to *its own* sensuous character. The moment we begin to wonder as to what *kind* it could possibly belong to, or try to think of its medicinal uses in Āyurvedic or Unānī preparations, our awareness of its own perceptual character, and so our aesthetic experience of it, tends to peter out weaken. But, one must add, the *immediate* and self-evident recognition that the flower in question is a rose does nothing to ruffle our aesthetic experience, for reference to the concept of rose is here implicit and effortless, and surely does not take our attention away from the object.

Secondly, though the object's parts and their relations are all here attended to, the total experience is not the cool, intellectual understanding that parts are possessed of their individual character *and are also* (so to say, subsequently) related to one another, but is rather the perception of a whole wherein the parts are *directly seen* to conduce to each other's impact, meaning or character, *instead of being merely thought of as doing so*; and also to acquire their own significance in part from the pheomenal interplay. Thus, if we read the following simple poetic line with due attention to all that it has: "an *untumultuous* fringe of silver foam," because of the very length of the italicized word, we at once get the sense that the lack of tumult visualized is the quiet *of a long and lingering wave*; and the experience (as envisaged) is here quite different from the *analytic understanding* that the word in question does not merely have a meaning but also a manifest length, and that the two aspects conjoin to evoke its aesthetic significance. Or again, it is one thing to read a specific poetic line, registering instantly the music that its alliterative words provide, and quite another to draw a friend's attention to the sibilants that open the successive words of the line and to explain that it is the repetition of an identical pleasing sound that makes for an overall likeable effect. A relatednss *as felt* is obviously different from the *thought or understanding* that some distinct things are presently held in a relation. The difference is similar to the one that obtains between the experience of being friendly and the statement that A and B are friends.

Thirdly, we have also to remember that where the object of aesthetic notice is a work of art, what we attend to is not only the sensuous content of the given, but a good deal more. Every work of art is a record of the artist's individual reaction to, or treatment of a particular item of reality or detail of experience; or (/and) an illustration of his unique way of employing the materials of his art. This uniqueness of meaning, reference or manner has also to be seized by intelligence. It is partly on the basis of this truth that a distinction may be drawn between two kinds of aesthetic experience: *participative* and *spectatorial*. The distinction may be brought out as follows.

By virtue of his keener sensibility and imaginative power, an artist is often able to seize the unique or essential character of things which we too may well be familiar with, but which we notice but casually. Cezanne once told Emile Bernard that "the landscape thinks itself in me and I am its consciousness." This may look odd at first sight. But is it not possible for a lover of nature to experience moments when, in states of utter freedom from human company and affairs of the world, one feels undivided from the quiet of the landscape and even like sucking in, so to say, the surrounding serenity? It is, however, only a poet who can externalize the feeling in terms of a WoA by virtue of his artistic skill and empathic intenseness. It is surely no mere talk when some aestheticians speak of "the unveiling of Being and insist that creativity depends upon "reverence to things."[109] Now, it is precisely this artistically revealed uniqueness of some aspect of life and reality that we come to apprehend where our experience of a WoA is *participative*. Generally, however, the beauty of things or nature is admired in the way of a *spectator*. This happens, for instance, when the poet registers a beauteous passage of the moon across the heavens externally, so to say:

> . . . Lifting her silver rim
> Above a cloud, and with a gradual swim
> Coming into the blue, with all her light.

Luckily, however, the participative attitude is also occasionally seen in relation to objects of nature. Thus, see the following from Wordsworth's "Lines Composed a Few Miles Above Tintern Abbey" (lines 95-104):

> . . . And *I have felt*
> *A presence that disturbs me with the joy*
> *Of elevated thoughts*, a sense sublime
> Of something far more deeply interfused
> A motion and a spirit, that impels
> All thinking things, all objects of thought,
> And rolls through all things . . .

Contrarily, everyday objects of beauty win but a few passing nods of approval. They may well tickle the eye whenever we look at them. But their capacity to *hold* our attention is very limited, partly because it is their utility which is what is mainly of interest to us, so that after the first few moments of aesthetic approval, we soon begin thinking as to how — or when or where — they could be best made use of. They do not provide any meaningful material to thought or understanding, and are

109. J. Stolnitz, *Aesthetics and the Philosophy of Art Criticism*, Houghton Mifflin, Boston, 1960, p. 37.

unable to so influence our imagination that it could be led to visualize what is likely to come next, as when we follow the growth of the plot in a play or of a novel's narrative; or to provide a fitting supplement in case the object does not itself project what it yet clearly suggests or demands, as in following an *anāgat* rhythmic pattern — where the listener provides the unmarked *sama* — or even in attending to the incomplete sculptures of Rodin. In other words, in experiencing the beauty of artefacts other than works of art the involvement of our apprehending powers is generally not as complete as in contemplating art. Every work of art has something to say, some meaning or significance, which permits and invites close attention, and can be eventually grasped as insight. Long and loving attention to the beauteous details of nature can surely give us deep and disinterested delight, and the experience may even abide in our memory for long. But the delight that we get on coming to see the meaning of — or "the single image" behind — a poem after piecemeal analysis, is quite different in quality. It is regenerative in the sense that our thought and imagination have not only been exercised, but enlivened in the process of attaining to an aesthetic experience of what the poem has to say.

It should now be easy to see that the aesthetic experience of art is not a simple or one-way relation between an individual and what he looks at. The truth rather is that, if in varying measure, a vital *interplay* of the two sides goes into the making of every such experience. On the one hand, it is *the contemplating subject* who authors the experience, in the sense that it is under the stress of his focused attention, trained sensibility, and imaginative powers that the object reveals its richness or beauty of content and structure; and, on the other hand, it is the object which not only draws but holds his attention by virtue of its details and overall form, quickens his apprehending powers, at times even forcing them to refine or stretch themselves, and quickens him, in part because of the very exercise of his faculties, with a happy feeling which makes the act of contemplation to run quietly along. In other words, an aesthetic experience of art always arouses us creatively, and is never a passive reception by us as we normally are. Here, indeed, we

> want to make the value of the object come fully alive in our experience. Therefore we focus our attention upon the object and "key up" our capacities of imagination and emotion to respond to it. . . . Aesthetic experience . . . is awareness, alertness, animation.[110]

But is this alertness or awareness directed only at the object? Does an individual forget *himself entirely* in art contemplation? Here, it is clear, our answer has to be negative. It is of course quite possible that a man may so forget himself in reading a good poem or in listening to the music of a master that not only his everyday worries, but even a local pain may seem to disappear for the time being. But even in such cases awareness of self does not quite disappear. After all, the individual is able to remember that the experience in question was *his*, and that he had this experience on a specific occasion and at a definite place. Aesthetic experiences do not float in the air. They occur to individuals who not only remember them happily, but turn to them, off and on, with longing and not a little love.

We may in the end discuss a question which has some bearing on the problem of art–reality relation. When we contemplate and "enjoy" an aesthetic object, is our experience dependent on the faith that the object is a real existent? Or is our attitude '"disinterested" in the Kantian sense that we are here not "in the least prepossessed in favour of the real existence of the thing?"

This question has to be answered by making two distinctions. First, being generally interested in the continued existence or preservation of *works of art* is not the same thing as the act of basing *one's aesthetic appreciation* of an object (partly) on a faith in its real existence. Second, the object's "real existence" may be taken to mean either that it is only something

110. J. Stolnitz, *Aesthetics and the Philosophy of Art Criticism*, Houghton Mifflin, Boston, 1960, p. 37.

before us, maybe as a mere appearance; or that it is there *as a real object* in the way of an everyday thing, that is, as related to our practical needs and to other contents of our actual spatio-temporal world. Now, the desire that works of art may continue to exist or be preserved properly is perfectly legitimate. We can hardly forgo such a wish, for we want to turn to many of them repeatedly. Bur when we *take delight in* an object of natural beauty or in an art work, we certainly do not demand that the "object" be real or existent in the same way in which things are there. The poignancy that the reading of King Lear may affect us with will in no way be ruffled by a researcher's rhetoric by way of insisting that such a person never lived. Nor is the poet's own rapture likely to dissipate if a physicist explains in due detail how the rainbow only *seems* to be hanging in the heavens because of the working of some atmospheric laws. All that is required for an aesthetic experience is that something be actually there *before* us, and as possessed of a structure or form and some qualities which enable it to draw and hold our attention, and to elicit reactions that betoken a rare quickening of our mental powers, a sweet stirring which of course does not incapacitate us for dealing with the real world, though it may well make us a little more indifferent to the grosser elements of life. In other words, though it need not be grounded in a faith in the actual existence of *the aesthetic object*, an aesthetic experience itself is surely too real to be dismissed as a mere passing whiff of imaginings. Is it not common to recall, in moments of quiet and leisure, the experiences we had of listening to some soul-filling music, or of walking through a moonlit glade at the dead of night, and to still feel caressed by the reminiscence?

APPRECIATION OF NATURAL BEAUTY

The way is now paved to pay some attention to our aesthetic experience of the beauty of Nature, especially as it differs from art contemplation. Writing on this subject appears under different heads, the more important of them being the following: (1) appreciation of natural beauty, (2) aesthetic appreciation of

Nature,[111] and (3) appreciation and the natural environment.[112] Though they all alike relate to "nature," by which we may mean "all objects that are not human artefacts,"[113] the three headings listed are not quite identical in meaning. So it is necessary to see how the one *we* have chosen differs from the rest.

Our subject (which heads the page) speaks only of beauty, not of sublimity which is a quite distinct concept (/quality). On the ohter hand, "aesthetic appreciation of Nature" (no. 2) must be taken to cover the sublime as well, for if the word *aesthetic* is taken in its primal sense — that is, as relating to sense-experience — the sublime would seem to be as much an aesthetic concept as the beautiful, for the sublimity of a lofty snow-clad mountain range surely rarishes the eye. As for no. 3 — that is, "appreciation and the natural environment" — it is *not* quite covered by heading no. 1, for what "environment" means is not just what is there — say, nature with its beautiful flowers and foliage — but the surroundings or conditions within which something *or someone* exists. Today, indeed, when environmental *pollution* is so freely talked about, the word signifies the relation of living beings and not of mere things to what surrounds them. It also does not mean the mere relation of a subject to object or of a passer-by to a scene. On the other hand, what we generally understand by appreciation of natural *beauty* is that someone *looks at* or traverses, say, a flower-laden tree or a verdant landscape, and takes delight in doing so. Appreciation of the many beauties that nature abounds in is, of course, not necessarily exclusive of a notice of environment. A walk across a mountainous region may well include a notice of the *surrounding* cliffs. Yet, by and large, the distinction holds; for, whereas the sense of being *encompassed* by what one

111. See, here, R.W. Hepburn's essay, "Aesthetic Appreciation of Nature" in *Aesthetics and the Modern World*, ed. H. Osborne, London, 1968.

112. Allen Carlson, "Appreciation and the Natural Environment' in *JAAC*, Spring, 1979.

113. Ibid., p. 53.

admires is a *neccessary* element of one's appreciation of natural *environment*, our *common responses to the beauty of objects of nature* — such as a rainbow or a row of daffodils — are often quite free from from this suggestion of encompassment.

What distinguishes *these* responses from our aesthetic experience of WoAs may now be brought out as follows:

1. Where what we admire is the beauty of Nature the "object" can very easily comprise a rich diversity of *heterogeneous* elements. Generally, these elements are: sights, sounds, and free, unchecked flow, as in the case of a rippling brook; quiet *fragrances*, such as the one emitted by the earth at the first rainfall; an enveloping quiet which the many little sounds in the region of Nature, such as the *rustle* of leaves or the occasional *chirp* of a bird, may only serve to deepen; undulating contours and sheer *lack of form*, say, in untrimmed shrubs; and the *sight* may be, of unbounded green space as it permits and invites an individual to move about, *generating a reflex feeling of freedom*, specially in healthy children who begin to dash or scamper the moment they find themselves in a vast, open field. The arts, on the other hand, project winsome *forms* which, as a rule, build upon material which tickles a *particular* sense. This is indeed why architecture, sculpture and painting differ so clearly from music. In dance and drama, to be sure, the ear and the eye are both alike tickled, so to say, and there is a measure of movement too in the presentation. But this movement, as also the intervening pauses, are all alike regulated, *and are apprehended as such*; and though, because of what we see and hear our feeling and fancy may both be quickened, there is no question here of that feeling of *somatic* freedom which distinguishes our moving about in fields or forests of abundant foliage, or even in going around a tree and wading one's way through an undergrowth of shrubs to get a better view of a butterfly.

2. It is common to experience works of art as being *expressive of* specific emotions. In our concern with Nature, however, though a sunrise may *seem* to gladden the sky and a flower may look jaded, we do not here think of objects as *expressing* any feeling — of joy or sorrow — as we register their beauty. The glories of Nature indeed recalcitrate the view that all beauty is also some expressiveness. Nor do we commonly think of any creative intention behind them when we relish them. We admire the given *as such*, and not as the product of the exercise of a skill. Art is inseparable from craft regarded as sheer manipulative skill in using given material; but the beauty of (raw) Nature is clearly not taken to be so grounded. Quite often works of art have to be *understood*, though they may also thereby produce some agreeable feeling. Nature is only to be contemplated, often with what has been called a wise passiveness by some poets.

3. Though surely in different ways, works of art are usually framed; and what lies beyond the "frame" does not generally become a part of our aesthetic experience of the work. A chance train-whistle from outside can only *disturb* our appreciation of music in a hall with a gate left ajar. But where there is no frame — that is, where nature is our aesthetic object — the occasional chirp of a bird or the sudden emission of a curl of smoke from the chimney of a homely cottage may not at all ruffle, but only enrich our appreciation, say, of the serenity and evenness of a vast and level landscape, though loud music from a transistor radio, may not be so tolerated.

4. Again, precisely because there are generally no such boundaries in Nature as may keep our attention tied down to a particular region — and also because of the caprice, say, of changes in light and shade — "any aesthetic quality in nature is always provisional, . . .

[modifiable] by reference to a different, perhaps wider context or to a narrower one realized in greater detail. In positive terms this provisional character of aesthetic qualities"[114] imparts to the contemplation of nature a sense of flowing openness which WoAs cannot provide so easily and liberally. "In a painting the frame ensures that each element of the work is determined in its perceived qualities (including emotional qualities) by a limited context";[115] and our reaction is here held in check, so to say, by the work's own *stability*. In our concern with Nature, on the other hand, even a gentle ray of the rising sun is enough to change the sombre look of the morning mists in a forest into a cheery one, dispelling the fogginess; and what appears *from afar* as the limpid, *seamless* flow of a rivulet may easily come to look a little broken if we get *closer* to it and peer at the pebbles it runs over.

5. It is also noteworthy that mere *absence* of sound and motion can be far more easily — and importantly — a positive source of delight in our appreciation of Nature than in our aesthetic concern with a work of art. The relish of the peace pervading the lonely hills or of the blue overhead at the dead of night is open to one and all. The arts charm us differently, and never essentially through *sheer* stillness and quiet. True, there is neither any sound nor any motion in the object even where what we admire is a work of architecture; but here the double lack is more than made up for by the projection of a created and *commanding form*. The locus of the charms of Nature, on the other hand, can be far more evenly spread out. This is not to suggest that privation of the kind we have referred to is never and not at all a source of appeal in the region of art. There may well

114. Hepburn's essay, p. 52.

115. Ibid., p. 51.

be pauses — or cessation of both sound and manifest passage — in a music or dance recital. But these are (as a rule) brief, and though they certainly contribute to the aesthetic character of the total work, they are of value to us not because of any independent charm, but only because they are made to relieve the running presentation adroitly or to project the close of an evolving form.

6. Appreciation of Nature does not obviously involve the unravelling of contrived forms, and so our responses here are not determined by any "built-in guides to interpretation and contextual controls."[116] Yet the shapes or designs that Nature freely presents, often in a fluid and fickle form, provide ample room for fascinated and determinate perception and imaginative play. The ready emergence and disappearance of concentric, widening ripples in a lake at the sudden impact of a pebble; the irradiation of a dark cloud by emerging sunbeams; the waves and the flowers on the bank appearing to move alike in tune with the breeze, as was once the prized experience of Wordsworth;[117] a chance cloud formation resembling the map of a country; and the very incurve of a wild elephant's trunk highlighting the projection of its tusks — these are some of the numberless features or happenings that lend both interest and a certain determinateness to our appreciation of Nature in the raw, and of what it provides.

---

116. This is what makes our aesthetic attitude, here, quite different from that of a paid gardener.

117. I have here in mind the following from the poet's: "I wandered lonely as a cloud":

> . . . A host, of golden daffodils;
> Beside the lake, beneath the trees.
> Fluttering and dancing in the breeze
> . . . Tossing their heads in sprightly dance.
> The waves beside them dance, but they
> Out-did the sparkling waves in glee; . . .

7. Further, it is important to see how exactly one can be both detached and involved in contemplating the beauty of Nature. The spectator is, of course, aesthetically detached in the sense that he is not using nature, manipulating it or calculating how to manipulate it. But where, as in the case of children, appreciation of Nature also includes, say, *chasing* a flitting butterfly or a frisky squirrel, one becomes involved in the sense of enjoying participation in the abandon that prevails in Nature. Of course, a *rasika* too can take delight in *following the onward course* of a play or of a music or dance recital; but in all such confluence in the region of art the sense of imaginative freedom never quite outruns the felt little constraints of meaning or technical criteria.

8. Incidentally, if appreciation of Nature be taken to cover a sympathetic openness to the diversity of form, bearing, colour and movement in wild *life* as well, it may be said to provide what the arts, barring the literary ones, never seem to furnish: that is, a fascinating insight into some quite unsuspected ways of adaptation to life, such as methods of warning to members of one's own pack against some imminent danger, saving a wound from infection by repeated licking, or emitting or heeding a call for mating. Of course, not all the ways of animal life are good to look at. The manner in which a tiger consumes its kill is in fact a gory and repulsive sight. But it yet seems necessary and proper to enlarge "appreciation to Nature to cover a sympathetic concern with wild life as well. The shadowy charm of deer grazing in the Sunderbans as a drizzle bedims the trees and the animals is rare and ethereal in quality. Again, the Indian tiger is indeed the world's most beautiful cat; it also looks picturesque in its natural habitat; and if a painting can be admired because "such use of *yellow* is rare in European art,"[118] and if *art* in general is to be

118. The reference here is to an acclamatory comment on Van Gogh's *Sun Flowers*.

regarded as specially important because (as Langer insists) it gives us *insights* into the life of feeling, why should not appreciation of Nature or of its beauty be taken to include the *wondrous interest* that we take in the "unusally broad *black* stripes" of a tiger; and, likewise, how can we deny that our *delight* at the prettiness of cubs biting twigs like playful children is quickened a little by the insightful thought that the exercise assists the teething of the young animals?[119]

9. Finally, appreciation of the beauty of Nature is, on the whole, more closely tied to considerations of real existence than the aesthetic contemplation of works of art. True, our enjoyment of the beauty of a rainbow does not suffer when we are informed that it only *appears to be* overarching the heavens. But, on the other hand, were we to see for ourselves what the moon really is, it is likely that from that moment on our ready reaction to its (seeming) beauty will cease to be as unmixed as it normally is. The *assumption* (as against conviction) in such cases of nature appreciation is that the "object" is really what or as it appears to be. The *fact* that they do not actually emit any fragrance is no bar to our appreciation of van Gogh's "Sunflowers." But we can hardly be said to enjoy the beauty of a flower unless we *actually* smell it and touch its petals; or the prettiness of a rabbit if we do not caress it. In other words, when we appreciate Nature it is our natural tendency to avoid a severance of its sensory qualities. Yet another point which may *seem* to distinguish such appreciation from our concern with the arts is that we do not ordinarily evaluate the beauty of raw nature in the way we determine the worth of WoAs by adopting what is called the aesthetic point of view to which we

119. For all this reference to wildlife I am all along indebted to the film: *Saving the Tiger* (4), photographed and directed by Naresh Bedi, and produced by Bedi Films Production.

may turn *after* we have distinguished aesthetic from religious experience.

AESTHETIC EXPERIENCE (AE) AND RELIGIOUS EXPERIENCE (RE)

All experience happens to individuals, singly or collectively. So its precise character depends not only on the object which evokes the experience and the situation in which it comes about, but on one's own quality as a person, as also on one's attitude at the moment when the experience actually occurs.

Now, the most obvious difference between these two kinds of experience, aesthetic and religious (AE, RE), lies in what they relate to, or what evokes them. For the average individual the object of AE is the beauty and sublimity of nature or art. In respect of art, however, AE is often also a pleasing realization of the *meaning or significance*, or expressiveness of the work contemplated. In respect of *nature* on the other hand, it does not make sense to raise the question of meaning, in case nature is taken simply as the non-human part of the world. RE is not essentially related to nature as such. It has rather to do with supernatural realities like *ātman*, *Brahman*, or God. Our praying to God, cultivation of faith in His attributes, and godliness in general — it is these that may be said to make or give rise to RE. Allied to this basic difference between AE and RE there are quite a few others which may be put as follows:

> As a rule, RE requires the prior (and concurrent) practice of some ethical disciplines, namely, those which make for abstention from evil in thought, word, and deed; and/or serious efforts to pray to, and to develop faith in God. AE does not call for any *such* discipline. No effort or training is required to register the beauty of a flowerladen tree or the starlit sky. Where the object is *a work of art*, AE requires no *moral* equipment but only a trained sensibility, capacity for imaginative following, and adequate knowledge of the basics of the art which the work contemplated represents.
>
> The object of AE is necessarily something *outside* of us, but RE is not subject to any such necessity. Mental prayer — that

> is, prayer which *does* not involve any speech, singing or reverent attention to an idol — and feeling *inwardly* grateful to God for the descent of His grace as sensed in the unexpected arrival of relief in an emergency, can be very genuine religious experiences. Further, a moment of intense personal suffering can easily make for religious experience by inducing soulful prayer. Aesthetic experience, on the other hand, is just not possible when one is actually sorrowing. The emotions and attitudes involved in AE can differ very widely from those that characterize quite a good deal of RE. Indeed, in AE there is nothing similar to the intense soul-searching and inward yearning involved in prayers of confession and repentance; or of petition, say, for release from one's own intractable weaknesses. Growth in personal humility is therefore a very common consequence of RE. Humility naturally enables one to see one's own weaknesses clearly, and so induces self-improvement. This is why, though both are important ingredients of what is called the good life, RE is far more likely to purify and ennoble one's everyday conduct than AE.

The object of AE *of art* is necessarily an artefact, that is, something which is the product of human effort. Oppositely, God to whom our prayers are generally addressed is our creator, not our creation. Communion with God, which is according to many the essence of RE, can easily assume the character of a kind of interpersonal dialogue. Men of intense and abiding religiousness often speak of listening to, and being guided by the voice of God. A work of art, on the other hand, is never regarded as a person, however great be its impact on one who contemplates it. A great man of religion — that is, one who is blessed with the right religious attitudes and is generally credited with authentic religious experiences — can easily become a great force for social welfare and uplift. This just cannot be said of "consumers" of art or *rasika*s, however rich and varied be their aesthetic experiences.

In spite of these differences, however, AE and RE cannot be said to be utterly unlike or unrelated to each other. Both can sometimes be distiguished by a touch of sublimity and make us feel not only subdued but uplifted. Engrossment in the object is (in principle) there in both AE and RE, and both call for withdrawal of attention from whatever is irrelevant to or discordant with the purpose of the moment. So both easily partake of the agreeable feeling which goes with all interested doing. There is another similarity which the two kinds of experience share, but which is not commmonly known. According to a traditional Indian point of view, devotion to God can take nine clear forms (*navadhā bhakti*); and our time-honoured *rasa* theory too, distinguishes nine exalted emotions (*nava-rasas*) in the region of aesthetic experience.

Further, both AE and RE admit of differences in depth *and* intensity. Some experiences, both religious and aesthetic, are simply tangential; others, overpowering and capable of transforming one's entire personality. Our response to a short and sweetly sung lullaby is one thing; our relish of the run of a film like Attenborough's *Gandhi*, quite another. Similarly, a *routine* morning prayer is quite unlike the soulful prayer of one who pines for relief from an intractable weakness, or from a serious ailment which threatens to darken whole lives of one's many dependants. The latter is a yearning, not a mere asking-for; and it may well be called "an experience" of Dewey's conception, just because it clearly stands out in our humdrum experiences of daily life.

THE AESTHETIC POINT OF VIEW

Here we may begin by considering how a *viewpoint* differs from an attitude. An attitude is the way in which *a whole person* is disposed towards things, situations, happenings or other persons. A viewpoint, on the other hand, is simply *an angle* from which we regard an object with a view to determining or judging its character and significance. Where our *attitude* towards a man in distress is sympathetic, we not only realize his need, but also *feel* for him, and at least *tend* to resort to a course of action that is likely to comfort him. If, however, we simply consider his case from the humanitarian *point of view* —

that is, without considering whether he really *deserves* any help — we may well be able to determine what precise help he needs, *and yet not feel moved at all,* neither as a feeling-for nor as impulsion to relieve. Here, it is clear, our concern is merely cognitive. In other words, *our attitudes involve us more fully than the viewpoints we may choose to adopt*. It makes fair sense to say that a man *is* his attitudes; but it would be clearly odd to suggest that a man is nothing but the many viewpoints from which he may look at persons and problems. Our attitudes colour the way we *behave* with fellow-beings in everyday life; our viewpoints only determine how we *judge* them. This is why we are better revealed in our attitudes than in the viewpoints we may choose. Further, insofar as it is simply the way a man is disposed towards life and people, an attitude can be markedly passive. The attitude of indifference is a case in point. A viewpoint at work, on the other hand, is always an active, if merely cognitive, concern with the object; hence there is nothing like a viewpoint of indifference. An attitude, like that of sympathy or aesthetic regard, can be *elicited* with ease. To illustrate, the sight of a very sick man may at once evoke our sympathy; and the aesthetic attitude may be our wholly effortless response to a spectacle of Nature like a glorious sunrise. A viewpoint, on the other hand, *has to be chosen and adopted,* more or less consciously. An attitude is often a discriminating *openness to impressions;* a viewpoint generally *seeks to determine the features or qualities,* if any, that square with some prefixed requirements. Therefore, whereas the aesthetic attitude makes for aesthetic *experience,* the aesthetic viewpoint enables us to give aesthetic *judgements;* and this is precisely why a viewpoint may be said to be generally more objective than an attitude. The sympathetic attitude is *a man*'s feeling moved and inclined to help. A viewpoint is itself *a determinate way* of looking at an object. We speak of *a man*'s sympathetic attitude. The seven viewpoints of the Jaina, on the other hand, are only *determinate positions* from which an object may be judged.

This should not, however, be taken to suggest that the aesthetic attitude must always keep away from the aesthetic point of view. In fact, they freely go together. Thus, a *rasika* may feel absorbed in a music recital, consciously revel in its accents of beauty, and put no question as to how it can benefit us or whether it is real, thus keeping truly to the aesthetic *attitude;* and yet he may also openly admire — though without a conscious formulation of the reasons for doing so — the structure of the *bandish* and the visible self-activation of the *āmad* so as to make for the *sama,*[120] registering at once the unity of form and a regional quality, both alike features which we mark while looking at a work of art from the aesthetic *point of view.*

As a pointed way of looking at things, a viewpoint is special and determinate; and therefore, because every individual viewpoint is different from the others, the aesthetic viewpoint too is clearly distinct from the viewpoints of utility and theoretical coherence which determine our practical activity and intellectual pursuits. To look at a painting aesthetically is surely not to care for such questions as the price it can fetch or the method of preserving it securely. What is more, in adopting the aesthetic point of view we positively decide to look for, and to base our value-judgement on some select features. What these features are should become clear presently, as we turn to discuss Beardsley's account of the matter which seems fairly applicable to works of art, if not to objects of Nature.

But consider, first, some other possiblities. Could it be held that to look at a WoA aesthetically is to ask if its form is "significant" or whether it *expresses* some feeling, or *communicates* a meaningful thought or a vision adequately? Alternatively, would it be fair to say that, insofar as concepts like "expression"

120. *Āmad* is that part of the first line (or *sthāyī*) of the song which seems to activate and direct itself so as to move towards the *sama* in a well-designed way. For a fuller understanding of the point see my essay: "The Fabric of Aamad — A Study of Form and Flow in Hindustani Music", *Sangeet Natak,* Journal of the Sangeet Natak Akademi, New Delhi, no. 16, April-June 1970, pp. 38-44.

and "communication" suggest a relative looseness of what is expressed or communicated from the work's perceptual elements with which it is in fact fused, the aesthetic point of view is that which seeks to consider if a work has been able to project some meaning as *embodiment*, that is, as the very look of the material out of which it is made? Such questions, it is clear, relate to the various theories of art which cannot be presently discussed at length. Here, we may only note that none of them appears to cover *every* kind of art. All art is not a delightful arrangement of lines and colours; and, as we have already seen in our discussion of Bell's view, content is so clearly important at least in the case of literature that *his* apotheosis of mere form appears to be overdone. Nor is expression of some feeling *necessary* for art. The whole *nṛtta* aspect of our classical dances is a witness to this truth. "Communication" is just as inadequate to art. No vision or thought is *communicated* by our instrumental music. The musician only makes a world of winsome patterns of melody and rhythm. "Embodiment" may be relevant to arts which use material which has solidity and which produce works that remain where we put them. But what shall we say of literature and music? In the former, it is meaning and images that dominate, and not the sensuous elements; and in the latter, restfulness is but an occasional, if likeable, feature. That which is common to all works of art is perhaps only the quality of being a complex whole. However, insofar as even objects of everyday use are found to possess this particular quality in fair measure, we have to add that a work of art has the extra capacity to provide aesthetic delight or gratification.

We may now turn to Beardsley's view. Briefly, it runs thus:

> To adopt the aesthetic point of view is to care only for the aesthetic value of the object. Such value lies in the satisfaction which the work of art in question gives (or *can* give) us by virtue of its formal unity and (or) regional qualities.[121]

---

121. Monroe C. Beardsley's essay, "The Aesthetic Point of View" in *Metaphilosophy*, vol. I, no. 1, January 1970.

This means, first, that aesthetic value is inseparable from, though not confined to a state of feeling; and second that, however various be the ways in which they occur in the different arts, formal unity and regional qualities admit of fairly clear identification. So these two concepts may be discussed at some length.

Formal Unity

Formal unity is the unity of form. As we have seen, the word "form" may either be taken to mean shape, which it does in ordinary discourse, or the unique inner organization of a work of art, which it is commonly taken to signify in aesthetics. As for the *unity* of a work of art, we have to remember that it means no mere singleness, but a complex wholeness that incorporates differences. A single note or pigment, however appealing in itself, is not as such a work of art. The question, whether a WoA's parts have any self-existence, may be difficult to answer. But this can hardly be doubted that they are not here rubbed indiscriminately into oneness. Taking both words together, *formal unity* may be taken to mean the completeness and coherence of a work of art.

Completeness

To adopt the aesthetic point of view in respect of art is at once to seek to ascertain whether or not the particular work is (or seems to be) complete. But what is *completeness*? Here, it is important to mark that the word does not convey identical meaning in respect of different arts. It makes sense to say that dramatic plays — or music and dance recitals — appear to be complete partly because we are able to make out their beginning and end. But, it is obvious, we cannot *so* speak of completeness in respect of painting, sculpture and architecture. With this preliminary note of caution, we may now turn to the various arts:

(a) In a somewhat superficial way, a painting may be said to be complete if it has a definite frame, and appears to stand out against the colour of the wall. This appearance will be checked if the colours of the work appear to run out into the wall's (similar) colouring. Such a risk is, however, minimal where the work being contemplated is an "assembly" of such diverse materials as tin and wooden blocks.

(b) In the case of plays, a beginning is (in principle) no mere matter of serial precedence. The opening scene here is also expected to convey the general feel or essential idea of all that is to follow. This *is* true of quite a few of the opening scenes of Shakespeare's plays. Thus, in his *Twelfth Night*, the relaxed and effusive manner of the very first speech[122] projects a character who blazons out his love, and so the opening goes well with a clear purpose of the whole play, that is, highlighting the kind of persons who tend to make a luxury of their sorrow or love, acquiescing in a mere pretence of deep feeling. In Macbeth, on the other hand, the beginning is designed to capture the eerie character of a good deal of what happens in the play. Very rightly, the first scene here opens thus:

An Open Place

Thunder and lightning. Enter three Witches

1. Witch. When shall we three meet again?
   In thunder, lightning, or in rain?

The point to be noted here is that where a play's very opening gives us a hint of something essential to the whole work, what we register is also *coherence*, and not merely a detail that assists our perception of its completeness.

(c) In the region of Hindustānī classical music the completeness of a recital is ascertained by distinguishing the four stages of *vilambit*, *madhya*, *drut* and *atidrut*. But

122. This speech open thus, "If music be the food of love, play on, play on . . ."

here too a remark may be made to reinforce the idea that our notice of the work's completeness cannot be kept apart from the thought of its coherence. At the *atidrut* (or very fast) stage, the inner accents of the *gat*[123] and the *ṭhekā*[124] alike get blurred; what is now provided to attention is generally a mere lump of hectic (and more or less) indistinct sounds; and those who react with hand claps to *such* music applaud only vigour and pace, not musical form which has now lost its inner clarity; and what they betray is mere excitement, and no real percipience. Such a way to complete a recital is clearly improper; it only cancels what is essential to the music, instead of bringing it to a beautiful close, because the *coherence* or inner shapeliness of form (or *bandish*) is annulled or bedimmed.

(d) Here, it at once seems necessary to mark off mere completeness from self-complete*ness* and self-complet*ion*. A figurative statue, no limb of which is broken, is obviously a clear case of literal completeness. This actual wholeness will be aesthetic as well, and not merely a matter of undamaged limbs and unbroken outline, *if* it also appears properly ordered on the inside. In case this proviso is met the statue will appear to be *self*-complete. The distinctness of such (aesthetic) wholeness becomes clear when we compare it with completeness that may *have to be* put on a work of art, so to say, from the outside. The latter *is* the case where, for instance, a danseuse has to cut short her last intra-form (or number), say, in the way of a *jugalbandī* just because the audience appears to be getting bored. This is also often seen in the case of instrumental music recitals. Thus, when the *atidrut* stage becomes unmanageable — and music, a mere flowing lump — the performers may *have to* bring it to a close, and (what

123. *Gat* is the basic composition in our classical instrumental music.

124. *Ṭhekā* is the rhythm-cycle as played.

is more) to signal that they are doing so, by openly patting their instruments to indicate the end. On the other hand, where a *sthāyī* attains to *sama* in a well-designed way, the musical flow may seem to be complet*ing* i*s*e*lf*.

> It would, however, be wrong to suppose that in art the two suggestions of completeness and self-comple*tion* always oppose each other. They may, on the other hand, be of mutual assistance. To illustrate, when a well-designed pattern freely completes itself at the *sama* (or the focal beat of the rhythm-cycle) a Kathak *danseuse* may herself pause for a while, assume a moveless posture, and so intentionally add to the seeming *self*-comple*tion* of the pattern, from the outside, so to say, but surely not arbitrarily. It may here be added that the suggestion that a work of art is complet*ing itself* is easier to secure in the case of occurrent arts, such as music and dance, where we see the work *being* made, than in the region of arts like sculpture, architecture and painting where, as a rule, we contemplate works that are already complete. In the case of the (non-occurrent) arts of vision just listed, the suggestion in question is secured only by making the work's inner disposition so dynamic that every detail may, more or less, seem *to make for* the import of the total work.

(e) That *self*-completeness is essentially a matter of the *dynamics* of internal design may be brought out by considering some works which are in fact incomplete, but which do not yet disturb us with their incompleteness. Rodin's well-known statue, "The Inner Voice," does not have arms. The artist himself justifies their absence on the ground that insofar as the title of the work is "The Inner Voice," signifying the *contemplative* life, arms which signify *action* would not have been in tune with the intended meaning of the work. For us, however, the point to be noted here is that the incompleteness is not really felt by the onlooker, probably because the expression which the work has been able to capture is fascinating in itself; and that, perhaps because of the coercive quality of the (measure of) form visibly secured in the work, the contemplator is able to put in the supplement himself — as an act of "concretion," as Roman Ingarden would say — and may even feel happy in doing so. Technically, the device of leaving a work purposely incomplete may enable the artist to overcome some inherent limitaion of his material. See, here, the following remarks of Walter Pater on a detail of Michelangelo's art:

> In a way quite . . . peculiar to himself . . . he secured for his work individuality and intensity of expression while he avoided a too hard realism, that tendency to harden into caricature which the representation of feeling in sculpture must always have. . . . Michelangelo gains by leaving nearly all his sculpture in a puzzling sort of incompleteness, *which suggests rather than realizes, actual form*. . . . That incompleteness is Michelangelo's . . . way of etheralizing pure form, of relieving its hard realism, and communicating to it breath, pulsation, the effect of life."[125]

Coherence

Completeness, however, is not all that we mean by unity of form. We have to consider *coherence* too. Only that work of art can be said to be a formal unity — or to have aesthetic value — the details of which seem to go well together. The materials it builds on may well be diverse; but within the whole work they should all seem to belong to, or even demanded by one another.

(a) The coherence we here speak of is, of course, *aesthetic*. Such coherence means that two (or more) details *in fact* make an agreeable unity. Theoretical coherence, on the other hand, is a matter of *meaning*. Thus, in music, a *svara* which pleases the ear when played along with, or quickly after, another note is *aesthetically* concordant

---

125. I am here reminded of the willed incompleteness of some Rodin's works.

(*saṁvādī*), not logically coherent, with the latter. No question of meaning is here involved. We go only by the evidence of fact. The difference between the two kinds of congruence can be easily exemplified. Take the case of *sound* and *silence*. In respect of meaning (or theoretically) the two are clearly opposed to each other. But in the art of music, or aesthetically, pauses of silence are often seen to add to the effect or beauty of its flowing sonant form.

(b) However, one cannot say that only some *select* materials can be properly blended in art. There is no real limit to the artist's creative power. Painters of class have often beautifully blended many such colours as were earlier thought to recalcitrate togetherness, and, in the region of Hindustānī classical music, masters have occasionally surprised us agreeably by incorporating notes which the grammar of the *rāga* being treated forbids — of course, *after* working up a spell so intense and sweet that the little, inessential detail does not ruffle the overall relish.[126]

(c) Nor can the *methods* of achieving coherence be fixed for ever. Great artists can always devise new ones. Here, however, we may just speak of some simple ways in which a work of art is made to look coherent:

It may have an aesthetic focus, that is, a central or distinctive point, figure or region around which everything else appears organized, or to the meaning or beauty of which the other details may appear to contribute variously. Here, however, it is important to see that an aesthetic centre is pivotal in respect of effect, and is not necessarily in the mid of an arrangement that is spatial or may be thought of as such. The *gandhār* of *darbārī*, so crucial to the *rāga*, does not divide the scale into equal halves; and if it yet sways attention, as it certainly does, it is only because of its own distinctive melodic character.

126. The reference, here, is to the deft use of *vivādī svaras*.

Generally, however, in Hindustānī music it is the *vādī-samvādī relation* that is really (or in principle) the focus of the *rāga*, though the *rhythm* of our music may be said to owe its cyclic or organized quality essentially to the single first beat (or *sama*). But it is here necessary to add that the impact of the *sama* itself may gain from what is called *āmad*, that is, a clear and well-designed reaching of the *sama* by the basic *gat* or *sthāyī*.[127] A similar disposition of content is often seen in the visual arts. Thus, quite a few paintings appear organized around one figure. A simple way to achieve this suggestion is to suitably slant the looks of the other figures. But even here, we may note, when we mark what is central in a painting we speak not so much of *a* figure as of a dominant *line* of look.

Again, in the region of art, a measure of coherence may also be achieved by balancing the different segments of a work. The aim, here, is also to ensure that no part of the work is wholly ignored. Positively, the purpose of balancing may either be to relieve the uniformity of a large part of content, or to lend some shape or tension to the work as a whole. Balance is, therefore, of different kinds. It may, for example, be symmetrical or asymmetrical. The first is provided by details that seem to be similar halves of a single shape, like the wings of a flying bird. Asymmetrical balancing, on the other hand, works through contrast or opposites. Its common instances are figures (or limbs)[128] put diagonally, or a white-black contrast at uneven levels. What is balanced may also be the *depth* of pictorial space. Thus, quite a few Cezanne landscapes employ not only such lines as take our attention to the picture's background, but also some other equally effective ones which lead the eye once again, to the front, so that, along with a due awareness of depth, we also take note of what is closer to us.

---

127. For an explanation of this point, see my essay, "Aesthetic theory and Hindustani Rhythm" in my book: *The Winged Form: Aesthetical Essays on Hindustani Rhythm*, Sangeet Natak Akademi, New Delhi, 1979, p. 17.

128. Say, in dance.

Sameness of parts is another simple device by which a work may be made to look unified. In poetry this end may be realized by using end-rhymes, or words that alliterate. The two may also work together, as they do in the following:

घन घमंड गरजत अति घोरा।
प्रिया हीन मन डरपत मोरा।।

In these lines from *Rāmāyaṇa* one cannot miss the alliteration of घ-sound in the first line. But it is not so easy to see that the comparative rhythmic brevity of *अति*, evidenced by the *hṛsva mātrā* of *ति*, is balanced by its contrast with the steadfast *घो* of the next word. In developing sensitivenesss to such details, attention to the rhythmic aspect of our music can be of great help. Grouping of similar is also freely seen in the region of *tāla*. *Tirmānamas* or *tiyā*s are well-known examples of this artistic device.

Finally, the singleness of a work of art may well be due, in part, to a clear and unremitting feature of the artist's individual manner. Thus, the works of Botticelli owe their uniqueness, in a measure, to a liberal use of graceful lines; Van Gogh's, to vibrant, even frenzied brushwork; and El Greco's, to the generally elongated, and often bony look of the figures.

Regional Qualities

As distinguished from the purely "local" character of a detail — say, the steadfast majesty or brevity of a note, or the intrinsic fineness of a pictorial curve — a *regional* quality is one which is based on a *relation* between parts or details. Such a quality may be purely summative, that is, the result of mere aggregation; *or* emergent, as being a quite new outcome of aesthetic configuraion. Thus, the greatness of a mural is, as a rule, merely additive; for, extension is a feature of its parts as well. So is the total duration of a music recital, because everyone of its segments — say, the total singing of *vilambit* and *drut* compositions as also the *sthāyī-antarā* and *taan*s they comprise — all take time. Here, it is clear, the regional quality — say, the extent or duration of the segments of the work — is always more than, but is *not necessarily* different *in quality* from its parts, for the repetitions of, say, the *sthāyī* that punctuate the volley to *taans* may look exactly similar to each other. Some other instances of additive qualities, again from the region of music, are: the sheer abidance of voice at a steadfast, single note that is sung long enough (and sweetly), or the repetitive, cyclic quality of a *drut tritāla thekā* that appears to go on and on.[129] On the other hand, the intentional deviation of a musical pattern as judged *in relation to* the rhythm-cycle, and the easy and intrinsic ebullience of a poetic line over an expected end-rhyme may be called emergent qualities; for, neither can be said to be there in the relata as such. Take, again, the case of painting or drama. In a landscape drawing no shape is near or remote in itself; and the suggestion of distance is due (in part) to the *relation* of superposition between figures. Nor can the *climactic* quality of a dramatic scene — such as that of the storm-scene in King Lear — be felt if we witness or read it alone, and do not relate it to *what precedes it*, and, so to say, makes the big dramatic moment appear something which the course of events has been heading for.

We may now see if Beardsley's conception of the aesthetic viewpoint is quite beyond question. In addition to formal unity of the whole work, he speaks (as we saw) of regional qualities too. But, what about such qualities as are different from both coherence and completeness, but can yet relate to the whole work, say, shapeliness and expressiveness? A building like Taj Mahal may seem to be shapely in every individual segment; and *bhajans* by (the late) Kumar Gandharva, all along expressive of devotional fervour. Would our viewpoint here be aesthetic if we ignore shapeliness in the former case, and expressiveness in the latter? Obviously not. But the answer (on Beardsley's behalf) could readily be that, though their value is in many

---

129. *Drut* is allegro, quick and lively pace. *Tritāla* is a rhythm-cycle of 16 beats; the 9th one is the offbeat. *Ṭhekā* is the basic cycle as drummed.

cases clear and undeniable, such qualities do *not* relate to *all* works of art, and so may well be ignored in our understanding of *the* aesthetic point of view. Nobody says a poem is good because it is shapely. Nor is a good rhythmic recital admired as being expressive. Coherence and completeness cover a far more extensive region of art.

Yet some may find it difficult to accept the phrasing of the following in Beardsley's account of the conception in question:

> To adopt the aesthetic point of view with regard to an object is to take an interest in whatever aesthetic value the object may possess or the value that is obtainable *by means of* the object.[130]

Here, exception may be taken to what the words in italics imply. It may be contended that when our experience of a work *as art* is completed for the present, it would be truer (to actual experience) to speak of the joy that we have found *in* the work than to say that we have felt gratified *by means of* it. But the point of the protest is dissipated as we turn to the following words with which Beardsley forthwith supplements the extract just cited:

> The aesthetic value of an object is the value *it* possesses in virtue of its capacity to provide aesthetic gratification.
>
> Gratification is aesthetic when it is obtained primarily from attention to the formal unity and/or the regional qualities *of a complex whole*, and when its magnitude is a function of the degree of formal unity and/of the intensity of regional quality.[131]

Here, it is obvious, Beardsley clearly speaks of the object's own gratifying character.

Objections may also be built around the "capacity" nature of our definition. We have held (with Beardsley) that to adopt the aesthetic point of view is to care for the satisfaction that an object provides or *can* provide by virtue of its formal unity and

130. Beardsley, "The Aesthetic Point of View", p. 43, My italics.

131. Ibid., pp. 43-46.

(/or) regional qualities. But is it not possible to conceive a work of art so subtle and exalted in significance that nobody may be able to see its greatness today? Shall we deny it aesthetic value merly because *we* do not have the capacity to appreciate it?

Here, as we turn to meet the objection, we must open with a distinction. The fact that quite a few men lack the power to admire a great work is one thing; the protest that the work in question itself lacks the power to satisfy us, is quite another. Our concern is here with the latter; and if this emphasis on the *work* be duly kept in mind, the protest can be easily met as follows:

We may consider the matter either abstractly *or* in the light of facts. To *think* (or conceive) of a masterpiece is at once to imply that it *can* give delight to at least some men of refined sensibility. What, otherwise, is the meaning of a masterpiece? It is self-inconsistent to think that a work is a masterpiece though it is not going to satisfy *anyone*. And if in his actual commerce with art, a critic speaks of an "unrecognized masterpiece," the meaning cannot be that it has satisfied nobody, but simply that, though it has not so far received the wide notice it deserves, *he* at least has been able to see its charm, and can be of help to others as well in gaining access to the same. To sum up: as a mere word, a "masterpiece" at once *means* a work which *can* satisfy (some of) us deeply; and as something that is *in fact* contemplated, it is one which has given deep and discriminating delight to at least some men, maybe pretty long after its being exposed to public view.

Lastly, one may ask, is it proper to assign aesthetic value to an object merely because it *has somehow come to appear* invested with formal unity and regional qualities? Does a heap of street sweepings acquire aesthetic value when it seems to be possessed of such features to a man who is drugged? Here, we have to turn to a detail of the logic of our talk about the aesthetic point of view. Whereas the *single* word "view" just means notice, *in relation to thought "a point of view"* means a way of looking that is more or less *consciously adopted*. Now, it is obvious that when a random heap of sweepings just *comes to appear* vivid and lovely to a man under the influence of, say, LSD, the appearance in question does not arise from any express resort to the aesthetic point of view. The entire happening is simply an instance of *a thing's coming to gain* some fictitious qualities; and it is hence no real threat to the view being put forth. Even in a normal situation when the landscape *itself* looks washed and freshened (so to say) in sun after a sharp shower, we do not say that the perception is a result of our having adopted the aesthetic point of view.

Yet one may find something questionable too in the extracts (from Beardsley) cited. They fail to provide for the truth that, at least in some cases, a work's formal wholeness is in part made by the *rasika*'s active sympathy; and that it is not always found as a readymade fact. A more serious difficulty, however, appears when we reflect that not merely art, but even nature too as untouched by man can be looked at aesthetically. Where the object is a grey and straggling, but majestic mountain range, we just do not raise any question of unity or self-completeness. The source of delight is here simply the massiveness and boundless appearance of the object. Nor can we here be said to care, in the main, for any regional quality. What is more, such objects of attention do not generally offer to the eye any beauty of detail. Yet our concern with them would be aesthetic if they keep us awestruck and fascinated by virtue of their very massive look, and of course without any thought of their being useful to us.

Here, again, it seems to us that Kant's view is here preferable. In his *Critique of Judgement* he argues that whatever be the object contemplated, a spectacle of nature or a work of art, when we find it aesthetically satisfying our feeling is not at all determined by the thought of its possible usefulness; and that we only dwell upon what is given to the eye.[132] In other words, the aesthetic viewpoint is that of disinterested delight.

132. This, of course is, not the whole of Kant's view here, but it will get due supplement as we proceed.

At this point, however, a question may be put at once. Is it at all proper to say that one can look *at nature* from the aesthetic *point of view*? Or does common sense permit us only to say that our *attitude* can here be aesthetic? Now, it is easy to argue that one *can* fairly speak of looking *at nature* from the aesthetic *point of view*. Consider an instance. Suppose a colonizer and his friend are both looking at a vast and lush green, undulating plot of ground around which some good flats can be built. Suppose further that when the colonizer avidly declares that it would not cost much to level *the plot* into a useful playground for the children of those who may come to occupy the flats, his friend suggests that it would be better to let it remain as it is, *for the sake of the sheer joy that it will give to the eye*. Here, the friend's way of looking at the matter would be clearly aesthetic. He would be judging that the ground is worth preserving *from the viewpoint of sheer disinterested delight*.

Our *attitude* to nature is aesthetic when in contemplating it we do not raise any question of utility, reality or meaning, and just remain lost in the beauty of the scene. But our *viewpoint* is aesthetic when we consciously ascribe value to the scenery *because of* its very look of delight. An attitude (we have seen) is a matter of how one is generally disposed towards an "object"; a viewpoint is a particular angle from which we consciously judge something. Both, of course, can be easily aesthetic in respect of physical nature; *but the viewpoint, in such cases, may not be one of formal unity*.

What is more, the point we are seeking to make is warranted by a form of actual *art* as well. Consider, for instance, the case of some really good *ālāpa*, as it is done by our *dhruvapad* singers of the orthodox kind.[133] Is our *overall* response here mainly determined by any *specific* regional qualities of the singing? We can hardly say, yes. A particular note or glide may well seem specially sweet and tranquil. But ultimately we judge the *ālāpa* essentially as a whole. And, in general, *as we follow it*, it

133. In specifying the kind of *ālāpa* I here wish to exclude the way it is done by *khyāl* singer of the Agra school.

looks like the build-up of a kind of musical atmosphere, "a serene and intense *diffusion*," and certainly *not a well-defined unity or composition*. In such cases when, at the end of the recital, we use words to acclaim it we do not generally say that the *ālāpa* was coherent or well-structured. We say rather that it was soothing or tranquil, and at places elevating, or even sublime; or that it created a virtual canopy of the *rāga* chosen, so to say, all around us. The point here simply is that so long as the aesthetic point of view remains tied down to considerations of formal unity, structural coherence and regional qualities, not merely the sublime beauties of nature, but even some *art* will not be given the right kind of notice.

Here, in passing, we may look at another detail of listening to music. *Ālāpa*, at its best, is often said to be *great* music. But how is this greatness estimated? Surely not in the way in which we praise a *vilambit khyāl*.[134] In the case of listening to *khyāl* of this kind, our awareness of the "high seriousness" of music is in part calculative. We go by the slowness of the cycle; and the adagio is here the *measured* stretch of a number of beats. But in *ālāpa*, as we know, there is no counted rhythm. How, then, do we manage to call it great? The answer may be had by turning once again to Kant. In his view, we experience the "absolutely great" when we open to something which appears to be greater than everything else, but the greatness of which is not known by resorting to measure. He calls such awareness *aesthetic*. Now, all this fits *ālāpa* to perfection. It is a fact that, if only for a while, good *ālāpa* makes us feel uplifted above everything else; and that, what is more, we never take the help of any calculative norms in estimating its excellence.

What is more, even in respect of the concept of "form," Kant's view is of some positive value. This will become clear, partly by virtue of contrast, as we turn to consider some recent thinking on the subject. S.K. Langer and L.A. Reid, though

---

134. *Vilambit* means adagio, or slow and reposeful. *Khyāl* is a distinct form of classical north Indian music, and is much more popular than its older form, *dhruvapad*.

they both pay due attention to the objective meanings and analysis of "form," agree in concluding that what the form of a work of art is cannot be wholly put in words and that it is truly known only in the direct contemplation of the work itself.[135] This means that every work of art has its own form. Now, this is a view to which few would object. But for the *theory* of art we need concepts too. We must have some *general* idea as to what *form* signifies in the region of art.

Langer uses two words to distinguish the general meaning of form in art: *expressiveness*[136] and *articulation*. But neither word, it appears, is applicable to every art. As already pointed out, expressiveness is not a feature of our art of rhythm. Yet, in its solo expositions, our rhythm *is* an independent art with its own material of beauty, criteria of excellence and creative principles.[137] *Articulation*, of course, should always be there in a rhythmic recital. By way of explaining this feature, we may note, Langer emphasizes that a work of art should be as good a balance as possible of distinctness of details and its own overall cohesiveness; or that neither the parts should be so individual as to tug and detract from the whole form, nor the unity so coercive that it may simply seem to swamp the parts into utter indistinctness. In the region of our rhythm we indeed always insist alike on the neatness and proper grouping of the syllables as played. But then there are works and features of art to which the word *articulation* can hardly apply.

But what do we really mean by form as *articulate*? Langer explains the word as follows, with reference to music:

---

135. Thus, see Reid's *Meaning in the Arts*, pp. 32-33; and Langer's *Problems of Art*, p. 68.

136. See, here the following, "The work of art is an expressive form created for our perception through sense or imagination, and what it expresses is human feeling." Langer: *Problems in Art*, p. 15.

137. As to the propriety of the (Indian) view that rhythm is an independent art, see my essay, "Aesthetic Theory and Hindustani Rhythm" in my book: *The Winged Form*, Sangeet Natak Akedemi, New Delhi, 1979, pp. 1-17.

> Music, like language, is an *articulate form.* Its parts not only fuse together to yield a greater entity, but in so doing they *maintain some degree of separate existence.* . . . The greater entity we call a composition is *not merely produced by mixture,* like a new colour made by mixing paints, but is articulated, i.e. *its internal structure is given to our perception.*"[138]

Two ideas are here implicit. First, an articulate form is not the unity of mere mixture. When a new colour [is] made by [merely] *mixing* paints, the latter, — that is, the different paints — can no longer be distinguished. In the articulate form of art, on the other hand, as in a musical composition, the parts do not wholly cease to seem individual. Second, what is again not possible in the case of a mere mixture, in the articulate form of art "the internal structure *is* given to our perception."

Now, what exactly does it mean to say that an artistic form is articulate because its internal structure *is given* to our perception? "Is given" can have two different meanings: is actually given, *or* given in principle; that is, directly manifest *or* capable of being perceived. Now, to take the first meaning, is the structure or organization of details actually *manifest* in the case of every work of art? We must answer in the negative, because of the evidence of a good deal of art. Consider, for instance, the masterpieces of Turner, the famous English painter of seascapes and landscapes. Take, in particular, his well-known work, *Snowstorm.* Turner himself feared its details would not be manifest to the onlookers. *That* indeed is why he had to exhibit the work with a long, descriptive rubric.[139] And yet the work is a masterpiece, "one of the vastest representations," as Ruskin said, "of the sea in motion, and of clouds and light."[140]

If it be said that the details are after all distinguish*able* or

138. S.K. Langer, *Feeling and Form,* Routledge and Kegan Paul, 3rd Impression, 1963, p. 31. Italics added.

139. This rubric run thus, "Snowstorm: steamboat off a harbour's mouth making signal in shallow water, and going by the lead."

140. Gieuseppe Gatt, Turner, *A Dolphin Art Book,* Thames and Hudson, 1960, p. 37.

that we *can* distinguish them with more or less effort, is not such discrimination possible, one may ask, even in the case of a mixture? Everyone may not be able to do it, but a gourmet may well be able to distinguish the many condiments that have to go into the making of a richly flavoured dish. In fact, what can be, *or* what cannot be made out in a given complex is undecidable *ab extra*. But one thing is clear and unchallengeable. In north Indian music, *mīṇḍ*s or glides, if suitably employed, are seen to make for rather than to weaken the form of music; and yet it would, on the whole, be untruthful to say that the notes in a *mīṇḍ* retain "some degree of *separate* existence." In fact, *such* existence is here neither present nor desired; for, what distinguishes a *mīṇḍ* as a formal device is a quite opposite feature: the notes it comprises or traverses seem *to flow into* one another. Notice may here also be taken of a remark that Langer herself makes in a different context:

> In artistic production, the composer's materials must be completely *swallowed up* in the illusion they create.[141]

And, to speak quite generally, where harmony dominates the music, constituent notes just cannot be credited with any *separate* existence. So we conclude: the form of *all* art cannot be said to be expressive or *articulate*.

Let us now turn to Reid. He speaks of artistic form as *embodiment*, amplifies it as "creative aesthetic embodiment," and finally projects the inseparability of "perceptua" from aesthetic meaning as a key emphasis in his thesis of embodiment. But such a view can hardly be said to cover *all* art. Whatever other meaning the words, *art is embodiment*, may be able to convey, they just cannot provide for the idea that a work of art may *develop directly* (if only occasionally) in response to suggestions from an audience; and insofar as this interactive openness is *often* a mark of our music at its best,[142] we cannot say summarily that the form of (all) art is embodiment.

141. S.K. Langer, *Problems of Art*, p. 39. Italics added.

142. Often, and not merely freakishly, as sometimes in the case of painting. I have here in mind the art of Michelangelo Pistaletto.

What, then, is the alternative left? How can we speak of "form" in such a way that *every* art could be covered? Let us see if Kant's views on the matter can here be of help. He believes that whereas in the case of arts like painting and sculpture form is a matter of spatial relationships between the *coexistent*, the form of music and dance lies in relations within the *successive*. Yet, we are further told, two occurrent arts may not be "formed" quite similarly. In the region of music, form is a fabric of successive *sensations in time*, but in dance it is successive *figures in space* that conjoin to give us *form*. In the case of every art, however, form — or relationship between sensations — is perceived "intellectually." According to Kant, the vehicle of our awareness of form is never mere sensation.

Now, the suggestion that "form" is not a direct feature of what is given to sense may seem suspect to many. But, on the other hand, it is not easy to question the idea, implicit in Kant's view, that apprehension of the form of an object is not a matter of mere sens*ing*. To take a simple instance, we can hardly hazard the opinion that *anyone who just lends his ears to* the sequence of *svaras* built upon is at once able to see the form of a music *composition*.[143] The right response here is in fact a discerning awareness of how the different notes go to make a whole which seems to be self-complete, or even self-complet*ing*; it is, in no case, the passive, undiscriminating awareness of a mere series.

Yet, it seems difficult to ascribe to Kant the view that perception of form is necessarily a matter of apprehending structural *relations and organization*. He holds that, as objects of

---

His "photographic, figures [are] fastened to mirror backgrounds in which the spectator sees himself reflected, thus completing the composition." Edward Lucie Smith: *Movements in Art Since 1945*, London: Thames and Hudson, 1969, p. 132.

143. Kant himself says that music is not merely an art of beautiful auditory sensations (*Critique of Judgement*, 190/Academy Edition, p. 325); and that here composition constitutes the proper object of the pure judgement of taste, (Ibid., 68/Academy Edition, p. 225).

sense, even colours and tones are successions of sensations;[144] that they are therefore relatively "formed"; and that what can be beautiful is not merely a rich and intricate symphony, but an individual note. Now, it is obvious that we have *no* excellence of *organization* in mind when we admire the beauty (or beautiful form) of a *single* tone. In short, the difficulty here is that by regarding form as a manifold of the *co-existent or the merely successive* — rather than as a matter of *interplay or dynamic organization* — Kant is not only enabled to speak of the beauty of individual tones and colours along with that of (complex) works of art, but is also a little weakened in respect of his own insistence that apprehension of form is *intellectual*.

However, in his emphasis *that* form is important, as distinguished from *how* he interprets it, Kant would perhaps be acceptable to many. He insists that "perceptua," such as bright colours in painting "only make (the) form more clearly . . . intuitable, as they excite and sustain the attention directed to the object itself";[145] that, in respect of the arts, "the fundamental prerequisite for taste is not what gratifies in sensation but merely what pleases by its form";[146] and that all such embellishments as do not "enter into the composition of the beautiful form" are mere finery which takes away from genuine beauty.

Such views, it is clear, foresee the contemporary emphasis on form in art. We may also note, in passing, that Kant emphasizes not only the universal forms of experience — that is, space-time and categories but the empirical form of objects[147] as well. For our present purpose, however, it is the following ideas of his that are of particular value:

144. Kant, *Critique of Judgement*, tr. by J. C. Meredith, Oxford: Clarendon Press, 1969 Reprint, 68/Academy Edition, pp. 225 ff.

145. Ibid., 67/Academy Edition, p. 225.

146. Ibid., 68/Academy Edition, p. 226.

147. Kant's remarks on "empirical form" have not received the notice they deserve. See, in the context, T.E. Uehling's *The Notion of Form in Kant's Critique of Aesthetic Judgement*, Mouton, The Hague, 1971, p. 79.

First, form is beautiful when we contemplate art — *or* not very big objects of nature — with disinterested delight. Second, the source of delight is here the mere presentation. In other words, the object is liked for its own sake. It is not regarded as a mere instance of some kind. Nor is it admired because it conforms to any plan or concept. Finally, when a man declares that a work of art is beautiful, the immediate ground of his judgement is no objective criterion, but only subjective feeling. This feeling, however, is one of restful contemplation, and no mere gratification of sense. At the same time, it is no inert state of awareness, but the reflex of an active, yet harmonious working of our cognitive powers. Kant insists that aesthetic delight issues from the accordant functioning of understanding and imagination. The beauty of form is essentially a matter of the object's being apprehended *in a particular way*.

Now, of all these emphases it is the final one that is distinctively Kantian; and it is essential to see this clearly, by reflecting on a passage from his *Critique of Judgement*.[148] Beauty, we have seen, is essentially a matter of form. The faculty which perceives beauty is *taste*, according to Kant. It estimates an object by judging that the imagination conforms to law freely. But what does this *free* conformity of imagination to law really *mean*? It means, to begin with, that the activity of imagination, here, is not merely reproductive. Reproductive imagination is not free, but subject to the laws of association. In a judgement of taste, on the other hand, imagination *is free* in the sense that it is productive and exerts an activity of its own. It is here seen to originate "arbitrary forms of possible intuitions."

Yet, on the other hand, where (in the region of nature or the arts) what is apprehended is a definite object of sense — unlike a poem, the form of which cannot be said to be essentially

---

148. The reference, here, is to the passage which opens the "general remarks on the First Section of the Analytic" on p. 86 (Academy Edition, p. 240), and covers almost the entire next page of *Critique of Judgement*.

perceptual — the activity of imagination is "to that extent" not free; for it cannot quite abandon, but has in general to conform to the object. This constraint, however, is not so rigid in the case of *beautiful* form as to deny all freedom to imagination; for the object, here, is such a readymade arrangement of the manifold *as would be projected freely by imagination itself,* were it allowed to do so, in *general* conformity with the law of understanding. To illustrate, a painting showing some figures, including that of Christ, may present the latter as distinctly, yet not mathematically central;[149] and, what is more, this could well be the way in which imagination may itself like to organize the figures as an intelligible unity. As an object of attention such a work would certainly control our apprehension by *imagination,* but it would do so without seeming to *constrain*[150] this faculty.

Here, it is important to mark, Kant is speaking of the freedom *of imagination,* not of the will. In the case of *the will,* it seems proper to say that its determination by (its) law does not detract from its freedom. In fact, according to Kant, freedom of will is nothing but autonomy — "that is, the property which the will has of being a law to itself."[151] But the freedom *of imagination* lies in its originating *"arbitrary forms of possible intuitions."*[152] So it would be a contradiction to say that imagination is both free and *of itself* conformable to law.

149. I may here refer to works like "Adoration in the Forest" by Fillippo Lippi (included in C. Bazin's *A Concise History of Art,* London: Thames and Hudson, 2nd Impression, part I, 1964, facing, p. 240); and "Resurrection" by El Greco (Ibid., part II, facing p. 308).

150. It would here be relevent to note that traditional Indian aesthetics takes pains to emphasize the point that, along with other features, aesthetic experience is at once a feeling of freedom. This is clearly implicit when *rasa* is said to be an experience which is *svātma parāmarśa svātma viśrānti.*

151. Kant, *Critique of Judgement,* op. cit., p. 242.

152. All these italicized *words* are Kant's own, but the italics are mine. (Ibid., 86/Academy Edition, p. 241).

Moreover, it is (in Kant's view) *understanding*, not imagination, which is the true source of law. So, instead of saying that imagination itself (directly) conforms to the law of understanding, we must say it *has to* do so. But, on the other hand, this *having to conform to law* cannot mean "being compelled to follow a course laid down by *a definite* law," for in such restrictive conformity, the form of the product is determined by particular concepts. To illustrate, where a figure is admired because it is wholly in accord with the definite concept of circularity, the likeable feeling relates to the formal perfection of the figure, not to its beauty.

So when we speak of the *free* conformity of imagination to understanding in a judgement of taste, we can mean only that imagination has here (roughly) to conform not to a determinate concept of the understanding, but to the (general) law of understanding, which is judgement. In other words, though the object *is* here judged, it is not judged according to a specific concept. This is what Kant means by "conformity (in general) to law without *a* law" or "finality apart from an end" or "a subjective harmonizing of the imagination and the understanding *without an objective end*."[153] And this is exactly what makes imagination "free." It is free in schematizing without a concept.[154]

To turn, again, to our earlier reference to painting, we may now say that when the work is found beautiful, it is only because of the feeling which results from the accord of imagination with the general discursive manner of understanding; or, with a rather indeterminate idea of centrality, and not with the precise concept of a mathematical centre. The play of the two powers is here "free" because it is not at all constrained by any *rigid or mathematical regularity*, "the contemplation of which *affords us no lasting entertainment*."[155] This is what Kant means by the general accordance of the *faculty* of

153. Kant, *Critique of Judgement*, op. cit., 143/Academy Edition, p. 287.

154. Ibid., 88/Academy Edition, p. 242.

155. Ibid., My italics.

imagination with the faculty of understanding. For him, "beauty" means "a free and indeterminately final entertainment of the mental powers."[156] Where it is pure, says Kant, a judgement of taste "combines delight or aversion immediately with *the bare contemplation of* the object irrespective of its use or of any end." "The subjective formal condition of every judgement is the harmonious accordance of the two powers of representation,"[157] but the *aesthetic* judgement is free in the distinctive sense that it is determined neither by any concept nor by the criterion of utility.

We may here add that where the unity of a manifold is apprehended by referring it to a *definite* concept, it is only grasped, not explored; and that such form is clearly abstractable. (This is so when, for instance, we simply speak of a table as being a round one, that is, without referring to its other actual features, such as colour and size.) Kant, on the other hand, speaks (we have seen) of "a free and indeterminately final entertainment of the mental powers." This means that, in his view, the unity in question is *experienced by indwelling*, and as a mutual quickening of imagination and understanding. A form that is thus experienced is clearly not abstractable; and, what is more, the emphasis is of help to us in avoiding the mistake of regarding aesthetic experience as merely an *inert* "absorption in the fullness of artistic meaning."[158] Kant's emphasis on the self-complete or autonomous *and active* character of aesthetic experience is indeed unmistakable. He says:

> We dwell on the contemplation of the beautiful because this cotemplation strengthens and reproducs itself.[159]

It may be noted, in passing, that the accord of imagination and

---

156. Ibid.

157. Ibid., 143/Academy Edition, p. 287.

158. Reid, *Meaning in the Arts*, p. 88. Reid, I may add, speaks of our actual experience of art as (merely) "a time to be silent." Ibid., p. 89.

159. Kant, *Critique of Judgement*, 64/Academy Edition, p. 222.

understanding of which Kant speaks does not mean a matching activity of the two powers. Kant, in fact, says openly that whereas in a cognitive judgement — such as: "This is a perfect circle" — imagination is at the service of understanding, in a judgement of taste, "understanding is at the service of imagination."[160]

In other words, Kant explains *beautiful* form in terms of subjective feeling,[161] and not by referring to objective properties. For him, the beauty of art or nature means that *the form of the objects* delights the contemplator because in apprehending it his understanding does not dominate, but rather subserves the working of his imagination. In other words, the unity of the given manifold is judged not as determined by any concept, *but in accordance* with whatever varying syntheses imagination may like to put on the given,[162] consistently, of course, with the overall unity of the object itself.

The accordance in question, we may further note, is merely formal. Understanding, according to Kant, is the faculty of the forms or rules of thought; and *that* content in imagination which corresponds with understanding is therefore nothing material or specific, but comprises only temporal and spatial relationships. The question as to what precise concept is an analogue of a synthesis of imagination is left open by Kant.[163]

---

160. Kant, *Critique of Judgement*, 64/Academy Edition, p. 222.

161. "The judgement of taste must found itself upon a mere sensation of the mutually quickening activity of the imagination in its *freedom*, and of the understanding with its conformity of law." Ibid., 143/ Academy Edition, p. 287.

162. This specific suggestion would appear to be warranted by Kant's own view that what distinguishes a judgement of taste is "a principle of subsumption, not of intuitions under concepts but of the [very] faculty of intuitions . . . i.e of imagination, under the *faculty* of concepts (Ibid.), provided we remember that imagination makes for the intuiton and the arrangement of the manifold of intuition." (Ibid.).

163. J.E. Uehling, Jr: *The Notion of Form in Kant's Critique of Judgement*, pp. 60-61.

But the act that an analogue is found is indicated by the resultant feeling of pleasure. The "analogue" is found in our dealing with the *object*. The two cognitive powers are not to be regarded as working *only in relation to each other*. Where "form" seems *beautiful* the *object* appears "preadapted to our power of judgement," though not to any plan or concept. In our experience of the *sublime*, on the other hand, the object may seem "to contravene the end of our power of judgement, to be ill adapted to our faculty of presentation, and to be, as it were, an outrage on imagination."[164] To sum up, the apprehension of a beautiful form means, first, that the object seems adapted to our powers; second, that the latter work in harmony with each other; and thirdly, that the delight here does not rest on any thought of utility, reality or accordance with a plan or concept. This is what Kant means by his emphasis on disinterestedness and by the "definition" of the beautiful he derives from the "third moment":

> Beauty is the form of finality in an object, so far as perceived in it *apart from the representation of an end*.

Such a way of speaking, it is true, gives us nothing detailed about form in the *various* arts; but, we may note, such detailing is not the business of general aesthetics. The alternative to Kant's way is to characerize form less abstractly, by turning to objects of art; and to speak of it, say, as "expressive" or "embodied." But the inadequatenes of such efforts has already been brought out.

Finally, we may ascertain the bearing of Kant's thought on the question of the relation of art to religion and morality. How exactly is the question problematic? We cannot, of course, doubt the possible togetherness of the good and beautiful. As we listen to good music, a well rendered note may seem to be not merely sweet, but quintessentially fine *and uplifting*; and the mixedness may not at all strike the listener as odd. Nor

---

164. Kant, *Critique of Judgement*, p. 91/Academy Edition, p. 245.

would anyone murmur if a concept from the good life is woven into an image of poetic beauty. The fusion, on the other hand, may only delight us. This is certainly what happens when Kierkegaard, for instance, visualizes the rainbow as "a portal of grace in the heavens."[165]

One feels like protesting only when art is subordinated to, and seems a mere vehicle of some ulterior purpose, moral or religious. Here, we may object, there is a weakening of aesthetic values, and an encroachment on the autonomy of art; and Kant would here readily support us. He in fact opposes all determination from the outside, or all objective finality. If a work of art appears to be made according to some formula, moral or merely technical, he would set little value on it. On the other hand, Kant's position is far removed from the view that beauty has nothing to do with the good life. But, to see how (in his view) the two are related, one has to reflect on some of his own key utterances.

His well-known concept, "purposiveness without a purpose," is here of help. It makes for the idea that art can be purposive in the sense of *being incidentally adapted to a* basic feature of the good life *without seeming to pursue any purpose*, moral or otherwise. Thus, it may well be — in Kant's view, it really is — that when one takes delight in the beauty of art or nature, his implicit approval is not determined primarily by any sensuous charm; and *that such relative freedom from the easy lure of sense is at once a necessary sign of, or a step towards being moral.*[166] This indeed is the meaning of Kant's own remark that the beautiful and the sublime are alike

> final in reference to the moral feeling; [and that whereas] the beautiful prepares us to love something, even nature, apart

---

165. P.D. LeFevre: *The Prayers of Kierkegaard*, The University of Chicago Press, Chicago and London, 1963, p. 27.

166. And also, Kant would like to add, an active step towards the good life. Thus see, "Taste makes . . . *the transition from the charm of sense to habitual moral interest* without too violent a leap, for . . . it teaches us to find, even in sensuous objects, a free delight apart from any

> from any interest, the sublime to esteem something highly even in opposition to our (sensible) interest.[167]

Kant's thought here may not be identical with, but if it is taken along with his emphases that our experience of beauty is not one of objective finality, and that, in both art and nature, form is or crucial value, it seems fairly akin to *the modern view* that if a (literary) work is morally interesting, in adopting *the aesthetic point of view* with regard to it we only mean to see if the moral theme is nicely interwoven with the plot, and does not appear to have been forced into it.[168]

---

charm of sense." Kant: *Critique of Judgement*, 225/Academy Edition, p. 354. Italics added. This perhaps explains why Kant regards "beauty as the symbol of morality."

167. Ibid., 119/Academy Edition, p. 267.

168. F.C. Coleman, *Contemporary Studies in Aesthetics*, McGraw-Hill Book Co., New York, 1968, p. 10.

4
Art and its Linkages: Meaning, Truth, and Reality

In some other directions, however, aesthetic theory today raises questions which go well beyond Kant. One of these is the question as to how art is related to *meaning*, truth and reality. Meaning is a key concept in present-day philosophy; and so we may focus on it before we turn to consider how art is related to truth and reality.

ART AND MEANING

The word *art* itself has three distinct meanings: *an* object or a work of art, artistic activity or art-making, and works of art taken generally. Thus, we may point to *a* painting or *a* piece of sculpture, and say: "it is art"; or in respect of a painter *at work*, "He is *doing* art"; or, if we choose to think of art quite generally, we may comfort ourselves with the thought that there is plenty of art in the world or remind warmongers that an armed conflict between nations always poses a threat to art museums and galleries.

For our purpose, however, it is more important to see how *works of art* may be said to be meaningful than to care for the precise sense in which we use the *word* art in a particular context, though such caring is also essential for clarity in our talk about art. Beauty, we may note, is no longer regarded as a necessary correlate of art; meaning *is*; and this changed emphasis is surely warranted by the actual evidence of a good deal of art today. If *beauty* be taken in its popular sense of that which tickles the eye, the word cannot be used in respect of Picasso's *Guernica* and Goya's *Colossus*. Yet these are admittedly great works of art, great because of their meaning or what they signify. *Guernica* is meaningful because it *expresses* Picasso's own actual revulsion and crushed feelings at the wanton bombardment of the village, Guernica; and Colossus may be said to *symbolize* the dark, ominous threat of large scale violence that looms large today.[1] The former articulates a deeply subjective reaction, though of course in a highly creative way; and the latter highlights a feature of the outer world which is truly a matter of widespread concern today.

Before, however, we set out to see how *truth* (as subjective or objective) relates to art, it is essential to make two points in respect of artisitic significance in the sense of expressiveness or symbolic meaning. First, whatever a work of art expresses or symbolizes is *inseparable* from its sensory elements, say, from the shapes, figures and colours that it presents to view. This is quite unlike the meaning of words as used in everyday discourse, for such meaning can always be, so to say, disjoined from the language which first expresses it, and just as well conveyed by a quite another language which is bound to look and sound very different.[2] Second, in spite of their dominance in the history of art making, expression and representation — which are two common ways of a anything's becoming meaningful — are no *essential* functions of art. A good deal of our classical instrumental music, for instance, is acclaimed only for its sweetness, fluency, and configuration, and not for what it may be said to express or represent.

1. A rough idea of how these great works actually look may be had by turning to the illustration that appears on pp. 264-65 of Harold Osborne's *The Art of Appreciation* (for *Guernica*) and to (for *The Colossus*) to Plate VII in Beardsley's *Aesthetics: Problems in the Philosophy of Criticism*, New York: Harcourt, Brace & World, Inc. 1950.

2. This is why Susanne K. Langer speaks of artworks as *presentational* symbols, as against *discursive* symbols by which she means language as ordinarily used.

ART AND TRUTH

In respect of the art-*truth* relation too, the question of meaning is important. What do we *mean* by *truth*? What *is* Truth? Now, it is admittedly difficult to define truth with finality. But this is obvious that it can be subjective or objective. For one who actually feels a pain, the experience is undeniably true, though not visible from outside. Truths of religious experience too are subjective, in the main. The fact that one feels both subdued and uplifted in a moment of fervent prayerfulness cannot as such be shown to others. This page, on the other hand, is open to public view. Its being before us is *objectively* true.

Besides these simple ways of looking at truth, its philosophical theories may also be given some attention. The simplest one of these is the correspondence theory of truth. It looks on truth as a matter of parity between what we think, say, or report and what is actually there. Those who regard imitation or representation as the essential function of art may well be said to subscribe to the correspondence theory of truth. The other, fairly well-known theory — that is, truth as coherence — is not so directly akin to coherence that we find in the region of art. In fact the two differ widely. Philosophical or logical coherence is an accord of meaning. Upon this theory, it would be *untrue* to say: "*A* is the best student in the class, but *B* is also *equal to* his (or her)"; and untrue because the word *best* means better than all the others (here, students), and so at once cancels the possibility of an equal. To make such a judgement, we may note, one does not have to look at the actual academic records of the students in question. In art, on the other hand, coherence is not such an abstract quality; it is a matter of visible agreement between actual particulars, not a relation of accordance in meaning. Where *one* colour or *svara* is actually seen to go well with *another* no question of meaning is involved; it is simply a matter of agreeable appearance to sense. In passing, we may also distinguish truth from *reality*, for our next step will be to see how art relates to reality. It is not uncommon to use the two words interchangeably. This happens, for instance, when we speak of God as ultimate reality *or* as

Truth which alone abides (*sat*). Even in everyday life, when we have to deal with a tough and tangled situation, we may either say: "Let us first determine what the problem *really* is" *or* "We have first to get at the *truth* of the matter." But, at the same time, the logic of common discourse also shows at least one way to distinguish the two concepts fairly clearly. Thus, one is advised to speak the truth, not to speak what really is the case. By and large, truth is quality of speech and apprehension; reality, a matter of being there.

Heidegger puts it all a little differently. Truth, in his view, is the manifestness of the Essent; and art facilitates the self-advent of Truth. Such a view may be difficult to grasp at once, but it is easy to bring it out. Generally, we have to make an effort to get at the truth what faces us, may be the pleasing façade of a man who is known to be deceitful, or just a complex state of affairs. *Speaking the truth* as a matter of habit is not easy either. In everyday life we generally fail to see that failure to keep an appointment is also a deviation from the norm of truth-speaking, if not intentional lying. But, on the other hand, the habitual veracity of a man may also be manifest, as sincerity, in his very looks. What is more, many vital truths relating to conduct just reveal themselves during the very course of living, and do not have to be striven for. One such simple truth is the value of patience. But whether we get at this truth after some effort, or just seize it when it reveals itself, manifestness is in either case a mark of truth. As for art's facilitating the self-advent of truth, the point of Heidegger's well-known remarks on Van Gogh's *Two Shoes* (cited in Chapter 1 of this work) may be noted with advantage.[3] It is true that we do not value a WoA because it serves a practical purpose. Yet it may be proper to consider if it clearly embodies and reveals the full practical serviceability — or the factual truth — of a thing of daily use. Van Gogh's *Two Shoes* does precisely this; and it is this which makes it admirable as a painting.

3. Heidegger's own view, in this context, has been cited in Chapter 1.

Yet, as we turn to focus attention on the relation between art and truth a little longer, we have to open with some cautionary remarks. It has never been asserted that it is the sole or basic function of art to tell the truth about the world. Such truth-telling is the admitted function of science.[4] Yet one cannot say categorically that art has nothing to do with truth. The fact rather is that works of literature often make *explicit* statements which are true because they are seen to work in life. That genre of Hindi poetry which goes by the name of नीति के दोहे (*Nīti ke Dohe*) is here a clear case in point. Consider, for instance, the following:

रहीमन देख बड़ेन को, लघु न दीजिए डार ।
जहां काम आवे सुई कहा करे तलवार ।।

This is surely a needed counsel to refrain from what we commonly do, that is, ignoring the lowly out of sheer fascination for the spectacular. Is it not true that we easily go in for an eye-catching bottle of Pepsi, as against the homely *aqua* even though the latter is better able to quench genuine thirst, and of course far more economically?

It can surely be contended that the kind of poetry we have just adverted to often gives us conflicting views. Thus whereas, on the one hand, we have couplets such as the following:

जो रहीम उत्तम प्रकृति का, का करि सकत कुसंग।
चन्दन विष व्यापत नहीं लिपटे रह्त भुजंग।।

The following apparent counter can also be produced from the same genre of poetry:

काजर की कोठरी में कैसो ही सयानो जाय
एक न एक लीख लागियै पै लागियै है।

However, a *close* look at the two couplets cited is enough to cancel the point of the protest. For whereas the first one speaks of a man who is established in goodness (उत्तम प्रकृति का) as firmly as sandalwood is ingrained with irremovable

4. J. Hospers (ed), *Introductory Readings in Aesthetics*, The Free Press (New York) and Collier MacMillan Publishers (London), 1969, p. 8.

fragrance, the second couplet envisages only a clever man (सयानो) in a room teeming with soot. But even without resorting to this somewhat subtle defence one could rejoin that a half-truth too is some truth, and that even the high-sounding truths of philosophy are often seen to collide with each other and so have to be taken as but partially true.

Nor is it difficult to pick obvious truths from the region of English poetry. Thus, who would disagree with Shelley when he says:

> We look before and after
> And pine for what is not;[5]

or with Grey's moving reminder that

> Even in our ashes live their wonted fires?[6]

It is indeed borne out by a considerable amount of human experience that hankering after objects of sense persists almost up to the last breath of our lives. The better known English essayists too have given us a host of indisputable truths. Here is a simple, but doubltess one from Roger Bacon:

> Reading maketh a man full; writing maketh a man definite.

However, no amount of such evidence can be allowed to suggest that its truth-giving potential is the sole or distinctive, or even a superior quality of art. As has been rightly pointed out,

> the ability to give us truth, which art does have, is an ability possessed in greater degrees by the sciences and by the vast

---

5. From Percy Bysshe Shelley's ode *To a Skylark.* The full stanza in which these lines occur is as follows:

   We look before and after
   And pine for what is not:
   Our sincerest laughter
   With some pain is fraught;
   Our sweetest songs are those
   That tell of saddest thought.

6. From Thomas Gray's *Elegy written in a Country Churchyard* (1751).

majority of statements made in daily life. As such . . . it can hardly be a distinctive feature of art.[7]

What this extract says, in effect, may be brought out as follows:

We freely make statements in life which convey definite truths. Some simple instances here are: "One must save for the rainy day"; "Prevention is better than cure"; and "There is no sense in crying over spilt milk." Futher, even the most trivial happening can give us some true knowledge. For instance, who does not know it to be true that a bout of eructations is generally a sign of some digestive disorder? So, provision of some truths cannot be regarded as the *distinctive function of art.*

On the other hand, it is the overwhelming evidence of actual art contemplation that works of art give us aesthetic delight, where they do, quite independently of any question of truth. What truths do we glean from Shakespeare's King Lear which is admittedly a great tragedy? That it is risky to allow one's vanity to be tickled by sycophancy; or that "filial ingratitude"[8] is very painful to a credulous parent? Probably, yes; but we sure do not admire the play because of such humdrum truths. The sources of charm are quite different here. We admire the exalted fury of King Lear's searing words on the Heath[9] or the

---

7. Hospers, *Introduction Readings in Aesthetics*, p. 9. The extract cited is from the editor's introductory summary of Douglas N. Morgan's essay,"Must Art Tell the Truth?" in the same volume, on pp. 225-41.
8. *King Lear*, Act III, sc. IV.
9. Ibid., Scene II. See, here, the following:

   Blow, winds, and crack your cheeks!
   rage, blow!
   You cataracts and hurricanes, spout
   Till you have drench'd our steeples, drown'd
   the cocks!
   You sulphurous and thought-executing fires
   Vaunt couriers of oak-cleaving thunderbolts,
   Singe my white head! And thou, all-shaking
   thunder!

build-up of the plot towards a moving climax; and we do not ask if the King's invectives, such as the following against Goneril, can materialize in actual experience:

> You nimble lightnings, dart your blinding flames
> Into her scornful eyes! Infect her beauty,
> You fen-sucked fogs, drawn by the powerful sun
> To fall and blast her pride![10]

Or take the case of listening to an absorbing music recital. It may well provide to an authentic *rasika a truthful* idea of the *gharānā* to which the vocalist belongs or of the progress he (or she) has made over the years. But all this is quite peripheral to the joy of actual listening, and one who finds himself spellbound by the music does not at all ask what truths are being unravelled to him. Of course, he may well at times acclaim: 'सुर कितने सच्चे लगते हैं इनके'; but the predicate सच्चे here does not signify any truth *delivered by* the notes, but their own *intrinsic* tunefulness. Our experience is here participative. It is no objective concern as to how the music in question could possibly add to our knowledge. We tend to flow with the music, to mark time with its beats; and to drink in the melodic sweetness, so to say, when the singer abides restfully, mostly, at the *taar ṣaḍja*.[11] Truth is here incarnate in the notes actually heard, not a quality of thought or speech.

ART, LIFE, AND REALITY

This is not to suggest that the relation of art to truth calls for deeper reflection than its relation to *life and reality*. Together, these two concepts, *life* and *reality*, cover almost everything that we experience or can visualize. It is therefore difficult to talk about them comprehensively. Works of art too are infinitely

---

> Smite flat the thick rotundity o'the world!
> Crack Nature's moulds, all germens spill at once,
> That make ingrateful man!

10. *King Lear*, Act II, Scene IV.

11. *Taar ṣaḍja* are our words for the upper tonic of the musical scale.

various. So only the main *forms* of art may be considered in brief, though some passing reference to many more will be unavoidable, because they relate to life and reality quite variously. We sure have different folk songs *for* important festive occasions in life. But life is not so clearly *reflected in* our classical music as in literature. Architecture too is essentially non-representational, quite unlike landscape or portrait painting. A distinction may also be made, if quite generally, between life and reality. Life is something to be lived; essentially, it is doing and suffering in time. As for *reality*, its simplest meaning is: all that is there. If the two, *life* and *reality*, are taken together, the occurrent arts of dance and drama would perhaps seem to need some special attention, for they not only freely build upon what is there or can happen in reality, but are possessed of a clear measure of the temporal and living character of our being in the world.

Now, as we turn to consider at some length how art is related to life and reality, two points have to be kept in mind. First, not only life but *reality* too is to be taken to mean not only what is outside of us, but our reality as persons, that is, our specific individuality, and our distinctive sensitiveness to life's varying situations. Secondly, this *personal* reality can relate to art quite variously. Thus we find that during his pacificatory walks across the frenzied Noakhali, when all his colleagues seem to have turned away from his own principled way of looking at things, Gandhi is *sustained* in spirit by his ideal recourse to Tagore's immortal song, *aiklā chālo rey*, quite as deeply as, in the general run of his life, by Narsi Mehta's poetic epitome of Vaiṣṇavite righteousness, *vaiṣṇava jana to taine kahiye*.[12] Maharṣi Vālmīki is *moved to* give vent to his intense anguish, in the form of an instant projection of the *ādi-śloka*, by the sight of a cruel interruption in the act of mating between

12. It is noteworthy that the first two lines of this devotional composition provide an echo of the definition of religion as given by our Hindi poet, Tulsīdās:

परहित सरिस धरम नहीं भाई

two birds.[13] The devout-poet Sūrdās *visualizes* uplifting moral messages emanating from such mute objects of nature as the lowly trees; and in his "barely ten years"of creative work Van Gogh *seeks an escape* from his dark and troubled life through an abiding love for the sun, "the symbol of warmth and light," the yellow of which "aroused ecstasy first as an idea in the man, then as a colour in the artist," impelling him eventually to produce his *Sunflowers* "which rise above the significance of ordinary still life," and which, as the painter himself puts it, "produce an effect like that of stained glass windows in Gothic churches."[14]

It should now be clear that *art and real life* often quicken each other, at times *providing sustenance and not mere substance, reciprocally*. Further, what is common to the making of art and the living of life is not only content which is generally open to view, but some personal attitudes *and reactions* which we, the outsiders, can only vaguely visualize unless we cultivate a kind of reverent closeness with those who actuallly create art, and also reflect on the way they talk about what they do, with insistent eagerness to get at the inner meaning that their (first order) aesthetic discourse may appear to glimmer with.

Such pro-artist attitudes can indeed deliver some insights that are not otherwise accessible. Thus if, when he has just concluded a glorious, spellbinding recital, an eminent vocalist is addressed with the complimentary wonder, *how could you do*

13. *Ādi śloka* means the "first verse." "Vālmīki, the traditional author of the *Rāmāyaṇa*, is said to have spontaneously produced the first metrical utterance, and thus is considered as the discoverer of poetry. Seeing the female of a pair of . . . curlews bereaved at the loss of her mate to the senseless arrow" of a hunter, Vālmīki . . . [expressed his instantaeous grief in terms of a Sanskrit *śloka* which may be translated as follows:] May you not rest for evermore, for you have killed this curlew distraught with love." S.K. De, *Sanskrit Poetics as a Study of Aesthetic*, OUP, 1963, p. 81.

14. L. Goldscheider and W. Uhde, *Vincent van Gogh*, Oxford and London, Phaidon Press Ltd., 1945, p. 12.

it, the maestro's crisp and quick answer may well be: "it just came about (बस हो गया)." What is more, a little closer talk on such occasions reveals that the artist not only feels deeply satisfied, but often a little subdued and even overawed at what has been created by him, *or rather through him* — at times, as a mere channel of the creative impulse. More or less similarly, in the non-aesthetic run of real life, the purer a man becomes by struggling along the path of goodness, the keener is his sense of felt humility as against the growing vision of the ideal he seeks to pursue. Why otherwise should a poet *and a saint* like Sūrdās exclaim in all humility: मो सम कौन कुटिल खल कामी, (Who can be so uttterly vile and vicious — and so thoroughly infested with carnal desires — as I am?)

However, the most obvious form of art-reality relation is the provision of content to art by life and reality as commonly understood. Moreover, it is precisely this form of relatedness which shows how the different arts build upon the same content variously. Take, for instance, a quite common experience from real life, say, the experience of consuming sadness when one has somehow to refrain from expressing one's intense love or is not able to elicit the fruition cherished. It is painful, to be sure. But a poet can easily turn it into a more or less abiding object of *our imaginative sympathy, and so help us in becoming a little more humane in real life, by investing the experience in question with a beauteous garb of word-bound images and rhythm*. Shakespeare, for instance, may be said to do so when he makes Viola speak thus in his play, *Twelfth Night:*

> . . . She never told here love.
> But let concealment, like a worm; i' the bud
> Feed on her damask cheek: she pined in thought;
> And, with a green and yellow melancholy,
> She sat like patience on a monument,
> Smiling at grief . . .[15]

What we have here is not only the representation of a possible

---

15. Shakespears's *Twelfth Night*, Act II, Scene V.

situation, but the expression of a sad and intense feeling as beautifully visualized. However, a much simpler mode of expression can also serve to project the painful state of being neglected in love — by one who really counts. An Urdu poet, Meer, does this artlessly, yet quite effectively, in terms of the following couplet which I have already cited earlier, and which is perhaps a little more widely known than any other lines of Urdu poetry:

> पत्ता पत्ता, बूटा बूटा, हाल हमारा जाने है।
> जाने न जाने, गुल ही न जाने, बाग़ तो सारा जाने है।।

The poet's lament is here clear:

> The beloved may well be unaware of my languishment in love, because I have not made it known — to the one who really counts. But how does it matter? The whole wide world is alive to my absolute self-effacement in love.

Take another feature of real life, near-absolute silence or quiet, which (as actually experienced) is often a felt unwinding of nerves and no mere absence of sound. As both outer absence of noise and inner tranquillity, silence is also demanded by steadfast prayer. *Be still, and know that I am God* — advises the Bible. Now, though silence is opposed to sound in respect of meaning, the art of music freely builds on pauses of sheer quiet, *not only to enable the performing artist to think of the next step*, but *to help the rasika to inhale, so to say, the melodic aroma, which is what tādātmya here is — as an actual experience*. What is more, there are some cadences in *vīṇā* music which seem to whisper into silence and *to capture the very interface between sound and silence*. A poet too can do the same, say, as follows:

> A little noiseless noise among the leaves
> Born of the very sigh that silence heaves.

We may note that it is no small service to seize and preserve in a rhythmic form such finenesses of actual experience. Couplets like the one just cited can sweeten our solitude as lingering reminiscence. Perhaps a painter can picture quiet even better, and in more ways than one. He takes care to distinguish the different appearances of serenity in life and reality; and so we find that the painted serenity of a vast uncluttered landscape, as heightened by *a long line of horizon*, is not the same thing as the poise that may be seen in a picture that shows a necklace of pearls *being weighed with steadfast care, and daintily*. The reference here is to the art of Cezanne on the one hand, and to that of Vermeer, on the other.

The way we have proceeded so far is however not the aestheticians' usual manner of discussing the relation of art to life and reality. They prefer to do it with the help of some select concepts such as *imitation*, *representation*, *expression*, *embodiment*, *abstraction*, and *symbolization*.

What these concepts mean and how they are all distinct will be brought out in chapter 5 which discusses the different definitions and theories of art. Here we may focus only on the following, in brief:

(a) The long and varied tradition of art-reality/life relation.

(b) The Marxist's additional emphasis on the need to relate art to *social* reality.

(c) Some contemporary attempts to disjoin art from life and reality.

A. Now, though the fact that art has for long been related to life and reality is common knowledge, the *variety* of ways this relation has taken is rarely thought about. Yet this variety deserves attention, specially of those who seek to unburden art *entirely* from the yoke of reality.[16]

The word *reality*, we may note, does not only mean the state or fact of being real — that is, being actually or physically existing, not imaginary — but has also been taken by philosophers in the sense of ultimate Reality, which is the metaphysical meaning of the word, and which does not

16. As has been attempted by Jośe Ortega Gasset whose view will be discussed a little later.

generally figure in our present-day discussion of the question of art-reality relation. Yet, to the history and different genres of art this meaning too is relevant. Thus, whereas the French Impressionists take *reality* to mean the world of smell, taste, and texture which is open to immediate inspection, the Gothic and Byzantine artists prefer to take the word in the sense of a supernatural world which is known not through sense experience, but through intuition or pure reason. On the other hand, a good deal of traditional *Indian* art is clearly related to acts and objects of everyday life. The miniatures of Mogul India give us a vivid idea of ceremonials at the courts of the emperors; and of their costumes, details of jewellery, weapons, and other accessories. Again, though quite a few of our ancient texts on the subject maintain that painting had a *divine* origin, this art has always played an important part in our *social* life. In the past, people of higher classes were required to cultivate it as a part of their education; and whether done on panels, scrolls or walls, pictures served as an important means to educate people, say, about the various episodes in Buddha's life and Brāhmanic epics. Further, the very details of a work of art may be traceable to things as used in real life on special occasions. A good instance here is the *toraṇa*[17] which is a common feature of our temple architecture. The impulse to it was provided by the popular practice of putting a stretch of leafy twigs between two posts as a mark of celebration or homage. The practice led to gateways first of wood, then of stone, such as the ones we find at Sāñchī; and finally, the cross-pieces were joined into one arch.

There is an even fuller way to see the relation of art to *reality*. Our habits and settled ways of thought are undeniably real. So they cannot be left out of "reality," for they determine our real life as clearly as our basic needs. Now, two notable habits of the traditional Indian mind have all along been a

17. As of the Mukteśvara temple, Bhuvanesvar. See Illustration no. 26 on p. 54 of Jeannine Auboyer Roger Geopper's, *The Oriental World*, London: Paul Hamlyn, 1967, p. 54.

penchant for *regulation* in every field of activity *and* the tendency to *assimilate* the many in one, as also to *diversify* the one into relative plurality. Both these habits had a clear impact on our artistic practice. "Canonical texts (*shāstra*s) set down clear aesthetic and iconographical rules, and artistes were also guided by a whole sculptural vocabulary composed of "speaking" gestures (*mudrā*s or *hasta*s)."[18] On the other hand, using his own creative imagination, the Indian artist did not hestiate to indicate the omnipresence of a god by giving him several faces; or his omnipotence, by projecting him as possessed of several pairs of arms. What is more, we find that

> the union of opposites is [freely] expressed . . . by a character being divided vertically into two halves and being given a double name. Thus *Harihara* unites Śiva and Viṣṇu and Ardhanārī represents Śiva and his female energy [Śakti].[19]

It is noteworthy that not only in the realm of painting and sculpture, but in that of ancient architecture, the influence of (the reality of) our beliefs on art is clearly visible. Temple architecutre has received great attention in India, and it is clearly linked with a spiritual conception of the universe. It in fact provides a rare instance of how a substantial part of a whole art-form can be basically *symbolic*. The temple is conceived as a microcosm, a model of the *universe*, and also as a miniature reflection of the whole world we live in. This is why sculptured representation of the major doings of everyday life is to be found in every temple. However, it is the symbolic character of the very *structure* of a temple, more than its content of direct representation, that strikes one specially. The temple's centre is the sanctuary which is the seat of the deity. This symbolizes the faith that a spiritual principle is there at the heart of the universe, controlling all that is or happens. Further, the wall that encloses the sanctuary represents the mountain ranges that tower over the earth; and the pools around the

18. Geopper's *The Oriental World*, op. cit., p. 81.
19. Ibid.

temple stand for the oceans which surround the world on all sides. Finally, the gates at the four cardinal points symbolize openings in the vault of heaven, — that is, the stars. The suggestion is that it is by fixing his gaze at the starry heavens — or, by means of commitment to lofty ideals — that man can rise up to the realm of divinity.[20]

Finally, how exactly we look at religion itself may determine the character of the structures we make. Take, for instance, our mosques *and* temples. The mosque has a quite open court for mass prayer; it is meant for the kneeling and prostration of a large number of people. They are not required to move towards any secret interior; and architecture is here simple, its essentials being a *mihrāb* (or "alcove") and a *mimhār* (or pulpit). The temple, on the other hand, is a half-lit, sombre mysterious cell before which each individual has to commune with the deity. What is more, the individual's relation to what is outside of, and greater than him is relevant not only to the appearance of completed works, but to the very process of their making. Artistes themselves are found to make such pronouncements.

> Every painting of mine is a definite social statement. I want to make that statement in as realistic and . . . direct a form as possible.[21]

It is however Marxism[22] which puts a sustained and reasoned

---

20. Geopper's *The Oriental World*, op. cit., p. 10.

21. This is an express statement of Bikash Bhattacharjee, a noted painter of today. See p. 17 of *Indian Painting Today*, 1981, Jehangir Art Gallery Publication.

22. Marxism is the economic and political theory and practice originated by Marx and Engels which holds:

    (a) that human actions and institutions are economically determined;

    (b) that the class struggle is the basic agency of historical change; and

    (c) that capitalism will be ultimately superseded by communism. Communism, we may note, is the advocacy of a classless

emphasis on the relation of art to *social* reality, and to which we may now turn.

THE MARXIST VIEW OF ART

Neither Marx nor Engels wrote any treatise on aesthetics. Their views on art and the aesthetic have to be culled from their passing remarks and occasional literary criticism. But unsystematic though they may well be, they are significant not only because of their own content, but because they may be said to provide a powerful corrective against some contemporary attempts to sever art *entirely* from life and reality. Now, both aspects of the matter — that is, what the Marxist view of art says and what it is opposed to — may be brought out by outlining the view in question in terms of the following points:

(a) Like every other cultural product, art and literature are shaped by social conditions. Of all these conditions, the economic ones — such as the means of subsistence — are most important.

(b) However, the determination of art and culture by economic conditions may not be said to be absolute. In his work: *A Contribution to the Critique of Political Economy* Marx[23] admits that

> certain periods of highest developments in art stand in no direct communication with the general development of society, or with the material basis . . . of its organization.[24]

---

society in which private property will just not be there and the means of production and subsistence will belong to the entire community, and not to some individuals.

23. Karl Marx (1818-83). German founder of modern communism, in England from 1849. With Engels, he wrote *The Communist Manifesto* in 1848. Developed his theories of class struggle and his economics of capitalism in *Das Capital* in 1861-95.

24. Cited in Melvin Rader's *A Modern Book of Esthetics*, 5th edn. New York: Holt, Rinehart and Winston, 1979, p. 484.

In this context Marx points out that Greek art, which we still value so highly, sprang out of Greek mythology, and not out of any economic conditions; and that [because] all

> mythology masters . . . and shapes the forces of nature in and through the imagination . . . it disappears as soon as man gains mastery over the forces of nature. . . . Where does . . . Jupiter . . . [come in] . . . as against the lightning rod.[25]

(c) Yet, an economic system which is fairer than the one we presently have may well be expected to be far more congenial to artistic activity and aesthetic contemplation. And it will only be in tune with Man's essential nature as *a conscious species-being,* if maximum scope is provided for the exercise of his creative faculties which distinguish him as an animal. How these faculties are distinctive is easy to see. Of course, lower animals also produce things.

> They construct nests, dwellings, as in the case of bees, beavers, ants. . . . But they only produce what is strictly necessary for themselves or their young . . . [and] only under the compulsion of direct physical needs. . . . Man [on the other hand] truly produces when he is free from physical need. . . . The needy man, burdened with cares, has no appreciation of the most beutiful spectacle. . . . [Further,] animals construct only in accordance with the standards and needs of the species to which they belong, while man knows how to produce in accordance with the standards of every species and knows how to apply the appropriate standard to the object. Thus man constructs also in accordance with the laws of beauty. . . . [Such variform production] is his active species-life.[26]

---

25. Rader's *A Modern Book of Esthetics*, op. cit. In Greek mythology Jupiter is regarded as the king and ruler of the Olympian gods. His Greek couterpart is Zeus who was believed to wield thunderbolts and to rule the heavens. A lightning rod, as we know, is a metallic rod for protecting buildings from lightning.

26. Rader's *A Modern of Book of Esthetics*, pp. 486, 488.

Today, in a society dominated by capitalism and industrialization, the masses employed in factories have no time for anything except for providing for their material needs. Their spiritual interests, such as the need for aesthetic gratification, remain utterly uncared for. In a mature communist system, on the other hand, everybody will have leisure to meet this need. There will be no specialist painters; but everybody will have time to paint, besides doing other things.

(d) Art does not merely *reflect* the actual state of society. It can also serve as a powerful social force for *the promulgation of revolutionary ideas*. Both these capacities of art, passive and dynamic, were further developed by Lenin, after Marx.

(e) After Lenin, the more vigorus exponents of Marxist dialetical materialism look upon art "*as a completely determined* form of cognition wherein the world in its actuality is reflected." Their emphasis is on thoroughgoing realism — or rather on *socialist realism* — in art. It is important to see what such realism truly is. It is not naturalism, for it does not slavishly follow nature quite without idealization. Nor is it a passive copying of life. Consider, for instance, the works of Shakespeare, Balzac, Tolstoy, Dostoyevsky and Maxim Gorky.[27] They all seek to reveal the innermost workings in the life and nature of Man, and his complex reactions to, or struggles with happenings in the outer world. It is true that they are all essays in realism; yet by no stretch of imagination can their authors be regarded as

27. Balzac, French novelist (1799–1850); Tolstoy (1828–1910), Russian novelist, short story writer and philosopher, author of two monumental novels: *War and Peace* and *Anna Karenina*. Dostoyevsky (1821-81), another Russian novelist, the psychological acuity of whose works has greatly influenced the subsequent development of the novel. *Crime and Punishment* is perhaps his best known work. Maxim Gorky, yet another versatile Russian literary artist, noted for his depiction of the outcastes of society.

mere copyists. Positively, socialist realism is an inquisitive investigation of life and man; and is therefore of great value.

> Creative investigation of the world presupposes not only exceptional sensitivity to what is going on within it, but also a determination by the artist to penetrate to the root of processes and phenomena, beneath mere appearance. It also presupposes the desire . . . to defend social progress and that which assists Man in his growth. In his book *Man as Purpose*, Alberto Moravia wrote that realism is courage . . . that the artist is a witness. "To witness means . . . to determine . . . the objective significance . . . [of things] for us."[28]

What is more, in socialist realism the artist is no mere observer of, but an active participant in social change. "He not only investigates life and recreates it in artistic images but also intervenes in life's conflicts, when he describes their causes and results and expresses his attitude towards them."

DISJOINING ART FROM LIFE AND REALITY

But if so much can be said to emphasize the relation of art to life and reality, how are we to deal with the view, such as that of Sartre, that art is a commitment to *un*reality, or with Gasset's thesis that the glory of "new" art lies precisely in an artist's ability to *de*humanize art, that is, to produce a work which, far from copying human reality, may eschew it maximally and yet have "substance of its own."[29] "Reality," Gasset warns,

---

28. Mikhail Khrapchenko, *Artistic Creativity, Reality, and Man*, Roduga Publishers (Eng. trans. 1986), p. 19.

29. José Ortega Gasset, "The Dehumanization of Art", Princeton, New Jersey: Princeton University Press, 2nd printing, 1972, p. 23. I have thought it necessary to cite the words "A substance of its own" because they say something more definite than the words "some substance" which provide the close of a big passage to be cited from the same source, a little later, as it occurs in Rader's *A Modern Book of Esthetics*, 5th edn.

"constantly waylays the artist to prevent his flight. Much cunning is needed to effect the sublime escape."[30]

Now, to turn first to Sartre, what he means by declaring that "a work of art is an unreality" is not that a WoA is a mere nothingness, but only that so long as our attention remains confined to the *actual* canvas and frame of, say, a portrait of Charles VIII, "the aesthetic object "Charles VIII" will not appear; and "that *this* Charles VIII . . . is an unreality so long as he is . . . the object of our aesthetic appreciation." Surely, *this* Charles VIII is not regarded as the agent of the various acts that are attributed to "his" real historical parallel. This negative emphasis is obviously sensible. Gasset's thesis, on the other hand, appears quite odd. Echoing the view of many *avant-garde* artists, whose techniques are markedly experimental or in advance of those that have been current so far, Gasset believes that the individual and social being of man is quite alien to art; and that everything that is related to human feeling interferes with the perception of pure form, or with *art as such*, and with *aesthetic pleasure* and *the contemplative attitude* as strictly regarded. Now, we cannot at once brush aside this radically innovative view. We have to see what it really says before we reject it, should reason so demand.

Let us first consider, in this context, the following from Ortega Gasset's widely discussed book: *The Dehumanization of Art*:

> To enjoy and suffer with human destinies, which perhaps . . . a [literary] work of art is presenting to us, is something very different from true artistic enjoyment. . . . These sympathies toward the human element in the work of art are in principle incompatible with strict aesthetic delight. . . . [Art that is increasingly "purer"] will be an art of caste, and not a democratic art. . . . [It will divide people] into two classes of individuals; those who understand it and those who do not; that is, the artists and those who are not. New art is artistic art. . . . The art of which we are talking is not only inhuman

30. Gasset, "The Dehumanization of Art", op. cit.

> because it does not contain human things, but because it actively consists of the dehumanizing operation. . . . The thing is not to paint something completely different from a man . . . but to paint a man with the least possible semblance of a man . . . which preserves of . . . [his] nature only what is strictly necessary for us to witness its metamorphosis. . . . Aesthetic pleasure for the new artist emanates from the victory over the"human"; for that reason it is necessary in each case to make concrete such victory and to show the strangled victim. . . . To be able to construct something that is not a copy of the"natural" and which nevertheless possesses some substance implies the most sublime gift.[31]

Now, to facilitate close attention to the above extract, we may explicate, as follows, the points which it makes without quite distinguishing them:

a. *New* art (we are told) is artistic art. It cares strictly for the values of art alone, and not for those of human reality, though the two kinds of values have freely gone together, traditionally. The *new* artist possesses — and reveals in his works — "the most sublime gift" of producing works which have "some [positive] substance," though they do *not* copy "the natural." It is important to see how (according to Gasset) the new artist's *art-making* is not merely negative, but positive. Such an *artist*, we are told, does not choose the easy way of, say, painting something "completely different from man," that is, of just staying away from humans. Instead, he ventures to paint a man in such a radically creative, yet controlled way (see here the word "*metamorphosis*" in the extract cited) that traces of the human in the work are kept intentionally minuscule, and are only so much evident as to serve a double purpose: first, to enable (not any one's, but) *this* artist's eye to identify that a man has been painted; and,

31. Gasset's essay, "The Dehumanizaition of Art" in Rader's *A Modern Book of Esthetics*, 5th edn., 1979, pp. 363, 365, 369.

second, to let him exult in the sense that (as an artist) he needs very little of the real man to paint a man artistically.

b. It is from this victory over, or maximal indifference to, the "human" that the new *artist's* (not anybody else's) *aesthetic pleasure emanates*. What *has been* our way of enjoying art so far is one thing; what it *should be in principle*, is quite another.

c. To the sceptical wonder, if this ideal of almost total indifference to human matters — including our joys and sources — really makes for the right attitude to art and art making, Gasset's answer may be put thus, largely in his own words which occur elsewhere in the same essay from which the extract in question has been taken:

Where the object of attention is "an illustrious man . . . dying" quite unlike his visibly concerned and grieving wife, the painter, as an artist

> merely glances sidewise at the human reality. What happens there does not worry him. His attitude is *purely contemplative* and one might even say that he does not contemplate the event in its integrity; the painful internal sense of it is left outside the field of his perception. He pays attention only to externals, to lights and shadows, to chromatic values. With . . . [such a] painter we have reached a point of maximum distance and of minimum sentimental intervention.[32]

Now, the points (about Gasset's view) that we have listed as a. b. and c. (before the extract just cited) are about three distinct matters relating to art: art making, aesthetic pleasure, and the ideal contemplative (or aesthetic) attitude to art. Let us see if these points can stand critical scrutiny:

Consider a. and c., to begin with. a. forbids us to enjoy and suffer with human destinies, say, when we read a novel or a play. c. prescribes "minimum sentimental intervention" in

32. Gasset's *The Dehumanizaition of Art*, op. cit., p. 366. Italics added.

contempleting even such situations as show people suffering and grieving. But, we may ask, even without actually rejoicing and sorrowing concurrently with changes in the fortunes of characters, cannot and should not the sympathetic reader of a tragedy yet follow the vicissitudes in question closely? If he does not do so, how will he realize, as Aristotle would expect him to, that the misfortune which has befallen an exalted personage, say, King Lear — is a bit too heavy for a simple human failing, that is, credulousness arising from love of self and sycophancy? And if our reader is required to abstain from taking cognitive note of the intense chagrin and anger behind the ravings of King Lear in the *Heath Scene* (Act III, Sc. II) is he (the reader) supposed to take them as "mere sound and fury, signifying nothing?" As Gasset visualizes, *a painter* may well be able to make do with the merely chromatic values of a scene which is painful in reality. But what about *the reader of a play* we have picked for attention? Is he to make do with such merely formal features of the play as consistency of characterzation, adroit inter-knitting of the main and subsidiary plots, and the relief which the Fool's seemingly light-hearted speeches appear to provide to the overall dramatic situation, highlighting its sombreness? Even if we answer this question affirmatively it would not lend any weight to Gasset's view, for the formal features we have distinguished cannot themselves be comprehended without a notice of the human elements. What indeed is consistency of characterization, if not the predictable quality of a *man's* behaviour in different situations? And what is a dramatic plot if not an interlacement of events with *human* attitudes and actions? Nor can the run of a plot appear plausible to the reader in a kind of philosophical vacuum. While reading a play the very feeling that a *present* state of affairs is an index of things to come is grounded in our everyday habit of anticipating the future in the light of what is presently before us. Similarly, the overall feel of a play — that is, whether it strikes us as a serious tragedy or as a light-hearted "comedy of errors" — cannot be sensed except in the light of analogous affective experiences in life.

However, the point that it is in fact impossible to leave out human realities while reading a play is not the only important objection to Gasset's view. A much more serious matter, by common consent, is that if we are expected to follow, in imagination, the turns and twists in the hero's lot in an attitude of perfect detachment, that is, without *at all* feeling for him, our hearts will not be enlisted, and the impact of the play on us will be merely cognitive. The chastening or inspiring aspect of great literature will be totally missed; and the Marxist would at once object to this truncated view of the role of art and literature in life.

It may of course be said by some artists, as indeed it has been by Albert Camus, that "we *as artists* do not have any need to interfere in the business of the world, . . . [however] *as people we* should." But does it make sense to suggest that in influencing the world around him, the artist should not avail of that very tool which he is most adept in handling, that is, the art to which he is committed and in the practice of which he is known to specialize?

What is more, as Lenin has rightly argued, an artist just cannot isolate himself from the world completely:

> One cannot live in society and [yet] be free from society. Are you free in relation to your bourgeois publisher, Mr. Writer, in relation to your bourgeois public, which demands that you provide it with pornography in frames and paintings? This absolute freedom is . . . an anarchist phrase.[33]

Romain Rolland has put the same point positively:

> Our work should strike root in the fertile soil of our present-day action and be nurtured on the content of the people of today, their passions, struggles and impulses.[34]

---

33. V.I. Lenin, *Collected Works*, vol. X, p. 48.

34. Cited by Mikhal Khrapchenko in his book: *Artistic Creativity, Reality and Man*, p. 28.

The *avantgardists* often claim that when they isolate themselves from everything that is temporary and transitory, they restore the real essence of art. But is a departure from the communicative function of art really warranted by the evidence of fact? Can theatre live without an audience *which obviously keeps changing*? Is the art of cinema merely a creative monologue? Lenin saw it clearly that a very important feature of socialist literature is its close links with the general public; and that

> The new literature will serve . . . not the bored "upper ten thousand" suffering from fatty degeneration, but the . . . tens of millions of working people — the flower of the country, its strength and its future."[35]

Gasset, we have seen, insists that the *new* or pure art "will be an art of caste, and not a democratic art." It is indeed contended by *avantgarde* artists generally that all such art works as appeal to the masses, just because they are easy to appreciate, cannot but be deficient in aesthetic value. But this is just not true. A work may be difficult to follow, but it may yet succeed in inducing large numbers to pay close attention to, and so to follow it, just because it gives eloquent expression to the problems and aspirations of people at large. Balzac, Zola, Dickens and Tolstoy are by no means puny writers; and what their writings cover of life and reality is pretty large in extent. Yet their works have in fact been very widely read.

35. Lenin, *Collected Works*, vol. X, pp. 48, 49.

5
Theories of Art

ART AS IMITATION

Of all the theories of art the imitation theory is the oldest. It may also be said to have enjoyed a pretty long spell of influence. In the form given to it by Plato, Aristotle and Plotinus, it was widely accepted in the Middle Ages. It was only after the Renaissance that it began to lose its dominance. The Romantic period attached very great importance to spontaneity, originality and self-expression in art; and so it often preferred the word *representation*. Presenting again, with some inevitable differences of manner and medium, is surely not the same thing as mere *imitation*. The theory that imitation is the essence of art is commonly associated with the names of Plato and Aristotle. Before, however, we set out to see if they really favour *imitation* in any literal sense, we may address some critical questions about it.

(a) Is it possible to imitate anything *in its entirety*, and *exactly as it is*, that is, quite objectively, without any imposition from our side?

(b) And would it be reasonable to reverse, as Oscar Wilde seeks to do, the basic emphasis of the theory in question? In other words, can we accept his ingenious thesis that Life and Nature imitate Art much more than the extent of their copying by Art?

Now, the first part of the first question may be ascribed to Nelson Goodman. See, in this context, his following words:

"To make a faithful picture, come as close as possible to

> copying the subject just as it is." This simple-minded injunction baffles me; for the object before me [let us say] is a man, a swarm of atoms, as complex of cells, a fiddler, a friend, a fool and much more. . . . [Surely] I cannot copy all these at once . . ..[1]

So, concludes Goodman, what one can copy is only "one of things the object is, or looks."[2] But which particular aspect of the subject is chosen for attention would surely depend on the onlooker's individual interest. This is the point in Emile Zola's remark that a work of art is but "a corner of nature seen through a temperament."[3] Gombrich amplifies the point as follows:

> The artist . . . can render only what his tool and medium are capable of rendering. His technique restricts his freedom of choice. The features and relationships the pencil picks out will differ from those the brush can indicate. Sitting in front of his motif, pencil in hand, the artist will, therefore, look out for those aspects which can be rendered in lines . . . while brush in hand, he sees . . . [the motif] in terms of masses.[4]

What is more, even eminent artistes have often faltered in respect of representational accuracy:

> A German ophthamologist who studied the eyes of Durer's portraits, which appear to the layman triumphs of painstaking accuracy, reports . . . such mistakes as representing [horses with] eye-lashes on the lower lid, a feature which belongs to the human eye, but not to that of the horse . . . [and even] the greatest of visual explorers, Leonardo himself, has made mistakes in his anatomical drawings.[5]

---

1. Nelson Goodman, *Languages of Art*, Indianapolis, Cambridge, Hackett Publishing Co., Inc. 4th printing, 1981, p. 6.
2. Ibid., p. 7.
3. E.H. Gombrich's essay, "Truth and the Stereotype" in Rader's *A Modern Book of Esthetics*, 5th edn. p. 33.
4. Ibid., p. 34.
5. Ibid., p. 42.

So, an absolutely faithful copying of all that an object is or appears to be on the outside cannot be said to be the basic emphasis of the imitation theory. This truth will be borne out further as we turn to the theory's main advocates.

In respect of the second question we may quickly list the main points that Oscar Wilde makes in support of his view, and also put our own critical reaction immediately after each individual point:

> (a) . . . The basis of life . . . is *simply* the desire for expression. . . . Art is always presenting various forms through which the expression can be attained. Life seizes on them and uses them, even if they be to her own hurt. Young men have committed suicide because Rolla did so, have died by their own hand because by his own hand Werther died. . . . [Hence the principle:] Life imitates Art far more than Art imitates Life.[6]

Now, it is easy to find reasons for disagreeing with what the extract cited says:

First, the basis of life is not "simply" (or only) the desire for expression. Far more essential for life is what has been called the instinct of self-preservation. Even a deaf and dumb person to whom the normal ways of expression are denied may resort to some self-defence the moment he is attacked physically.

Secondly, if (as Oscar Wilde himself insists) the desire for expression is intrinsic to human life, and if — as is unquestionally true — Art is created by Man, are we not logically driven to say that the various forms provided by Art, of which Oscar Wilde makes a pointed mention, are important channels through which Man expresses himelf? To say *yes* to this question would only be to acknowledge a patent fact. But if art arises or results from a basic impulse *of life,* it must be said to *follow* life; and so the latter (or life) cannot be said to imitate art; for, as is quite obvious, whatever is imitated must *precede* the act of imitation.

6. Oscar Wilde's essay, "Nature's Imitation of Life" in Rader's *A Modern Book of Esthetics*, p. 27.

One may of course here protest that this kind of arguing is merely general. We should not indeed ignore the specific instances that Oscar Wilde cites of those who have actually ended their lives *in imitation of literary characters*. Even in this day and age teenage boys, obsessed with the body image of a superstar of the film world, are known to have developed anorexia nervosa in their effort to become thin.[7] But such cases, we rejoin, are greatly outnumbered by those typical characters in literature who are *not* known to have served as role models for people in real life. We may well *find* many persons who are "sick of self-love," or who tend to oscillate between giving in to, or wrestling with, life's overwhelming odds, but they cannot be said to be *imitating* such Shakespearean characters as Malvolio and Hamlet.

(b) Nature too may be said to imitate Art.

> She is our creation. . . . Things are because we see them, and what we see, and how we see it, depends on the Arts that have influenced us. . . . At present [in London] people see [the beauty of] fogs, not because there are fogs, but because poets and painters have taught them the mysterious loveliness of such effects.[8]

Now, this again is a clear failure to go to the root of the matter. It may well be that quite a few people have become a little more prompt in noticing the beauty of a *rainbow* after reading Wordworth's ecstatic poem on this showpiece, so to say, of Nature's charms. But what are we to say about Wordsworth *himself*? Did *he* register the beauty of the wondrous spectacle *after* reading some poem or seeing some picture? With him, as

---

7. The reference here is to a report that appeared in *The Times of India* of 3.6.2002. It quoted a finding by Dr. Savita Malhotra, Head of Psychiatry at PGI, Chandigarh, that two ten-year-old boys, both obsessed with the body image of Hrithik Roshan, developed *anorexia nervosa* because they tried to starve themselves for the sake of losing weight.

8. Oscar Wilde's essay, p. 28.

he himself says in the poem, the enrapt reaction has been his way since the very dawn of his life. Indeed, does not every child's heart leap upon beholding "a rainbow in the sky," well before it has developed interest in the arts?

PLATO AND ARISTOTLE

The thesis that imitation is the *essence* of art is commonly associated with the names of Plato and Aristotle. Today, however, this view cannot be accepted without qualification, because of the following arguments advanced by scholars like R.C. Lodge, Herbert Read, and C.J. Ducasse, especially with reference to Plato.

There is no doubt that Plato admits the presence and popularity of imitative art in his day. In the tenth book of Republic he says:

> A painter will paint a cobbler, carpenter, or any other artist, though he knows nothing of their arts; and if he be a good artist, he may deceive children or simple persons, when he shows them his picture of a carpenter from distance, and they will fancy that they are looking at a real carpenter.[9]

But the "artists" of whom Plato here speaks seem pretty similar to what today we would prefer to describe "vaudeville entertainers."[10] Their sole gift, as he depicts them, is cleverness in imitation. Of such an imitator Plato says:

> He will be ready to imitate anything, not as a joke, but in right good earnest, and before a large audience . . . he will attempt to represent the roll of thunder, the rattle of wind and hail, or the various sounds of pulleys . . . of flutes . . . ; also he will bark like a dog . . ..[11]

9. Jowett's translation pp. 288-29,.
10. C.J. Ducasse, *The Philosophy of Art*, New York: Dover Publication, Inc, 1966, pp. 72-3.
11. Ibid., p. 74.

Now, the skilfulness of such "artists" is not to be denied. Plato in fact acclaims such an imitator openly, "as a sweet and . . . wonderful being"; but, in the same breath, he refuses to accommodate such an "artist" in his state.[12] Positively, he says:

> . . . We mean to employ for our soul's health the rougher and severer poet . . . who will imitate the styles of the virtuous only.

Now, if all this be taken along with Plato's unqualified praise for what may be called "inspired" art, he cannot be said to hold that, as it is commonly understood, imitation is the essence of art. "Inspired" art, he believes, proceeds from a vision of the pure celestial forms of Beauty, Goodness, Truth and the like; and such a vision, we are told, is given only to that soul which occupies the highest of the nine levels to which human souls can possibly belong "according to the measure of truth they have seen before birth."[13] . . . Only such art, Plato adds, can be said to arise truly from the mimetic *impulse.* The mere imitator does not act in obedience to any *inner impulsion;* he imitates only "for the sake of applause, or perhaps of gain."[14]

What is more, those who ascribe to Plato the view that imitation is the *essence* of art ignore another vital fact. In Philebus, on an explicit request from Plato to clarify a view which he holds but is not himself able to put properly, Socrates explains, as follows, what he means by those pleasures "which arise from the colours we call beautiful and from shapes . . . true pleasures [which] arise from all those things the want of what is not felt as painful but the satisfaction from which is consciously pleasant and unconditioned by pain":[15]

> Well, I mean such sounds as are pure and smooth and yield a single pure tone . . . [and so] are not beautiful relatively to

---

12. Republic Bk. III, p. 221.
13. Ducasse, *The Philosophy of Art,* p. 74.
14. Ibid.
15. Philebus, 51B.

> anything but in their proper nature, and produce their proper pleasures.[16]

This is, as Herbert Read points out,

> a definite abandonment of the theory of mimesis [as commonly understood] or of art conceived as a technique for the direct imitation of the appearance of things . . ..[17]

Further, Plato clearly admits a distinction between representational and *non-representational art*. For him, the highest kind of "mimesis" is to imitate the Good by living in accordance with it, and such "imitation," it is obvious, is a matter of self-discipline, and no mere representation as ordinarily understood. Aristotle too, in respect of poetry, like Joshua Reynolds with regard to the art of painting,[18] propounds the ideal of representing the individual *as a type*.

Of Aristotle, however, we have to speak at some length, specially with reference to his view of tragedy and his concept of *Katharsis* which have long engaged the minds not only of philosophers of art but of literary theorists too.

ARISTOTLE ON TRAGEDY

What is more, it is by reflecting on his theory of tragedy that we can clearly see how Aristotle differs from Plato in respect of the concept of mimesis or imitation. The definition runs thus:

> Tragedy is *imitation* of an *action* that is *serious, complete, and of a certain magnitude;* in language embellished with each kind of *artistic ornament,* the several kinds being found in separate parts of the play; in the form of action, not of narrative; through

16. From *Philebus,* as translated by E.F. Carritt in his *Philosophies of Beauty*, Oxford, 1931, pp. 29-30.

17. Herbert Read, *Art Now,* London: Faber and Faber, 1960, p. 73.

18. The famous English portrait painter (1723-92). He was the first President of the Royal Acdemy (1768). The annual lectures he gaves there, published as Discourses, are important contributions to art theory and criticism.

> *pity and terror* effecting the proper *katharsis* or purgation, of these emotions.[19]

The key concepts in this definition (all put in italics) may now be treated at some length. To begin with *imitation*, Aristotle believes that it is both a necessary and pleasant activity. The instinct of imitation is implanted in man from childhood. Man is indeed the most imitative of all living creatures. Further, when we find that a copy is quite similar to the object it imitates, we look at it steadfastly, identify it definitely, and also feel happy at the versimilitude.[20]

But, as an *aesthetic* concept, imitation is not a literal transcript of the world of reality.[21] In Book XXV of his *Poetics* Aristotle openly concedes that the artist may imitate things *as they ought to be*.[22] Even apart from this we could say, in the light of his full definition of tragedy, that if the imitation of an action is to be done in "language embellished with" artistic ornament, it cannot be regarded as a literal copy of reality as it is, that is, in its naked character. Further, the fact that for Aristotle imitation is no mere superficial copying of the given is also borne out by his conception of the true *objects* of imitation in art. These objects are distinctly three: first, the characteristic moral qualities, the permanent dispositions of the mind, which reveal certain disposition of the will . . . [; secondly,] the more transient emotions, the passing moods of feeling . . . [; and thirdly,] actions in their proper . . . inward sense. So imitation in art cannot be said to relate only to the outside of things. Aristotle is indeed emphatic on this point:

> An act viewed merely as an external process or result, one of a series of outward phenomena, is not the true object of aesthetic imitation. . . . [What] art seeks to reproduce is mainly

---

19. S.H. Butcher's tr. of *Aristotle's Theory of Poetry and Fine Art*, with a new Introduction by John Gasser, New York: Dover Publications, Inc., 4th edn., 1951, p. 240.
20. Ibid., p. 15.
21. Ibid., p. 122.
22. Ibid.

> an inward process; deeds . . . events . . . situations, being included under it [only in] so far as these spring from an inward act of will, or elicit some activity of thought or feeling.[23]

Only that which reveals a rational personality is for Aristotle the object of aesthetic imitation. This is why he does not regard landscapes and animals as proper objects of mimesis.[24] At the same time he would like to add that though it is not a literal or superficial imitation of anything, a work of art has to be identifiably and quite naturally faithful to the original, so that we may not have to probe as to what it is about:

> A work of art is a likeness . . . or reproduction of an original and *not a symbolic* representation of it.[25]

Between a symbol and what it symbolizes — say, between *spoken words and mental states* — the connection is only conventional, not natural. No word in any way *resembles* what it signifies. On the other hand, *mental impressions* are virtual copies of external reality; and it is these impressions which a work of art seeks to capture. In other words, "art does not attempt to embody the objective or original reality of things, but only their sensible appearances."[26] To be sure, a portrait does not capture a man in flesh and blood. If it is yet taken to be the picture of a real person, a measure of make-believe or illusoriness must be said to be clearly involved. Further, when a work of art represents something in actual reality, the object is relieved of its practical relations with our everyday needs; and our interest in it (as represented) becomes aesthetic.[27]

In actual life, because we need them, things interest us only so far as they remain usable. No such constraint is there when

23. S.H. Butcher's tr., op. cit., p. 123.
24. Ibid., pp. 123-24.
25. Ibid., p. 124. Emphasis added.
26. Ibid., p. 127.
27. Ibid., p. 128.

we contemplate art; and so the delight here is in this sense free. Yet, Aristotle insists, all works of art have [some identifiable] reference to a world independently known. It is noteworthy that this basic thesis of Aristotle covers even music and dance. Music, he believes, is the most imitative or representative of the arts . . . [It is] a copy of character.[28]

> In rhythms and melodies we have the most realistic imitations of anger and mildness as well as of courage, temperance and all their opposites . . . and in reflecting . . . [all this, music] moulds and influences [character].[29]

Dancing too "is [held to be] descriptive of every shade of character and emotion."[30] But, one may ask, what shall we say of poetry? Does it not use words, and are they not symbols? To questions such as these Aristotle's answer is that, if only for a particular culture or country, the words which poetry avails of *relate to real life quite clearly*. They are the natural and familiar medium by which thought and feeling are revealed.[31] They are images of things, situations, and experiences of real life. They are not purely symbolical, but partly representational as well. So, even though it uses verbal symbols which have to be interpreted by the mind, poetry is no exception to Aristotle's principal thesis that all fine art is representational in character.[32]

What is more, poetry (according to Aristotle) is imitative art of the highest kind, because "it is an expression of the universal element in human life."[33] Life is everywhere governed by design or purpose. This design is a co-ordinated working of the several parts "for the good of the whole."[34] The actual

---

28. S.H. Butcher's tr., op. cit., p. 129.
29. Ibid., pp. 129-30.
30. Ibid., p. 137.
31. Ibid., p. 138.
32. Ibid.
33. Ibid., p. 150.
34. Ibid., p. 152.

working of this design is, however, often hampered by some specific, accidental, and extraneous factors; and it is in this context that the value of art becomes apparent.

> Fine art [and, above all, poetry] eliminates . . . [these obstacles] and reveals the permanent and essential features of the original. . . . It discovers the form . . . towards which an object tends, the result which nature strives to attain, but rarely or never can attain. Beneath the individual it finds the universal. It passes beyond the bare reality given by nature, and expresses a purified form of reality disengaged from accident, and freed from conditions which thwart its development. The real and the ideal from this point of view are not opposites. . . . The ideal is the real, but rid of contradictions, unfolding itself according to the laws of its own being, apart from alien influences and the disturbances of chance.[35]

All life, we are told, moves towards an improving co-ordination of the parts for the good of the whole; and, taking this cue from life and reality,

> the artist in his mimic world carries forward this movement to *a more perfect completion*. . . . He too aims at something better than the actual. He produces a new thing, not the actual thing of experience, not a copy of reality, but a . . . higher reality. . . . Art, therefore, in imitating the universal imitates the ideal; and we can . . . describe *a work of art as an idealized representation* [and so no mere imitation] *of human life — of character, emotion, action — under forms manifest to sense.*[36]

But the *relation* between the real (as given) and the ideal (or the abiding, and so truly real) is conceived very differently by Aristotle and Plato. Reality, as *we find or experience it*, is a mass of phenomena or happenings and appearances, all in a state of flux, so to say. Science, on the other hand, seeks to discover laws that determine and abide through phenomenal changes in the region of plant and animal life, and also in physical reality.

35. S.H. Butcher's tr., op. cit., pp. 150-51.

36. Ibid., pp. 152-53.

Thought too cannot do with the merely particular. It needs concepts; and morality also needs some regulative *principles* of conduct. All these laws, concepts and principles are posited to *be* there and to abide, though they may not be directly manifest, and though we overselves may have to suffer changes in order to avail of them. How are these ideal realities related to the phenomenal world? Plato, who speaks of the abiding, non-sensuous realities as Ideas, believes that the relation is but tenuous, and that the contents of the world are at best a vague and fleeting reflection of the world of Ideas. This is why he thinks of *that* art which represents our everyday concerns as but an image of what is itself a shadow, so to say, of the world of Ideas, and therefore as two steps away from Truth.

> The poet or painter holds up a mirror to material objects — earth, plants, animal, mankind — and catches a reflection of the world around him, which is itself only the reflection of the ideal. [So] fine art is a copy of a copy, twice removed from truth. . . . A painter may paint a table very admirably without knowing anything of the inner construction of a table, a knowledge which the carpenter, who would fashion it for its proper end, must possess. And poets too, whose ideas of men are formed on a limited experience, cannot pass beyond the range of that experience; they have no insight into the nature of man, into the human soul as it is in itself; this can be had only by philosophic study.[37]

Of Aristotle's thought, on the other hand, the focus is on Becoming, not on Being. To him Becoming is not a fleeting shadow, but the unfoldment of what is already there in the germ, an actualization of what is potentially present in things and happenings. Butcher puts the point quite clearly as follows:

> [For Aristotle] the concrete individual is not a shadowy appearance but the primary reality. The outward and material world, the diverse manifestations of nature's life, organic and inorganic, the processes of birth and decay, the manifold forms of sensuous beauty, all gained a new importance for

37. S.H. Butcher, op. cit., pp. 159-60.

> his philosophy. Physical science, slighted by Plato, was passionately studied by Aristotle.[38]

Therefore, for Aristotle, fine art is "no longer twice removed from the truth of things"; but is

> the manifestation of a higher truth, the expression of the universal which is not outside of and apart from the particular, but [is] presupposed in each particular. The work of art was not a semblance opposed to reality, but the image of a [given] reality which is penetrated by the Idea [or the higher Reality, the universal] and through which the Idea becomes more apparent than in the actual world. Whereas Plato had laid it down that "the greatest and fairest things are done by nature, and the lesser by art, which receives from nature all the greater and primeval creations and fashions them in detail,[39] Aristotle saw in fine art a rational faculty which divines nature's unfulfilled intentions, and reveals her ideal to sense. The illusions which fine art employs do not cheat the mind; they image forth the immanent idea which cannot find adequate expression under the forms of material existence.[40]

Consider, for instance, a truth which is often glibly talked about and accepted as obvious, though in actual life we may not generally see it clearly and convincingly verified, say, the truth that the arrogance of status, love of sycophancy — and the consequent inability to correctly judge how far one's near relatives are credible — can make for painful results. Is it anywhere more clearly borne out, and more indelibly impressed upon our minds, than by a close reading of Shakespeare's *King Lear*, which is admittedly a great tragedy? And does the dramatic presentation of the King at all delude us into the belief that such an individual, with three daughters of uneven truthfulness, ever lived in fact? Surely not. The impression we are left with is only that of a truth which in life

---

38. S.H. Butcher, op. cit., p. 160.
39. Plato, *Laws:* X. 889A; Jowett's translation.
40. Butcher's tr. pp. 160-61.

we see but fitfully, and not of a fable of doubtful credibility.

But however important it be, a single character does not make a whole tragedy. A tragedy, we are told, is the imitation of action that is richly qualified, say, as follows. First, this action is serious, complete, and of a certain magnitude; and, secondly the language in which it is represented is embellished with "each kind of artistic ornament." Here, again, *King Lear* is a good illustration. The play's completeness is obvious, for it has a clear beginning and an equally definite end. What is more, the two are in a way opposed to each other, and so gain in distinctness by virtue of contrast. The opening is provided by a subject of moment, that is, "the division of the Kingdom" which is being actively contemplated by the King and looked forward to by others; and the end, by a situation of "general woe" and an attitude of resignation following some deaths, including that of the King himself:

> The weight of this sad time we must obey,
> . . . The oldest hath borne most; we that are young
> Shall never see so much nor live so long.[41]

Nor is the play's *magnitude* any less manifest. It comprises five distinct Acts, and no Act contains less than three Scenes. As for the actions' seriousness, it is manifest in such grave matters as the king's intense and shattering unhappiness not only at being let down by those daughters who first profess to love him deeply, but at the death of his dear Fool which he bemoans expressly and which makes him quite distraught:

> And my poor fool is hang'd! No, no, no, life!
> Why should a dog, a horse, a rat have life,
> And thou no breath at all? Thou'lt come no more,
> Never, never, never, never, never![42]

Here, the jerky run of the last line itself indicates intense despair; and the final feeling effected by the play is indeed one of

---

41. Shakespeare's *King Lear*, Act V, Sc. III. These are in fact the closing lines of the play.

42. Shakespeare's *King Lear*, a little before the closing lines.

"solemnity and awe."[43]

The artistic "ornaments" which Aristotle deems essential for the language of a tragedy are metre (and rhythm which relates as much to words and sounds as to bodily movements and melody). Yet, though he admits their importance, Aristotle assigns to these ornaments only "a subordinate rank." The essence of poetry, he believes, is just *imitation*; "the melody and verse are [but] the seasoning of the language."[44]

In dramatic poetry indeed imitation is evident *even* in its rudimentary form;

> speech has its counterpart in speech, and, if the play is put on the stage, action is rendered by action . . . acting or recitation . . . [all this here produces] an impression allied to that of mimicry.[45]

This is however but the surface of what imitation here really is. According to Aristotle, imitation is essentially

> a creative act. It is the expression of the concrete thing under an image which answers to its true idea. To seize the universal, and to reproduce it in simple and sensuous form is not to reflect a reality already familiar through sense perceptions; rather it is a rivalry of nature, a completion of her unfulfilled purposes, a correction of her failures.[46]

As for the "ornaments" that Aristotle speaks of, rhythm is present in the play we have referred to, *King Lear*, even in the form of *repetition* — of impassioned invectives and curses, say, against Goneril or ingratitude generally, or as King's intense grieving at his own unhappy lot. Thus, see the following:

(a) Hear, nature, hear! dear goddess, hear.
Suspend thy purpose if you did'st intend

---

43. Butcher's tr., p. 271.

44. Ibid., p. 146.

45. Ibid., p. 138.

46. Ibid., p. 154.

To make this creature fruitful!
Into her womb convey sterility!
Dry up in her the organs of increase;
. . . If she must teem,
Create her child of spleen, that it may live
And be a thwart disnatur'd torment to her!
Let it stamp wrinkles in her brow of youth . . .;[47]

(b) Blow, winds, and crack your cheeks! Rage, blow
You cataracts and hurricanes, spout
Till you have drench'd our steeples, drown'd the cocks!
Vaunt – couriers of oak – cleaving thunderbolts,
Singe my white head; and thou, all-shaking thunder,
Strike flat the thick rotundity o'th' world!
Crack nature's moulds, all germens spill at once,
That make ungrateful man![48]

Such exaltation of sheer passion, even if it does not aim at any noble purpose, serves two clear ends. It obviously puts an edge on our sense of the seriousness of the king's disconsolateness, and evokes in us a feeling of pity for the sufferer. But how the impact of the play is a *Katharsis* or purgation of our pity and fear has to be brought out at some length.

Pity and fear are two basic emotions in the life of Man. They may be said to be related, respectively, to the instincts of protective love and self-preservation. To put the matter simply, provided our basic nature has not been made insensitive by some extraneous factors, we all have a natural tendency to feel moved by, and to give some relief, if possible, to any one who is suffering, weak, or helpless, but not disgustingly evil; and also to fear and somehow get rid of whatever poses a threat to our life and security. Like the impulses to know a little better of whatever is new and striking, and to generally relish the company of fellow-beings, which go naturally with the instincts of curiosity and gregariousness, the impulses to sympathize with and feel for others also need exercise in ways that may

47. *King Lear*, Act I, Sc. IV.

48. Ibid., Act III, Sc. II.

give us some relief. Aristotle realized this, whereas Plato perhaps did not. It is true that as incidental to his attack on drama, Plato said that "the natural hunger after sorrow and weeping which is kept in check in moments of our own suffering, is satisfied and delighted by the poets." But in the same Dialogue — that is, Republic — he also speaks thus:

> . . . Through its tearful moods . . . [poetry] enfeebles the man by temper; . . . makes anarchy in the soul by exalting the lower elements over the higher, and by dethroning reason in favour of feeling.[49]

Aristotle, on the other hand, holds that

> it is not desirable to kill or starve the emotional part of the soul, and that the regulated indulgence of the feelings serves to maintain the balance of our nature. Tragedy . . . is a vent for the particular emotions of pity and fear. In the first instance, it is true, its effect is not to tranquillize but to excite. . . . [But] it excites emotion . . . only to allay it . . . [Tragedy] . . . at least . . . [expels] *such elements in* . . . [*our real life experience of pity and fear*] *as are disquieting.*[50]

What these disquieting elements could be is easy to see. In actual life whenever we feel moved to relieve a man's suffering, the lack of requisite means at our disposal or the sufferer's own exaggerated sense of self-respect may bar the way, and so leave us dissatisfied at our inability to provide actual relief. Similarly, where we are not able to find a way out of a threatening situation — say, of being blackmailed by an evil person who possesses some such secret of ours as cannot be divulged without disastrous consequences to us — we continue to feel unhappy and afraid because of the threat of exposure. But here, in the case of contemplating a tragedy (like *King Lear*), we are not faced by any actual threat to our own security; and so the fear that we here experience is only a kind of apprehensiveness for the aged King's lot, say, when we come

49. Butcher's tr., p. 246.

50. Ibid.

to read of a drastic reduction of his normal comforts and facilities. Similarly, the pity that we feel for him — especially where he himself bemoans his fallen state and finds himself pathetically at the mercy of his daughter, Goneril — relates only to a situation as imagined; it does not involve any impulse to provide relief to any actual sufferer; and so there is no question here of our feeling unhappy because of our inability to provide effective relief.

Therefore, the experience of pity and fear in contemplating a tragedy does not make us feel as unsettled as it easily can in a real life situation. On the other hand, when we have completed the act of reading or witnessing the play, we experience a kind of pleasureable relief, just because two basic impulses of our nature have been given a chance to come into play, if refinedly. It is, in this context, helpful to note that even after a bout of violent anger, caused (it may be) as a natural reaction against as undeserved infliction, one feels *directly* relieved, though the extremity of reaction may be rued on *subsequent* thought. But even apart from this, the suggestion that the emotions of pity and fear are allayed into a felt quietude by first being excited[51] is supported by an everyday experience which Plato has emphasized in the context of the useful art of nursing. A restless infant is generally lulled into sleep by the agitation of external swaying.[52] In other words, tragedy is a form of homoeopathic treatment, curing emotion by means of an emotion like in kind, *but not identical.*[53] Here, two distinct points have to be noted with care:

(a) First, "the feelings called forth by the tragic spectacle are not indeed permanently removed, but are quieted for the time [being], so that the system can fall back upon its normal course."[54]

---

51. Butcher's tr., op. cit., p. 246.

52. Ibid., p. 250.

53. Ibid., p. 248.

54. Butcher, op. cit., p. 245.

(b) Secondly, the emotions of pity and fear are here *purified* in the sense that, instead of being felt as a part of the contemplator's own personal life, they here appear integral to "the picture of human destiny in all its significance,"[55] and so utterly free from the disquiet or sense of being ill at ease with the world which accompanies their experience in real life.

So *Katharsis* as brought about by our contemplation of tragic play is no mere discharge of the pent up emotions of fear and pity, but is their aesthetic refinement. This is what Butcher means by the following:

> As the tragic action progresses, when the tumult of the mind, first roused, has afterwards subsided, the lower forms of emotion are found to have been transmuted into higher and more refined forms. The painful element in the pity and fear of reality is purged away; the emotions themselves are purged. . . . Tragedy . . . does more than effect the homoeopathic cure of certain passions. . . . Its function is not merely to provide an outlet for pity and fear, but to provide for them a distinctively aesthetic satisfaction, to purify and clarify them by passing them through the medium of art.[56]

How it makes sense to *couple* pity with fear is easy to see.

> Pity . . . turns into fear where the object is so nearly related to us that the suffering seems to be our own. We pity others where under like circumstances we should fear for ourselves.[57]

ART AS FORM

In spite of its association with Plato and Aristotle, however, the imitation theory of art has hardly any supporter today; and opposition to it comes to it largely from those who regard *form* as the key source of artistic value. But what exactly do we

55. Butcher's tr., p. 241.

56. Ibid., pp. 254-55.

57. Ibid., p. 256.

mean by form in art? A basic aesthetic meaning of it — that is, a meaning which seems to be relevant to all art — has already been proposed and explained earlier. But *form* has been interpreted in other ways as well. Further, as related to our earlier account of *form* there are some other concepts too, such as that of organic unity, of which we have taken no note so far. So some detailed attention may now be given to the theory of art as form.

Clive Bell puts forth the view that "*significant form* is the only thing that is common and peculiar to all the work of *visual art*. . . ."[58] What he means by form so regarded may be put in his own words:

> . . . Lines and colors combined in . . . [such a] way . . . certain forms and relations of form [so put together that they may] stir our aesthetic emotions . . . [this is what] I call "Significant Form."[59]

If it be asked why he does not regard *beauty* as the essence of all art, Bell's ready answer would be:

> Every one sometimes uses "beauty" in an unaesthetic sense, . . . in the minds of many the sexual flavour of the word is stronger than the aesthetic . . ..[60]

And to the possible protest that, insofar as he has painting especially in mind when he formulates his history of art, Bell is not justified in speaking only of form, and "*not of colour*" as well, his rejoinder is explicit:

> The *distinction* between form and colour is an unreal one; you cannot *conceive* a colourless line or a colourless space; neither can you conceive a formless relation of colours.[61]

---

58. Bell's essay, "Significant Form" in *Introductory Readings in Aesthetics*, edited by John Hospers, The Free Press and Collier Macmillan Publishers, 1969, pp. 88-89. Italics added.

59. Ibid., pp. 89-90.

60. Ibid., p. 89.

61. Ibid., p. 91.

Here, however, one can fairly complain of an ambiguity. The word *conceive* is commonly taken to mean, to think or *to imagine.* Now it is surely impossible to *imagine* a line without colour, or space without colour. But a *distinction* is only the state of being different *to thought*; and when we merely *think* of form — say, as the unity of diverse elements — we just omit colour. Taken as such, the form-colour *distinction* is by no means unreal. We can make it even if we take *distinction* in the sense of being *noticeably* different. Who finds it difficult to *see* the difference between the form and the colour of an orange? To distinguish is one thing; to separate, quite another. But even apart from this verbal challenge, Bell's theory is unsatisfactory, because it is admittedly confined to visual art, and so cannot be said to provide the essential (or basic aesthetic) meaning of *form.*

What is more, if in accordance with current trends in the field of art appreciation, we decide to look at cultures other than those that dominate the West, Bell's theory would appear inadequate even in respect of the purely formal elements that he focusses on. As explained in *Vāstusūtra Upaniṣad* (*VSU*) attributed to the Paippalāda Kalpa of the *Atharvaveda,* in the case of image-making, the basic geometrical diagram is called *pañjara,* "cage" or "skeleton," and it consists of [not only] lines, [but] points, circles, squares, triangles and diagonals.[62] Now, a point is not a line. Nor is a circle identical with a line. A single line can of course be used to produce a full circle, but whereas a line as such merely runs through or divides space, a circle appears to *encompass* space. Further, every circle must have a centre. In respect of a line, on the other hand, we are not bound to think of its middle point. Above all, the following insistence of Bell, which issues from his keenness to emphasize the value of form, is clearly a bit too categorical:

> If a representative form has value, it is as form, not as representation. The representative element in a work of art may or may not be harmful; always it is irrelevant. For, *to*

62. Boner-Sarma-Baumer, *Vāstusūtra Upaniṣad: The Essence of Form in Sacred Art,* Delhi: Motilal Banarsidass, 4th rev. edn., 2000, p. xi.

> *appreciate a work of art we need bring with us nothing from life, no knowledge of its ideas and affairs,* no familiarity with its emotions. Art transports us from the world of man's activity to a world of aesthetic exaltation. For a moment we are shut off from human interests; our anticipation and memories are arrested; we are lifted above the stream of life.[63]

Surprisingly, Bell's thesis that "to appreciate a work of art we need bring with us nothing from life, no knowledge of its ideas and affairs" is stretched by Fry to cover even literature. See, here, his following emphatic words:

> . . . The essential of great tragedy . . . [is] not the emotional intensity of the events portrayed, but the vivid sense of the inevitability of their unfolding, the significance of the curve of crescendo and diminuendo which their sequence describes, together with all the myriad subsidiary evocations which, at each point, poetic language can bring in to give fullness and density to the whole organic unity.[64]

Besides the important concept of "organic unity" which may be discussed a little later and at some length, the other general ideas that occur in the extract just cited may be put simply as follows:

> determination of (represented) events that come later (in the course of play) by those that precede them; rise and fall of fortune, and intenseness (density) of the events that make the fabric of the play.

To this list we may add two other features, both essentially formal; and of which literary critics freely speak, namely, consistency of characterization and the inter-knitting of the main and subsidiary plots.

All these features, we may note, may either be merely thought about in the abstract and quite generally, as Fry here appears to do, *or* actually seen to characterize a particular play

---

63. Hospers, *Introductory Readings in Aesthetics,* op. cit., p. 7.

64. Roger Fry's essay, "Art as Form" Ibid., p. 104.

as it is read or witnessed as presented on the stage. Now, a very clear and quite *non-human* instance of "inevitable" determination of an act or event by what precedes it, and also of rise and fall, is provided by the simple descent of a ball which is first tossed up high into the air. Are we to take the "inevitability" and "crescendo and diminuendo" of which Fry speaks in this purely skeletal form? Nobody would here say *yes*. In fact, we just cannot. As represented in a play, happenings generally create a situation to which the represented characters react in their individual ways, and out of varying motives; and if these diverse attitudes and modes of behaviour yet hang together it is essentially because they issue from personalities. The represented characters here are surely no mere pegs to hang characteristics on. What is more, they all bear names, as we do in real life. If, following Bell and Fry, we have to take literally *nothing from life* as we turn to contemplate art, not even the habit of distinguishing persons partly with the help of names, would it at all be possible to follow a play which cannot do without characters? Reid is therefore justified in denying the "exclusive importance" of formalistic considerations in art, though (as he is careful to add) it is just as wrong to look "at art *solely* for the things in the world (people, mountains, trees and so on) that it represents."[65]

The truth surely is that we have to regard the form of WoA as the *organic unity* of all that it comprises. It is indeed quite common to look on art "as an organized complex of sensuous and expressive elements," and to regard this organization itself as the form of art.[66] So the concept in question, *organic unity*, may be discussed at some length.

Organic Unity

Organic unity is commonly regarded as a key feature of works of art which are admittedly good. The concept is generally

65. Rader, *A Modern Book of Aesthetics*, 5th edn., p. 283. Italics added.

66. Osborne's essay "Organic Unity" in Rader's *A Modern Book of Aesthetics*, 5th edn., p. 307.

traced back to classical antiquity, to Plato and Aristotle in particular. Loosely, it is often spoken as "unity in variety." But it is by focusing on the word, *organic,* that we can get at the real meaning of such unity, say, as follows:

(a) The different parts of a living organism do not merely go together but are intimately interconnected. The moment any part or limb is hurt, the entire organism may be adversely affected. Similarly, a work of art is no mere aggregate but a living unity in the sense that, if any detail or element of it — say, a mere line in a painting — is erased or even altered, the entire work will suffer a perceptible change. As Aristotle pointed out long ago, in a truly "unified whole . . . any change in any part produces changes in the nature and relations of all the remaining ones *as parts of that whole.*"[67] No such pervasive determination occurs when we change the details or content of a mere aggregate. If one hockey stick is taken out of a bundle of similar sticks, the remaining do not suffer any change. Yet another way to show that a WoA is an organic unity is to argue, as Susanne Langer does, that just as it is not possible to tell exactly how much life a particular organ contributes to the living character of the whole body, so we cannot precisely determine *how much* (*not only how*) a particular element contributes to the beauty or significance of the WoA which comprises it.

(b) Further, because by virtue of its organic character a work of art is not a loose whole, it admits of "synoptic" awareness, as against "atomic perception" which was once the ideal of British associationist psychology. This ideal "emphasizes the qualities of acuity and precision"; synoptic awareness, on the other hand, values the richness and unity of content. Baumgarten was keen on this difference. He in fact took pains to highlight

67. Osborne's essay, "Organic Unity", op. cit., p. 309. Italics added.

the contrast between the vital fulness of perceived reality ["intensive clarity"] which is caught and communicated by the artist in all its richness *and* the discursive analytical processes [extensional clarity] of science.[68]

Osborne clarifies the above as follows:

> By breaking down experience into its elements, searching for laws and physical causes, analysing and generalizing, scientists gain much useful knowledge; but the original vital richness of the experience is dissolved and lost. The geologist can tell us much in a scientific way about the landscape we see: but in his explanations the landscape itself disappears. Conceptualization . . . sacrifices the life of experience by reducing it to an aggregate of features in which only the common and repetitive aspects are retained, letting slip the original and the unique.[69]

(c) This does not however mean that the unity in question is vacuous on the inside or a bare identity. It is a unity in diversity, and so it satisfies us.

> The human mind has a need for variety as a relief from dullness and monotony, but unless [it is] balanced by unity, variety will lead to confusion and fatigue.[70]

(d) Further, its being an organic unity means that a WoA is a dynamic interrelatedness of diverse elements — *dynamic* in the sense that each element contributes something, some effect or suggestiveness to others. So the elements (in an artistic whole) all come to acquire something which they do not possess in their original, independent character; and, what is more, the whole too is seen to wear a look which does not belong to any of the elements, nor even to their mere aggregate. To illustrate, a note of music is neither *high nor low* by

68. Osborne's essay "Organic Unity" in Rader's *A Modern Book of Aesthetics*, 5th edn., p. 309.

69. Ibid., p. 308.

70. Ibid., p. 311. Bracketed words added.

itself. It is only in the *āroha* and *avaroha* (ascent and descent) of a melody that the notes acquire the semblances in question (that is, appearing high or low); and the melody itself, if it ends at the focal beat of the rhythm-cycle, may easily appear to be completing itself. This suggestion of self-completion, we may note, cannot relate to any note exactly in the same way as it does to the whole melody. In this respect indeed "a whole in apprehension is more than the sum of its parts."[71] The *phrases* too in a melody may seem to be crisp and tense or relaxed and meandering; but the *notes*, taken individually, can hardly do so.

(e) It is important also to see as to what "wholeness" as implicit in the concept of organic unity really is. It is not literal completeness. As aestheically contemplated, a work of art has only to *appear* self-complete, even if it is not actually whole. The point is well illustrated by the sculptures that Rodin left incomplete intentionally. We can explain it further as follows:

> In aesthetic appreciation, the art object is isolated from its environment and framed apart in attention as a single individual, apprehended as a single complex impression and not as an aggregate [that is, not discursively] . . . [;] ideally, [here] we become aware of a total presentation manifesting qualities which are not built up from, or fully analysable into, the properties and relations of the constituent parts. . . . The contained parts . . . [can of course] be attended to separately in the . . . process of becoming acquainted with the total work of art . . . [but] they become fully articulate [or reveal their aesthetic character] only when they are perceived as parts of the particular whole in which they occur, in the completed act of appreciation. . . . [In the words of Coleridge, a WoA is] is whole that is presupposed by all the parts.[72]

71. Osborne's essay "Organic Unity" in Rader's *A Modern Book of Aesthetics*, 5th edn., p. 311.

72. Ibid.

Art as Expression

"The successive displacement of 'imitation' by 'representation,' and of 'representation' by 'expression' is a striking feature of the way philosophical thinking on art has followed its course in history; and it is hardly an exaggeration to say that from the close of the eighteenth century to the present, 'expression' and its cognates have dominated both aesthetic theorizing and the critical appraisal of the arts. . . . Words such as 'communication' (Tolstoy), 'objectification' (Santayana), 'embodiment' (Bosanquet and Reid) and 'symbolization' (Langer and Arnheim) . . . are not alternatives to 'expression' but are cognate terms."[73]

Now, advocates of the view that art is essentially a kind of expression are some of the best known names in the philosophy of art. However, the way they argue for this view, or interpret the very concept of *expression*, is by no means identical. Thus, whereas Croce emphasizes the essentially internal or spiritual character of expression, Langer defines art as a symbolic expression of the "forms of feeling." A detailed discussion of the views of these two thinkers, and of quite a few others who also regard expression as the essence of art is not possible here.[74] We have to be content with only a general account of the views of some of the relevant thinkers.

Now, the main acknowledged meanings of *express* (as a verb) are the following:

(a) to put one's thoughts into words;

(b) to show or reveal;

(c) to represent something with looks, actions or symbols; or

---

73. Alan Tormey, *The Concept of Expression*, Princeton, N.J.: Princeton University Press, 1971, p. 97.

74. Luckily, however, the views of these two thinkers have been discussed by me, at fair length, in my book: *Art and Philosophy: Seven Aestheticians*, Indian Council of Philosophical Research, 1994.

(d) to press or squeeze out something.

What is common to the meanings, barring perhaps (c), is the thought that to express is to externalize some inner content. Croce and Collingwood, on the other hand, put a quite different meaning on the word. They think of expression in art as an *internal activity, inseparable from intuition.* Intuition, as Croce regards it, is not the passive reception of what is directly presented to us. It is rather the spiritual (or inner) *activity* of having a *vivid* image or perception, "To intuit is to express, and nothing else [nothing more but nothing less] than to express."[75] This is indeed a recurring emphasis in Croces's philosophy of art. See, for instance, his following words:

> . . . Intuition is only intuition insofar as it is, in that very act expression. An image that does not express, that is not speech, song, drawing, painting, sculpture or architecture — speech at least murmured to oneself, song at least echoing within one's own breast, line and colour seen in imagination and colouring with its own tint the whole soul and organism — is an image that does not exist. . . . The *identity of intuition and expresssion* . . . is [not only a] profound philosophical doctrine . . . [but] a principle of ordinary common sense.[76]

Here the emphasis is obvious. But is it possible to agree on all that the above extract says? We may accept the suggestion that insofar as he is very sensitive to, because his mind habitually dwells on, the character of the material and elements of his art, when a painter intuits a colour he does it very intensely —

75. B. Croce, *Aesthetic as Science of Expression and General Linguistic*, tr. D. Ainslie, Rupa and Co., p. 11.

76. Intuiting the melodic form of a *whole song* at once is a very rare happening, if it ever takes place. It is surely not the experience of the generality of composers in the field of Hindustani music. What first flashes on the mind, as if from nowhere, is only the opening line, the basic *gat* or *sthāyī*, or initial collocation of *bol*s that open a rhythmic pattern. From them on, one has to proceed in a piecemeal way. Here I speak partly on the basis of my own experience as a composer of sorts.

with his whole being, so to say; and that therefore the colour is not only imagined by, but is clearly expressed ("in that very act") or is made manifest to him. However, so to interpret *expression* and to insist on its identity with the act of intuiting (or imaging) cannot be regarded as proper by "common sense" as this sense is generally understood. It may be accepted, as we have already done, that the word *expression* is used in quite a few different senses, and that if it is used (in its everyday senses) in respect of art, it is likely to cause confusion. But, as Ducasse rightly contends, if this is so, Croce should have avoided this word altogether and "coined some new term to designate 'the spiritual aesthetic synthesis' which is what . . . [he] means when he talks about 'expression.' . . . But . . . far from thinking of doing so, Croce on the contrary considers himself free to do as he likes with the word . . . and expects the rest of us to regard our use of it as metaphorical."[77]

Nor is it possible to accept Croce's thesis that art is intuition-expression as a purely *internal* or spiritual (and indivisible) activity. It may be conceded that where a composer visualizes a song, or rather its first line, it echoes "within . . . [his] own breast." But a mere opening line is not a whole song; and what is more, a musical phrase *as visualized*, howsoever intensely, is just not identical with the selfsame phrase *as heard*, in a particular voice or on a specific instrument. This indeed is why those who compose music — say, for our films — are generally seen doing so with a harmonium in their laps, and with a *tablã* player by their side. Those who can do without this outer aid can only be said to be glorious exceptions to the generality of composers.

However, quite apart from the question as to how a work of art is created, the *word* art itself calls for a little pointed attention. As we noted earlier, this word may be taken in three main senses: first, as the activity of art making; second, as an individual work that results from this activity; and third, as all art-works taken generally. Corresponding to these meanings

---

77. C.J. Ducasse, *The Philosophy of Art*, Dover Publication, 1966, p. 45.

of *art*, the expression theory may be said to put forth three distinct theses:

I. Art is essentially *the artist's activity* of expressing his own emotions.

II. *A work of art* is art insofar as *it* is expressive of, or embodies (or projects) some emotion.

III. All genuine art is expressive to those who contemplate it properly — "expressive" here in the sense that it is able to evoke in them the same emotion as is embodied in the work.

The last of these, we may note, is a key idea also in the Indian theory of *rasa*. According to this theory, the right response to art is not merely the *rasika*'s recognition, but a living re-evocation in him, of the emotion which the work itself expresses. However, insofar as we cannot have a work of art without an active exercise of *the artist's* creative ability, it would be proper to begin by attending to the first of the three forms of the expression theory as we have listed them.

According to Veron, who precedes Croce,[78] a work of art is "an emotive symbol," as distinguished from a "cognitive symbol." An emotive symbol enables the artist to express his feelings and emotions. A cognitive symbol, on the other hand, is a means by which we all freely express what we *know or believe*, not what we *feel*. The assumption here clearly is that if emotion is to be properly *expressed — and not merely felt and naturally evinced or betrayed* — the right kind of symbols must be created for the purpose. It is this *creation of symbols for emotional expression* which distinguishes art as an activity. But, important though this emphasis is, it is not everything about Veron's philosophy of art. On the one hand, he argues against the views which look on emotion or even the creation of beauty as the essence of art making; and, on the other hand, he takes pains to put forth the view, with due reasons, that the making in

78. Eugene Veron, 1825-1889; Croce, 1866-1952.

question is a vital self-expression on the part of the artist. All this may be put as follows, as a simple summary of his essay, *Art as the Expression of Emotion,*[79] at places in his own words.

The imitation theory is superficial; it does not go to the root of the matter. What exactly do we admire when we find that a work of art imitates or is faithful to its object markedly? Its seizure of the *object's* appearance or character, or sheer "resemblance"? If that is so, why do we need the work at all? The appearance (or character) in question is already there in the object. The truth is, and this is what the imitation theoy misses, that what we here really admire (in the case visualized) is the *artist's* skill in imitating the object. Further, how can "the similitude of an *ugly* object . . . be beautiful"?[80] Beauty fascinates us; ugliness by itself tends to repel the onlooker. So if an ugly object as painted yet appears beautiful or likeable to us, clearly the painter must have done something in "imitaing" it. (It may be that if the object painted is a rickety beggar in rags, the picture has been so made that the face appears to wear a pathetic expression that moves and so attracts us readily.[81] Therefore, once again, the value of the artist's own skill is highlighted.)

Consider, next, the case of beauty or what gives us "pleasure of sight and hearing." (It is already there in plenty, in the world around us, say, in flowerladen gardens and in the chirping of birds and lisping of infants.) So what is the point in going to art for pleasures which are merely sensuous? Such pleasures *are* important; and *art as expressive* is by no means indiferrent to them. But, by way of affirming its own distinctive value, so to say, "it sees something beyond them." The very logic of art-making compels us to speaks thus. It is the artist who creates art. At times

> he is struck by . . . [a] vivid impression — whether moral, intellectual, or physical — [; he then] expresses that

79. Rader, *A Modern Book of Esthetics,* 5th edn., pp. 50-57.

80. This is my question, not Veron's.

81. This explanation, again, is mine.

> impression by some outward process — by poetry, music, sculpture, painting, or architecture — in such a way as to cause its communication with the soul of spectator or auditor [listener?]; . . . [and in doing so he produces] a work the beauty of which will be in exact proportion to the intelligence and depth of the sentiment displayed, and the power shown in giving it outward form. . . . A work of art is beautiful when it bears strong marks of the individuality of its author, of the permanent personality of the artist, and of the more or less accidental impression produced upon him by the sight of the object or event rendered. . . . [By] way of general definition . . . [we may, say] that art is the manifestation of emotion, obtaining external interpretation now by expressive arrangements of line, form or color; now by a series of gestures, sounds, or words governed by particular rhythmic cadence. . . . [Above all,] art is the direct and spontaneous manifestation of human personality [; and] aesthetics is the science whose object is the study and elucidation of the manifestations of artistic genius.[82]

Now, by way of clarifying and estimating Veron's account of art-making as given above, we may make the following comments:

1. The very first point with which we opened our account of Veron's philosophy of art — namely, the view that every authentic work of art is an *emotive* symbol (p. 334) — appears suspect when we look at it from the viewpoint of actual art. Consider, for instance, the *Naṭarāja Bronze,* The Dancing Śiva, admittedly a sculptural marvel. Of the two scholarly reactions to it given below, the first one is from Ananda Coomaraswamy, the well-known Indian philosopher of art, and the second is from one whose interests are shared by modern physics and Eastern mysticism:

---

82. Veron's essay in Rader's *A Modern Book of Esthetics*, op. cit., pp. 51-53, 57. The order of words as cited here differs from the way they occur in the original essay, but the words themselves are Veron's own.

(a) How supremely great in power and grace this dancing image must appear to all those who have striven in plastic forms to give expression to their intuition of Life! . . . No artist of today . . . could more exactly or more wisely create an image of that Energy which science must postulate behind all phenomena. . . . Nature is inert, and cannot dance until Śiva wills it. He rises from His rapture, and dancing sends through inert matter pulsating waves of awakening sound, and lo! matter also dances appearing as a glory round about Him. Dancing, He sustains its manifold phenomena. . . . This is poetry; but nonetheless, science.[83]

(b) The dance of Śiva is *the dancing universe,* the ceaseless flow of energy going through an infinite variety of patterns that melt into one another. Modern physics has . . . revealed that every subatomic particle not only *performs* an energy dance but also *is* [itself] an energy dance; a pulsating process of creation and destruction. . . . For the modern physicists, then, Śiva's dance is the dance of subatomic matter. . . . The bubble-chamber photographs of interacting particles, which bear testimony to the continual rhythm of creation and destruction in the universe, are visual images of the dance of Śiva . . ..[84]

Neither of the extracts cited above looks on the work in question as essentially an emotive, as distinct from a cognitive symbol. Susanne Langer just makes one comment on this bronze, simply with an eye to illustrating her emphasis on the virtual in art:

> [In spite of its left foot's looking dangling in the air] its motion seems perfected, not suspended, in the image.[85]

---

83. A.K. Coomaraswamy, *The Dance of Śiva,* New York: The Noonday Press, pp. 77f.

84. Fritjof Capra, *The Tao of Physics: An Exploration of the Parallels between Modern Physics and Eastern Mysticism,* London: Fontana, 1976, pp. 258f. Italics added.

85. S.K. Langer, *Mind: An essay on Human Feeling,* vol. I, Baltimore

It is noteworthy that there is no attempt here to see any *form of feeling* expressed in the work.

2. The way Veron opposes the imitation theory of art is obviously proper. But it is difficult to accept the suggestion that art is "*direct* and *spontaneous* manifestation of human [that is, the artist's own] personality." If, as we are here required to believe, a WoA proceeds straight from the artist's personality (or is *direct*); and, what is more, if it occurs wholly by itself, and is not caused or influenced from outside (and is therefore *spontaneous*), how can Veron say, in the same breath (as he does) that a WoA "bears strong marks . . . [also] of the more or less accidental impression *produced on him by the sight of the object or event rendered*"? Even apart from this semantic protest, there is a solid fact which opposes Veron's view. As Osborne points out, there is no one *straightforward* way in which art-works could be related to the emotional life of their creator. Perugino was a villain and an atheist. How could he then imbue his pictures with the intense religious emotions that they visibly embody? To suggest, as Bernhard Berenson does, that Perugino could do it bacause, insofar as he found them "easier victims," he "preferred them (devout men) in real life" is hardly convincing.[86] In any case, such expiations fail to relate emotions in the artwork to emotions *in the artist's own life.* It is be contended, as has been done in some writing defending surrealism, that "great works take shape at the lowest and most inaccessible regions of the unconscious mind and therefore carry echoes and reverberations of the whole psychical being of the artist" with unusual completeness, our ready rejoinder could be: "so do the products of psychotics and

---

and London: The John Hopkins University Press, 2nd printing (paper), 1975, p. 234.

86. Osborne, *The Art of Appreciation*, op. cit., p. 99.

backward children express the content of their subconscious minds."[87] How then does the defence in question account for the *distinctive* significance of art?

3. Some other objections too can be made to all those Western theories (including Veron's) which look on art as an expression of the artist's own emotions or feelings:

(a) Firstly, how are the artist's own emotions any more important than those of the average man? The fact rather is that there is little evidence to prove that by and large and on the whole . . . [artists] are better men or emotionally more balanced or profound than the generality of mankind.[88] Closer at home, the reaction which the conferment of the prestigious *Bharat Ratna* award on Pandit Ravi Shankar elicited from Pandit Jasraj hardly did justice to the latter's own eminence as a musician. If an artist's emotive reactions are so similar in quality to those of average men, how is the distinctive importance of art provided for by saying that what is here expressed is the *artist's* own emotion?

(b) Secondly, if art is essentially the expression of (the artist's) emotions, we get committed to the view that during the course of creation he must be (supposed to be) in the grip of some *strong* emotion, specially if we accept Veron's emphasis that a WoA must show "power" in giving "outward form" to the artist's sentiment. But, first, this is not borne out by the evidence of fact. Speaking in the light of his own experience, T.S. Eliot declares that emotion does not play any part in the creative process; and, as Ryle has ably argued by distinguishing the various meanings of the word, the only "feeling" which may be said to be there in all artistic creation is that of "feeling absorbed in" what is being done, a feature which can be present in any kind of serious activity, and is therefore not uniquely relevant

---

87. Osborne, *The Art of Appreciation,* op. cit., p. 99.

88. Ryle's essay, "Feeling" in *Aesthetics and Language.*

to the making of art.[89] Indeed, if at the end of a recital, a *tablã* maestro is asked to describe his mental state during the act of playing, he will never rejoin by saying that he wanted to express an emotion that possessed him. His answer would rather be that he was all along keen to project the proper design of the patterns he played, without letting the clarity of individual syllables suffer; that, just as ceaselessy, he felt *attuned with* the steady cyclic extent of the basic rhythm; and that if, at some rare moment of such attunement, he felt transported with a quiet delight at the subtle insertion of *a syllable* into the flowing fabric, or at the purposely wayward design of *a whole pattern*, that feeling of delight only accompanied, but did not produce any change in the design of the compositions played.

(c) Thirdly, if the artist at work is in fact subject to a strong emotion, be it sorrow or anger, he will just not have the composure that is needed for a careful use and organization of his material, and so his creation will suffer. In a letter to his father Mozart once wrote: "I who must always be composing, need a clear mind and a quiet heart."[90] To turn to our classical dances, if a danseuse — presenting the number known as *navarasamālikã*, in which different emotions have to be *expressed* in quick succession — somehow becomes actually subject to a flitting experience of real love, anger, sorrow and joy, one after the other, she would find it impossible to concentrate and to meet the rigorous demands of rhythm and meticulous *abhinaya*, and so will hardly be able to proceed according to the plan of the intra-form (or number[91]) in question. And is any emotion

89. Ryle's essay, "Feeling" in *Aesthetics and Language*.

90. Cited by Susanne K. Langer, as the third footnote on p. 176 of her book, *Feeling and Form*, Routledge and Kegan Paul, 3rd Impression, 1963.

91. For reasons why I prefer to use the word *intraform* in place of *number* or *item* for the individual contents of a dance recital see my essay, "Kathak — Some Terms and Distinctions" in *Sangeet Natak*, January–March, 1979, pp. 5-8. My word, I may add, has

needed for *vilambit* singing which we all so highly value in the region of Hindustani music? A self-possessed attunement of mind with the details of *rāga-tāla* fabric, and with the form of the vocal *bandish*, is the only requirement here, besides of course a duly trained voice.

(d) Fourthly, if an art-work is, in essence, the expression of the artist's own emotions, the critic will have to consult the artist as to what his emotion during the act of creation was, before he (the critic) formulates his own judgement as to the value of the work. But this is something that the critics never do.

(e) Fifthly, as Hospers rightly points out, the relation of art to feeling is by no means necessary:

> In the house of art there are many mansions. Some works of art hardly touch the life of feeling at all, but simply tease the eye or the ear: their impact is perceptual rather than emotional; consider some of Gauguin's and Matisse's colour-harmonies or Mondrian's arrangements of straight lines intersecting at right angles. On the other hand, there are many works . . . especially [of] literature that appeal to the intellect and not to senses, such as the long stretches of informational material in Tolstoy's *War and Peace*. . . . [we must] resist [the tendency to say] that there is just one function of art, to be expressive . . . of some aspect of the life of feeling.[92]

In case we choose to focus on art that *is* expressive, and have to determine what exactly is that which is expressed, perhaps the most sensible choice will be to accept the following from L.A. Reid:

---

already become a part of dance critics' language. See, for instance, Shanta Serbjeet Singh's review of the Kathak performance of Rani Karna, in *The Hindustan Times* of 16.10.1988.

92. The essay, "Hartshorne's Aesthetics," by John Hospers in *The Philosophy of Charles Hartshorne*, ed. L.E. Hahn, The Library of Living Philosophers, vol. XX, Illinois: La Salle, 1991, pp. 128-29.

> It is not facts or ideas as such, nor feelings or emotions as such that try "to get expressed," but feeling-about-things, or things (facts, ideas, anything) — as-felt. Things-we-are-interested in . . . objects of interest (or *values* as R.B. Perry regards *value*). . . . [it is these which may be regarded as] the life-resources of art.[93]

(f) Finally, there is an obvious incompleteness not only in Veron's view of art, but perhaps in all other kindred theories, including that of Susanne Langer, which look on expressiveness as the key feature of a WoA. Veron speaks of art-making as the artist's expression of an inner impression "by some outward process . . . in such a way *as to cause its communication with the soul of spectator or auditor.*" Now, if the WoA is to speak to the *soul* of, or to make it a very deep appeal to, the contemplator, will the actual effectuation of this appeal depend on the work *alone*? Is not the contemplator's own cultivated sensibility expected to contribute something? To say that we need percipience to get at the aesthetic meaning of WoA is hardly enough. In this context it is noteworthy that Bharata has listed more than thirty requirements for a true *rasika,* including even such imperceptible factors as predispositions (or helpful *saṁskāras*) inherited from the previous birth.

ART AS TRANSMISSION/COMMUNICATION OF EMOTION

Let us now see if concepts like *transmission* or *communication* are able to seize the essence of art any better than *expression.* We have spoken of these words as cognate concepts. But they (all italicized) cannot be taken to be identical in meaning, and it is easy to visualize situations to which only one of these terms can be suitably applied. *To communicate* is to impart ideas or information, or to make something known or intelligible. Here, a suggestion of transmission of some ideal content from one individual to others is necessarily implicit. The verb *express,*

---

93. L.A. Reid's essay, "Values, Feelings and Embodiment," in Rader's *A Modern Book of Esthetics,* 5th edn., pp. 182-83.

on the other hand, is not subject to any such necessity. A sad, *lonely* man who gets some emotional relief by weeping surely *expresses* his grief; but he is obviously not *communicating* anything to anyone, just because no one else is present there. We may add, following Osborne, that it is "not nonsense to say that a man expressed himself in a work of art which was not understood by [or which could not *communicate* anything to] anyone . . . until after his death."[94]

But this attention to single words is hardly enough, and it seems necessary to consider a whole theory of art, such as Tolstoy's, which builds upon the concept of *communication* at some length and not without a show of reason. The essence of Tolstoy's philosophy of art may be put in his own words:

> To *evoke in oneself* a feeling one has experienced and having evoked it in oneself then by means of movements, lines, colours, sounds, or forms expressed in words, *so to transmit that feeling that others experience the same feeling* — this is the activity of art. Art is a human activity consisting in this, that one man consciously, by means of external signs, hands on to others feelings he has lived through, and that others are infected by those feelings, and also experience them. Art is not . . . [merely] the expression of man's emotions by external signs; . . . it is not mere pleasure; but it is a means of union among men joining them together in the same feelings . . .. Thanks to man's capacity to express thoughts by words, we may know all that has been done for him in the realms of thought . . .. So thanks to man's capacity *to be infected with* the feelings of, [and] means of art."[95]

Kandinsky, the father of Abstract Expressionism, speaks in almost the same vein:

> A work of art consists of two elements, the inner and the outer. The inner is the emotion in the soul of the artist; this emotion has the capacity to evoke a similar emotion in the

94. Osborne, *The Art of Appreciation*, p. 96.

95. Tolstoy's essay, "The Communication of Emotion" in Rader's book, *A Modern Book of Esthetics*, 5th edn., p. 61.

> observer. . . . The sequence is: emotion (in the artist) — the sensed — the artwork-emotion (in the observer).[96]

Now, to turn first to *Tolstoy's* view as cited above, how exactly are we to interpret the very opening words: "to evoke in oneself?" Do they mean that as he sets out to create a work of art, the artist first (somehow)[97] makes himself *experience* anew the feeling which he had suffered earlier *or* that the experience in question has only to be vividly *recalled*, or brought back before the mind as an *object* of contemplation? It is obvious that if the feeling in question is a powerful one, its actual re-activation as a felt state (somehow brought about) may so agitate the artist's mind as to make him unable to concentrate on making the art-work properly. If, on the other hand, what is required is only a *recall* of the emotional experience for the sake of *attending to* its felt character, so that the materials of art could be suitably shaped and used to incarnate and reveal it, why can't we speak similarly also of the *rasika*'s right reponse, that is, as just a clear imagining, and not as an actual re-enactment of the felt state which is assumed to have set astir *and* shaped the process of creation? Be that as it may, it is the evidence of fact that we do not react, say, to "fear" in a novel or film, with the same oppressive directness as may be seen in a crowd's fleeing in panic pell-mell at the rumour that a tiger at large is approaching the spot where they presently are. So it does not seem quite proper to look on the aesthetic response as our geting "infected with the [red-hot] feelings" of the artist as he once actually experienced them in the real course of life.

Further, as Ducasse rightly points out, "transmission to, or evocation in, others" is by no means essential to art:

> Whether transmission of the emotions expressed occurs or not . . . is largely accidental; for a given work of art may never happen to come to the attention of persons other than the

---

96. Osborne, *The Art of Appreciation*, pp. 94-95.

97. This word, *somehow*, has been used to suggest that an exact re-evocation of a past emotional experience can never be easy.

> artist himself; and yet it remains a work of art. Moreover, the *individual psychological constitution* of persons other than the artist is one of the variables that determine whether the feelings those persons then experience are or not the same as the feelings the artist intended the object he has created to express. Evidently the activity of the artist *as artist* terminates with his creation of the work of art.[98]

Further, whether or not a *particular* person is emotionally stirred by a work of art is no sure index of its aesthetic merit or demerit. One may be too easily moved to tears by even a slightly "sad" *ghazal* if it happens to be the one that he has himself freely hummed in his moments of despair, or if it projects an image that reminds him of some unhappy, actual experience of his own. This is precisely why some aestheticians require the *rasika* — say, a reader of poetry — to find joy and sweetness in the very words of the poem, rather than to admire its expressiveness only if it makes *him* happy or sad. Or again, if the focus of a listener's attenion is really on some "sad" music itself, it would be truer to his immediate experience to say that "the music *is* or *looks sad to him*" than to say that it is *expressive of sadness in his view*, or that "it may be taken to be expressive *because* it makes *him* sad." It would here be of help to remember that to *identify* the emotion in an object is not necessarily to *experience* that emotion oneself. If we can easily read the sadness in a man's face without being saddened ourselves, why should it be otherwise in the case of our response to expressiveness *incarnate* and *embodied* in a work of art? The word *embodiment*, incidentally, is a keyword for L.A. Reid. In his theory of art it is meant to emphasize the inseparability of a work's expressiveness or meaning from its "perceptua"; and it is precisely the intense cohesion of a work's "expression" with its material elements which Tolstoy seems to miss where he speaks of a work's emotion as being transmitted or "handed on" to others. To transmit is to pass or hand on some message

98. C.J. Ducasse, "Art and the Language of the Emotions," in Rader's *A Modern Book of Esthetics*, 4th edn., p. 69.

or meaning — to others; and though to *hand on* is not exactly the same thing as to *hand over*, Tolstoy's way of speaking is not quite true to the fact that a work's expressiveness is ingrained in its perceptual elements. A letter which transmits or communicates some ordinary news to us is generally put aside once the message is caught. To a poem, on the other hand, we may have to turn repeatedly even after we have happily grasped the meaning it seems to express (*and embody*) at the very first look, maybe because of its easy run and winsome rhyme. Do we ever complain that the sweet little lines that speak of twinkling stars, and of our wondering what they are, have begun to bore us?

Felicity of expression is something that we all value, and this partly explains why the expression theory of art has received very wide and varied attention at the hands of art theorists. Whereas, on the one hand, there is "a very widespread assumption (in the West) that appreciation of art is emotional in character . . . [or that] it consists . . . mainly in experiencing an appropriate affective response towards it,"[99] on the other hand, we have the well-known Indian doctrine of *rasa* which speaks of aesthetic experience as a "tasting," and which, Osborne rightly acclaims as "the most subtle of the emotional theories of appreciation."[100]

Yet, even as *Western* aestheticians, artists and literary critics present it, the expression theory of art is by no means lacking in subtlety and we find a great variety of views not only on what exactly is expressed, but on the precise character of the emotion expressed or evoked. Dr Johnson, for instance, is said to have held the view that

> the thing to be communicated was not emotion in all the flux and flurry of its original presence in the human soul. It is never a stream of consciousness. It is emotion selected and generalized into the simple universals that move all men everywhere. To generalize animation was not, as the

99. Osborne, *The Art of Appreciation*, p. 108.

100. Ibid., p. 116.

romantics tended to believe, to evaporate it but rather to make it available.[101]

Now, what the above extract says towards its close is very similar to what the Indian *rasa* theorists mean by *sādhāraṇīkaraṇa*, and it is easy to illustrate the point. Thus, where Gray speaks thus in his well-known Elegy:

Full many a gem of purest ray serene
The dark, unfathom'd caves of ocean bear
Full many a flower is born to blush unseen
And waste its sweetness on the desert air,[102]

the sadness quietly expressed by the last two lines is easily sensed by one and all, because it does not relate to any specific individual. But a more striking view of expression in art is provided by Kandinsky's insistence that though

> abstract and formal elements of art do not express the precise articulations of emotion and feeling experienced in ordinary life . . . they do embody equally precise articulations of basic modes of feeling . . . [and that] a person who would cultivate powers of appreciation beyond the most elementary stages . . . must acquire a delicate and true sensibility for the precise crystallizations of mood and feeling which are embodied in the formal and non-representational aspects of visual art.[103]

Clive Bell also emphasizes the emotional impact of the formal elements in visual art. He begins with the following emphasis:

> The starting point for all systems of aesthetics must be the personal experience of a peculiar emotion. The objects which provoke this emotion we call works of art. This emotion is called the aesthetic emotion.[104]

---

101. Osborne, *The Art of Appreciation*, p. 115.
102. Thomas Gray, "Elegy written in a Country Churchyard", in *Master Poems of the English Language*, New York: Trident Press, 1966, p. 306.
103. Osborne, *The Art of Appreciation*, p. 107.
104. Clive Bell, *Art Now*, p. 21.

Later, in his books, *Art* and *Enjoying Pictures,* Bell explains "the aesthetic emotion" as a kind of thrill or shock which only the formal beauty of lines and colours can evoke. Now, we may agree that the purely formal elements of a work of visual art can have their own expressiveness. Lines can appear taut or relaxed, even as colours can look angry. But to regard the formal or structural elements of an art-work as the *only* source of its appeal, or significance — or cause of a "shocking" impact, as Bell expressly does — is surely an exaggeration. Consider, for instance, the following testimony in support of the truth that even the very *material* of art, as transformed in a work, can produce a sudden and powerful impact:

> We stood gaping and struck speechless at the sight [of a bronze statue] when we saw the bronze leaving its proper province and accomplishing the works of nature. For though bronze, it blushed; and though hard by nature, it melted into softness yielding to the artist's skill; and though devoid of living sensation, it created the impression that sensation dwelt within it.[105]

Further, a *shock* is a kind of momentary impact; it cannot be regarded as a reaction that develops and endures. So, though the "shock" view of aesthetic emotion may well be relevant to some visual art, it is obviously inadequate to the reading of a novel or to musical listening, for in such cases of art contemplation our aesthetic delight takes quite some time to emerge in its fullness.

It would here be relevant to point out that, according to the Indian theory of *rasa*, at least in respect of witnessing a good play the right aesthetic response is not one of a momentary shock, but simply a deeply satisfying awareness of the emotive roots of our being, so to say; and a feeling of liberation from the inhibiting factors which make us look upon ourselves as merely limited egos. Ultimately, we are told, our response here is "a state of serenity and repose." Vishwanatha characterizes

---

105. Osborne, *The Art of Appreciation*, p. 107.

rasa as a relish which is at once "an expanding of the mind . . . [and] and extraordinary pleasure inherent in contemplation itself." Indeed, our experience of listening to good (*dhruvapad*) *ālāpa* is, on the whole, one of elevation to a kind of contemplation serene; and it is only rarely that the singer's occasional and impressive use of a particular formal device, such as *gamak* or *anuraṇātmak* singing, gives us a gentle *shock* of wondrous delight. Even in respet of visual art we have to admit the truth of critical reactions such as the following:

> Every painting of Vermeer's is bathed in . . . serenity. . . . There is no violence in his work of thought or action. There is an eternal stillness, of music that dies on the echo, of the mind entranced by a message of love, of fingers that gently guide a thread of lace, of a tiny pearl suspended in delicate scales. Even Clio's eyes are downcast, as if embarrassed by the symbols of Fame she is compelled to hold.[106]

We may end this section with a brief account not only of how and where the expression theory of art is obviously relevant, but of its overall inedequacy. There are at least two kinds of art the success of which is surely to be judged by their ability to evoke the intended emotions: first, detective and adventure literature, which must arouse the emotion of suspense; and, second, humorous art which is just as inseparable from the end of evoking the emotion of amusement.[107]

But apart from these two cases — that is, if we consider the generality of art-forms — it does not appear correct to say that it is the *essential* function of art to arouse some emotion, or that art appreciation is, in essence, a kind of affective reaction. The truth rather is that whereas, on the one hand, there is a good deal of art which is admitted to be good as art though it does not express or evoke any emotion — besides, of course,

---

106. Sir Herbert Read's "Critical Appreciation", in *Vermeer* (The Masters) Paulton, Nr. Bristol: Knowledge Publications, Purnell and Sons Ltd., 1965, p. 6.

107. Osborne, *The Art of Appreciation*, pp. 110-11.

the agreeable feeling of self-absorption in whatever one is engaged in doing — there is, on the other hand, considerable evidence to prove that the affective tone or likeable quality of art appreciation is merely a reflex of the effective exercise of percipience. According to the traditional Indian view, the distinctive flavour of an art-work can be relished only by a *rasika,* and the *rasika* is a person who is thoroughly trained for art contemplation because he meets the many conditions required for the job. Even today, in our musical parlance *the right kind* of response to artistic beauty and significance is said to be a matter of *nigāh* or discriminating attention; and one who lacks the ability to make such responses is dismissed as a *koorh* or an *ignoramus,* not as a merely impassive person. It is to be noted that where, in our traditional writing on poetry, "a fit reader" is required to be *sahṛdaya,* the meaning is not that he should be possessed of a marked tendency to emotional excitement, but only that he should have the same kind of temperament as the poet whose poetry is being read. Further, insofar as the actual making of a poem, as distinguished from the creative impulse which drives it, is no mere ebullience of feeling, the same negation must hold of our aesthetic response to it as well. It may well be true that, unlike an average man, a poet reacts "intensely and vividly" to "the finer influences of life"; but he is also a *kavi,* "a man who shows" — and so must "have himself seen"; and he is therefore required, in addition, "to fashion something better than . . . the [imperfect] world of Nature . . . so that in his work at least man may find joy untainted by sorrow."[108] If the reader of poetry is to be similar to a poet *so regarded,* he too must train himself to react sensitively to the details of fact, feeling and fancy; and be capable of unravelling and re-composing in idea the whole fabric of an art-work. All this is bound to make pretty heavy demands on his cognitive powers, and is clearly not a mere wallowing in feeling.

It in fact seems correct to say in respect of every major art

108. M. Hiriyanna, *Art Experience,* Kavyalaya, pp. 18, 20.

that "aesthetic enjoyment . . . is a form of percipience transfused in various degrees with feeling and that it may also include apprehension which assumes the form of feeling when feeling mediates cognitive insight."[109] Because the meaning of art-works is in fact not abstractable from their individual "perceptua," their proper appreciation as art cannot but be grounded in the "delicate perceptions of sensory qualities."[110] But it is important to see how exactly these *perceptions* are special. They are the fruits of years of repeated communion with art-works and intimate conversance with — if not actual practice of — their technique; and are therefore both quick and unerring in art contemplation. The immaculate tuning of the *tānpūrā*; the ongoing steadiness of rhythm-*ṭhekā* as marked by the drummer, and felt as the gently supportive matrix of the whole music; the subtlety of a sudden rhythmic turn in the "unfoldment" of a *quāyedā* on the *tablā*; the balancing of a *mudrā* with the whole figural posture in sculpture; the poignancy of comic relief in a Shakespearean tragedy; a hardly perceptible suggestion of violence to the grammatical identity of a *rāga* arising from just a little longer stay at a *svara* than is permissible; dynamic symmetry in architecture; and the touch of *animation* provided by a slight torsion of shapes in a painting, or by the minimal but intentional shift of a pre-fixed vocal emphasis from its corresponding beat in the rhythm of a *tarānā*[111] — aesthetic details such as these reveal themselves to the *rasika* with the immediacy of feeling, indeed as instantly as the readiness with which the proportions of a bird or a tree are taken to betoken, respectively, the quality of nimbleness or of a lasting rootedenss. But whereas the "meaning" of everyday objects accrues without effort in the normal course of living, the perception of aesthetic qualities, such as the ones we have listed

109. Osborne, *The Art of Appreciation*, pp. 109-10; Italics added.

110. Ibid., p. 108.

111. A *tarānā* is vocal composition in a specific *rāga-tāla* frame. Its content, generally, is provided not by words, but by letters or their combinations, all alike meaningless.

above, is given to attention that is not merely close at the moment, but has trained itself for long and lovingly in the art of directed listening, seeing, recitation, and analytic understanding, along with sympathetic perception of the wholeness of artistic form.

In brief, the feeling of delight or satisfaction that we get in appreciating art *as art* is only a reflex of the active exercise of percipience, and the fact that (in some cases) it evokes an affective mood in us is not an unfailing index of a work's artistic quality.

> A tear-jerking film is not considered to be artistically good in proportion to the intensity of the emotions it arouses, and those persons are not thought to have appreciated the aesthetic qualities of a film most adequately who have wept *copiously* during its performances.[112]

We must, however, explain why the word "copiously" has been put in italics. *Uncontrolled* tears may well be said to betoken a *non*-aesthetic response to a tragic play. But shall we say the same even of a slight moistening of the eyes? The point may be discussed with reference to the following remark *of Hospers* (which differs from that *of Osborne* just cited) insofar as it does *not* take care to emphasize the point that our response, in the case in question, will be non-aesthetic (only) if the tears are *copious*:

> Those who respond to a drama or novel [even] with [a few imperceptible] tears have not developed aesthetic distance; they are responding to the work of art as they would to a situation in real life; they are still in the position of the yokel in the gallery who shoots the villain on the stage as he is about to capture the heroine. We should not respond to art with the emotions of life.[113]

---

112. H. Osborne, *The Art of Appreciation*, p. 110. Italics added.

113. John Hospers, "The Concept of Artistic Expression", in *Introductory Readings in Aesthetics*, ed. John Hospers, The Free Press and Collier MacMillan, 1969, p. 152. Words within brackets have been added to highlight the point I am seeking to make.

Here, it appears, the way aesthetic response is sought to be kept away from "the emotions of life" is a bit too categorical. But let us explain why we say so, with the help of a simple instance. Suppose in a representational work — say, in a novel or a film — a tragic incident, the like of which we freely come across in life, is *convincingly* depicted. What would the requirement of aesthetic distance here mean? Surely not that we should refuse to regard it as a true-to-life happening, and dismiss it instead as utterly improbable; for such negativity would only be a failure to respond to the "object" properly. On the other hand, if the representation in question is rightly registered, and due notice is taken also of its content of feeling (say, grief) by means of imaginative sympathy, it may be quite natural for a *sahṛdaya* (or sympathetic) contemplator to grow a little tearful himself. And why should we object to thus feeling gently moved so long as it does not disturb our exercise of percipience? One is not of course expected to, and even an average *rasika* surely does not try to offer actual relief to a character represented as distressed in a play. In art contemplation we all easily remember that what we are attending to is an imaginary representation and not a content of real life; and so we do not think of *dealing with* an emotional situation in art in the same way as we may do in response to an identical situation in life. In this respect certainly, we do "not respond to art with the emotions of life." But so far as the *feel* of the emotion in art is concerned, as distinguished from the *overt* behaviour that the same emotion may bring about in real life, there is no reason why the *rasika*'s actually getting infected with it *in a measure* should interfere with a proper appreciation of the work. What otherwise is the meaning of the traditional Indian insistence that a *rasika* has to be sensitive and not merely perceptive? The alternative would be to believe that an ideal contemplator has only to identify, in an act of quite unfeeling attention, that the situation represented projects a particular emotion. But such a simple cognition would hardly make any demands on our capacity for *sympathetic imagining*, and so can hardly be called aesthetic. We may here add that the following declaration of personal preference by Hospers does not quite square with his own categorical remark, cited earlier, that we should not "respond to art with the emotions of life":

> . . . I want art to move me, not merely to titillate my senses or inform my intellect; I want art . . . to impinge on me "at the gut level" . . . to derive from it a memorable emotional experience.[114]

On the whole, however, though it is very common to look on art activity as a kind of expression, and so to admire works of art for their expressiveness, expression cannot be said to be *essential* to every kind of art. True, we freely speak of good music as soulful or as (at least) tranquil and sweet; and we all readily acclaim a convincing projection of the nine basic sentiments in the dance number known as *navarasamālikā*. But, in either case, what the artist himself does is not to serve as a mere channel for the self-driven spilling, so to say, of an actual emotion that is directly and powerfully felt. He has rather to visualize its character vividly, and to so organize the material at his disposal that, as it takes shape, the work may come to wear the "look" of a particular emotion, and may be identified as such by the *rasika*. Where the effort succeeds, the art-work itself appears to be expressive. But here, in such consummate moments, our attention is focused on the work itself. We do *not* go beyond it to its maker, the artist, and regard the work as a mere medium of *his* self-expression. Nor does the state of *our* immediate experience warrant the use of such language as: "How well is sadness *expressed by* music." What we here naturally say simply is: "How sad the music looks!" In other words, *in the actual contemplation of art* which projects some emotion, the thought of expression *as activity* is hardly ever present.

But, what is more, even the look of expressiveness is not there in a good deal of art that is yet acknowledged as excellent.

114. Hospers, "Hartshorne's Aesthetics", in *The Philosophy of Charles Hartshorne*, p. 128.

How is the Taj Mahal *expressive*? What look of emotion does it seem to wear? It just looks lovely, superlative in its shapeliness in spite of its actual hugeness. Indeed, there is a considerable amount of art which we admire only for its structural excellences, and for such qualities as adroitness, fluency and sparkle. A good *vilambit gat* has nothing to do with emotion. What it expresses, or rather projects, is the chosen *rāga*'s distinctive character within a rhythmic frame. Of course, it has also to square with the demands of *sur* and structural oneness and flow; but the appearance that such many-sided rightness comes to invest the *gat* in question with is not that of an emotion's substrate, but that of a measured, sweet-sounding and self-completing flow. And, as we all know, the entire *nṛtta* aspect of our classical dances is acclaimed for its rhythmic richness, not for expressiveness. But, of course, the art which is most clearly and consistently removed from the canon of emotive expressiveness is that of *tablā* or *mṛdaṅgam* rhythm.

Art as Symbol

The way we have proceeded so far should have made it clear that the expression theory of art is quite close to those views which emphasize the value of communication and symbolization in art. Yet, because it does not take *expression* in its everyday sense, and also because it has evoked some animated aesthetic controversy today, Susanne K. Langer's view that a work of art is an expressive and presentational *symbol* may now be given some separate attention.

How expression can relate to symbols is easy to see. When we express our thoughts and feelings in everyday language each word contributes its own fairly determinate meaning; the sequence is relaxed, so to say; and we get at the total import by just adding up the individual meanings, quickly and easily. In most cases there is little, if any, involvement of imagination. But expression can also be fairly tight on the whole and concentrated at places, say because of the use of symbols. This happens, for instance, when a poet characterizes a feminine figure as *lily* white, suggesting not mere fairness of complexion, but chastity or purity of character without, of course, distinguishing the two. Here whiteness may be pictured in the mind as an actual attribute of the figure, whereas purity is to be *understood* as what is meant or expressed by *lily* as a conventional symbol. Of course, not every symbol is conventional; poets and artists are freely seen to create new ones. But because it is not possible to consider all of them we may confine ourselves to some of the better known conventional symbols. Further, we may also highlight a distinction. To speak of symbols as used *in* art is not the same thing as characterizing complete works of art as symbols. To clarify all these points we may address the following questions:

(a) What exactly is a symbol? And how does a symbol differ from a sign or signal?

(b) How do symbols *in* art differ from the symbolic character, if any, of a total work of art?

(c) What does it mean, and is it fair to speak of art-works generally as being symbolic in significance, as Susanne Langer does?

Now, to speak quite simply and generally, a symbol is something concrete or material representing or standing for an idea or emotion. The red colour, for example, is taken to symbolize danger; and a set of scales, justice. The lotus, according to Indian cultural traditions, is a symbol of purity and detachment even during the course of everyday living. Now, real *danger* can appear in various forms; so what it means is not quite determinate. *Red*, on the other hand, is a specific colour; the eye registers it easily; so by relating it to danger we get alerted, so to say, to think of or face some unwelcome happening. Similarly, justice in action is more than a single attitude. It is evenness of temper or not getting confused and agitated in the heat of opposing arguments; balance in considering rival claims; and avoiding an undue tilt in favour of, or against any of the warring parties. Now, all this can be easily brought to mind by seeing or visualizing a set of scales as steadied by a level beam. The image of a lotus too is similarly helpful. Lotuses bloom in mire, without getting sullied themselves. So this flower is an apt symbol for what it is taken to mean. In fine, symbols enable us to economize and articulate *thinking;* hence their value, which is not merely representational. There is indeed eminent sense in Langer's following emphasis:

> The great importance of *reference and communication* by means of symbols has led semanticists to regard these uses as the defining properties of symbols, that is, to think of symbol as essentially a sign which stands for something else and is used to represent that thing in discourse. This preoccupation has led them to neglect . . . the more primitive function of symbols, which is to formulate experience as something imaginable in the first place — to fix entities, and formulate facts and the fact-like elements of thought called fantasies. This function is articulation . . . symbols articulate ideas. Even such arbitrarily assigned symbols as mere names serve this purpose, for whatever is named becomes an entity in thought. Its unitary symbol automatically carves it out as a unit in the word-pattern.[115]

What Langer here says is not quite easy to follow; so we may clarify the extract cited, importantly because it warns us against ignoring what she regards as the "more primitive function of symbols."

True, a symbol *stands for* what it is taken to mean. In Indian culture, for instance, the symbol *svastika* stands for expectation (or assurance) of prosperity. But this "standing for" or reference is possible only because, by virtue of its "unitary" form or shape, the symbol enables us to focus on the thought of prosperity, leaving out everything else in the welter of experience, and thus turning the thought in question into a virtual entity, that is, something which has a kind of self-existence of its own. This is what is meant by saying that a symbol articulates ideas or isolates them for attention. What exactly a symbol refers to in different situations may vary; but its ability to help us in focusing on specific thoughts remains

115. S.K. Langer, *Problems of Art*, p. 132.

constant. For example, as used in a *pūjā-kī-thālī* when a student-member of the family is about to leave for the examination hall, the *svastika* symbol is a quiet prayer for the candidate's academic success; but when it is used similarly in welcoming a couple of newly weds, it symbolizes a hope and prayer for their marital happiness. On the occasion of Dīwālī *pūjā* the same symbol expresses a hope and longing for *material* welfare. But in everyone of these cases what is meant, expected or wished for is isolated for attention by means of the symbol, *though the form of the symbol itself may recede into the margin of consciousness as we avail of its meaning.*

The words we have just put in italics need a little comment. As they operate in contributing to overall meaning, symbols as such do not dominate attention equally in the regions of different arts. In paintings that relate to Christian saints, the halo around their faces is not only seen as such all along but is also taken to *signify* divinity. The same is true of *abhaya-mudrā,* signifying assurance of protection from threatening situations, in the region of Indian sculpture, say, in some works representing the Buddha. But where the object of attention contains a verbal image — such as *charaṇ saroj* in the line: *śrī guru charaṇ saroj raja, nija mana mukur sudhār*[116] — though what the word-symbol *saroj* (lotus) signifies (that is, purity) is readily understood, the form of the symbol — that is, the image of the lotus as such — is not held on to. Here the symbol effaces itself, so to say, in the very act of conducing to what it means.

The point may be made a little more clear by considering the use of *mudrā*s (or gesture symbols) in the classical dances of India. Take, for instance, the *patākā-mudrā* or the symbol of a flag, *unfurled* or *open.* In actual dance it is used to make us *think* of many diverse situations or happenings, such as the beginning of a dance recital, welcoming an honoured guest, or the undulating waters of a river. In the first case the open palms of outstretched arms face either side; in the second case, the

---

116. This is the opening line of Ayodhyā-Kāṇda in *Rāmāyaṇa.*

open (and skyward looking) palm of a slightly outstretched right arm — bent a little at the elbow and coupled with a slight, reverent bow — is made to represent the act of welcoming a special guest; and in the third case the palms, again quite open, face the ground and suggest the undulating waves with a fairly imitative movement of the hands. But though what exactly is represented or suggested by the *mudrā* differs in the three cases — not of course without an accordant configuration of look, stance, and limbs — the *mudrā* in every case lends a little definiteness to, and so may be said to articulate what is sought to be represented. However, the noteworthy point here is that when a *rasika* is actually watching an ongoing dance recital, *a flag* is never really thought of when the palms are being used in the way they are. Just as the linkage, *a-for-apple* — often used in making an Indian child learn the English alphabets — is quite forgotten as the child's knowledge of the actual use of language develops, so the literal image of *patākā* (or a flag) is never visualized when one has learnt to follow the flowing fabric of dance, of course with the help of understanding provided by the theme or verbal text of the number being danced.

But, we may note, whatever be the sharpness of focus with which a symbol is apprehended, what it symbolizes is never expected to be *co-existent* with it. We do not hope to actually find justice in a set of scales, or the living quality or attitude of purity and *anāsakti* (non-attachment) in a lotus. On the other hand, what a *sign* signifies may well be found to go along with it. (Why we here use the words *may well be*, in place of the categorical *is*, will be clear when we have considered different kinds of signs.) Smoke is a sure sign of the presence of some fire nearby. Signs of improvement in a patient's condition may also be said to signify some actual present changes in his bodily and mental health, such as better appetite; sound refreshing sleep; and general cheerfulness. But there are some other signs, such as the mathematical ones of addition and multiplication, which do not make us expect to *find* anything, but only direct the mental activity of calculation.

Nor is it any less difficult to draw a *clear* distinction between sign and *signal.* It has been contended by some that, quite unlike many a sign, a signal is always *intended* to convey some message or to direct activity or its suspension. The signalling done by scouts and the signals that regulate traffic are some obvious illustrations of the point. But if we speak thus, as we freely do in daily life: "Their arrival was a *signal* for the party to begin," the signal — or *their arrival* — cannot be said to *intend* anything. As for *symbols in art*, perhaps the least questionable way to distinguish them from signs and signals is to say that, along with their being conducive to the import of the total work, symbols in art can be generally more striking and winsome than the other vehicles of reference and communication: more striking, we may say, because of what Beardsley speaks of as the Principle of Prominence;[117] and winsome in themselves because of the artist's unremitting concern for shapeliness and design.

> Goya's *The Colossus,* though it is surely not a recognized conventional symbol, becomes a natural symbol [because] its presence is . . . unusual [and] striking. . . . There [the Colossus] sits, enormous, on the edge of the world, towering over the plain; there is no explanation of his coming and going, he is just a giant out of place. We can hardly refrain from regarding him as a powerful symbol . . . [of] a potential destructive force . . . like something in our own unconscious, an embodied *id.*[118]

And, as for symbols that are readily winsome, they are freely found in the arts of India.

Symbols in Indian Art

Of all its traditional arts, it is perhaps the classical dances of India that make a very systematic use of gesture symbolism. A symbolic gesture is called a *mudrā*, and in the making of it the

117. Beardsley, *Aesthetic: Problems in the Philosophy of Criticism*, New York, Harcourt, Brace and World, Inc., 1958, p. 292.

118. Ibid., pp. 292-93.

dancer's hands (*hastas*) generally play a prominent part. But, we may note, the two words, *hastas* and *mudrā*, are by no means identical in meaning: *hasta* mean *hand*. A *mudrā*, on the other hand, is (as a rule) an expressive use of hands conveying a definite, commonly identifiable meaning, though the overall expressiveness here also depends on the accordant use of stance and bodily parts, specially the face in many cases. *Any* occasional positioning of hands in real life cannot be said to be a dance *mudrā*. For example, if a man casually probes with his fingers the right side of his lower jaw, say, with a view to ascertaining where a suspected swelling on the gums really is, the hand involved would surely assume some position; but such a random use of hands cannot be called a *mudrā*, because it is neither meant nor suited to convey any definite meaning *to others*. At the same time, just as in real life, so in the case of *mudrās* in art, for the purpose of expression a measure of accordance between the look of different bodily parts is essential. Thus, neither in real life nor in the world of art can anyone wear a frown while assuring protection to others (*abhaya-mudrā*). In sum, a *mudrā* is always *a meaningful detail of an integrated setting*. But, it is noteworthy, a *mudrā* is not always the *focus* of the setting which encompasses it.

Consider, for instance, the ninth-century Pallava-Choḷa bronze, *Kālīya-Kr̥ṣṇa*, presently housed in the National Museum of India. Here the *abhaya-mudrā* assumed by Kr̥ṣṇa's right hand is of course harmonious in effect with the *firm* placement of the left foot and the equally *secure* grasp of the serpent's tail with the left hand; and it is also visibly parallel, as a vertical, to quite a few other details: say, the (right) upper arm, the suspended right foot and the *añjali-mudrā* of the figure under the hood. Yet the *mudrā* in question is not the *focus* of what goes along with it happily, because it does not actually dominate the onlooker's notice. Rather, one is impelled to survey *the whole figure vertically*, because of the following: the pronounced stretch of the tail; the lissom stance of Kr̥ṣṇa with a *curvature* which not only permits but induces a passage of the eye; and the *añjali-mudrā* (of the nether figure) which, as we follow its look of self-gathering arising from the elbows, prompts our vision to move upwards beyond the hooded barrier. Quite contrarily, where what is artistically built upon is the *alpadma-mudrā* suggesting (in our dances) the blooming of a lotus — the danseuse is so clearly seen to lavish care in *shaping and projecting* the *mudrā* that the whole dance, for a moment, appears concentrated in the symbol which therefore captivates the *rasika*'s eye. In fine, a *mudrā* may either be the effective focus of, or just contribute incidentally to the expressiveness of the total figuration.

What this contribution precisely is would of course depend on the thematic context provided by the number in which it occurs, exactly as a word may suffer some changes in meaning in accordance with variations in its verbal setting. But what gives a definite identity, and makes it usable intelligently, is the name which it bears — a name which is shared by some object of everyday experience, and so makes the *mudrā* identifiable with ease. Thus, nobody who knows a little Hindi finds it dificult to see that the *abhaya-mudrā* is meant to symbolize assurance of safety, or that where fingers are held like the crescent moon the *mudrā* being used is *ardhachandra*. In the case of some other *mudrā*s too — such as *soochī* and *añjali* — it is easy to see that they are abstracted from everyday life.

At this point, however, a question may well be put. If some *mudrā*s, like the ones just mentioned, have only been lifted from real life, how are they symbols and not mere imitations of everyday objects? To be sure, a photocopy is a mere reproduction and not a symbol. The answer, however, may well be that even where a *mudrā* is quite similar to what we find in real life, its essential purpose is to contribute some meaning to the number which employs it, and that the similitude is but a means to this semantic purpose. This explanation will hold also where the *mudrā* chosen for attention is strikingly beautiful in itself. Ordinarily, even where handwriting is very beautiful, does the essential purpose of the written words cease to be communication of meaning?

But the emphasis we have put on the ease with which quite a few *mudrās* can be comprehended should not make us think that symbols in art are all alike easy to follow — for us as we are; and that art contemplation does not involve any effort of active imagining on our part. In the case of some peculiar symbols we *have to determine* what precise meaning tradition has invested them with. Take, for instance, the figure of *yakṣiṇī*, the tree-woman, which is sculpted on the eastern *toraṇa* of *stūpa* I at Sāñchī, with all the grace of Indian womanhood, and very winsomely in the canonic pose of triple flexion (*tribhaṅgī*). It symbolizes fertility, and it is precisely in this sense that it came to be included in Buddhist iconography. As for the possibility that the meaning of art may only be suggested, and that the needed complement may therefore have to be supplied by us, we may consider the case of an Amarāvatī medallion, housed in the British Museum, which conveys the idea of Buddha's crossing the river Nairañjara *without* actually showing the Master's own figure. The end is achieved by depicting some happenings, both real and mythical, which are commonly associated with the event: namely, the movement of the *nāga*s towards the river bank (which suggests that the Master is approaching); the circular movement of the birds which bespeaks their recognition of the glory of the Master; and the *drooping* look even of the trees and plants which signifies that they not only revere Buddha, but are (so to say) concerned about the safety of his venture.

It is, however, to be noted that the meaning of a WoA is secured not by merely adding up what its different elements signify *individually*, but by determining how their *interplay* both invests them with some extra significance *and* makes for the overall import of the work as an indivisible, significant unity. It is with the purpose of projecting this truth that Langer distinguishes the use of *symbols in art* from *the Art Symbol* or the work of art regarded as a symbol itself:

> Symbols certainly do occur in art . . . [for instance,] the familiar halo of sacrosant personages . . . the terrible figures of the

> Guernica, . . . the obvious rose of womanhood . . . the lily of chastity . . . [or] the personal symbols of T.S. Eliot . . . These are all genuine symbols . . . [in the sense that] they mean something beyond what they present in themselves. . . . [But they all] lie on a different semantic level from the work that contains them. Their meanings are not [directly a] part of its import, but [mere] elements in the form that has import, the expressive form. . . . *The elements in a work are always newly created with the total image, and although it is possible to analyse what they contribute to the image, it is not possible to assign them any of its import apart from the whole.* That is characteristic of organic form. The import of a work of art is its "life," which, like actual life, is an individual phenomenon. Who could say how much of a natural organism's life is in the lungs, how much in the legs . . . ? The Art Symbol is a single symbol, and its import is not compounded of partial symbolic values.[119]

The extract just cited is only partly clear. What it says about "a natural organism's life" is evidently true. But the words in italics have to be clarified. We may do it as follows, with the help of a simple example from the region of poetry.

Consider the following couplet of Kabīr:

हम घर जारा आपना, लिया मुराड़ा हाथ।
अब घर जारों तासुका, जो चलै हमारे साथ।।[120]

Here, (as translated literally) *the three "elements"* — that is, such complexes of words (all relating to the poet himself) as may be taken to be more or less self-complete in meaning — are:

(a) I have burnt my home

(b) I have taken a burning torch (मुराड़ा, or मशाल) in my hand

119. Langer, *Problems of Art*, pp. 134-36. The order of words, as they are here cited, differs from the way they occur in the book referred to; but the words are Langer's own.

120. Hazari Prasad Dwivedi, *Kabir*, Rajkamal Publications, 3rd edn., 1976, p. 165. For accuracy of wording and publication details of the couplet I am here indebted to Mrs. Smrti Srivastava.

(c) Now, I am ready and willing to burn the home of anyone who is willing to follow me.

However, as we have put them above, they are all independent sets of words, not really "elements in" the couplet. They become its elements only when they are taken as related to the (import of the) whole couplet; and the moment this is done they are "newly created" in the sense that they come to acquire a meaning which is quite different from what they mean independently. Now, if we only bear it in mind that Kabīr was a saint and not a militant, the whole couplet's meaning could be put thus:

> I have burnt my home *or all my local ties*, and have taken a blazing torch (or मशाल) in my hand — the torch of enlightenment, of which detachment from worldly ties is a natural reflex, and which emits both *light* (to illumine the path) and has intense enough *heat* to burn out all mundane ties. Thus liberated from the bondage of egoity, or of "me and mine," I am now equipped and willing to give similar help to all those who agree to follow me.

Now, if they are taken as elements of the total meaning as we have just put it, (a) would mean not what it literally does, but absolute renunciation of all local ties; (b) not "I have taken an ordinary torch in hand," but the torch of enlightenment; and (c) not the perverse intent to initiate general home-burning, but to guide one and all along the path of renunciation. So all the three elements — a, b, and c — will be "newly created." Yet, we may note, this new meaning cannot be given to any one of them unless they are all alike seen in the light of the overall import.

But is it at all proper to speak of a WoA as a symbol? It is perhaps Susanne Langer alone who not only says *yes* to this question but argues for her view at fair length; and because she does not speak of art as symbol unreservedly, her view has to be taken with care, and so partly in her own words:

> The art symbol . . . [or the work of art regarded as a symbol] is not a symbol in the full familiar sense, for it does not convey

> something beyond itself. Therefore it cannot strictly be said to have a meaning; what it does have is *import*. . . . Its import is seen in it . . . the art symbol is the absolute image [or important because of what it shows in itself, not because of what it points to]. . . . [It is] the *image of* what otherwise . . . [that is, without this imaging] would be irrational . . . [an image of] direct awareness, emotion, vitality, personal identity . . . [or, to put it briefly, an image of] life lived and felt. . . . [The Art Symbol] is a symbol in a special and derivative sense . . . *it formulates and objectifies experience for direct intellectual perception.*[121]

What the extract cited says may now be clarified — and also discussed incidentally — in terms of individual points:

(a) A work of art is not a symbol "in the full familiar sense" because its essential function is not to mean or convey anything beyond itself. But then, one may ask, what shall we say of works that are clearly representational in character, say, portraits, landscape paintings, and poems that relate to specific occasions (such as Eve of St. Agnes by Keats), or to periods of actual human growth say, from infancy onward (such as Wordsworth's Ode to Immortality)? Now, Langer's answer here is clear. Nobody can deny the presence and importance of *representation* in art. But representation cannot be said to be art's *essential* function. It is only one of the many principles of constructing art.

> Representation in painting, diatonic harmony in music, metrical versification in poetry are [all] . . . major devices of composition. They are exemplified in thousands of works; yet they are not indispensable. Painting can eschew representation, music can be atonal, poetry can be poetry without any metrical scaffold.[122]

(b) But if representation is not regarded as the basic function of art, can we say, as is actually held by many

121. Langer, *Problems of Art*, p. 139.

122. Ibid., p. 137.

practitioners and connoisseurs of painting today, that what really counts in art is only the effective (or significant) organization of its formal elements? No, we hardly can; for such a view of the essence of art would leave out a good deal in the region of literary arts, because what words here mean or refer to — that is, things, people, situations, and happenings — makes the bulk of what we relish and react to in contemplating a literary work. True, formal devices such as consistency of characterization, skilful interlacement of the main and subsidiary plots, and comic relief all make for the excellence of, say, a good tragic play. But how can we ignore the interplay of motives and reactions, and the changes of fortune that the words of the play make us visualize?

(c) However, yet another question may be put against Langer's attitude to representation. If in making a portrait the essential purpose of a painter is not to represent the model, what exactly does he aim at in the act of creating the work? Langer's answer would be that the artist's purpose here is to capture on the canvas how or what the individual being portrayed directly appears to him, or is felt by him, not what the individual in question intrinsically is. Langer insists that, as he sets out to create, an artist must ignore every other point of view except that of appearance. But, we may note, she does not *oppose* appearance to reality. How things directly appear to us is itself immediate reality. Our seeking to understand or deal with them comes later.

Two other points may be made in this context. First, insofar as our immediate experience (or intuition) of things, or of life as actually lived precedes *and defies* understanding — *defies* in the sense that the discursive or analytical mode of thinking cannot really *capture,* though it may well *talk about* the non-relational manner of direct experience — it may be said to be "literally ineffable" or indescribable, inexpressible in words, though surely not (Langer would add) in terms of works of art. Second, insofar as all cognitive activity is itself *felt* as interesting, exciting, rewarding or as a mere convoluted wheeling (say to say) on the selfsame axis, it should seem fair to speak of immediate experience (or feeling) as the very "*matrix* of mentality."

(d) But if feeling is the very matrix of mentality, there can be no limit to what it may comprise. Langer is indeed explicit on this point:

> The word *feeling* must be taken here in its broadest sense, meaning *everything that can be felt,* from physical sensation, pain and comfort, excitement and repose, to the most complex emotions, intellectual tensions, or the steady tones of a conscious human life.[123]

Yet though *feeling* is here said to cover anything that can be felt, what lends a distinctive value to *art* is, according to Langer, its capacity for articulating

> the character of so-called "inner life" which discourse — the normal use of words — is peculiarly unable to articulate, and which [that is, "inner life"] therefore we can only refer to in a general and quite superficial way: The actual felt process of life, . . . the drive and directedness of desires, and above all the rhythmic continuity of our selfhood, defies the expressive power of discursive symbolism. The myriad forms of subjectivity, the infinitely complex sense of life, cannot be rendered linguistically, that is, stated. But they are precisely what comes to light in a good work of art . . . not necessarily a "masterpiece". . .. A work of art is an expressive form; and vitality, in all its manifestations from sheer sensibility to the most elaborate phases of awareness and emotion, is what it [the work] may express.[124]

---

123. Langer, *Problems of Art*, p. 15

124. Ibid., p. 133.

Now, Langer may well be acclaimed for drawing our attention to "the myriad forms of subjectivity" which we surely experience, but rarely objectify for explicit attention. It may also be admitted that a semblance of "the drive and directedness of desires" and of "the most elaborate phases of . . . emotion" can be evoked in music. Targeting the *sama* (the focal beat of the rhythm-cycle) and designing varying approaches to it may well be able to objectify a kind of directedness for our notice, and as for the projection of (virtual) emotion in music, we cannot ignore eloquent testimonies such as the following one, cited by Langer:

> If I could be as sad as certain passages in Mozart, my glory would be greater than it is. . . . The fact that I know as much as I do of the essence of pathos comes from meeting with such music . . . from moments . . . when I have seen sadness before me released from entanglements with contingency. . . . We do not read into [the work of our greatest artists] . . . some petty emotions we ourselves have experienced and can readily name. Rather we learn from them what an emotional reality of the greatest stretch *can* be . . . the calm, the spirit of eternal rest, that comes to birth in an Egyption statue. . . . Such are the emotions unnamed perhaps, but expressible and realizable in art. Those, and not personal emotional excitements, are what great artists give.[125]

But even if, on the basis of first hand experiences such as the one given above, we agree to the view that "music sounds *as* feelings feel,"[126] how is it fair to insist that music is a *symbolic* expression of the forms of feeling? Would it not be better to say that music at its best may well appear quite *similar to* some form of feeling? Is not the relation here involved one of simple resemblance? What otherwise does the word *as* here suggest? Langer's answer here would be that though the word *as* certainly means "just like," the two terms which are here said

125. Langer, *Mind — An Essay on Human Feeling*, vol. I, p. 88. Italics added.

126. Langer, *Problems of Art*, p. 26.

to be very similar to each other are, in their wholeness, also quite unlike mutually. This is easily seen when we pay due attention to "sounds" and "feel." A sound is heard; a feeling is felt. What can yet be common to them is a specific emotive impact, virtual in one case, and actual in the other. Music is just a tonal *analogue*, not a photocopy of feeling; and the word, *analogue* is to be taken to mean "that which corresponds in certain respects with something else *which is otherwise different.*" So if music seems similar to feeling it is only in the way of a symbol, exactly as the level beam of a pair of scales, a physical object, may be said to be similar (I repeat) to qualities of being well-balanced or freedom from bias, both implicit in the idea of justice; but with this difference, to be sure, that whereas the set of scales symbolizes something external, the meaning of music, or the feeling it may express, is wholly within its own fabric of tones and rhythm. Indeed, where we actually find some feeling in music, our attention does not shift to anything beyond the music. Music is here a symbol only in a "derivative" sense; it just objectifies the feeling in question for our explicit notice and understanding.

But to turn from music, in respect of which we freely use the words "expressive of feeling," to the other arts which are not occurrent, such as paintings and works of architecture, how can *they* be said to be expressive of (run or life) feeling? Langer's answer here is as follows:

> In good painting, sculpture, or building, balanced shapes and colours, lines and masses look as emotions, vital tensions and their resolutions feel.[127]

What is here said is clearly difficult to accept, nay even to understand. One can only wonder what exactly is there in our subjective life to match the colours and masses that we find in works of painting and architecture; and there is indeed a good deal which can be said to oppose Langer. As we experience it in daily life, resolution of tensions gives us a definite feeling of

---

127. Langer, *Problems of Art*, p. 26.

relief. Perhaps a feeble analogue of this experience is to be found in how a *rasika* at a concert of *tablā* or *pakhāwaj* recital reacts when a long and intricate rhythmic pattern — say, a *chakkardār paraṇ* — attains to the *sama* with split second accuracy. But where, if anywhere, are the arts of architecture and sculpture seen to provide a semblance of the feeling of relief that follows the resolution of a tension? And to take the case of a painting, which "form of feeling" may be said to be symbolized by El Greco's *View of Toledo*?[128] It is simply an expression of the artist's apocalyptic vision of the city of God; and it is for *this* end, and not for the sake of providing any analogue of our inner life as we experience it that the artist rearranges the very topography of Toledo.

To conclude, one may agree that, as Langer points out, representation is not the essence of art; and that what is in every case essential is the immanence of artistic meaning in the work itself. But as for art's being symbolic in significance, what one can fairly concede only is that some music may well be said to *symbolize* our subjective life in the sense of objectifying some of its various forms for our explicit notice. But the grandiose thesis that all art is *necessarily* symbolic of, or in any other way related to, the life of feeling is not supported by the actual evidence of art, a good deal of which, as Hospers rightly observes, is significant essentially because it provides some interesting historical material, or is sweet to the ear or the eye, or just a teaser to perception.

There is, however, yet another relation in which art may be put. Our *rasa* theory is an elaborate attempt to ground artistic activity, specially as it operates in the areas of drama, music, and dance to some basic dispositional modes of emotion with which we are all born. It is precisely this theory which makes the content of the chapter that follows, the final one.

---

128. *El Greco,* Spanish School: 1541-1614. This work is the first great landscape in Spanish Art, and a proud possession of New York's Metropolitan Museum.

6
The Rasa Theory
Its Meaning and Relevance[1]

THE Rasa theory of Bharata Muni has evoked at least as much scholarly debate as the Aristotelian theory of tragedy. What is more, its run as a determinative force of actual artistic practice has perhaps been longer that of the Greek theory. The more systematic classical dances of India still take pride in keeping to Bharata's injunctions in respect of the details and basic function of artistic creation. It is true that both Aristotle and Bharata seek to ground the charm of the art-forms of their choice in some inborn tendencies of humanity as a whole. But whereas Aristotle, in this context, focuses only on our natural proneness to pity and fear, Bharata chooses many more original propensities as bases for his account of the way of evoking *rasa* which is his word for how the impact of a proper presentation *and* contemplation of plays, dance and music actually feels. Bharata's account is also distinguished by the fact that it gives meticulous attention to the details of experience *and* expression of subjective states in respect of both actors who actually create the stage presentation *and* those who follow it knowledgeably, that is, those who make the audience. He is also careful not only to list the various factors that prevent us from adopting

---

1. This chapter only reproduces what has already appeared, under the same title, in *Sangeet Natak*, vol. XXXVII, no. 2, pp. 3-39. The reproduction of this chapter, as of the opening one, appeared essential to me because I wanted this work to serve as a balanced, if brief, account of both contemporary Western and traditional Indian aesthetical thinking.

the right aesthetic attitude, but to relate variations in aesthetic response to differences in age, sex, and temperamental characterstics. Above all, our systems of philosophy, Vedānta and Sāṁkhya in particular, have been more actively concerned with the *rasa* theory than the Western philosophies with Aristotle's view of tragedy.

My purpose in this eassy is essentially interpretative. But it is also exploratory in the sense that it seeks to consider if Bharata's theory is applicable also to some such art-forms as non-dramatic poetry and Kathak dance, to which it has not been convincingly related so far. If other art-forms have to be left out, as is indeed unavoidable, it is due to two main factors: first, my own limitations; and, second, the fact that Kathak is perhaps the only one of our major dance-forms in respect of which no one has tried *to show in detail* and plausibly the relevance of the *rasa* theory. But even generally I have to proceed very carefully for, as has been pointed out by Harold Osborne, one of our top aestheticians today, the theory in question is an extremely intricate one.

So I have to reflect on it piecemeal, say, by trying to answer some key questions, if not exactly in the same order in which they are listed below:

1. What exactly is *rasa*?

   (The answer, to begin with, may be given as a quick listing of the main emphases of the *rasa* theory.)

2. How is the evocation of *rasa* brought about?

   (This will require us to distinguish and explain the various objective and subjective factors that make for the eventual emergence of *rasa*.)

3. How does *rasa* really feel to one who actually experiences it?

   (Here, the answer will call for attention to some of the more important ways in which *rasa* has been spoken of by our traditional theorists *in a manner which is today the well known idiom of phenomenology*.)

4. Finally, can the relevance of the *rasa* theory be fairly extended to cover arts *other than* drama say, non-dramatic poetry and *sangeet* or music and dance as they flourish today?

I. To turn now to the first question, we may begin by noting that *rasa* is not exactly the same thing as aesthetic experience taken quite generally. We often grow ecstatic at the beauty of nature. *Rasa*, on the other hand, is (said to be) produced by contemplation of *art* alone, specially of drama, dance and poetry; and the *what* and *how* of it may be put, quite briefly, as follows:

> *Rasa* is the aesthetically sublimated,[2] yet direct and deeply satisfying experience of *a basic determinative mode of our emotional life* (*sthāyībhāva*). The process of sublimation here consists in so treating this mode with a configuration of some essential factors — namely, *vibhāva*, *anubhāva*, and *vyabhichārī bhāvas* — that the resulting emotional experience appears in utter freedom from those factors that tend to delimit, bedim, and disturb our experience of emotions in daily life; and may therefore be said to be quite otherworldly, nay, even a close approximation to the bliss of realizing ultimate Reality.

Almost all the major emphases of Bharata's view of *rasa* have been noted above, if rather tightly. They may now be brought out at some length. However, before we set out to do so some immediate comment is needed in respect of the way *rasa* has been commonly spoken of, that is, as an exalted emotion. The word *exalted* not only means noble, but *exaggerated*. On the other hand, the word we have chosen, *sublimated*, can only be taken

---

2. The psychoanalytic meaning of sublimation — that is, the channelling of a morally or socially unacceptable impulse, especially a sexual one, towards something creative and more appropriate — is here irrelevant, for even the *sthāyībhāva* of *rati* is (for Bharata) only our natural liking for delight or enjoyment (R. Gnoli, *The Aesthetic Experience According to Abhinavagupta*, Varanasi: Chowkhamba Sanskrit Series Office, 2nd edition, 1968, p. xv), and not the sexual impulse.

to mean *purified* or refined. Even generally, it does not carry any derogatory sense. Positively, *rasa*-experience has indeed been regarded as pure and refined because the emotion here sensed is utterly free from linkages with particualr individuals, places or occasions in real life. Yet, in spite of its being quite different from our mundane emotional experiences, it feels as a very personal experience; and is, what is more, deeply satisfying not only because the process of its evocation involves a good deal that fascinates the ear and the eye, both aesthetic senses according to Bharata, but because it presents to us, for vivid contemplation, the primal determinants of our emotional life and behaviour. Nor is it difficult to see why we have thought it necessary to qualify *sublimated* with *aesthetically*. It is easy for a poet to invest his poems with a sublime look by just packing them with words and thoughts of profound ethical import. The bulk of our saint poetry is a case in point. Indeed, who can deny the exalted look of *bhajan*s like that well-known one of Narsi Mehta which fixes the essential marks of Vaiṣṇava jana?[3] Bharata, on the other hand, looks on *śṛṅgāra* as the pre-eminent *rasa*[4] and entertainment as the essential function of *drama*. So, from his point of view, the sublimation of a *sthāyībhāva* (into *rasa*) is to be secured aesthetically, that is, through the principal artistic device of so integrating the constituent elements (*saṁyoga*) that they may all help each other in making the whole work significant. In respect of the *rasa* theory, indeed, it only means such an interlacement of the various *bhāva*s that the resulting complex or the dramatic presentation as a whole may, so to say, liberate the onlookers from all such factors as delimit experience to individual concerns or specific time-place settings,

3. The reference here is to the *bhajan* which opens thus: "वैष्णव जन तो तेने कहिऐ (*vaiṣṇava jana to tene kahiye*)."

4. Thus, the 16th *sūtra* of Chapter VI of Babu Lal Śukla's *Nāṭyaśāstra*, 2nd edn., Saṁvat 2040 (Hereafter referred to simply as *NŚ* 2nd, part I) as given on p. 218 which lists the eight *rasa*s (that relate to the art of drama) opens with a mention of *śṛṅgāra* and the reason why this *rasa* has been regarded as pre-eminent is simply that it appeals to the generality of mankind. Ibid., p. 220, f.n.

and so provide them with an exalted *or purified* emotional experience.

As for the total meaning of the way we have distinguished, if in brief, the main ideas implicit in the *theory* of *rasa*, it will emerge by degrees as we proceed. But the word *rasa* itself provides some clues to what the *theory* may be taken to say. Traditionally, this word has been commonly translated as *taste*, not in the sense of cultivated or poor taste — say, in respect of clothing or the arts — but in that of the relish of what we eat or drink. Even in this everyday sense, however, the word "taste" may be taken as a noun *or* as a verb: that is, as what is tasted (*rasyate iti rasaḥ*) — namely, *something* edible as it feels to the tongue — or as the *act* of taking the taste of the edible in question (*rasānām rasaḥ*). As that which is tasted, *rasa* may well be the juice of a fruit. *Juice* is also, as we know, a commonly acknowledged meaning of *rasa*. Taken in this sense *and* as an aesthetic concept, the word *rasa* would mean that just as its juice is the very essence of (the value of) a fruit, so *rasa* is the secret of the charm of a work of art as contemplated. The analogy, however, should not be pressed too far, for whereas the pulp of a fruit is commonly thrown away after its juice has been extracted, a work of art — say, a good poem — remains a single, undivided object of relish even after many careful readings.[5]

We have also to remember that every act of tasting is not welcome to the palate. Very few, for example, relish the taste of bitter gourd. *Rasa*, on the other hand, is said to be always a felicitous experience. Partly because of this one consideration, *relish* would probably be a better word for *rasa* (taken as a verb) than *taste*. What is more, *relish* does not only mean "to enjoy something greatly," but "with discrimination"; and this again makes the word *relish* more accordant with Bharata's real view than *taste*. What justifies our saying so is an analogy which he expressly uses and which may be put as follows. Just

5. T. Gnoli, *The Aesthetic Experience According to Abhinavagupta*, I[st] edn., Rome, 1956, pp. 60f.

as a dish, in the making of which various spices have been used, must be tasted *by a connoisseur* of food if its distinctive taste is to be rightly perceived, so, because it is no simple property of any given object — but is rather a kind of rich and elevated delight which arises from the interplay of various factors — *rasa* too is an object of relish only for those who can contemplate works of art knowledgeably.

But even when it is so interpreted the sensuous analogy is open to a question. If, as the theorists insist, in experiencing *rasa* we do not *severally* identify the various factors which have gone into its evocation, how are training and discrimination necessary (as they are emphatically said to be) for those who expect to experience *rasa*? An answer is however possible, and we may put it thus. What is demanded and exercised in the case of *rasa*-experience is *intuitive* discrimination, and no explicit analysis. Yet such discrimination, though it here *works* instantly, is the *product* of a long course of discipline of our apprehending powers. It would not be proper to doubt if discrimination can ever be *intuitive*,[6] for differences can certainly be felt as such without being blown up into clear distinctions. It is, in fact, an everyday experience for a gourmet to sense the various condiments that have gone into the making of a dish *without* letting his overall relish suffer for a moment because of abidance of attention at a particular condiment.

At the same time, as sensitiveness to a relish, *tasting* is not mere *eating*. The latter can be done absent-mindedly; the former, never.[7] There is yet another way in which the metaphor of tasting is of help to us in the present context. Just as the

---

6. See, here, the following statement by Susanne K. Langer in *Problems of Art*, London: Routledge & Kegan Paul, 1957 (p. 166): "There are certain relational factors in experience which are either intuitively recognized or not at all, for example, distinctness, similarity, congruence, relevance. These are formal characteristics which are protological in that they must be seen to be appreciated."

7. R. Gnoli, *Aesthetic Experience According to Abhinavgupta*, 1st edn., p. 66, 4th footnote.

experience of tasting is so immediate that the truth of what is tasted, along with that of the experience itself, is quietly admitted in the very act, so *rasa*, as a kind of tasting, is itself a witness to its own truth.[8] *This* tasting, however, is no mere isolated act of *momentary* relish (or चखना). It is the *course* or process of enjoying an experience. In spite of the charm that may be there in the aesthetic presentation itself, the person involved has to put in some effort, though he is also impelled to hold on to the act. This is why the dual ability to concentrate on, and to adopt an impartial attitude towards the aesthetic object is regarded as one of the essential preconditions for experiencing *rasa*. But, of course, once *rasa* has come into being as the experience of a relish, the *rasika*'s effort operates as just a quiet impulse to keep himself open or available to the bliss. It is because of this (partly deliberate) attitude of effortless attention and *self-surrender* (of a sort) that when the experience is over, the *rasika* is often able to *recall* it all as his, not with any self-conscious sense of having been its agent, but as one who was, so to say, just blessed with, and enlivened by the experience — a fact which explains why we cannot be prompted by a play to take recourse to righteous actions that make for felicity if it could *not* evoke *rasa*,[9] and so has failed to impress us deeply.

In other words, in the act of "tasting" *rasa* the ego is only submerged, *not utterly undone* as it is in mystical experience. It may seem odd to speak thus, but we cannot dismiss the suggestion outright; for if the *object* can be perceived with varying degrees of distinctness, why should we find it difficult to believe that in having an experience the *ego* can be more or less self-conscious? The truth indeed is that, in the experience of *rasa*, one's own self is neither quite eclipsed (*tiraskṛta*) nor in a state of tending to cut into (*ullikh*) the felt unruffledness. Were the self here wholly eclipsed, the cognition would be not merely aesthetic, but mystical or utterly free from distinct

8. R. Gnoli, *Aesthetic Experience According to Abhinavgupta*, p. 38, 2nd footnote.

9. Babu Lal Śukla, *NŚ*, 2nd, part I, 3rd footnote on p. 228.

apprehensions (*vikalpa*); and were it to remain a distinct, self-conscious ego, the experience in question will tend to take the form of subject-object relatedness, or be merely discursive, like the bulk of everyday experience, dissipating *tādātmya* without which *rasa* can neither arise or continue. Here, as a fair analogy, we could point to the possibility of an intensely devout man's *regarding himself as a mere channel of His Will*. Here his *ego-sense* is not wholly rubbed out, for he truly feels both humbled and nourished by the attitude, and so happily lets himself be imbued with it ever deeper; but, on the other hand, the sense of being the bearer of an experience does not obtrude upon the feeling of surrender, and so keeps up the beatitude.

We may not here wonder if our recourse to an instance of *non*-sensuous experience is not a mere leap, for Bharata is quite explicit on the point that, though he surely uses the analogy of tasting food, *rasāsvādana* (in his view), is *mānasāsvādana*[10] in reality, and that the analogy in question is meant only to heighten the immediacy, or the self-certifying, presentational character of *rasa*-experience.

All this has been repeatedly pointed out by learned writers on *rasa*, both in the past and in our own day. What has, however, perhaps not been quite clearly seen is *the relation* between Bharata's recourse to the metaphor of tasting and the other emphases of his theory of drama. The point is that what is tasted is not only directly sensed but directly *presented*. It is this which explains Bharata's unremitting and extremely detailed emphasis on the presentational side, and not merely on the inner details of the art of drama; and so necessarily on *overt* physical changes that make for effective *abhinaya*. This is also what makes the *rasa* theory pre-eminently relevant to drama (as staged) and dance. In both these arts what directly meets the eye is of paramount importance, and the ideal content or what is expressed never looks disembodied. It is this which can easily make our experience here *sākṣātkarātmaka*, or of the

10. Babu Lal Śukla, op. cit., p. 287.

nature of encountering a *presence* (as Marcel uses the word).[11] Phenomenologically, there is no gap here for *rasikas* between sensing and the seizure of expressiveness. Yet, we may note, it would be wrong to assume that Bharata is indifferent to the actors' need to be watchful in respect of the subjective aspect of *abhinaya*. What he speaks of as *sāttvika abhinaya* is impossible without the actors' intense imaginative oneness with the ideal content being expressed.[12] It would here be pertinent to note that even today our better known directors and writers of plays regard intensity as a key requirement of effective acting.[13]

Nor can we say that Bharata's emphasis on the paramount need to train actors in the art of making the requisite *gestures and movements* is wholly irrelevant today. Our classical dancers educate themselves in both; and some of our directors of plays today have thought it necessary to subject their actors to a regular course in body discipline. See here the following emphasis of Kavalam Narayana Panikkar in respect of his presentation of (a part of) *Shākuntalam*:

> The body is of paramount importance to an actor. So we chose the Kalaripayattu system as the basic method of training. Kalari is the martial art of Kerala. . . . In our process of training, we try to combine body movements with the *bhāva*, the inner state of being.[14]

Our main concern, however, is with Bharata's own formulation of his *rasa* theory and not with the measure in which it still

11. That is, something which is not only directly encountered, but is at once a benign influence.
12. Śukla, *NŚ*, 2nd, part I, p. 84 of editor's own Preface, and p. 222.
13. The reference here is specially to the following words of Utpal Dutt: "Intensity is the most important thing. Actors cannot act [effectively] if they don't find joy in the acting. The moment acting in a rehearsal or a performance feels like a torture, one has to stop it." *Contemporary India Theatre: Interviews with Playwrights and Directors*, New Delhi: Sangeet Natak Akademi, 1989, p. 17.
14. Ibid., p. 62.

holds good today. So we may now turn to what we have listed as the second question relating to our task.

II. How is the experience of *rasa*, which is said to be other-worldly, actually evoked? To be sure, it does not arise on its own, and quite as definitely it is very different from our everyday emotions. The joys and sorrows of our daily life occur quite easily; they do not need that happy, yet controlled interplay of subjective and objective factors without which *rasa* cannot arise. Now, the factors that make for the emergence of *rasa* are put thus in the famous *rasa sūtra*:[15]

vibhāvanubhāvavyabhichārīsaṁyogādrasaniṣpattiḥ.[16]

According to this *sūtra*, *rasa* results from the *saṁyoga* of three factors, namely, *vibhāva*, *anubhāva* and *vyabhichārī bhāvas*. *Sthāyībhāva* does not here figure in this list, though it is undoubtedly regarded as the basis of the whole aesthetic configuration. But, then, how are we to account for its omission in the *sūtra* itself? Some answer to this question may perhaps be had by considering the very order in which Bharata proceeds in the sixth chapter of his *Nāṭyaśāstra*, and by reflecting on it expressly in relation to some key questions, say, as follows:

What is the ultimate objective of the artist's (or dramatist's) creative effort?

It is evocation of some *rasa*. So, in the 16th *sūtra* Bharata lists all the eight *rasas*.[17]

15. The common belief that this *sūtra* is an utterance of Bharata has, however, been challenged. Thus, see the following statement in Dr Radhavallabh Tripathi's review of Prof. Kapil Kapoor's book, *Literary Theory — Indian Conceptual Framework*, in the *Journal of Indian Council of Philosophical Research*, Special Issue ("Life-Worlds"), March 2002, p. 160. "The fact is that the theory of *rasa* does not originate with Bharata's *Nāṭyaśāstra*. The famous *rasa sūtra* . . . was not given by Bharata, it was handed over to him by the tradition of earlier *ācāryas*."

16. 32nd Sūtra of ch. VI on p. 228 of Sukla's *NŚ* 2nd, part I.

17. Sukla's *NŚ* 2nd, part I, p. 218.

As against the ultimate *aim*, what is the basic, fundamental *ground* on which art creation is to proceed?

It is (in Bharata's view) some *sthāyībhāva*. So, in the 17th *sūtra*, Bharata lists the eight *sthāyībhāvas*.[18] *What* exactly he means by making *sthāyībhāva* the very anchor of the creative process, and *why* he does so can be brought out quite simply. Is the dramatist to begin by choosing any subject straight away? No; if he wishes to make his work acceptable to *rasika*s at large (as he surely does), and not to any highbrow penchant of some people who may choose to affect a cultural stance superior to the common man's attitude, he has to begin by picking a subject which admits of a particular *sthāyībhāva* for artistic treatment, because these *bhāva*s are integral to our being, and are already familiar to us as common determinants of our emotional life. Everything else that is needed to make a good play has to follow subsidiarily, — that is, in such a way that the *sthāyībhāva*'s aesthetical potential, or its openness to be exalted into a super-personal and deeply unified (*niravacchinna*) emotion may be duly realized. This is *the essential logic* of artistic creation, as distinguished from its *devices of construction*.

Finally, after the ultimate goal and the regulative principle of artistic creation have both been fixed, how is one to proceed? What are the elements to be built upon or the creative devices one may use? These are, we are told, *vibhāva*, *vyabhichārībhāvas* (*sūtras* 19-22), *sāttvika-bhāva*s (23), and *abhinaya* of four kinds (24).[19]

As components of the creative process (which integrates them) they may be called *elements;* but in so far as they have all to be *created* — that is, projected or performed by actors or provided by the stage manager — they may also be called devices of construction. None of these elements can work in a kind of philosophical vacuum. Like emotional reactions in our daily lives, they become meaningful *only* as related to some *specific* situation or pre-existing factors, essentially objective or

18. *Sūtra* 18, Ibid., p. 221.

19. Sukla's *NŚ* 2nd, part I, pp. 222-3.

subjective, or both at once (*vibhāva*). Yet, they are to be creatively visualized (in writing a play) or actively presented on the stage, *and* integrated in either case, for the sake of exalting a *sthāyībhāva* (which is already there is us as human beings) into *rasa*. This is why where (as in the *rasa-sūtra*) Bharata speaks of elements which are to be brought together for the purpose of evoking *rasa*, *sthāyībhāva* is not included. The omission cannot be taken to suggest that he here undervalues *sthāyībhāva*. In fact, in the two *sūtras* (33, 34) which naturally follow the *rasa sūtra* (32) pretty quickly,[20] we are told that just as those who have expert knowledge of the *rasas* found in food can relish the delicacies made out of various ingredients, so *sahṛdaya jana* (non-sensuously or mentally) taste the *sthāyībhāvas* as *rasa* in dramatic compositions. Here, it is obvious, the primacy of *sthāyībhāva* is reaffirmed.

It is, in this context, noteworthy that Bharata relates (the individual emotive character of) every *rasa* to a specific *sthāyībhāva*, and not to any particular *vibhāva* or detail of *anubhāva*. However various be the factors that go into the rise of, say, *śṛṅgāra rasa*, it must have the feel of *rati* (sheer delight or amorous enjoyment); and, similarly, the *rasa* known as *karuṇa*, though of course it is not our immediate response to any actual tragic news or event, must induce in us a serious and sympathetic mood, as can easily happen when we actually find someone in a sorry state. For abstract understanding it may suffice to think of *rasa* in terms of its *general* attributes, such as tranquillity or repose and freedom from desire or from thoughts of reality and utility; but when we experience *rasa*, it is always a *specific rasa*, and its distinctness arises from, and retains and evokes the unique feel of the particular *sthāyībhāva* which it builds on. This is a vital part of Bharata's meaning when he fixes specific *sthāyībhāvas* (s.b.) as the bases of different *rasas* as follows:

s.b. *rati* (desire for happiness, amorous or general) — *rasa, śṛṅgāra; hāsa* (innate love of mirth or laughter) — *rasa, hāsya;*

---

20. Sukla's *NŚ* 2nd, part I, pp. 286-7.

śoka (tendency to grieve) — *rasa, karuṇa; krodha* (tendency to get angry) — *rasa, raudra; utsāha* (impulse to feel enthused) — *rasa, vīra; bhaya* (propensity to feel afraid) — *rasa, bhayānak; jugupsā* (tendency to dislike, abhor) *rasa, bībhatsa;* and *vismaya* (proneness to wonder) — *rasa, adbhuta.*

But what exactly is a *sthāyībhāva*? It is obvious that whatever be the way we put it in English, it should go well with the literal meaning of the Sanskrit word. Now, the word *sthāyī* means *permanent* or *abiding;* and as for *bhāva,* we have to go by the way Bharata interprets the word at the very start of the seventh chapter of his treatise.[21] Derived from the causative of *bhu,* to be, it is also intended to mean *to cause to be, create, or bring about.* So, taking the two meanings together, *bhāva* may be taken to signify something which (already) is and which also brings about something, say, the projection of dramatic meaning through speech, bodily limbs and *sāttvikabhāvas*. The complete word *sthāyībhāva* therefore comes to mean an original or already present tendency or disposition in the mind which makes for the *experience and expression* of some ideal content.[22] So to understand the *concept* of *sthāyībhāva* is however not the same thing as an *actual sthāyībhāva.* The latter always bears a specific character. This is why Bharata takes pains to distinguish the different *sthāyībhāvas*. The *sthāyībhāva* of *rati* inclines us to rejoice and seek happiness generally; that of *śoka,* to commiserate with others; and so on. Words *we* have chosen for *bhāva* — that is, *tendency, disposition* — are both open-ended in the sense that they alike mean the supplement *to do* or *bring about.* So they may both be taken to facilitate Bharata's passage from a *sthāyībhāva* to its corresponding *rasa*. Even apart from this semantic consideration, actual experience bears out the way Bharata here speaks. Relating the *sthāyībhāvas* of *śoka* and *utsāha,* for example, to *karuṇa* and *vīra rasas* (respectively) is obviously proper. The sight of someone sorrowing may easily make us

21. Sukla's *NŚ* 2nd, part I, pp. 368-9.

22. Here too I follow, in part, what Gnoli says about *bhāva* in the first footnote on p. xv of his *The Aesthetic Experience According to Abhinavagupta*, 2nd edn., op. cit.

feel moved; and how can anyone be a hero without being enthused for the pursuit of some definite objective? Further, in so far as the *sthāyībhāvas*, regarded as dispositions, are here taken to *operate* as tendencies that (can) *produce* emotional experiences of different kinds, instead of merely *being* this or that, their full meaning may be put thus: dispositional *modes* of emotional experience.[23]

At this point, however, a question may be put. Emotion is also an acknowledged meaning of *bhāva*. So why can't *sthāyībhāva* be translated as "permanent or fixed *emotion*"[24] rather than as "permanent *disposition*"? To this our answer would readily be that the word *emotion*, as commonly understood, stands for something that is merely occurrent, something which comes and goes; and that therefore it cannot go with the word *sthāyī*. Precisely for the same reason it is difficult to accept the suggestion, put forth by both Ananda Coomaraswamy[25] and S.K. De,[26] that *sthāyībhāva* may be taken to mean "permanent mood." A mood is always *felt*, however dimly.[27] A *sthāyībhāva*, on the other hand, is said to abide in us as a *latent* disposition.[28] Further, whereas any stray object can quicken a mood (say, a gloomy one) into re-awakening its parent emotion (say, grief)

---

23. Harold Osborne, *The Art of Appreciation*, OUP, 1970, p. 116.

24. "Fixed emotion" is S.K. De's translation of *sthāyībhāva*. See his *Sanskrit Poetics as a Study of Aesthetic*, OUP, 1963, p. 103. (From now on this work is referred to simply as *Sanskrit Poetics*). Yet, as we have just suggested, it does seem proper to translate *sthāyībhāva* as "permanent or dispositional mode of emotion." Cf. K. Krishnamoorthy's essay, "Traditional Indian Aesthetics in Theory and Practice" in *Indian Aesthetics and Art Activity*, Shimla: Indian Institute of Advanced Study, 1968, p. 44.

25. Ananda Coomaraswamy, *The Dance of Śiva*, Asia Publishing House, 3rd printing, 1956, p. 53.

26. Cf. S.K. De: *Sanskrit Poetics*, 1963, p. 53.

27. This is obviously implied when we say, as we freely do, "Please do not disturb me; *I am not* in a good mood."

28. Or, as a *vāsanā*.

quite easily — as when a bereaved parent, still close to the loss, starts crying at once on recovering a dress which the toddler used to wear — a specific *sthāyībhāva* is *made to* bloom into its corresponding *rasa* through a close, skilful and creative mixing of diverse elements. Finally, a mood is often the gradual way in which an emotion is seen to taper. So it does not abide, or is *asthāyī*. Surely, the irritable mood which comes in the wake of violent anger, and the blues which may follow intense grieving, both generally pass off quickly. Nor can a *sthāyībhāva* be identified with *sentiment*. *Sentiment* is of course an admitted meaning of *bhāva*. What is more, sentiments like friendship and patriotism work as fairly *stable* determinants of our attitudes and behaviour. However, they cannot be said to be a part of the *original* equipment of our minds. We *develop* sentiments. Two men become friends by experiencing, say, joy, sorrow, or anxiety with regard to each other in different situations. Nor can anyone be said to be born with the patriotic sentiment. A *sthāyībhāva*, on the other hand, is (for Bharata, and quite rightly) a part of our mental make-up from the very beginning of our lives. This is borne out by the way in which he posits the reality of *sthāyībhāva*s. All human beings, he argues, desire the company of those whom they love, enjoy making fun of others, and are saddened when their loved ones depart. So it would only be proper to believe in the universal (if uneven)[29] presence of *sthāyībhāva*s like *rati*, *hāsa* and *śoka*, and also of the other ones, following the same line of argument. It would here be relevant to add that the deeply satisfying character of actual *rasa*-experience — distinguished by the feeling that though it is (in the main) objectively evoked, the experience strikes a chord in our hearts, instead of appearing as an imposition from outside — is better explained on the assumption that *sthāyībhāva*s are inborn. So, because of their being original, they cannot be regarded as being identical with sentiments. In case it is protested that *sentiment* can also be taken in senses other than the one we have focused on — say, as refined feelings expressed in art or literature — our answer would be the same as we

29. Śukla, *NŚ* 2nd, part I, p. 266.

have already given in respect of taking *sthāyībhāva* as (permanent or fixed) emotion.

Nor can we equate *sthāyībhāva* with instinct. The difference is, in fact, easy to see. As a native capacity to *deal with* a situation in terms of some overt and relatively determinate action, an instinct is essentially conative in character.[30] A *sthāyībhāva*, on the other hand, is essentially an original tendency to *feel*. To speak of a *sthāyībhāva* as being original to human nature is simply to mean that we have an inborn tendency to become sad, angry or happy in appropriate situations. On the other hand, where we act out of (what have been regarded as) the instincts of sex, pugnacity or self-preservation, the resulting feeling is one of having been able *to do* what we wanted to do. The aesthetic evocation of a *sthāyībhāva* in terms of *rasa* just gives one the *feeling* of emotional exaltation,[31] or *sublimation* (as we have interpreted the word); and so long as it is not evoked, it may be said to remain in a state of latent abidance, or as *vāsanā*.

At this point too, a sceptical question is possible. Can we not produce a good play without relating it to any specific *sthāyībhāva* or *rasa*? A negative answer cannot be given here at once, especially if we take care to go by contemporary evidence. On December 31, 1959, under the banner of Little Theatre Group, Utpal Dutt produced *Angār* "the immediate provocation" of which was simply the occurrence of some coal-mine disasters, and which was yet a definite commercial success.[32] Again, *Ādhe Adhūre*, a well-known play of Mohan Rakesh, has been successfully produced more than once. In

---

30. The commonly acknowledged meanings of "instinct," we may note, are an involuntary prompting to *action*, and the natural impulse by which animals are guided *in their behaviour* apparently without the help of reason or experience.

31. M. Hiriyanna, *Art Experience*, Mysore: Kavyalaya Publishers, 1954, p. 38.

32. *Contemporary Indian Theatre*, p. 14.

1970, it was directed by Shyamanand Jalan;[33] in 1976, by Amal Allama from the National School of Drama;[34] and yet again on 8 September 1989, by Jalan, in connection with the Nehru Shatābdi Nāṭya Samāroha. But the underrunning theme of this play, as of all the other plays of Mohan Rakesh, from *Āṣāḍh kā ek Din* onwards, does not conduce to evocation of any definite *rasa*, but is simply the contemporary

> breakdown of communication in human relations and the consequent tragedy . . . observed and experienced at its direct and most delicate in man-woman relations.[35]

Are we then to say that the *rasa* theory has now utterly lost the value it has been so widely attributed to it?

A fair answer here would simply be that though a play can surely be good in itself and also as a stage presentation without owing allegiance to the *rasa* theory, it is doubtful if such works can have as *wide and abiding an appeal*, as distinguished from merely contemporary acclaim, as (say) *Shākuntalam* of Kālidās or Shakespeare's *Romeo and Juliet*.[36]

On the other hand, it would be wrong to believe than an element of merely contemporary interest is necessarily a barrier to the evocation of *rasa* by a work of art. Consider, in this context, the widely (and rightly) acclaimed film *Lagaan*. The *rasa* theory seems to be quite applicable to it. Even generally, it would be odd to hold that a theory which holds good for drama and dance is necessarily irrelevant to films. It is true that drama and film differ in some quite clear ways. In the former we look at a stage; in the latter, at a screen; and the diverse visual effects

---

33. *Contemporary Indian Theatre*, p. 69.
34. Ibid., p. 68.
35. Ibid., p. 67.
36. If I do not here mention the great Shakespearan tragedies like *King Lear, Hamlet and Macbeth*, it is simply because (in my present state of understanding) I find it difficult to relate them to the *rasa* theory.

produced by the actual entry and exit of actors, or by their living movements across the stage, are obviously missing for those who watch a film. Further, it is only in the presentation of a play that an actor may seem to be addressing the audience directly. But, on the other hand, the two arts of drama and film also share a great deal. Both are instances of occurrent art. Stability is not the dominant character of what here meets the eye. Again, there is plenty of *abhinaya*, even of the *sāttvika* kind, in both. Music and dance, included by Bharata in *āhārya abhinaya*, are perhaps even more pronounced in the majority of our films today than in contemporary theatre. Again, in respect of films like *Ānand* one could even speak of a continual undercurrent of the *sthāyībhāva* of *śoka*, say, because of a manifest all-round apprehensiveness at the thought of what is imminent for the sick and overly cheerful hero; and so also of an effective evocation, finally, of *karuṇa rasa*. In respect of *Lagaan*, perhaps even more convincingly, one could speak of the *sthāyībhāva* of *utsāha* and of the corresponding *rasa*, *vīra*. Violence, we may note, is *not* one of the essential *vibhāva*s that make for the evocation of this *rasa*. According to Bharata, these *vibhāva*s are rather the following:

> highly exalted and enthusiastic nature; freedom from confusion, insensibility, and ignorance (*a-sammoha*); mental effort (*adhyavasāya*); *bala* (strength, power); *parākrama* (enterprise, courage); *śakti* (capability); *pratāp* (reputation); *sthairya* (steadfastness, perseverance, tranquillity); *dhairya* (patience): *śaurya* (heroism, valour); *tyāga* (giving up, resigning, sacrificing one's life, liberality); and *vaiśāradya* (expertness, wisdom).[37]

None of these means physical violence. It is true that at least one commentator has translated *bala* as an army which

37. Sūtra 68 in Śukla's *NŚ* 2nd, vol. I pp. 336-37. Bracketed English equivalents of listed words have been taken from *A Sanskrit–English Dictionary* by M. Monier Williams (hereafter referred to simply as *MW*), Motilal Banarsidass, Corrected edition, 2002.

comprises horses, elephants, and soldiers.[38] But this is not one of the acknowledged meanings of the word;[39] and to insist on this meaning is just being driven by our chronic, but mistaken, tendency to take the word in question in a merely physical sense. Do we not speak of the strength of will quite as freely (and as justifiably) as of a strong body? Indeed, anyone who pursues or struggles for a noble objective persistently and patiently, without being discouraged by opposition, criticism, or difficulties like lack of resources, deserves to be regarded as *vīra*.

Now, to turn again to the film in question, right from its beginning to the very end what strikes the onlooker is the determined and perfectly fair opposition to the imposition of a quite unfair tax (*lagaan*), spearheaded by the hero Bhuvan, and gradually taken up by most of the villagers. They may all be said to be acting *nobly* not only because of the manifest rightness of the cause they are fighting for, but because of their recourse to fervent collective prayer — rather than to any devious means or sheer abdication of the fight — in a life-and-death situation. The hero, Bhuvan — highlighted not only as the target of the British army officer's venomous challenge, but as the central rallying force that galvanizes almost the whole village into action — is here the *ālambana vibhāva*; and the ominous situation created by the challenge, and the thought of the ruinous consequences that are bound to follow the failure to meet it, are *uddīpana vibhāva*, because it is these factors that quicken and intensify the hero's resolve. The cricket match, where the challenge comes to a head, is of course an element of contemporary interest for urban Indians, most of whom are cricket crazy; but the way it is fought out against some very heavy odds and machinations of the opponents, overriding occasional moments of despair, is so manifestly courageous

38. The reference here is to Śukla's own footnote on p. 337 of vol. I., *NŚ* 2nd.

39. I say so on the basis of the way the word has been interpreted in *MW*, p. 722.

that the finale is not the mere winning of a game, but the very climax of a fight for justice which we *all* hail happily, because of our innate propensity to get enthused for a noble cause;[40] and so experience *vīra rasa*.

In thus reflecting on the film in question, however, we have used some terms, such as *vibhāva* (*ālambana* and *uddīpana*) and *āhārya abhinaya*, the precise significance of which is yet to be brought out. It is this defect which we may now try to remedy. Like our everyday experience of emotions, *rasa*-evocation needs appropriate pre-conditions or *vibhāva*. Generally, *vibhāva* is taken to mean an objective situation[41] which is more or less lifelike by virtue of having a distinct emotive character, yet without representing a real, living individual. It is lifelike also in the sense that it comprises a human focus (*ālambana*) and a context which is commonly known as *uddīpana* because it is favourable for the self-revelation of (a particular *sthāyībhāva* in terms of) an emotion. Thus, where (a semblance of) the *sthāyībhāva* of *rati* is to be evoked, the togetherness of the *nāyak* and the *nāyika* can easily appear as the focus (or *ālambana*) of the situation, and details like a moonlit night and a bower in the garden may be said to serve as *uddīpana* or stimulus to love-making. To make the point clearer, an example may here be taken from the well-known classic of Kālidāsa, *Abhijñāna Shākuntalam*. At a particular juncture in the course of the play, King Dushyanta, as he moves about the hermitage of Kaṇva Ṛṣi, gets his first glimpse of the lovely Śakuntalā watering the plants of the garden, accompanied by her two close friends. When she casually asks one of them to slightly loosen her improvized bra of bark which, she complains, has been tied a bit too tightly by the other friend, the latter retorts: "Why do

40. See here the following relevant remark of Śukla: "उत्तम वर्णों का उत्साह सर्वत्र आस्वाद्य होता है।" *NŚ* 2nd, part I, p. 336, footnote.

41. Thus, in his *Sanskrit Poetics*, De is seen to explain *vibhāva* as follows: "Conditions appropriate to the emotion to be evoked, as a garden or a beautiful woman" (p. 88). The word is explained similarly on p. 104 as well.

you pick me for blame? It is rather the blooming of your own youth which is at fault."[42] Now, here Śakuntalā may be said to be the *ālambana vibhāva* because she has been brought to a focus by the pleasantry; and the beautiful natural surroundings of the hermitage and the amiable friends, the *uddīpana vibhāva*, because they conjoin to bestir the king's ardent love for Śakuntalā.

However, if we stop here, as has indeed been done by some scholars,[43] our account of *vibhāva* will be incomplete and even misleading. In Bharata's total view *vibhāva* is not always merely objective. As already pointed out, he includes the following *essentially subjective* qualities or attitudes in the list of *vibhāva*s that make for the quickening of *utsāha* which is the *sthāyībhāva* of *vīra rasa: adhyavasāya* (mental effort, apprehension) and *asammoha* (freedom not only from confusion but also from insensibility, ignorance, folly, and bewilderment).[44] So, *vibhāva* has to be taken to mean all those factors — subjective or objective, or both at once — which serve as essential *pre-*conditions of the very start of the creative process whereby a *sthāyībhāva* is made to bloom into its corresponding *rasa*. Both the points here made in respect of *vibhāva* have to be borne in mind, that is, not only its being essential as a pre-condition, but its being related to our subjective attitudes. A pre-condition is simply a condition to be satisfied in advance, like just getting properly set at the blocks for running a race. *Vibhāva* too does not itself evoke *rasa* directly, but only facilitates or prepares the ground for evocation of the experience. So, as compared to the manifestly active character of *abhinaya* (acting and dialogue,

42. This example has been taken from K.C. Pandey's *Comparative Aesthetics*, vol. I (Indian Aesthetics), 2nd edn. 1959, Varanasi: Chowkhamba Sanskrit Series Office, p. 25. The way I have put it, however, differs from the way it appears in the work referred to.

43. Śukla, for instance, interprets *vibhāva* as simply the situation or occasion which makes for the awareness of *sthāyībhāva* in the *nāyak*. *NŚ* 2nd, part I, p. 67.

44. In translating *asammoha* into English I have again followed *MW*, p. 118.

in particular) included in *anubhāva*, the due value of *vibhāva* is likely to be missed. But a simple example should suffice to make us see that the effectiveness of *abhinaya* itself depends on *vibhāva*, if but partly. A mere class-room lecture (by a danseuse) on *abhinaya* relating to *śṛṅgāra rasa* may be accompanied by the most accurate "illustrations" in terms of actual bodily postures, gestures, and movements; but because the only figure present here is that of the danseuse herself, and further because what here surrounds her — say, the barren walls of the room — is not at all suggestive of *rati bhāva*, the impact of the entire exercise will be much less than that of similar *abhinaya*, say, during the course of an actual dance involving a (male-female) couple of performers, and supported by appropriate singing and stage decoration.

On the other hand, *vibhāva* itself needs the supplement of *anubhāva*, specially as movement and speech. Even in the case of the instance we cited from *Śākuntalam*, what appears to put life into the visualized setting of man and nature is the sweet little bout of words between Śakuntalā and her friends, the gestures which naturally go along with such talk, and the act of watering.

It is indeed quite easy to see the value of the second factor listed in the *rasa sūtra*, that is, *anubhāva* which comprises *abhinaya* of different kinds, say, the following: *āṅgika* (or bodily, as movement, gesture, and posturing); *vāchika* (relating to utterance, dialogue); *sāttvika* (or involuntary) comprising those bodily changes which serve as unmistakable signs of some actual emotion; and *āhārya*, or those superadded things which are not really a part of the psycho-physical being of the actors, namely, costumes, lighting arrangements and *sangeet* (that is, vocal and instrumental music, and dance). It is noteworthy that *āhārya* can add substantially to the effect of stage presentation. This is borne out by the practice of both dance and drama even today. Thus, where a Kathak danseuse begins the dancing of a *trivat* composition which, we may say, opens with the syllable *kṛān* (क्ड़ान) after a flourish of some prefatory music, the sonant suddenness of the syllable would be greatly enhanced if, exactly when it is uttered (by the vocal accompanist), the stage lights are also switched on promptly. And, to turn to contemporary ways of presenting *plays*, directors have been seen to use.

> the proscenium stage itself, the apron, the ramp . . . [extending] from the stage down to the middle of the auditorium, allowing for . . . [actors'] entrances and exits, from one of the side doors of the auditorium. . . .[45]

What is perhaps not quite heeded today in the presentation of plays is Bharata's emphasis on *sāttvikabhāva*s which have been put as follows: stupefaction, loss of consciousness, horripilation, sweating, loss of lustre or colour, tremor, tears, and changes of tone. The neglect may be due to the consideration that some of these *bhāva*s can be noticed only by those who are seated in the first one or two rows in today's large halls, and are therefore not relevant to the bulk of the audience.

Here, however, a question may be put. The last three of the *sāttvikabhāva*s we have just listed — namely, tremor, tears, and tonal changes — can also be simulated or projected without the actual presence of related emotions on the inside. How, then, is it proper to regard these three *bhāvas* as *sāttvika* or truthful expressions of actual feelings? To this our answer may be that Bharata is all along keen on genuineness, as against mere manifestness of expression, which is exactly why he justifies the practice of enlisting *actresses* to play such roles as involve portraying typically feminine reactions;[46] and that, therefore, though they can *also* be simulated, Bharata would like the *sāttvikabhāvas* in question to be genuine indices of what is actually felt, and so to invest *abhinaya* with a (more) natural and convincing look. What we truly feel easily spills into identifiable gestures; and so from Bharata's point of view, we may note, it would not be right to hold (as Susanne K. Langer

45. *Contemporary Indian Theatre*, p. 14.

46. K.C. Pandey, op. cit., p. 34.

seems to do) that *all* artistic expression is wilfully controlled. At the same time, with a view to lending some balance to what we have just said about Bharata's view, it is necessary to add that, in the 24th chapter of his *Nāṭyaśāstra*, Bharata not only details how the different kinds of *nāyikā*s have to act (positively), but what they may *not* be allowed to show on the stage, such as bathing and robing themselves. In other words, decorum is not to be sacrificed for the sake of representational accuracy.

Yet, by and large, Bharata's emphasis on such fidelity is unremitting; and he takes care to add that the convincing quality of *abhinaya* also needs *vyabhichārībhāva*s (33 in all) which are so called because, as opposed to *sthāyībhāva*s that form an *abiding* part of our mental equipment, they just flit across the run of an emotional experience, adding to its true-to-life look. These fickle *bhāva*s include the following: self-disparagement, apprehension of encountering what is (nonetheless) desired, depression due to poverty and pain, perplexity, shrinking from censure, agitation caused by pleasant happenings, and drowsiness.

Now, it is common to speak of all these as *sañchāribhāvas* too. However, a close look at what the word *sañchāra* means does not allow us to identify the two *bhāvas*, *vyabhichārī* and *sañchārī* straight away. *Sañchāra* does not only mean transition or passage, but transference and transmission as well. The last of these (or sending-out) is indeed the meaning of this word when, for instance, we speak of *dūrsanchāra*. This, again, is the meaning of that segment of *dhruvapad*-singing which is called *sañchārī* as distinguished from the other three segments, namely, *sthāyī*, *antarā* and *ābhog*. *Sañchārī* here is the more or less free unfoldment of the aesthetic range of a *rāga*, as against the mere indication of its basic, grammatical character. So the word *sañchārībhāva* may be said to point to the disseminating or expressive, as distinguished from the merely fleeting character of *vyabhichārī bhāvas*.

Some thought may now be given to the two remaining

terms in the *rasa sūtra*, namely, *saṁyoga* and *nishpatti*, the meanings of which have perhaps not been quite clearly brought out anywhere in the *Nāṭyaśāstra*.[47] Now, as for *saṁyoga*, some of its acknowledged meanings are: conjunction, connection, combination, and absorption-in. The first three meanings[48] make obvious sense in the light of what the *rasa sūtra* as a whole may be taken to say quite generally. If, as is evident, *rasa* is not said to arise from any *one* of the factors listed in the *sūtra*, it would only look proper to hold that they all *conjointly* evoke *rasa*. But, we may note, to indicate *what* goes into the evocation of *rasa* is not the same thing as to explain *how* it is evoked in the presentation of a play. The latter, or the "how" of evocation, has got to take into account the work of the actors too; and from this viewpoint of actual stage presentation, to which Bharata is all along very clearly alive, it is (what we have listed as) the fourth meaning of *saṁyoga* — that is, *saṁyoga* as absorption-in — which seems preferable. A good actor does not merely find himself in, *or* conjoin himself with a specific situation (or *vibhāva*), but is sensitized by it; and the way he reacts is importantly determined by his imaginative attunement with what the situation (or *vibhāva*) does not merely show but suggests. *Sāttvika abhinaya* would otherwise be impossible.[49] Even apart from this specific consideration, it is easy to see that the *vibhāva* which a good actor finds himself in, inspires, or at least prompts him to act appropriately.

A simple example from the region of musical practice should make the point clear. The right setting (or *vibhāva*) for a classical vocalist as he gets set to begin singing is an attentive, expectant audience and a well-tuned *tānpūrā*. But this prefatory getting-

47. Śukla, *NŚ* 2nd, part I, p. 229, 1st footnote.

48. Which are not quite identical. In fact, they can be distinguished easily. In "I am no longer connected with that company," *connected* cannot be replaced with "in conjunction with"; and words like *and, but, if* and *because* are neither combinations nor connections, but conjunctions.

49. Śukla, *NŚ* 2nd, part I, pp. 84, 222.

set is not merely to get conjoined with the sounding *tānpūrā*; the latter rather inspires him, or puts him in the right mood to sing; and the vocalist, in turn, remains so continually open to the impact of the sound that its slightest deviation from the correct tone disturbs him instantly. In other words, the instrumental sound and the singer here interact. Hence, from the actors' point of view, it is by no means odd to interpret *saṁyoga* as absorption of the different *bhāva*s into each other. This may be said to be the dramatic parallel of what is called *form* in the region of other arts. But, quite differently from the interplay of elements in arts like painting, architecture, sculpture, and literature — where the locus of integration of elements is canvas, stone, wood, or language — here, in the presentation of a play, it is the sensitiveness and imaginative powers of living actors which serve as the efficient cause of integration, and so we have to speak of their getting imbued with, and activated by what *vibhāva* as outer situation demands or suggests, and what the language of dialogues means and is expected to convey. It is because of this close integration of utterance, meaning, accordant movement, music and spectacle (*āhārya abhinaya*); and, above all, because of the *presentational* character of the entire complex that the *rasa* thereby evoked acquires a *prismatic* look which is not to be found in any one of the *bhāva*s taken individually or even in their mere aggregation. This is what Bharata means where he likens the aesthetic configuration which makes for *rasa* to a dish emitting a new flavour which is not to be found in any one of the condiments used;[50] and what *we* have said here about the integration in question should provide a clue to why Bharata speaks of *rasānubhūti* as *ujjavalveṣātmakaḥ* and as *sākṣātkarātmaka*.

Saṁyoga, however, calls for three more comments. First, it is not a blending of the various constituents *in equal measure*; for, with an eye to evoking the specific *rasa* aimed at, any one of them may be emphasized. Consider, for instance, the following verbal stimulant of *śṛṅgāra rasa:*

50. Śukla, *NŚ* 2nd, part I, p. 83.

> O lovely damsel! your body is the locus of the honey that love-making exudes; the shapely arch of your eyebrows is the bow of the love-god, Kāmadeva, with its striking bend; and the wine that oozes from your lotus-face quickens desire by its very aroma — that is, without being drunk. In all the three worlds, indeed, you remain unmatched as a specially beautiful creation of Brahmā.

Here, obviously, the word-bound images and the overall meaning both alike heighten the charm of the *nāyikā* who is the *ālambana of the vibhāva*. *Vyabhichārī bhāva*s may be projected as follows:

> This lady, possessed of liquid eyes, is repeatedly impelled to throw away the water cupped in her hands; for, though she is impatient to bedew her lover with it, she is disturbed by the presence of fish in the water as it mirrors the shape of her own eyes.

Here, it is clear, the emphasis is on *vyabhichārī bhāva*s. Liquidity of eyes at the passing thought of a mischief, impatience, and agitation are obviously all transitory states. So *saṁyoga* admits of uneven emphasis on the factors that make for the evocation of *rasa*.

Second, the way we have interpreted *saṁyoga* — that is, as an interplay, and not merely as a putting together of the various *bhāva*s — is favoured by the basic consideration that all the details of the creative process have to aim at sublimating the *sthāyībhāva*. It is this common, underrunning reference which determines what these details are going to be. Thus, where the *rasa* aimed at is *śṛṅgāra* and the *sthāyībhāva* is *rati*, a moonlit garden alone cannot serve as *vibhāva*, for such a garden may well be used also for an after-dinner leisurely stroll. A pair of lovers too have to be shown; and they have to *appear* to register (mainly through *mukhaj* or facial *abhinaya*) the charm of the setting, and to be stimulated by it. The greater their attunement with the precise suggestiveness of the *vibhāva* the more effortless and convincing will their *abhinaya* be, aided of course by the import of dialogues and the due measure of *vyabhichārī* and *sāttvikabhāva*s.

Thirdly, to turn now to those who are watching the play, their self-identification with what they see on the stage goes on waxing as they follow the *intense knitwork of bhāvas*, essentially because it is perceptibly true to their common experience of how the *sthāyībhāva* being built on (in the dramatic presentation) actually determines the inner run and expression of emotions in their own actual lives. The result is that the deepening of this attunement (or *tādātmya*) is at once an experience of the *ekaghanatā* (or intense unity) of the *rasa* ultimately evoked. This word, *ekaghanatā* has to be taken with care. Derived from the root *ghana* (to strike) it simply means unity of impact. Some scholars, like Coomaraswamy and Gnoli, ignore this derivative meaning and prefer to translate *ghana* as "a condensation of multiple factors without extension in space;"[51] and *ekaghanata* as the quality of being "dense, compact, uniform," or as the character of "a state of consciousness which does not allow the interference of obstacles"[52] (or *vighnas*). But the prefix *eka* makes better sense when related to *ghana* in the sense of *impact* than as conjoined with *ghana* taken as *condensation*. Moreover, whereas the negative remark that, as an experience, *rasa* is not discursive or analytical (or is *niravacchinna*) — or not separated by distinctions — seems perfectly warranted, the positive insistence that the experience in question is utterly dense or compact would tend to make *rasa* appear as a static something, and to merely ignore the flow that *rasa* as experience necessarily is, as also its quickening and illuminative effect on the audience.

It is indeed important to realize how *what the rasikas* see on the stage relates to *how* they see it. Generally, of course, care has to be taken to ensure that *vibhāva* is so structured that it may appeal to the generality of *sāmājikas*,[53] and not to any

---

51. A.K. Coomarasway, *The Transformation of Nature in Art*, Harvard, 1934, p. 209.
52. R. Gnoli, *Aesthetic Experience According to Abhinavagupta*, 1st edn., p. 71. 2nd footnote.
53. A *sāmājika* is "One of the assembly." De, *Sanskrit Poetics*, p. 99.

particular person. To illustrate, whereas in a man's personal life even the passing thought (say) of how his wife reacted happily when he teased her endearingly on her last birthday may excite the *rati bhāva*, on the stage the *vibhāva* — that is, a setting which is expected to be duly evocative — must be typical of lovers in general, for otherwise it would fail to engage the attention of the majority of onlookers. Yet, however true it be to our general experience, *vibhāva* in itself is by no means enough to have the requisite effect. The audience too has to be of the right age and attitudes. No amount of effort to make the *vibhāva* in question meaningful — say, emblematic of *rati bhāva* — would succeed where the audience is of young children only. In other words, the perception of *vibhāva*s (as significant) is not merely objective. It draws upon or awakens the latent traces — *saṁskāra*s or *vāsanā*s — already present in the spectators. A young male member of the audience will not perceive the representation of a young woman quite impersonally, or in the way of *tāṭasthya* or *neutrality* which is the exact opposite of *anupraveśa* that is, intimate and active participation. The truth rather is that the very description of a beautiful woman easily arouses the pre-existing sexual interest in male readers. But, on the other hand, the (knowledgeable) *rasika* surely does not *behave* erotically in this context, as he might in his personal life, but is only led *to comprehend and follow the growth of a specific kind of emotive situation*, so that, instead of experiencing *rati* in the everyday manner, he is drawn out to contemplate how *rati* feels.

The other term *nishpatti* too calls for some critical attention. Its more important meanings are: (a) going forth or out; (b) being brought about or effected; (c) completion; and (d) consummation. Now, from the viewpoint of stage presentation as such, *rasa*-evocation may well be said to crown the creative effort of actors with success, and not merely to bring it is a close. Or the terminus here may be called a climax. But *for the audience*, the evocation of *rasa* is no mere culmination of an outer process. It comes to pass not only because of proper integration of the different *bhāva*s on the stage, but because, as *sāmājikas* (spectators), they have been following the presentation in question all along, attentively and knowledgeably; *and* because the *sthāyībhāva* which the entire play builds upon is already there in them as an inherent emotional disposition. This is why, in spite of the rich and elaborate outer process that goes into its evocation, the actual experience of *rasa* or *rasānubhūti* is felt by the spectators not as an imposition from outside, but as a deep and delighted expansion of their own sensibilities, a creative quickening of the very springs of their emotional nature. It is partly in this sense too that *rasa*-experience is a *nishpatti*, a going-forth or a welling-up. Even in our daily lives there is no dearth of situations where experience does not seem to be produced only by what is external to us, but is at once felt by us as inner enlivenment. The poet's heart leaps up when he beholds a rainbow in the sky, and we too often *pine for*, and not merely think of *what is not*.

Yet, it is important to note that the way in which the *sthāyībhāva*s are made to conduce to the evocation of *rasa* is different from their working in real life. In the everyday world a person feels angry or sad generally in accordance with his *uniquely* developed attitudes. To illustrate, whereas the man who has meticulously trained himself to put everything always at its proper place may at once grow a little angry or sad at the sight of even a slight displacement of books from their proper positions on his study table, his friend who believes, let us say, that some disorder serves only to lend an informal or lived-in appearance to the place of work — and so is likely to make him feel relaxed — would remain quite unaffected by the displacement in question. Further, when we experience an emotion in real life, which always happens in a specific situation, our emphasis (as a rule) is on *behaving* in a particular way, so as to deal with the situation properly, not on *contemplating* how the emotion itself feels. Thus, if a man feels afraid at the sight of a snake, he will either run away from the place or try to kill the reptile somehow. Here the urgent need for personal safety demands quick action, and just does not give him time to attend to his feeling of fear. In other words, the emotions of real life remain tied down to individual persons; and though they are certainly felt, and even quite intensely at times, our awareness of their own inner character is only incidental to, and so is bedimmed by the demands of personal adjustment.

But, one may ask, is the complex dovetailing of various elements, which we have taken pains to explain and justify, really necessary? Why can't we say that *rasa* is our more or less direct response to a theme or subject of a specific emotional hue? Now, questions such as these may be answered as follows:

An emotive subject is not by itself enough to generate *rasa*, for the way it is dealt with may be just philosophical, that is, the way of serious, meaningful statement or reasoning which is only to be understood and accepted as true or rejected as false. This is the case, for instance, where a Shakespearean sonnet speaks of love as "an ever-fixed mark," and asserts that

> . . . Love is not love
> Which alters when it alteration finds . . .[54]

Here the subject is love; yet the whole sonnet only induces us to *think* of love, instead of enabling us to experience *Śṛṅgāra rasa*. The same may be said of (Urdu) poet Jigar's famous poem on love which opens even more philosophically than the sonnet from which we have just cited. Here, in one daring sweep the poet professes to sum up the whole story (*fasānā*) of love as follows: quintessentially, it appears in the heart of a lover; and should it decide to unfurl itself, it can cover the whole wide world — as love of humanity.[55]

Nor is a poem on a *sad* subject necessarily evocative of *karuṇa*

---

54. Sonnet No. 116 in *Master Poems of the English Language*, ed. Oscar Williams, New York: Trident Press, 1966, p. 55. Hereafter, this work is referred to simply as *Master Poems*.

55. The reference is to the following opening lines of the poem:

    इक लफ्ज़े मोहब्बत का अदना ये फ़साना है।
    सिमटे तो दिले आशिक़ फैले तो ज़माना है।।

rasa. Tennyson's poem: *Tears, Idle Tears*[56] is also only *about* the commonest expression of acute sadness; and though, in both its first and closing stanzas, it bemoans with "idle tears . . . the days that are no more," it gives us at the most a fitful feeling of sadness at what has ceased to be, which is quite different from the *bhogīkaraṇa* (or enlivening, making available for relish)[57] of *karuṇa rasa* which is a single, undivided run of emotional experience. This is so also because, like the sonnet already referred to, this poem is pretty short in length. Tennyson's lament comprises only twenty lines; and Shakespeare's poem, being a sonnet, even less, just fourteen. So, though the sentiments they express are true and even noble, their reading fails to make us feel that we are being led over the build-up of an emotion, instead of being merely provided with some readymade statements of truth or images of longing or reminiscence.

This does not, however, warrant the view that *all poetry other than its dramatic genre* is necessarily incapable of evoking *rasa*; and we must duly heed Vishwanath's account of how poetry *can* well evoke *rasa*, if not the sweeping way he *appears* to decree that *rasa* is the soul of poetry.[58] This is how he himself explains (a part of) his view in brief:

> When *sthāyībhāvas* like *rati* (which are already there in us as *vāsanās*) become manifest (as transformed) for the blissful, immediate relish of *sahṛdaya jana* through the poet's depiction

56. *Master Poems*, p. 658.

57. De, *Sanskrit Poetics*, p. 103.

58. That Vishvanath actually does so is the view of S.K. De. See his *Sanskrit Poetics*, p. 90. If I have yet thought it necessary to italicize the word "*appears*," it is simply because it has been suggested (and I think quite rightly) by at least one eminent scholar that the utterance in question should be taken as an eulogy of the poetic art *rather than as an assertion of its essential character*. The reference here is to p. 11 of Vishvanatha Kaviraja's *Sāhityadarpaṇa*, ed. Dr. Satyavrata Singh, Varanasi: Chowkhamba Vidya Bhawan, New edn., 1992.

of *vibhāva, anubhāva*, and *sañchārībhāva*, they are said to be *rasa*.[59]

How exactly this can happen in our concern with (*non*-dramatic) poetry may now be brought out by considering two well-known English poems: Keats' *The Eve of St. Agnes* (for *śṛṅgāra rasa*) and Shelley's *Adonais* (for *karuṇa rasa*). The former tickles the *sthāyībhāva* of *rati* repeatedly and all along, through images and thoughts of love, longing, and beauty, such as the following:

a. . . . These let us wish away
And turn, sole-thoughted, to one Lady there,
Whose heart *had brooded, all that wintry day,*
On love . . .[60]

b. They told her how, upon St. Agnes' Eve
Young virgins might have visions of delight
Upon the honey'd middle of the night
If ceremonies due they did aright;
As, supperless to bed they must retire
And couch supine their beauties, lily white;[61]
. . . .

c. *Full of this whim* was thoughtful Madeline
The music, *yearning* like a God in pain,
She scarcely heard . . .
. . . her heart was otherwhere:
She *sigh'd* for Agnes' dreams, the sweetest of the year[62]

d. . . . Meantime, across the moors.
Had come young Porphyro, *with heart on fire*

---

59. *Sanskrit Poetics*, p. 69.

60. *Master Poems*, p. 60.

61. Ibid.

62. Ibid.

For Madeline . . .[63]

It is easy to see that, along with making a quiet appeal to the *sthāyībhāva* of *rati* (as desire for amorous bliss), the lines cited above also at once make for the needed *vibhāva* by inducing us to visualize situations and happenings relating to *rati*. As for *anubhāva*, we are not of course expected to see any actual acting here, as we do in witnessing a play; but, on the other hand, there is no dearth of word-bound images which prompt us to visualize movements, action, postures, and even such details (of stage management, basically) as disposition of things and figures in space. Thus, see the following:

> . . . *Beside* the portal doors,
> Buttress'd from moonlight, *stands* he, and implores
> All saints to give him sight of Madeline,
> But for one moment . . .
> That he might *gaze* and worship all unseen;
> Perchance *speak, kneel, touch, kiss* — in sooth such things have been,[64]

Or again:

> Ah, happy chance! the aged creature *came,*
> *Shuffling along* with ivory-headed wand,
> To where he *stood, hid from the torch's flame,*
> *Behind* a broad hall-pillar, far *beyond*[65]

What is more, even *vyabhichārī bhāva*s are traceable in some such lines of the poem as the following:

> a. She danc'd along with *vague, regardless eyes,*
> *Anxious her lips, her breathing quick and short*:
> . . . : she *sighs*[66]

---

63. *Master Poems*, p. 60.

64. *Master Poems*, p. 601. In the second quote, here, most of the words italicized are obviously such as signify positioning in space.

65. Ibid.

66. Ibid., p. 601.

b. . . .; with aged *eyes aghast*
From fright of dim espial.[67]

c. She clos'd the door, . . .
No uttered syllable, or, woe betide!
But to her heart, her heart was voluble
Paining with eloquence her balmy side;
As though a tongueless nightingale should swell
Her throat in vain, and die, heart-stifled, in her dell.[68]

The *regardless eyes* which (*a*) speaks of are *śūnya dṛṣṭi*, and "*eyes aghast*" (in *b*) are *śaṅkitā dṛṣṭi* in Bharata's account of how eyes can be made to express *bhāva* and *rasa*; and both are meant to express *sañchārībhāvas*.[69] Further, the *pain* of having to hold searing longings of love which press for fulfilment is a deeply subjective *vyabhichārī bhāva* in the course of being in love. It may not last long, but it feels excruciating. On the stage it may well be expressed through some subtle bodily signs of felt inner discomfort through *mukhaj* (or facial) *abhinaya*.[70] But *āngika abhinaya* is clearly not a part of poesy's resources; and so, in the lines just cited, the poet has to use an endearing image of anguish — that is, the *nightingale* image, with such specificity that the reader can easily visualize the *vyabhichārī bhāva* in question, and so quietly do without the prop of actual *abhinaya*.

This, however, is not all that may be said to support our view that the poem makes for evocation of *śṛṅgāra rasa*. Two more points can be made. First, quite in accordance with one of Bharata's basic emphases, the locus of *rasa* in question is here kept free from sensuality; nay, it is even made to look ethereal, both at its core, that is, in the heart, *love*'s *fevrous citadel*,[71] and in respect of its overall setting. Secondly, care has

67. *Master Poems*, p. 604.

68. Ibid., pp. 604-05.

69. *Sūtras* 40, 41, 42 in ch. VIII of Śukla's *NŚ* 2nd, part II, p. 11 *of the text*.

70. *Sūtra* 11. Ibid., p. 5 *of the text*.

71. 84th line of the poem in *Master Poems*, p. 62.

been taken to ensure that our relish of the poem is almost as immediate an experience as that of witnessing a play. The former end is secured, first, by providing the poem with a very chilly (or passion-free!) and devout opening:

> St. Agnes' Eve — Ah, bitter chill it was!
> . . .
> Numb were the Beadsman's fingers while he told
> His rosary, and while his frosted breath,
> Like pious incense from a censer old,
> Seem'd taking flight for heaven without a death,[72]

and, secondly, through some express projections of purity directly in relation to those who are yet indissolubly in love:

> a. "I will not harm her, by all saints I swear,"
> Quoth Porphyro: Or may I ne'er find grace
> . . .
> If one of her soft ringlets I displace,
> *Or look with ruffian passion in her face*[73]
> . . .
>
> b. Full on this casement shone the wintry moon
> . . .
> As down she knelt for heaven's grace and boon;
> . . .
> And on her hair a glory, like a saint:
> She seem'd a splendid angel, newly drest,
> Save wings, for heaven:- Porphyro grew faint:
> She knelt, so pure a thing, so free from mortal taint.[74]

The past tense of the second quote (b) balances Porphyro's solemn swearing in the present (Quote a). Such balancing is in fact a recurring device which the poet uses all along. Further, whichever be the temporal mode of what the poem says, past or present, pinpointing of details that make our real life experience is all along immaculate:

---

72. *Master Poems*, p. 600.
73. Ibid., p. 603.
74. Ibid., p. 605.

a. Her falt'ring hand upon the balustrade,
Old Angela was feeling for the stair,[75]
. . .

b. Out went the taper as she hurried in;
Its little smoke, in pallid moonshine, died:[76]

It is precisely these two poetic devices, present-past equipoise and fidelity to detail, that lend to the whole poem an air of presentational immediacy, in spite of the fact that it is meant to be "a dream, in olden times."[77] Indeed, "the power of language to overcome distance . . . looms throughout the poem";[78] and this is how a poet provides a parallel of our direct attention to what is shown on the stage. The two are in fact by no means disparate. We should not forget that, as we have already said earlier, what Bharata speaks of as *rasāsvādana* by *sahṛdaya jana* (or persons of responsive sensibility) is not a physical, but essentially a mental act (*mānas-asvādana*).

In respect of Shelley's *Adonais* too it is not difficult to show how the interplay of different *bhāva*s makes for the evocation of *karuṇa rasa*. What makes our task here easy is the fact that, in dealing with this *rasa*, Bharata includes separation from a loved one and death importantly in the list of requisite *vibhāvas*; weeping and lamentation in *anubhāva*s that make for proper *abhinaya* of the *rasa* on the stage; and attachment (*moha*) and dying (*maraṇa*) among the relevant *sañchārī* and *sāttvikabhāva*s.

Now, all this is traceable in *Adonais*, as follows:

The very title of the poem is significant. It opens with the word *Adonais* — "a name that partakes of Adonis, the youth *slain* by a wild boar and hence a sacrificed seasonal god, and Adonai, the Hebrew name for Supreme Being";[79] and quickly

75. *Master Poems*, p. 604.

76. Ibid.

77. Ibid., p. 612.

78. Ibid., p. 610.

79. Ibid., p. 540.

follows it up with a sub-title which says that the poem is an elegy on the death of John Keats, author of *Endymion, Hyperion,* etc. Now, the slaying of a youth and death taken generally are both common causes of making us commiserate. But such moments of compassion produced by isolated thoughts are fickle and merely personal; and it is important to see how our everyday experiences not only of pity for others but of our own grieving differ from *karuṇa rasa*. This *rasa* is no mere prolongation of sorrow. One may keep wallowing in grief because of the death of a child for days on end, but it would not be nameable as an experience of *karuṇa rasa*; for such an actual experience is not only personal, but painful. The feeling of compassion has to be released from concern with those who matter in one's merely individual life — and sustained through a pleasing organization of such factors as are common to all — before it can truly claim the status of *karuṇa rasa*; and this is precisely what the elegy in question does. Our innate propensity to grieve (*sthāyībhāva* of *śoka*) over the death of a loved one (*vibhāva*) is repeatedly quickened by verbal invitations to mourn — in ways which we are *all* familiar with, and which are therefore trans-individual or *sādhāraṇa* (general). Phenomenologically, the course of actual sorrowing is never uniform; it runs in waves, so to say, which surge up and subside; and here (in *Adonais*) the accents of poignancy are provided by two factors: thoughts of the brute finality of the ceasing-to-be, and the glory *and ardent interior* of the one who has ceased to be. Hence the lifelike quality of the following word-pictures of (invitations to) lamentation (*vibhāva*) that may be taken to parallel its bodily presentation on the stage:

a. Oh, weep for Adonais! *though our tears*
Thaw not the frost which binds so dear a head![80]

b. Oh, weep for Adonais — he is dead!
. . .
For he is gone, where all things wise and fair

80. *Master Poems,* p. 527.

Descend: oh, *dream not that the amorous Deep*
Will yet restore him to the vital air;[81]
. . .

c. *He will awake no more, oh, never more!*[82] —

But, one may ask, what are the *sañchārī* and *sāttvikabhāvas*, if any, in this poem? Now, one of these is *āvega* which we have already spoken of as the occasional swell of pathetic feeling in actual lamentation. What is more, the selfsame *bhāva* — along with some other *sañchārī* and *sāttvikabhāvas*, such as *moha, dainya,* and *maraṇa* (that is, attachment, wretchedness, and death or the act of dying) — is there also in such ardent, pathetic lines as the following:

1. Lament anew, Urania![83] . . .
2. . . . now, thy youngest, dearest one has perished
3. . . . , who grew
4. Like a pale flower by some sad maiden cherished,
5. And fed with true love tears, instead of dew;
6. Most musical of mourners, weep anew!
7. Thy extreme hope, the loveliest and the last,
8. The bloom, whose petals nipt before they blew
9. Died on the promise of the fruit . . .
10. The broken lily lies — the storm is overpast[84]

In these lines evocation of the *bhāva*s we have set out to trace is all clearly there in the only way that poetry admits of, that is, in terms of verbal meaning and word-bound images. The last three lines (8-10) bespeak *dainya*. It sure feels wretched to contemplate the premature passing away of a peaking genius; and the fourth and fifth lines clearly add to this feeling by

81. *Master Poems*.

82. Ibid., p. 528.

83. Urania is the muse of astronomy; and another name for Aphrodite, goddess of love and beauty in Greek mythology, daughter of Zeus. Its Roman counterpart in Venus.

84. *Master Poems*, p. 528.

providing a virtual picture of sadness. Words like *youngest*, (so) *dearest*, and *loveliest* smack of attachment (*moha*); and *has perished* and *died* are the poet's obvious words for what is called *maraṇa*. So, building on our innate disposition to grieve (*sthāyībhāva* of *śoka*) the poet adroitly interfuses the *vibhāva* of the premature death of a loved one with four transient emotions of *āvega*, *dainya*, *moha* and *maraṇa* to make us experience *karuṇa rasa*.

This *rasa*, we may note, is not the same thing as *our* feeling sad in real life, say, because of loss of prestige, riches, or a dear relative. Such unfortunate situations are only the *vibhāva* or apt occasions for sorrowing, though the easy rise of the experience here is due to our innate and abiding disposition to grieve (*sthāyībhāva* of *śoka*). Nor can the *rasa* in question be identified with our feeling moved spontaneously when we see someone suffering — say, due to sickness or sheer poverty — because, though the reaction here may well be wholly selfless, it can also cause some actual discomfort if, maybe because of the absence of needed resources, we are unable to give practical vent to our impulse to help. Further, insofar as the way *the object* appears to us, as distinguished from how *we* react to it, is not actively controlled here, our kindly attitude may vaporize the moment we are told that the misery of the person before us is a sequel to his own chronic and ruinous vices. What is more, though the actual impulsion to help is surely felt as a sweet expansion of our being, a sort of going out in love, this blissful core of the experience does not become *a steady object of contemplation for us*, because, though it can surely recur freely if one is committed to a life of helping the needy, its individual occurrences are all at the mercy of many contingencies. Preoccupation with our own pressing problems may come in the way; or, as already indicated, some new information about the suffering one may dampen our very will to help.

Now, all this is quite transformed in the creative process of *rasa*-evocation as Bharata envisages it. One enters the theatre with the explicit intent to watch the presentation of a play; and what he sees on the stage — and hears what emanates therefrom, that is, the music and the dialogues — is all (in principle) such a compact blend (or *saṁyoga*) of *abhinaya* of different kinds that he is readily freed from the confines of his own joys and sorrows (*nijasuḥkhaduḥkhādivivaśibhāva*); and is enabled, in the case of a *karuṇa rasa* presentation, to relish the bliss of being perfectly in tune with what is presented (movingly) on the stage, and so to experience the particular *rasa*. Nothing that is presented on the stage is uniquely related to any one member of the audience. The various *bhāvas* are a part of everybody's being and behaviour in life, which is exactly what makes them easily and commonly intelligible. Yet the impact of the objective and integrated presentation of the various *bhāvas* on the stage (or in the text of a play) is *quite unlike our everyday experience* which is largely humdrum, often merely individual — at times even aggressively so; and rarely quite regulated. This is partly why *rasānubhūti* is said to be a beyond-the-world (or *lokottara*) experience.

But is not the poem avowedly about someone who *actually* lived? Sure, it is, about the poet, John Keats; but the way he is visualized in the present poem is such a palpitating blend of the real, the celestial, and the patently mythological; and the images that illumine the poem all along collocate quite disparate elements of our everyday experience in such novel and winsome ways that references to matters of fact nowhere seem to jar with what the poem seeks to do, that is, sanctifying the spirit of Keats[85] and making him appear virtually stellar in glory. This is why the reader just acquiesces in this movement away from real life.[86]

At the same time, in spite of its powerful, elegiac impact —

---

85. *Master Poems*, p. 540.

86. See, here, references to Urania, the mythical goddess of love and beauty who is visualized as having her seat in Paradise (*Master Poems*, pp. 527-28) and also such pictures of real life as the periodic renewal or reappearance of "the airs and streams . . . ants, bees . . . swallows . . . fresh leaves and flowers" (Ibid., p. 532).

and its recurring "invitations" to mourn, and abounding references to death and tears — the poem is by no means a vehicle of maudlin sentimentality. *Karuṇa rasa* is an exaltation *and no mere intensification* of the *sthāyībhāva* of *śoka*. The poem achieves this end partly by seeking to locate good poets in the heavens as stars, and partly by dotting the poem with such gems of philosophic solemnity as the following:

> The One remains, the many change and pass;
> Heaven's light forever shines, Earth's shadows fly;
> Life, like a dome of many-coloured glass,
> Stains the white radiance of Eternity,
> Until Death tramples it to fragments . . . [87]

Here, we seem to *see, and not merely to follow* what the poet says, if not in the way of watching a play. Indeed, as in reading Keats' *The Eve of St. Agnes*, the experience generated here is by and large immediate; or, as the *rasa* theorists would say, *sākṣātkārātmaka*, though not of course an actual *sakṣātkāra*.

What is said in the lines just cited from Shelley's poem is clearly of general significance. Further, of all the human beings visualized in the two poems we have dealt with, only one — that is, Keats — has actually lived; and (in *Adonais*) he too has been so beautifully idealized and framed in a setting of myth that, instead of being disturbed by lack of historical detail, we just chime happily with this rarefaction of the real — a typically romantic device which is also at work where even some real life objects of Keats' poetic artistry are pictured as phantoms, so to say, and are thus half denuded of reality:

> . . . Desires and Adorations
> Winged Persuasions and veiled Destinies,
> Splendours, and Glooms, and glimmering Incarnations
> Of hopes and fears, and twilight Phantasies;
> And Sorrow, with her family of Sighs,
> And Pleasure, blind with tears
> Like pageantry of mist on an autumnal stream

87. *Master Poems*, p. 539.

> All he had loved, and moulded into thought
> From shape, and hue, and odour, and sweet sounds[88]

Yet, on the whole, the poem is no real strain on our credence. It only exalts the idiom of reality without quite deserting it. The vein of lament which is all along visible, and thus holds the poem pretty tightly as one, is so freely relieved by expressions of praise, love, and longing that the whole picture appears quite close to the common features of the way we all in fact tend to mourn the loss of our dear ones because of something admirable in them. There are some, it is true, who live through their heartaches in silence and solitude, whereas quite a few others choose to mourn quite openly and even so expressly for a definite period that they seem to be making a luxury of their grief.[89] These are, however, but individual differences; the common core of mourning is provided by the features we have listed. It is these that the poet builds upon; and it is precisely this seizure of essentials of both experience and expression that makes the picture of (say) grieving acceptable to all. What *rasa* theorists mean by *sādhāraṇīkaraṇa* is no laboured simplification of what is originally obscure or profound. It is rather the device of so regulating an artistic presentation that, as a whole, it may neither appear related to any real person, nor to anybody's merely individual concerns; and may be positively relished by the *generality* of knowledgeable people. The whole process of *rasa*-evocation makes for both these ends, because *rasa* arises from an integration of situations and modes of expression which relate to human life *generally* and because what appears (in an exalted form) as the substance of the resulting (*rasa-*)experience is something that is already there *in one and all*, in the form of *sthāyībhāva*s.

Yet, as Abhinavagupta points out, the quality of being generally acceptable *and appealing* (or *sādhāraṇya*) is quite

---

88. *Master Poems*, pp. 530-31.

89. Say, like Olivia in Shakespeare's *Twelfth Night*.

different from, and independent of, the *logical* concept of generality (*sāmānya*).[90] The logically general is that which is *understood or thought of* as being applicable to all or most members of a class or category. The aesthetically *sādhāraṇa*, on the other hand, is that which is not the private experience of any one individual but is accessible, as a *presentation*, to all those who are suitably equipped to attend to it; which is why the senses which enable a whole gathering of people to attend to the same art object at once — namely, the ear and the eye — are (for Bharata) pre-eminently aesthetic. A simple analogy should make the distinction clear. The *concept* of a public park *subsumes* all parks which are open to the public; an *actual* public park, on the other hand, *serves* as such simply because it is not any one individual's personal property. A stage presentation too, if it is to be experienced aesthetically, must be presented (according to Bharata) in such a manner that it may not appear as relating to any one real person alone, though its details may well be identified on the basis of our *general* experience of life and reality. It is precisely because of this absence of explicit reference to our individual concerns that, while watching a play, we are able to attend to situations presented on the stage wholeheartedly, that is, without being disturbed by any such *purely individual* reactions on our part as could easily arise were we faced with similar situations in real life.

Here, again, we may take a simple example to make the point clear. If one of the two young and friendly neighbours one is known to be rather shy by temperament, and if he yet succeeds in carrying on with a lady in their locality, the other one may feel *happy* because, after all, his friend has been able to overcome shyness; *envious* because he has lost to one whom he had always regarded as inferior in love-making; or *angry* because the affair is likely to disturb the peace of their locality. But if the same shy young man impersonates an ardent lover in a dramatic performance, his friend will care only for the

90. Gnoli, *The Aesthetic Experience According to Abhinavagupta*, 1st edn., p. 29, 5th footnote.

truth and subtlety of *abhinaya*; and, as a *sāmājika*, his attention to the play will not at all be disturbed by the real life reactions we have just visualized.

Yet, a little more care is needed to see how exactly the self is related to its object in aesthetic experience. On the one hand, it is surely not a state of indifference (or *tāṭasthya*); in fact it is rather "an active participation (*anupraveśa*) of the cognizing subject in the event represented."[91] How otherwise can we explain the fact that after we have witnessed a good play or dance recital, quite a few moving scenes or expressive postures continue to haunt the mind? Yet, on the other hand, our attention to what we see on the stage does not impel us into the broad, overt reactions of daily life. The whole point has indeed to be taken in a duly balanced way, partly by holding on to Bharata's own views on both aesthetic attitude and variety of aesthetic responses, along with due attention to the otherworldly character of *rasa* emphasized by commentators on his views. Bhaṭṭa Nāyaka insists that the essence of *rasa* is "a pleasure which has no relationship with any real individual"; and that

> the images contemplated on the stage or read in poetry are seen by the man of aesthetic sensibility independently of any relationship with his [own] ordinary life or with the [normal] life of the actor or of the hero of the play or poem; and appear, therefore, in a generalized [*sādhāraṇīkṛta*] way, that is to say, universally and released from individuality.[92]

Abhinavagupta goes even further when he says that during the course of aesthetic experience the individual raises himself above time, space and causality; and so also above the very basic character of practical life (or *saṁsāra*). He believes that such an experience, even "like . . . a flower born of magic, has, as its essence, solely the present; it is correlated neither with what came before nor with what comes after. This experience

---

91. Gnoli, op. cit., pp. xx-xxi. *Anupraveśa* means "entrance-into."

92. Ibid.

is therefore different both from the ordinary experience and from the religious one."[93]

Now, what is meant here simply is that we do not situate our aesthetic experiences in the space in which we actually move about or in the time by which we measure delays or premature ageing. Where a danseuse traverses the stage in a series of quick and tight-knit steps the space covered appears greater than it really is. Oppositely, if the recital is absorbing, the seventy-five minutes or so it usually takes may not appear as a *passage* at all. In neither case, it is true, the difference disturbs us. But, on the other hand, our reactions on such occasions can be *basically* quite true to life. It is true that "the proverbial unsophisticated yokel whose chivalrous interference in the play on behalf of the hapless heroine [because he could not abstain from behaving as one is expected to, in response to a similar situation *in real life*] is not the ideal type of theatrical audience."[94] But, at the same time, the audience would be less than human if it reacted to emotive situations in a play *quite dissimilarly* to how we react to them in real life. Bharata does not visualize any such audience of bizarre onlookers; and where he speaks of the reactions of *prekṣaka*s (the audience) to presentations of different *rasa*s, he very rightly says that if the *rasa* evoked on the stage (effectively) is *adbhuta, śṛṅgāra* or *vīra*, the audience reacts with an audible *ahā* (or *vāh*, expressing wonder); and where the *rasa* is *karuṇa*, with tearful eyes or a mournful utterance of *hāi*.[95] What is more, with his uncanny eye for detail, Bharata even distinguishes the objects of aesthetic response from the viewpoint of age, sex and personality types. Children and ladies, we are told, generally react positively to a *hāsya*

93. Gnoli, *The Aesthetic Experience According to Abhinavagupta*, 2nd edn., Chowkhamba Sanskrit Series, vol. LXII, 1968, pp. xxxiii, xxxvi.

94. Edward Bullough's essay, "Psychical Distance" in M. Rader's *A Modern Introduction to Esthetics*. (Holt, Rinehart and Winston, 1979, 5th edn.) p. 350.

95. Śukla's *NŚ*, part III, 1st edn., 1983. *Sūtras*, 9-11, of chapter XVII, p. 324.

rasa presentation; and the elderly, to a religious or Purāṇic theme. By and large, however, Bharata's emphasis is on *prekṣakas* of "parallel" sensitiveness:

> Only those should be provided as audience to a play who feel happy when they find a blessed person in the play and feel sad on seeing a grieving character in the play. . . .[96]

Such writing provides a needful supplement to quite a few contemporary (and fairly sensible) definitions of the aesthetic attitude (and response) such as the following:

> [The aesthetic attitude] is disinterested and sympathetic attention to and contemplation of any object of awareness whatever for its own sake alone.[97]

How the aesthetic attitude is disinterested in the sense of being free from determination *by the very basic character of reality* — that is, by distinctions of time and space, you and I, or subject and object, thereby providing release from our everyday concerns, if only for a while; and how it is "sympathetic" as vibrating with parallel sensitiveness to what is shown on the stage — all this is clear in Bharata's account concretely, that is, as an explict mention of the details of artistic practice and art experience.

Drama and poetry in general, however, are not the only arts to which the theory of *rasa* seems relevant. As has been suggested by Hiriyanna, it may even be possible to construct, on the basis of *rasa* theory, an Indian aesthetics of fine art in general around the data provided by quite a few Sanskrit works on poetics, though "their set purpose is only to elucidate the principles exemplified in poetry and . . . drama."[98] Now, though the task here visualized has not been accomplished so far, it is undeniable that the theory in question is quite evidently at

96. Śukla's *NŚ*, part III, 1st edn., 1983, *sūtra*, 54, p. 350.

97. Jerome Stolnitz's essay, "The Aesthetic Attitude" in *Introductory Readings in Aesthetics*, ed. John Hospers, The Free Press & Collier MacMillan, 1969, p. 19.

98. Hiriyanna, *Art Experience*, p. 2.

work in the majority of our classical dance-forms. Quite a few of them, in fact, regard *navarasamālikā* as an important number. Kathak, however, is so far an exception to this. Indeed, of all the major classical dances of India it is probably the only one which has charmed its numberless fans without claiming that it derives its character or content fundamentally from Bharata's *Nāṭyaśāstra*. A careful look, however, at the great variety of its representational and expressional numbers (that is, *nṛtya*) makes one wonder if it has not borrowed, if perhaps unknowingly, quite a good deal from the time-honoured classic of dramaturgy. A brief account of some such numbers — or *intra-forms*, as I prefer to call them[99] — as have been actually presented on the Kathak stage in contemporary India should make the point clear.

Consider, to begin with, that well-known *nṛtya* number which opens with the words, *Vṛndāvana kuñjana racho rāsa āli*. Here, the *sthāyībhāva* of *rati* is manifest pretty quickly not only because of the general awareness among Indians that a *rāsa* is essentially an artistic essay in playfulness, figural charm as manifest in dancing, and variform expression of love, but because of what the text of the pattern in question itself actually provides. Thus, its very opening words that we have cited (in italics) enable the *rasika* to visualize the relevant *vibhāva*, that is, a celebration of *rāsa* in Vṛndāvana featuring the Rādhā-Kṛṣṇa duo as *ālambana* and the verdant charm of a *kuñja* as *uddīpana vibhāva*. Further, along with quite a few *bol*s of pure dance — such as *dig, dig, trām* — the figural representation of such meaningful words as *laya gati dikhāvat* or *chaplā si chamkat*

99. My reason for this preference may be put thus. In so far as every Kathak number has to be internally well organized *and also* to appear self-completing (importantly because it follows a cyclic rhythm), it may be said to a *form* itself. But because a whole Kathak recital from the opening *thāṭ* to the closing *tatkār* — and including all the other "items" — is also (in principle) internally well organized, what it includes, that is, the individual numbers, may well be said to be *form within the recital*'s *overall form*, or just *intra-forms*.

chandramukhī Rādhā may be said to provide what Bharata speaks of as *anubhāva*; and, above all, the accordant dancing of details like *kasak-masak, chanchal nain bān*, and *bhanva-kaṭāksh* exemplify what he says about *vyabhichārī bhāvas* (as incidental to the evocation of *saṁyoga śṛṅgāra*) in chapter VI of his treatise.[100]

What is more, on a number of occasions even a close and balanced presentation of both *saṁyog* and *vipralambha* (or *viyog*) *śṛṅgāra* in terms of two separate compositions — and in fair accordance with Bharata's view of *rasa*-evocation — has been effectively presented in the Kathak idiom. This is how I recall the way it was done. [101]

The danseuse first picks a sad and moving composition for presentation. The text for singing (as accompaniment) is provided by a Mīrā *bhajan* which opens with the words, *horī piyā bin lāgey khāri*. *Khāri* may here be taken to express *glāni* which is one of the *vyabhichārī bhāvas* of *viyoga śṛṅgāra*.[102] The song is set in *rāga pūriyā* which is admirably suited to express how one pines in love unrequited, and lives through endless stretches of waiting for the dear one, here Murārī or Kṛṣṇa. The rhythm chosen is *tritāla* at a reposeful pace. The *sthāyībhāva* of *rati* is manifest straight away, because of the very opening line, a refrain throughout the course of dancing, which says that even a gay and *frolicsome* festival like *horī* feels distasteful *in the absence of the loved one*. The next line speaks of the loneliness that pervades the village — nay, the whole neighbouring region — and makes even the *saij* and *aṭārī* look forlorn, that is, sad and deserted.[103] Words such as these, we may note, lend extra explicitness to both *sthāyībhāva* and *vibhāva*, at once indicating how the two interrelate or colour each other in an actual

---

100. Śukla's *NŚ*, 2nd, part I, p. 308.

101. Pretty freely, by Rani Karnaa, winner of the prestigious Sangeet Natak Akademi Award for excellence in classical dance for 1997.

102. Śukla's *NŚ* 2nd part I, p. 309.

103. The Hindi words here are: "सूनो गांव, देस सब सूनो, सूनी सेज अटारी।"

situation. *Anubhāva* has, of course, to be there all along as *abhinaya*; and glimpses of *vyabhichārī bhāvas* are provided by (a verbal mention) of such fleeting, but genuine indicators of an agonizing and seemingly unending wait as *andesā*[104] (or anxiety duly reflected in the dancer's face) and the eventual disappearance of the very lines that segment the fingers because of incessant counting of days spent in forlornness.[105] The closing words duly signify a helpless admission of what must be endured, that is, lingering loneliness.[106]

The next composition which follows very quickly is an essay in evoking *saṁyoga śṛṅgāra*. The *rāga* chosen is *hindol*; the rhythm, *dhamār*, at *madhya laya*; the vocal form, also a *dhamār*; and the text of the song visualizes *holī*-playing at its sportive best, as indicated by the text of the very first line which runs thus: *khelat holī shyām chapal madmātī*. Quite a few other words like *abeer gulāl ki dhoom machi hai, nāchat dey dey tālī* not only project the occasion or *vibhāva* (*holī*) and the *sthāyībhāva* of *rati* (as sheer rejoicing), but the *vyabhichārībhāva* of (an aspect of) dancing regarded as regulated movement of beauteous limbs.[107]

In respect of all such numbers, however, the following objection is possible:

It takes but a few minutes to complete their dancing; the staging of a play, on the other hand, lasts much longer; how then can we expect such dances to evoke the *sustained* emotive experience that *rasa* is said to be? Now, our answer may be that though the proper staging of a play is of course characterized by *saṁyoga* or due integration of the different *bhāvas*, good dancing is *more tightly* and more noticeably

104. Anxiety (or, चिन्ता), we may note, is (according to Bharata) one of the *vyabhichārībhāvas* in the evocation of *vipralambha* (or *viyoga*) *śṛṅgāra*. Sukla's *NŚ*, 2nd, part I, p. 309.

105. This is my translation of the following words in the *bhajan* in question: "गिणता गिणता घिस गई रेखा, आंगुरिया की सारी".

106. Signified by the words, "अबंहु न आये मुरारी."

107. Or, "ललित अंगो का परिचालन". Śukla's *NŚ*, part I, 2nd edn., p. 308.

organized on the inside, and so is quicker in producing an impact than a play. The point may be argued as follows:

Rhythm in Hindustānī (north Indian) music is necessarily cyclic in character; and so, because it here envelops and regulates both music and the dancing, the entire presentation appears visibly gathered. This appearance is also determined, in part, by the fact that the rhythm here is not a mere cycle, but a cycle with a distinct centre, namely, the *sama*, from where the *laya*-flow begins and to which it returns, *directing the rasika*'s *attention accordingly*. Above all, the two senses which are eminently aesthetic according to Bharata — namely, the ear and the eye — are much more conjointly and continually tickled by the dances we have referred to than by a play. No mere dialogues here detract from the fascination of senses; and the ideal content — that is, the meaning of the text of the songs — is generally too familiar to *rasika*s to make any heavy demands on their understanding. The *rasa* here evoked may not last long, but so long as it does, its impact is definite; and its character, quite easy to identify.

To turn now to classical music, in our talk about this art we freely — and confidently — speak of the *rasa*s of (at least) some *rāga*s. It is quite widely accepted that a recital of *rāga Aḍānā* has to evoke a semblance of *vīra rasa*, or at least of aggressiveness; and that the proper singing of *Jogīyā* and *Sohnī* has to wear a look of *karuṇa rasa*. But, on the other hand, there is a good deal in the forms, structural features, and practice of our (Hindustānī or north Indian) music today which distances the art from the *rasa* theory. What we call *sthāyī* in our *dhruvapad* and *khayāl* singing is not at all the same thing as *sthāyībhāva*. Whereas such a *bhāva*, we have seen, is an innate disposition to have *emotional* experiences of a particular kind, a *sthāyī* in vocal music is, for theory, just the first (steadfast) line of a composition and in practice (also) the *structural* anchor of a whole recital. The text of a *khayāl-sthāyī* may have nothing to do with emotion; and even where it has some emotive import, like the well-known *Sadāraṅg* composition (in *rāga Miyān ki Malhār*), *Karīm Nām Tero*, its opening devotionl air may be, in fact it usually is, quickly dissipated by the *taans* in which a *khayāl* recital usually abounds. Further, *tarānās* which only use mnemonic syllables, and no words at all, do not aim at evoking any emotion; and the whole genre of *tappā* singing is distinguished only by the vocalist's ability to execute quite sudden and difficult vocal turns, and not at all by evocation of any emotion.

Yet this is undeniable that where our *classical* singing — specially as *ālāpa* of the *dhruvapad* manner and *vilambit khayāl*-singing — is really top class, it *is* able to provide us with an experience which is delightful and unruffled by distinctions that characterize our everyday experience; which lifts us, temporarily, above the concerns of our real life; and, above all, which leaves us finally, if momentarily, with the feeling that we, who were just a random gathering of separate listeners at the start of the recital, have somehow become not merely akin, but one in the fellowship of art contemplation. How the evocation of this experience results from an integration of the various *bhāvas* which the *rasa sūtra* speaks of, is extremely difficult, if not impossible, to trace in respect of *our music today*; but as to the quality of the experience it *can* evoke, what we have just said is indubitable. This should become clear as we turn to consider how the experience of *rasa* actually feels — a task which calls for a fair amount of phenomenological analysis. Happily, our task is made easy by such succinct accounts of what *rasa* distinctively is as the following one by Vishvanath:

> *sattvodrekād akhaṇḍasvākāsānandachinmayaḥ* ।
> *vedyāntarasparśaśūnyo brahmāsvādasahodaraḥ* ॥
> *lokottarachamatkārapraṇaḥ kaiśchit pramāṭṛbhiḥ* ।
> *svākārvad abhinnatvenāyam āsvādyate rasaḥ* ॥[108]

Gnoli translates the above as follows:

> *Rasa* is tasted by the qualified persons. . . . It is tasted by virtue of the emergence of *sattva*. It is made up of a full

108. R. Gnoli, *The Aesthetic Experience According to Abhinavagupta*, 2nd edn., p. 47, f.n. 1a.

> Intelligence, Beatitude and Self-luminosity. It is void of contact with any other knowable thing, [and is the] twin brother to the tasting of *Brahman*. It is tasted as if it were our being, in indivisibility.[109]

Now, this translation may well be true to the essential features of *rasa*, but it is unable to account for their being interrelated in the unity of *rasa*-experience. Perhaps we could make it a little more enlightening too by reflecting as under:

There are three basic considerations which have to be borne in mind. First, however different it be from our everyday emotional experiences, *rasa* is not *alaukika* in the sense of being *utterly* independent of *every* kind of context, though, as Abhinavagupta insists, aesthetic experience does disconnect us, if temporarily, from the spatio-temporal awareness and utilitarian interests of our everyday life. It is emphatically said to happen *as the result of* a proper integration of the different *bhāva*s in the presentation of a play, in good poetry or in a dance recital — all as contemplated by a *rasika*. Second, though *rasa* is surely dominated by *sattva*, as against *rajas* and *tamas*, we cannot hope to see how exactly the operation of the three *guṇa*s interrelates in the blissful experience which *rasa* is, because it is (insistently said to be) thoroughly unified or *niravacchinna*. Further, the locus of *rasa* is always the state of *tādātmya*, that is, the *rasika*s' imaginative self-identification with what they see on the stage or read in a play. Finally, though the experience of *rasa* may well be taken to release the *rasika*s (temporarily) from preoccupation with their own individual lives and problems, it does not efface their temperamental characteristics and ingrained likes and dislikes, and sense of values, which is precisely why Bharata thinks it necessary to point out that *sāmājika*s do not all react identically to plays projecting different *rasa*s, and that differences of sex, age, and individual tastes necessarily determine their aesthetic responses. We have to resist being swept off the ground by references to light,

109. R. Gnoli, *The Aesthetic Experience According to Abhinavagupta*, 2nd edn., p. 47, f.n. 1a.

beatitude, and composure (*viśrānti*);[110] and to refrain from the temptation to think that *rasa* is a kind of luminous cloud floating all by itself in mid air.

Bearing all these precautionary attitudes in mind, let us now turn to the first keyword in Vishvanath's definition, that is, *sattvodrekād*. *Udreka* is here to be interpreted as predominance, not as mere abundance; for to say that a quality is abundant is only to mean that it is there in plenty, not necessarily that it also rules over other qualities. *Sattva* must here be taken to dominate *rajas* and *tamas*; otherwise it will not be possible to relate *sattvodrek* with other attributes that are made to qualify *rasa*. But how is *sattva* to be taken as distinct from *rajas* and *tamas*? According to the *Gītā*,[111] *sattva* makes for purity, light as heightened awareness and keener powers of apprehension, right knowledge, overall purity, and so for happiness. *Rajas* is at the root of self-serving actions; (hence) it makes for attachment to consequences, greed, fickleness of mind, desire for sense-indulgence, which is why it causes *duḥkha*. The third *guṇa*, *tamas*, is regarded as the principle of *pramād* (or useless, wasteful activity), ignorance, and *moha*. Therefore, *sattvodrek* or ascendance of *sattva* over *rajas* and *tamas* here means that, as experience, *rasa* is characterized by purity (as freedom from cravings, sensuous desires, and mental fickleness), and so by composure and beatitude, because (as according to Sāṁkhya) it is *aviśrānti* (or lack of composure) which is the *immediate* cause of *duḥkha*. But, we may note, the ascendance in question does

110. "*Viśrānti*, rest, denotes the fact of our being absorbed in something, immersed in it, to the exclusion of every other thing (*vigalitavedyāntaratayā*), without, that is, having any mental movement, any extraneous desire (in other words, no obstacle, *vighna*) which . . . [may come] to break into that state of consciousness. In . . . the . . . language [of aesthetics] *viśrānti* denotes, at the same time, the fact of being absorbed in the aesthetic object, and the sensation of pleasure *sui generis* which accompanies that state of consciousness." R. Gnoli, *The Aesthetic Experience According to Abhinavagupta*, 2nd edn., p. 47, f.n.

111. Chapter XIV.

not mean that *rajas* and *tamas* are thereby made inoperative for good, or even for the duration of *rasa*-experience itself. It is an obvious fact that after the most gripping aesthetic experience the normal tenor of our selfish pursuits, cravings and dissatisfaction — with spells of sheer lethargy and boredom — reappears pretty soon. What is more, even during the course of *rasa*-experience *rajas* and *tamas* do not become entirely ineffective. The luminous character of *rasa*-experience is not to be confused with the inert, changeless glow of a torch. *Wondrous* though it is surely said to be, *rasa* is not to be regarded as a *benumbing* experience. Nor is it accompanied by the incredulous feeling, *how could it happen*, which is partly why *rasa* is said to be a miracle *of a quite uncommon kind*. In spite of being very different from our everyday experiences, it elicits credence because what it builds on, basically, is a *sthāyībhāva*, a disposition which we readily identify as our own. What is more, it is a *course* of blissful experience; and it cannot but be so because it is largely confluent with our attention to the stage presentation, or with our reading of a play, both alike sequential necessarily. Now, this pervasive fluidity (*druti*) is provided by a contact of *sattva* with *rajas*.[112] Where *sattva* operates by itself — that is, where its sway is absolute — the resulting state of consciousness is *vikās* or expansion; but where its working is tempered with a touch of *tamas*, we get moments of mere dilatation or *vistār*.[113] This distinction, which can be drawn only by *recalling* how we felt in experiencing *rasa*, and not *during* the course of the experience itself, may be clarified thus:

First, out of this world though it may well be, *rasa* is after all an emotional experience; and, in point of fact, every emotion can be felt in two ways; as a flow, so long as it is allowed to express itself; and as a trifle uneasy block-cum-swell if it is denied due vent. Now, where the stage presentation appears to be heading for a denouement, and the *prekṣaka* holds his breath in *mounting suspense* or apprehension, the passing arrest

112. R. Gnoli, *The Aesthetic Experience According to Abhinavagupta*, 2nd edn., p. 46, footnote 1a.

113. Ibid.

in the varying flow of experience is due to the impact of *tamas* on *sattva* (or is *vistār*, a mere bloating of the present state of experience, so to say); and the moment uncertainties are clarified, and previously unresolved problems and mysteries are unravelled, *sattva* may be said to reassert its supermacy over *tamas*, undoing the hold on the flow of experience, providing fuller understanding (*vikās*) and deepening *viśrānti*.

The ascendancy of *sattva* over *rajas* — the *guṇa* which is the cause not only of overly oriented activity, but of haste, impatience, and unrest — accounts for the presence of tranquillity, as also for the absence of willed overt activity in the experience of *rasa*. As we have already hinted, some reflex bodily changes, such as bated breath and accelerated heartbeat, may well occur in *rasānubhūti*, but here we do not *seek to do* anything; and, generally, serene contemplation of what is presented to us is our only intentional, yet effortless activity.

Some features of *rasa*, however, relate directly to *sattva* itself. This *guṇa* is commonly regarded as the principle of *purity*; but here this quality cannot be said to characterize our motives and conduct. It has rather to be taken in a sense which is partly, but importantly negative. Just as *ālāpa* of the *dhruvapad* way of singing is said to be pure music because it is free from admixture with language and beat-measured rhythm, so the purity which *sattva* lends to *rasa* means that the experience here is not at all ruffled by preoccupation with one's *own* joys and sorrows (*nijasukhaduḥkādiviveśibhāva*) and cravings and desires, because of the *sādhāraṇīkaraṇa* brought about by the aesthetic configuration of different *bhāvas*; and is therefore *chinmaya* or consisting of pure awareness.

But, one may ask, what exactly is the point in relating this awareness to *prakāsh* and *ānand*? Here, we may answer thus:

It is quite proper and surely not uncommon to speak of feeling lit up with understanding, say, after we have given close and fruitful attention to an intricate train of argument. Now, though quite differently evoked, this feeling is importantly there in *rasa*-experience as well, because of the tightly focused and so exclusive quality of our attention. We feel gripped by the integrated and expressive form of what is presented on the stage, as also by its appeal as much to the ear and the eye as to understanding, not a little because of *āhārya abhinaya*. Further, by virtue of being authentic *rasikas*, we are not merely willing but *able* to follow the presentation. This ability is due to two main factors: first, our own past training and experience in watching plays; and, second, the passing release from preoccupation with our *own* joys and sorrows presently brought about in the way already indicated, so that our attention is here "exclusive" in the sense of not being ruffled at all by concern with any other object of knowledge (*vedyāntarasparśa śūnyo*). Be that as it may, this is a matter of actual experience that one who tastes *rasa* rests in a state of pure contemplation bereft of all practical interest (*saṁvit*), which is at once a feeling of composure (*viśrānti*). Such tranquil and undivided attention naturally makes for very clear perception which enlivens understanding. What is, in this context, spoken of as *prakāsh* is obviously no physical light, but

> The inner radiation of being which accompanies delighted understanding, a joyous state of heightened awareness.[114]

Correspondingly, Bharata's characterization of *rasa* as *ujjvalaveśātmakaḥ* may be translated as "whose essence is a look of splendour and clarity (rather than of *burning*!)" The italicized word within brackets has been taken from S.K. De's translation (of the Sanskrit word) which runs thus: "whose essence is an appearance of burning." By way of explaining what this *burning* is he has cited the case of "inflamed" passions. Now, this interpretation creates a problem if we take *it*, obviously a way of characterizing *rasa*, along with De's other view that *rati*, the *sthāyībhāva* of *śṛṅgāra rasa*, is "physical passion."[115] Are we to

114. S.K. Saxena, *Aesthetical Essays*, Delhi: Chanakya Publications, 1981, p. 159.

115. Cf. S.K. De, *Sanskrit Poetics as a Study of Aesthetic*, p. 109.

believe that *śṛṅgāra rasa*, as *ujjvalaveśātmakaḥ*, is simply the inflamed or violently excited (because *burning*) evocation of an animal appetite?

Anyway, to turn now to *prākash* and *viśrānti*, important though they surely are, these terms do not exhaust the meaning of *ānand* in Visvanatha's definition of *rasa*. Taken along with *sattvodrek*, *ānand* cannot be interpreted as everyday happiness, and surely not as sensual pleasure, though these are both acknowledged meanings of the word. The "emergence of . . . *sattva*, limpid and mirror-like" always makes for a clearer reflection of "the light and beatitude proper to the self."[116] So, taken in the light of this truth, *ānand* can here be taken to mean pure happiness alone, that is, happiness which is utterly free from impulses to do or to get, and from all domination by pull of the senses. It is this beatitude — that is, happiness with absolute peace — which brings *rasa* very close to the bliss of realizing *Brahman* (*Brahmānand sahodaraḥ*), for *ānand* (as we have interpreted it) is also regarded as one of the three attributes of *Brahman*. Another clue to this closeness is provided by the fact that just as *brahmānubhav* is a very deeply satisfying experience because it answers a basic need of the *ātman*, so is *rasa* because of its grounding in *sthāyībhāva*s which are a part of our native equipment of tendencies to have emotional experiences of specific kinds. In neither case does the blissful experience appear as the attainment of a merely objective end.

This is, we may note, not only an important emphasis of the theory in question but a point of some theoretical value, insofar as it enables us to meet an obvious and quite sensible objection. Can we not experience, one may ask, utter and blissful tranquillity even in looking at a beautiful detail of natural beauty, be it even a little foam at the moonlit bank of a lake? We surely can. What is more, intense and reverent communion with nature has even enabled some sensitive poets, such as Wordsworth and Sūrdās, to receive (or elicit) some

116. Gnoli, *The Aesthetic Experience According to Abhinavagupta*, 2nd edn., p. 46.

quiet, but ennobling impulses of vital moral significance.[117] Yet such experiences cannot be summarily likened to *rasa* because of two clear differences. First, our attention to a beautiful object of nature can hardly ever be *so sustained and so manifestly engaging to the mind* as our knowledgeable contemplation of a dramatic presentation which does not merely tickle our eyes and ears, but provides, as a rule, a full-blown plot packed with almost every element of real life, namely, thought, emotion, and variform interplay of character with situations. Secondly, to receive elevating influences from outside is not the same thing as seeing something that is essential to our own being reflected in an outer object with charm and convincingness, as really happens when we witness plays which present our own *sthāyībhāva*s as creatively exalted for objective contemplation. It is this projection of what is intrinsically within us as human beings which enables us to taste *rasa* with a degree of intimacy which is hardly ever there in Man's communion with Nature, except perhaps in the case of some religious mystics. There *are* moments when we feel perfectly *at peace with* the beauty that Nature presents, but the beauteous objects of Nature are surely not felt *as reflecting us*; and it is no mere rhetoric to say, as Vishvanath does, that "*rasa* [alone] is tasted as if in indivisibility."

Our experience of listening (knowledgeably) to good music

---

117. Wordsworth, for instance, voices the faith that

> One impulse from a vernal wood
> May teach you more of Man;
> Of moral evil and of good
> Than all the sages can.

And, in a much more enlightening *bhajan* which opens with the words: "वृक्षन से मति ले मन तू", Sūrdās reads in the existence and function of trees quite a few moving messages of selfless service and transcendence of the duality of aversion and attachment; for, do not these stately objects of Nature drop fruits precisely for those who throw pebbles at them; and do they ever get angry with those who cut them or attached to those who water them?

can perhaps be said to be closer to Vishvanath's characterization of *rasa* than our contemplation of Nature. There are reasons why I refer to such experiences again. They have a definite and illustrative, if yet partial, value for the purpose of this essay. So far as I know, in independent India just one explicit attempt has been made to *relate drama* to the *rasa* theory. This happened in 1980 when Shyamanand Jalan tried to explore the theory with a multi-disciplinary production of *Abhijnānaśākuntalam* with the assistance of Guru Kelucharan Mohapatra as choreographer and the famed vocalist Girija Devi as music composer — a venture which subsequently enabled Jalan to organize comprehensive workshops such as Indian Dance Traditions and Modern Theatre (1983) with seminarists, classical dancers and theatre actors. I have no idea of the result of this creative effort. Further, because the dramatic art of Bharata's day, to which the *rasa* theory might well have been very relevant, is no longer accessible to us, and also because it is not the general practice of our playwrights and directors of today to consciously adhere to all the injunctions of Bharata, we may turn to a visualized instance of listening to a top class music recital for getting some idea of how the various qualities distinguished by Abhinavagupta in his succinct characterization of *rasa* could in fact interrelate in a single experience.

With such an instance in mind we may proceed quite simply, say, as follows:

The clear *and discriminating* perception (by a knowledgeable listener) of sweet-sounding (and correctly placed) *svara*s as making the distinct wholeness of a single *rāga* provides some joy *and* also a little thinking simultaneously. What is clearly and appealingly perceived at once makes the listener feel enlivened or (so to say) lit up on the inside (*prakāsh*). All this is aided by intenseness of attention which is, in turn, helped not only by the ability and willingness of the (qualified) listener to care for nothing but the music (*vedyāntarasparśaśūnyo*) but (in principle) by the pull of the music itself. This perfect accord of *what* he listens to and *how* he does so makes for the undivided (*akhand*) quality of the experience which is wondrous (or of the nature of a miracle, *chamatkāra*) because it is quite unlike our everyday experiences insofar as it is not all disturbed by considerations of utility, or of location in real space or time and is therefore *vītavighna*. It may well be — in fact it often is — quite without the semblance of *a distinct full blown emotion* (which is not the same thing as a little happy wonderment); and this is indeed what prevents it from becoming an exact parallel of *rasānubhūti*. But this is incontrovertible that, as I have already said earlier, at least for a while after the listening is over, or even during the course of listening, such an experience lifts one out of the sense of being just a limited "I" as opposed to the others.

Yet, in spite of all that is said for it, *rasa*-experience is only very similar to, or a twin brother of (*sahodaraḥ*) so to say, but not exactly identical with the bliss of realizing *Brahman*; and the differences are easy to see. Even our most fascinated watching of a play is quickly followed by a return to the humdrum tenor of life; the recurring eclipse of *sattva* by the other two *guṇa*s begins all over again; and, as we resume it, our normal living generally does not show any marked improvement in its moral tone. The bliss of realizing *Brahman*, on the other hand, ennobles our lives markedly and loosens our bondage (more or less) to sheer worldly concerns. What is more, besides of course a modicum of moral decency — say, by way of discipline as members of an audience — no such rigorous psycho-ethical disciplines are needed for experiencing *rasa* as are generally essential for achieving the relish of Brahmānanda.

However, the

> limitations of the experience of art, to which we have just alluded, do not affect the conclusion that it is of the same [*sattva*-dominated] order as . . . the ideal [spiritual] state; . . . [what is more, it even makes *that state* appear feasible] . . . art experience [as visualized by the *rasa* theory] is well adapted to arouse our interest in the ideal state by giving us a foretaste

> of it, and thus to serve as a powerful incentive to the pursuit of . . . [that] state. . . . It is not given to the ordinary man to transcend [merely individual concerns] . . . ; art by its impersonalized forms appears the best means for a temporary [yet educative] escape from the ills of life arising from such [self-serving interests].[118]

Such a view which posits an essential relation between art experience and humanity's ethico-religious interests is obviously a far cry from those trends in present-day aesthetics which seek to *dehumanize* art completely; but though it seems most clearly relevant only to the more systematic of our classical dances today, it has surely been the traditional Indian conception of art.

---

118. Hiriyanna, *Art Experience*, Mysore: Kavyalaya Publishers, pp. 13, 28.

Bibliography

Abrams, Harry N., *Art Treasures of the Metropolitan*, New York: INC, Publishers, 1st edn. 1952.

Archer, W.G., *Indian and Modern Art*, George Allen & Unwin, 1959.

Auboyer, Jeannine and Roger Geopper, *The Oriental World*, London, Paul Hamlyn, 1967.

Audi, Robert (ed.), *The Cambridge Dictionary of Philosophy*, Cambridge University Press, 2nd edn., 1999.

Bazin, C., *A Concise History of Art*, London: Thames and Hudson, 2nd Impression, part I, 1964.

Beardsley, Monroe C., *Aesthetics from Classical Greece to the Present*, The MacMillan Co., 1966.

Beardsley, Monroe C., *Aesthetics — Problems in the Philosophy of Criticism*, New York: Harcourt, Brace and World, Inc., 1958.

Beardsley, Monroe C., "Redefining Art" in *The Aesthetic Point of View*, eds. M.J. Wren and D.M. Callen, 1982.

Beardsley, Monroe C., "The Aesthetic Point of View" in *Metaphilosophy*, vol. I, no. 1, January 1970.

Bell, Clive, *Art*, Grey Arrow edition, 1961.

Bell, Clive, "Significant Form" in John Hospers ed. *Introductory Readings in Aesthetics*, The Free Press and Collier Macmillan Publishers, 1969.

Best, D., "The Aesthetic in Sport", *British Journal of Aesthetics*, 14 (1974).

Blanshard, Brand, *On Philosophical Style*, New York: Greenwood Press, 1969, rpt.

Boner-Sarma-Baumer, *Vāstusūtra Upaniṣad: The Essence of Form in Sacred Art*, Delhi: Motilal Banarsidass, 4th rev. ed., 2000.

Bradley, A.C., *Oxford Lectures on Poetry*, MacMillan, 1970 rpt.

Bullough, Edward, "Psychical Distance" in Melvin Rader's *A Modern Book of Esthetics*, 5th edn., Holt, Rinehart & Winston, 1979.

Bury A. and C.R. Cammell, *World-Famous Paintings*, London: The New Educational Press, 1958.

Butcher, S.H., translation of *Aristotle's Theory of Poetry and Fine Art*, with a new Introduction by John Gasser, New York: Dover Publications Inc., 4th edn. 1951.

Capra, Fritijof, *The Tao of Physics: An Exploration of the Parallels between Modern Physics and Eastern Mysticism*, London, Fontana, 1976.

Carlson, Allen, "Appreciation and the Natural Environment" in *Journal of Aesthetics and Art Criticism*, Spring, 1979.

Carritt, E.F., *Philosophies of Beauty*, Oxford, 1931.

Coloman, F.C., *Contemporary Studies in Aesthetics*, New York: McGraw Hill Book Co., 1966.

Collingwood, R.G., *The Principles of Art*, OUP, 1963.

Contemporary Indian Theatre: Interviews with Playwrights and Directors, New Delhi: Sangeet Natak Akademi, 1989.

Coommaraswamy, A.K., *The Dance of Śiva*, New York: The Noonday Press.

Coommaraswamy, A.K., *The Transformation of Nature in Art*, Harvard, 1934.

Cordner, "Grace and Functionality", *British Journal of Aesthetics*, vol. 24, no. 4, Autumn 1984.

Croce, B., *Aesthetic as Science of Expression and General Linguistic*, tr. D. Ainslie, Rupa & Co.

Daix, Pierre, *Picasso*, London: Thames and Hudson, 1965.

Dawson, Sheila, "Distancing as an Aesthetic Principle" in *Australasian Journal of Philosophy*, vol. 39, 1961.

De, S.K., *Sanskrit Poetics as a Study of Aesthetic*, OUP, 1963.

Dewey, John, *Art as Experience*, New York: Capricorn Books, 1958, 7th impression.

Dickie, George, Richard Scalfani and Ronald Rabbin (eds.), *Aesthetics — A Critical Anthology*, Boston and New York: Bedford/St. Martin's, 2nd edn., 1989.

Dickie, George, "Reconsiderations", *Journal of Aesthetics and Art Criticism*, XLII, Fall, 1983.

Dickie, George, "The Myth of the Aesthetic Attitude", in John Hospers ed., *Introductory Readings in Aesthetics*, 1969.

Dissanayake, Ellen, "Aesthetic Experience and Human Evolution" in *Journal of Aesthetics and Art Criticism*, Winter, 1982.

Ducasse, C.J., "Art and the Language of the Emotions," in Rader's *A Modern Book of Esthetics*, 4th edn.

Duccase, C.J., *The Philosophy of Art*, New York: Dover Publication, Inc., 1966.

Dudley, Louise and Austin Faricy, *The Humanities*, 3rd edn., revised by Louise Dudley, McGraw Hill Book Co., 1960.

Dwivedi, Hazari Prasad, *Kabir*, Raj Kamal Publications, 3rd edn., 1976.

Elsen, Albert (ed.): *Auguste Rodin*, Prentice-Hall, 1965.

Elton E. (ed.), *Aesthetics and Language*, Oxford: Basil Blackwell, 1970.

Findlay, J.N., "The Perspicuous and the Poignant" in *Aesthetics*, ed. Harold Osborne, OUP, 1972.

Flew, Antony, *A Dictionary of Philosophy*, Pan Books Ltd., 1984 edn.

Fry, Roger, "Art as Form" in John Hospers ed. *Introductory Readings in Aesthetics.*

Gasset, Jośe Ortega Y., "The Dehumanization of Art," in M. Rader (ed.), *A Modern Book of Esthetics*, Princeton, New Jersey: Princeton University Press, 2nd edn., 1972.

Gatt, Gieuseppe, *Turner, A Dolphin Art Book*, Thames & Hudson, 1969.

Gaunt, W., *A Companion to Painting*, London: Thames & Hudson, 1967.

Gnoli, R., *The Aesthetic Experience according to Abhinavagupta*, Varanasi: Chowkhamba Sanskrit Series Office, 2nd edn., 1968.

Goldscheider, L. and W. Uhde, *Vincent Van Gogh*, Oxford and London: Phaidon Press Ltd., 1945.

Gombrich, E.H., "Truth and the Stereotype" in M. Rader *A Modern Book Esthetics*, 5th edn., Holt: Rinehart & Winston, 1979.

Goodman, Nelson, *Languages of Art*, Indianpolis, Cambridge: Hackett Publishing Co., Inc. 4th edn., 1981.

Guyer, Paul, "Disinterestedness and Desire in Kant's Aesthetics" in *Journal of Aesthetics and Art Criticism*, Summer 1978.

Haezrahi, Pepita, *The Contemplative Activity*, George Allen and Unwin, 1959.

Hamilton E. and H. Cairns, *The Collected Dialogues of Plato*, Bollingen Series, LXXI, Princton University Press, 7th edn., 1973.

Hammermeister, Kai, *The German Aesthetic Tradition*, Cambridge University Press, 2002.

Hampshire, Stuart, "Logic and Appreciation" in *Aesthetics and Language*, Oxford, Basil Blackwell, 1970.

Hart, Frederick, *The Paintings of Michelangelo*, London: Thames and Hudson, 1965.

Heller, Reinhold, *Munch — The Scream*, The Penguin Press, 1973.

Hepburn, R.W., "Aesthetic Appreciation of Nature" in H. Osborne ed., *Aesthetics and the Modern World*, London, 1968.

Hiriyanna, *Art Experience*, Mysore: Kavyalaya Publishers, 1954.

Hook, Sidney (ed.), *Art and Philosophy*, New York University Press, 1966.

Hospers, John, "Hartshorne's Aesthetics", in L.E. Hahn ed. *The Philosophy of Charles Hartshorne*, The Library of Living Philosophers, vol. XX, La Salle, Illinois, 1991.

Hospers, John, ed., *Introductory Readings in Aesthetics*, New York: The Free Press and Collier MacMillan, 1969.

Hospers, John, "The Concept of Artistic Expression" in John Hospers ed., *Introductory Readings in Aesthetics*, op. cit.

Hospers, John, "The Esthetic Attitude" in Melvin Rader's *A Modern Book of Esthetics*, Holt Rinehart and Wiston, INC, 4th edn. 1935.

Jain N. & P. Shankar (ed.), *Ādhunika Hindi Samikṣā*, Sahitya Akademi, New Delhi, 1985.

Kant, *The Critique of Judgment*, tr. J.C. Meredith, Oxford: Clarendon Press, 1964 rpt.

Khrapchenko, Mikhail, *Artistic Creativity, Reality and Man*, Roduga Publishers (Eng. translation), 1986.

Krishnamoorthy, K., "Traditional Indian Aesthetics in Theory and Practice" in *Indian Aesthetics and Art Activity*, Shimla: Indian Institute of Advanced Study, 1968.

Langer, *Mind: An Essay on Human Feeling*, Baltimore and London: The John Hopkins University Press, 1967, vol. I.

Langer, S.K., *Feeling and Form*, Routledge and Kegan Paul, 4th Impression, 1967.

Langer, S.K., *Mind: An Essay on Human Feeling*, vol. I, Baltimore and London: The John Hopkins University Press, 2nd printing) 1975.

Langer, S.K., *Problems of Art*, London: Routledge and Kegan Paul, 4th Impression, 1967.

Legfevre, P.D., *The Prayers of Kierkegaard*, Chicago and London: The University of Chicago Press, 1963.

Levinson, Jerrold, "Aesthetic Uniqueness", *Journal of Aesthetics and Art Criticism*, Summer 1980.

Lokke, Karl Elise, "The Role of Sublimity in the Development of Modernist Aesthetics", *Journal of Aesthetics and Art Criticism*, Summer 1982.

Macdonald, Margaret, "Arguments used in Criticism of the Arts" in E. Elton ed., *Aesthetics and Language*, op. cit.

Makkreel, Rudolf, "Imagination and Temporarlity in Kant's Theory of the Sublime" in *Journal of Aesthetics and Art Criticism*, Spring 1984.

Maritain, Jacques, *Art and Scholasticism and the Frontiers of Poetry*, tr. J.W. Evans, University of Notre Dame Press.

Martin, F. David, *Art and the Religious Experience: The "Language" of the Sacred*, Lewisburg: Bucknell University Press, 1972.

Matias, Michael H., "What makes an Experience Aesthetic" in *Journal of Aesthetics and Art Criticism*, Winter 1982.

Monroe, C. Beardsley, *Aesthetics from Classical Greece to the Present*, The Mac Millan Co., 1966.

Monroe, C. Beardsley, *Problems in the Philosophy of Criticism*, New York, Harcourt Brace & World, Inc., 1958.

Monroe, C. Beardsley, "The Aesthetic Point of View" in *Metaphilosophy*, vol. I, no. 1, January, 1970.

Mothersill, Mary, *Beauty Restored*, Oxford: Clarendon Press, 1984.

Nagendra, "Kāmāyanī kā Mahākāvyatva," in *Adhunik Hindi Samīkshā*, New Delhi: Sahitya Akademi, 1980.

Nwodo, C.W., "Philosophy of Art vs Aesthetics", in *British Journal of Aesthetics*, Summer 1984.

Osborne, Harold, "Organic Unity" in M. Rader ed. *A Modern Book of Esthetics*, 5th edn.

Osborne, Harold, (ed.), *Aesthetics and the Modern World*, London, 1968.

Osborne, Harold, *Aesthetics and Art Theory — An Historical Introduction*, New York: E.P. Dutton & Co., INC 1970.

Osborne, Harold, *The Art of Appreciation*, London: OUP, 1970.

Osborne, Harold, *Theory of Beauty: An Introduction to Aesthetics*, New York: Philosophical Library.

Pandey, K.C., *Comparative Aesthetics*, vol. I (Indian Aesthetics), 2nd edn. 1959, Varanasi: Chowkhamba Sanskrit Series Office.

Parker, De Witt, *The Analysis of Art*, New Haven: Yale University Press, 1926.

Passmore, J.A., "The Dreariness of Aesthetics" in W. Elton ed., *Aesthetics and Language*, ed. W. Elton, Oxford: Blackwell, 1954.

Plato, *The Collected Dialogues of Plato, Bollingen Series LXXI*, Princeton University Press, 7th Printing, 1973.

Poore, H.R., *Composition in Art*, The Oak Tree Press, 1967.

Prasad, Jaishankar, *Kāmāyani*, Bharati Bhandar, Allahabad: Leader Press, 14th edn. Saṁvat 2026.

Price, Kingsley, "The Truth About Psychical Distance", *Journal of Aesthetics and Art Criticism*, Summer 1977.

Price, Kingsley, "What makes an Experience Aesthetic", *British Journal of Aesthetics*, vol. 19, 1979.

Puppi, Lionello, *El Greco*, A Dolphin Art Book, London: Thames & Hudson, 1967.

Rader, Melvin, *A Modern Book of Esthetics*, New York: Holt, Rinehart and Winston, 5th edn., 1979.

Read, Herbert, *Art Now*, London: Faber and Faber, 1960.

Read, Herbert, "Critical Appreciation" in *Vermeer* (The Masters) Paulton, Nr. Bristol: Knowledge Publications, Purnell & Sons Ltd., 1965.

Reid, L.A., *Meaning in the Arts*, George Allen & Unwin, 1969.

Reid, L.A., "The Communication of Emotion" in Rader's book, *A Modern Book of Esthetics*, 5th edn., op. cit.

Reid, L.A., "Values, Feelings and Embodiment," in Rader's *A Modern Book of Esthetics*, 5th edn.

Reinhold Heller, *Munch — The Scream*, The Penguin Press, 1973.

Ryle, "Feeling" in *Aesthetics and Language*, op. cit.

Sartwell, Crispin, "Aesthetic Dualism and the Transfiguration of the Commonplace" in *Journal of Aesthetics and Art Criticism* (*JAAC*), Summer 1988.

Saxena, S.K., *Aesthetical Essays*, Delhi: Chanakya Publications, 1981.

Saxena, S.K., *Art and Philosophy: Seven Aestheticians*, New Delhi, ICPR, 1994.

Saxena, S.K., *Hindustani Sangeet and a Philosopher of Art*, New Delhi: D.K. Printworld (P) Ltd., 2001.

Saxena, S.K., *Avenues to Beauty*, Sangeet Natak Akademi and D.K. Printworld, 2009.

Saxena, S.K., "Essentials of Hindustani Music" in *Diogene*, 45, Paris, 1964.

Saxena, S.K., "Kathak — Some Terms and Distinctions" in *Sangeet Natak*, January–March, 1979.

Saxena, S.K., "The Fabric of Aamad — A Study of Form and Flow in Hindustani Music," in *Sangeet Natak*, no. 16, April-June 1970.

Saxena, S.K., "The Spiritual and Hindustani Music", in *Sangeet Natak, Journal of Sangeet Natak Akademi*, New Delhi, nos. 131-32, 1999, pp. 3-14.

Saxena, S.K., *The Winged Form: Aesthetical Essays on Hindustani Rhythm*, New Delhi: Sangeet Natak Akademi, 1979.

Scarre, Geoffrey, "Kant on Free and Dependent Beauty" in *The British Journal of Aesthetics*, vol. 21, no. 4, Autumn, 1981.

Schott, Rolf, *Michelangelo*, London: Thames and Hudson, 1st edn., 1964.

Smith, Edward Lucie, *Movements in Art Since 1945*, London: Thames & Hudson, 1969.

Sparshott, F.E., *The Structure of Aesthetics*, University of Toronto Press and Routledge & Kegan Paul, 1963.

Stolnitz, J., *Aesthetics and the Philosophy of Art Criticism*, Houghton, Mifflin, Boston, 1960.

Stolnitz, J., "The Aesthetic Attitude", in *Introductory Readings in Aesthetics*, ed., J. Hospers, New York: The Free Press, 1969.

Tagore, Rabindranath, "The Religion of an Artist", in *Angel of Surplus*, ed. Sisir Kumar Ghosh, Vishwa Bharati, 1978.

Tolstoy, "The Communication of Emotion" in Rader's book *A Modern Book of Esthetics*, 5th edn., op. cit.

Tormey, Alan, *The Concept of Expression*, Princeton, N.J.: Princeton University Press, 1971.

Tralbaut, M.E., *Van Gogh*, London: Thames & Hudson, 1955.

Tralbaut, M.E., *Van Gogh: A Pictorial Biography*, London: Thames & Hudson, 1959.

Tripathi, Surya Kant (Nirala), "Parimala kī Bhūkmikā" in *Ādhunik Hindi Samīkshā*, ed. Nirmala Jain and Prem Shankar, New Delhi: Sahitya Akademi, 1985, p. 63.

Uehling, T.E., *The Notion of Form in Kant's Critique of Judgement*, Mouton, The Hague, 1971.

Vishvanatha Kaviraja, *Sahityadarpaṇa*, ed. Satyavrata Singh, Varanasi: Chowkhamba Vidya Bhawan, new edition, 1992.

Whittick, Arnold, "Towards Precise Distinctions of Art and Craft", *The British Journal of Aesthetics*, Winter, 84.

Wilde, Oscar, "Nature's Imitation of Life" in M. Rader ed. *A Modern Book of Esthetics*, 5th edn., op. cit.

Williams, Oscar (ed.), *Master Poems of the English Language*, New York: Trident Press, 1966.

Wimsatt, W.K., Jr. and Monroe C. Beardsley, *The Verbal Icon*, Noonday Press, 2nd edn., 1980.

Index

(Of chapters and pages where the different accents of reflection occur)